RUSSIA/USSR/RUSSIA

Russian Peasant and Soviet Power (1966)
Lenin's Last Struggle (1968)
Political Undercurrents in Soviet Economic Debates (1974)
The Making of the Soviet System (1985)
The Gorbachev Phenomenon (1990)

Russia/USSR/Russia

THE DRIVE AND DRIFT OF A SUPERSTATE

Moshe Lewin

THE NEW PRESS
NEW YORK
1995

PUBLISHED IN THE UNITED STATES BY THE NEW PRESS, NEW YORK.
DISTRIBUTED BY W. W. NORTON & COMPANY, INC.,
500 FIFTH AVENUE, NEW YORK, NY 10110.

LIBRARY OF CONGRESS CATALOGING-IN-PUBLICATION DATA

Lewin, Moshe, 1921–
  Russia/USSR/Russia : the drive and drift of a superstate /
Moshe Lewin.
    p.   cm.
  Includes bibliographical references.
  ISBN 1-56584-123-9:
  1. Russia—History—1801–1917.   2. Soviet Union—History. I. Title.
DK246.L484   1995
947.08—dc20   93-46922

BOOK DESIGN BY CHARLES NIX

PRODUCTION MANAGEMENT BY KIM WAYMER

ESTABLISHED IN 1990
AS A MAJOR ALTERNATIVE TO THE LARGE, COMMERCIAL PUBLISHING HOUSES,
THE NEW PRESS IS THE FIRST FULL-SCALE NONPROFIT AMERICAN BOOK PUBLISHER
OUTSIDE OF THE UNIVERSITY PRESSES.
THE PRESS IS OPERATED EDITORIALLY IN THE PUBLIC INTEREST,
RATHER THAN FOR PRIVATE GAIN;
IT IS COMMITTED TO PUBLISHING IN INNOVATIVE WAYS
WORKS OF EDUCATIONAL, CULTURAL, AND COMMUNITY VALUE
THAT, DESPITE THEIR INTELLECTUAL MERITS,
MIGHT NOT NORMALLY BE "COMMERCIALLY" VIABLE.
THE NEW PRESS'S EDITORIAL OFFICES ARE LOCATED AT
THE CITY UNIVERSITY OF NEW YORK.

PRINTED IN THE UNITED STATES OF AMERICA.

95 96 97   9 8 7 6 5 4 3 2 1

CONTENTS

ACKNOWLEDGMENTS

———

*Grateful acknowledgment is made to the following for permission
to reprint previously published material:*

"The Village and the Community" appeared in Roger Bartlett, ed., *Land,
Commune, and Peasant Community in Russia: Communal Forms in Imperial and Early Soviet Society* (London: Macmillan, 1990).

"Civil War: Dynamics and Legacy" appeared in Diane P. Koenker,
William G. Rosenberg, and Ronald Grigor Suny, eds., *Party, State, and
Society in the Russian Civil War* (Bloomington and Indianapolis: Indiana
University Press, 1989).

"Russia/USSR in Historical Motion" appeared in *The Russian Review*
50 (1991).

"The Disappearance of Planning in the Plan" appeared in *Slavic Review*
(June 1973) as a comment on Holland Hunter's "The Overambitious
First Soviet Five-Year Plan."

"On Soviet Industrialization" appeared in William G. Rosenberg and
Lewis H. Siegelbaum, eds., *Social Dimensions of Soviet Industrialization*
(Bloomington and Indianapolis: Indiana University Press, 1993).

"Bukharin's Bureaucratic Nightmare" appeared as "Bukharin and the
Problem of Bureaucracy" in Theodor Bergmann and Gert Schafer, eds.,
Liebling der Partei: Nikolas Bucharin (Hamburg: VSA-Verlag, 1989); it
has been translated into English as *Bukharin in Retrospect* (Armonk,
N.Y.: M. E. Sharpe, 1993).

The following texts were initially presented as conference papers:

"Workers in Search of a Class" was presented at a conference on Russia's
working class which took place October 9–11, 1990, at Michigan State
University, the proceedings of which have been published as Lewis H.

Siegelbaum and Ronald Grigor Suny, eds., *Making Workers Soviet: Power, Class, and Identity* (Ithaca, N. Y.: Cornell University Press, 1994).

"Bureaucracy and Despotism" was presented at a conference on "Germany and Russia in the Twentieth Century in Comparative Perspective" held at the University of Pennsylvania, September 19–22, 1991.

"Nationalism in Our Times: The Case of Russia" is an elaboration of a paper presented at a conference on nationalism in Eastern Europe that took place in Le Mans, France, December 12–14, 1992.

GLOSSARY OF RUSSIAN TERMS

apparat	an administrative machinery, hence the term *apparatchik*—a member of an important (mostly Party) administration
brak	defective output
burlak	barge hawler
byvshie liudi	remnants from the past, has-beens
chernorabochij	an unskilled worker
chinovnik chistka	a term used in tsarist Russia for an official state purge (of Party members or government officials)
delovitost'	the quality of being businesslike
derevnia	a village
dvor	a family farm
gramotnost'	literacy
kantseliarsko-biurokraticheskie metody	bureau-pathological methods
karatel'	someone bent on punishing others
khoziain	a boss or owner
khozraschet	the cost-accounting principle
komsomol	Communist Youth League
idejnost'	dedication to ideological values
letun (letuny)	shirkers, dead weight
mir	the rural society, the bearer of communal institutions
mnogotsentrie	pluri-centrism
muzhik	a peasant (often pejorative)
nachal'nik (nachal'stvo)	a superior or boss
nas za liudej ne schitaiut	"they do not consider us as human beings"
nomenklatura	the system that exercised control over top-level nominees to the Party
obrazovanie	education
obshchina	a general term for "the rural community"
ogosudarstvlenie	assuring that state ownership is total
okrainy	the outlying regions, outskirts
orabochenie	assuring the prevalence of nominees of working-class origin in governmental and Party institutions
otpravnoj	a starting blueprint or variant of a plan
otvetrabotnik, otvet-politrabotnik	a holder of a political job

piatiletka	the five-year plan
pererozhdenie	degeneration
perezhitki	vestiges of the past, leftovers
pomeshchik, pomest'e	a landowner (and estate) of aristocratic origin
praktik	a holder of an important job who lacks the necessary professional schooling
prodrazverstka	the system of grain requisition used during the civil war
proslojka	a social layer or stratum
proval	a flop
rabsila	a contracted form of *rabochaia sila*, labor force, connoting fearless brute force
rassoglasovannost'	a lack of coordination
razbukhanie	a burgeoning of personnel
rvach	someone who is self-serving
ryvok	a jolt
samoderzhets	an autocrat
shtat (shtaty)	the actual personnel—or the officially prescribed numbers and specifications—of employees in an office
skhod	a gathering of the rural commune
sliianie	a merger
sluzhashchie	employees or functionaries
soglasovyvanie	the act of coordinating
snaby, sbyty	the agencies dealing with supply and marketing of the output of enterprises
stikhia	spontaneity, an elemental development
strojki	building sites
uchraspred	the Department of the Central Committee that dealt with registering and distributing cadres
vashe vysokoblagorodie, vashe velichestvo	a formal way in which one addresses the tsar or a prince (the equivalent of "Your Majesty" or "Your Highness")
vedomstvo, vedomstvennost'	an administrative body, such as a ministry or state committee
Velikaia Rus'	literally "Rus' the Grand": *Rus'* was the historical predecessor of Russia which nationalists in Soviet Russia endowed with a mythical grandeur and propounded as a symbol of the "real" Russian nation
votchina	the patrimonial property

vozhd'	a leader or chief
vreditel'stvo	sabotage
Vy, Ty	the formal terms used to address another directly
vysshyj komsostav	a military term for higher-ranking commanders, often used for the higher-ranking party and state cadres
zagradotriady	roadblock detachments
zalimitirovat'	to straitjacket
zastoj, zastojnye gody	stagnation, a time of stagnation
zek (zeki)	concetration camps (inmates)

PREFACE

This volume grew out of the inquiries I pursued in *The Making of the Soviet System*. This time, though, "the unmaking" is in the forefront, although not under the impact of the Soviet regime's downfall alone. The seeds of the downfall were amply present when I wrote *The Making*, as well as the earlier *Political Undercurrents in Soviet Economic Debates*. It goes without saying that the downfall of the Soviet system cannot but be foremost on the mind of a historian of twentieth-century Russia, and this is why most of the chapters in this volume are often traveling the whole historical road through the century, sometimes from the past forward and sometimes from the present back in time—as far back as the particular topic demands.

The chapters of this work comprise six essays that were previously published in different outlets and ten more that were written for this volume or developed from lectures and conference papers. The chapters are grouped in four sections. The first deals with "The Hard Nuts of Russian History," and the reader will not be surprised that peasant society is counted as one of them and the Civil War is another. This section is concluded by a summarizing essay in which I overview the whole process "In Historical Motion."

"Prometheus Unbound," as in the title of a well-known book on worldwide industrialization, is supplemented by the phrase "and Chained Again" in section two to fit the Soviet version of the process. Soviet industrialization under Stalin was a gigantic affair, but it was marred not only by its brutality but also by the appearance of internal "mechanisms" that would prove deadly for the system in the long run.

"The Faces of Leviathan," section three, is about the state system that was erected during the "big drive." Bureaucracy is a central theme here—as it is, to my mind, for the whole span of the Soviet period. It justified the subtitle of this volume—the "Superstate" predictably referring to the sprawling bureaucratic establishment that could not change, even when it faced extinction. It seemed becoming to include here an essay by Nikolay Bukharin, the man who prophetically dubbed the emerging system a "Leviathan" and only a few years later had seen enough of its ominous manifestations.

The last section deals with "The Springs of Demise" and the very peculiar way the regime passed away. The crisis this regime legated to the country is a very difficult one for the citizens to live through, and it is also quite a hurdle for anyone who tries to grasp its moving forces. Because each chapter attempts a broadly synthetic treatment of its topic, the recurrence of certain ideas and terms is unavoidable. Source overlap and repetition likewise proved difficult to avoid; it is hoped, the reader's patience will not be unduly tested. Whether the effort to gain some insights with the help of a historical interpretation was fruitful will be determined by the critical reader and by the unfolding events.

I would like to thank IREX (the International Research and Exhange Board) which supported two study trips to Russia, in 1987 and 1989 that allowed me to observe the development of the perestroika and to gain access to many previously unavailable publications, as well as to archival materials that impacted on many ideas contained in this book, even if the new material itself is quoted sparingly. There is no need to encumber these essays with an extensive scholarly apparatus that belongs more properly in monographs. I should also mention the importance of current Soviet publications—from newspapers to books—and the new openness introduced by perestroika that makes it possible to learn a wealth of things from endless encounters with citizens from the ex-USSR, who are not only invaluable sources but also often friends (although, obviously, in a number of cases, they proved no friends at all).

Over the years I enjoyed support from the Kennan Institute, which offered me a 1986–87 fellowship, and I received a six-month humanities fellowship from the National Endowment for the Humanities in 1989. André Schiffrin, the managing director of The New Press, was the one who persuaded me to produce *The Making of the Soviet System* when he was still managing Pantheon. It is a pleasure for me to do my new book with him in his new publishing venture.

RUSSIA/USSR/RUSSIA

THE HARD NUTS OF RUSSIAN HISTORY

CHAPTER I: USSR FROM A TO Z

An Introduction

A SOCIOHISTORICAL APPROACH THAT PROMPTS US TO LOOK AT large-scale social changes as being formative of social systems (not unlike geological shifts that shape landscapes, though certainly much slower) also enables us to identify some main features and the basic direction of such changes. In this case, the last seventy-five years of Russian and Soviet history (or a somewhat longer period if one begins the count, plausibly, from 1905) can be encompassed in a sweeping, but hopefully useful, generalization as a transition from a muzhik country to an urban one. The "sociology" of the country was rural well into the post–World War II period, and turned predominantly urban from the mid-1960s on, although not yet, to the same extent, in the Central Asian republics and some other areas. This sounds simple, but the whole time span during which the turning point occurred was actually extremely rich in complicated events and convolutions. This is why a book dealing with Soviet history cannot but continue to dwell on aspects of the rural past even while concerning itself with the processes that did the transforming—namely, collectivization of the peasantry, more fully treated in my earlier volume,[1] and industrialization, which is better represented in this one. But we do not forget the factor called "the state." In this context, the changing political regimes—Bolshevism, Stalinism, post-Stalinist political patterns, the changing character of the party, the bureaucracy and the relations among them—can be seen as piles of a political bridge

---

1. Cf. Moshe Lewin, *The Making of the Soviet System: Essays in the Social History of Interwar Russia* (1985; reprint, New York, 1994).

built over the transitional period, expressing its complexities, contributing to them, and then clearing the way for other forms evolving.

The latest changes, which involved the downfall of the previous system and now offers a bewildering picture of a society in crisis and in search of a new system, cannot but be uppermost on our minds. In this framework, the very character of the urbanization—its speed, spontaneity, and constraints specific to the Soviet conditions—becomes a key factor in understanding the difficulties that keep piling up on the way to reforms. The massive and large-scale uprooting that such an urbanization would, predictably, imply was not easily reabsorbed into a well-rooted urban society and culture, creating not only enormous difficulties for those who participate in the making or remaking (or even mere enduring) of the country, but also a challenge for those who try to contribute to the understanding of what is going on. As we endeavor to mobilize all our insights—notably those that history can, eventually, offer—we are also aware that what is happening and what is going to emerge in Russia and the whole area will force us to rethink the past as we knew it. This is why many of the essays in this book, whatever their central theme, tend to travel between some point in the past and land in or near the current situation.

Still, one should not be too hasty about drawing lessons from the ongoing changes. Today, many excited, even frenzied observers plunge into this now-accessible present and imagine that it is self-explanatory. The openness and accessibility of the ex-Soviet territory, as compared to the previous restrictions, do not automatically deliver clear and self-evident explanations about the past and the present. The millions of files now available from the archives do not do it either. The rush into current analyses and away from the longer-term historical approaches (away, actually, from the historical profession) may produce many intellectual bubbles and frustrations. The current events are still inconclusive, and it is too early to dismiss continuities and debts to history, including the so-called Soviet leg of it.

In this volume we will continue a line of thought that kept revising the weight, place, and character of ideology in the Soviet process, and we will concentrate on actual social changes of which ideology is an ingredient. Sometimes ideology preceded those changes, but usually it followed them, notably, the interests of the ruling strata; and it finally ended up in fragmenting or recomposing into different streams and amalgams.

Grasping the phenomenon and stages of Soviet bureacracy—its different layers, echelons, and pyramids—is a particularly important and new aspect in this context. We realize that bureaucracies and bureaucratic systems present many versions and patterns, and one of our key tasks is to reflect on what was specific about the Soviet bureaucracy, never, of course, disregarding its co-relations with the changing social realities around and inside it. As our attention focuses ever more on this tentacular force that, to my mind, was the most important feature (and "classifier") of the regime, the ideological differentiations inside bureaucracy take on a renewed meaning and weight. Even when study shows the system's inability to cope with the big socioeconomic problems of the country and, in this sense, its divorce from reality, such a divorce does not mean independence from broader historical transformations. To the contrary, the causes of the regime's inability to cope may well be found in the changing broader picture.

Anticipating a more expanded treatment of Soviet ideology in a subsequent chapter, we can say that Soviet socialism had no chance, not only because the conditions were not ripe for it in Russia but also because the system that was created there became, early on, adamant in refusing it. The appearing and hardening bureaucratic networks sought socialist credentials for themselves in the principle of nationalization, and their power was, in fact, a product of this principle and practice. But the same bureaucracy was the main force interested in thwarting any socialist development, but also refused capitalism and thus contributed an additional source of ideological confusion. By refusing democratization, this supposedly anticapitalist—hence, seemingly left-leaning—system in fact provided a powerful argument in favor of even faltering market economies by successfully claiming for itself socialist credentials—but running, equally successfully, a conservative, at times reactionary system.

The Soviet downturn is sometimes presented in a catchy title such as the "transition from socialism to capitalism." In this characterization, the sequence of "modes of production" once considered leftist and immutable is thus reversed (as some say it with sadness and others with glee). We will argue that such an interpretation is misleading. The sequence as it actually occurred is quite different—and no less intriguing.

Among the other crucial and recurrent historical themes, we have to mention the aspirations of the intelligentsia, which made it politically restless and active, but often also sterile and passive. Depending on who is talking and from what point of view, the intelligentsia is either the glory and pride of the country or its curse, as accusers from a group of rather conservative thinkers in the *Signposts* book and controversy had it.[2] The manifestations of the same dual picture can be seen in today's Russia, and the manichean vision of the intelligentsia is evident again. Is today's intelligentsia doing the job it traditionally claimed as the spearhead of freedom, or is it a hatchery of irresponsible anarchists, incurable Oblomovs, sterile political intriguers, and privilege mongers?

It is not the least of a whole system of paradoxes we are exploring that ex-Soviet intellectuals—some of them longtime critics, but most of them actually dependable mainstays of the previous regime—rushed into heralding the demise and end of "communism," "Socialism," and "Marxism," none of which they had actually ever practiced or known. Many also came out with sweeping "revisions" of Soviet history; but the past, liked or disliked, is a serious matter that does not just go away. It is especially pernicious to engage in misrepresenting or falsifying the past, which is a bad answer to the falsifications the previous regime was guilty of. Misrepresentation would amount to a self-inflicted wound rather than produce the badly needed clarification that historical analysis can offer.

The circumstances of the past cannot be redone, and actors have to be seen as doing what was feasible and possible at a given time. Talking about the past mainly in terms of "blame" or "guilt" to be apportioned, without a serious study of all the circumstances and forces involved, is an exercise in exorcism, not study.

As an example, I surmised in a recent book that conditions may be ripening in Russia for the fulfillment of the basically failed promises and hopes of both the March and the October revolutions of 1917.[3] There were actually three key constituencies on the historical arena of 1917, each one of them carrying a different prospect for Russia. The first was, in substance, the constituency that coagulated around the Provisional Government. It hoped for and carried the message of a Western-style democracy-cum-market economy. It should be remembered that the whole Marxist wing of the Russian left, including the Bolsheviks, fol-

---

2. *Vekhi* (Moscow, 1909). This source includes essays by an array of thinkers and public figures who attacked the Russian intelligentsia for their irresponsible radicalism and lack of understanding of the higher principles of statehood.

3. Moshe Lewin, *The Gorbachev Phenomenon* (rev. ed., Berkeley, Calif., 1991).

lowed Plekhanov's two-stage prognosis and hence belonged—or should have belonged—to the same constituency.

A "bourgeois-democratic" revolution was to be the next stage, to be followed by a socialist one at some time in the future. It was precisely because the Bolsheviks began to doubt whether such a stage was possible, in view of the perceived or actual weakness of this camp, that they parted company with the more moderate (though equally, if not more, orthodox) Marxists of the Menshevik wing and developed their own brand of radicalism. This rift became final in 1917. But the downfall of this bourgeois-democratic perspective began well before the Bolsheviks could capitalize on it, because the Provisional Government was not capable of handling the processes unfolding in the plebeian masses, whose radicalization was both a cause of and a response to the government's weakness.

Thus arose the other huge constituency whose radicalization fueled the phenomenon of Bolshevism, which espoused the basic requests emerging from the urban and rural plebs. The core requirement could best be characterized as "social justice" for the majority of the people who were underprivileged and deprived. Such yearnings existed independently of the actual amount of direct support that many of the common people offered the Bolsheviks; they could and often did revert to anti-Bolshevik moods and actions. The key to their response lay in the satisfaction of expectations that 1917 created. The great drama of those years stemmed from the fact that the ideals and ideas of the broadly democratic camps and those of the plebs did not find the needed common ground. In fact, the cleavages clearly and dangerously deepened.

The cause of the cleavages could be found, to some extent, in the fact that modern capitalist development created leadership groups that were naturally oriented either to the middle classes or to the many workers who appeared in the wake of the industrialization drives. In contrast, the enormous masses of the still "unmodern" Russia—mainly the peasantry—somehow were not viewed seriously as shapers of the future and of democracy, and this oversight caused the Provisional Government's downfall. Somewhat later, in different circumstances the Bolsheviks' own ideological stance toward "the proletariat" in the same plebs-dominated society was no less disappointing than the hopes the Mensheviks and social revolutionaries pinned on the middle classes.

The third constituency was the core of the "Whites," the forces rooted in the monarchist-nationalistic and imperial past and therefore equally hostile to both the Provisional Government and the "plebeian justice" perspectives. Their failure does not look very astonishing; rather, it was in the order of things—even if many in today's ex-USSR, especially in Russia, are trying to restore those doomed forces to some lustre.

The Bolsheviks, unlike the two other constituencies, could handle and could offer much to plebeian Russia. They were responsive to the mass yearning of the time—peace and land, in the first place—and some of them even had a theory about the genuine revolutionary potential of the peasantry. But as we know, they could handle this sometimes passive, sometimes explosive political sphinx only through the power of the state. In the process of building this state and using its might to make Russia move into the industrial age, the ruling party reinstated—in many ways and on a much larger scale—the statist-bureaucratic traditions of the previous regime.

The result was the "classical" Soviet double-header: First, the lifting of rural Russia into literacy, schooling, and industry had an emancipatory character. At the same time, the statist arsenal used—authoritarianism, indoctrination, and coercion—produced a disparity of power and privilege, an overgrowth of bureaucracy, and the dampening (and later, dumping) of much of the plebeian perspective and, eventually, also the proletarian "social justice" one. The first victim of this process was to be the Bolshevik Party itself. Soon thereafter, the socialist ideology also died, although somewhat more slowly. But this is not the whole story of the later—notably, post-Stalinist—development. The fact is that "perspectives" of a similar character—the bourgeois-democratic, the virulently nationalistic, and the different responses to popular demands for social justice—are here again today, facing each other and fighting for the future of Russia. The outcome is anyone's guess.

The Bolsheviks successfully tapped the sources of class hatred, national aspirations, and the additional and important resource that stemmed from their ability to produce a statehood amidst the wreckage of the Civil War. This, too, was a source of political capital that no other faction could harness. Once they won, Russia began to move in directions that were available or accessible to it, and Lenin began immediately to search for an appropriate new strategy, the gist of which consisted in toning down the older ideological radicalism and adapting the methods and objectives to Russian realities. However, death prevented Lenin from trying or implementing the new line. From then on, notwithstanding Stalin's "correction" that socialism can be built in Russia alone, pre-capitalist Russia (falsely presented after the October Revolution as post-capitalist) made a full circle that took the next sixty to seventy years and led back to the capitalism it had not managed to preserve earlier.

The initial doctrinal (Marxist) approach was actually vindicated. Capitalism, being in many ways superior to any previously known noncapitalist system, was supposed to prepare the ground for its replacement. Not only Marx and Plekhanov but also Lenin firmly believed in this. Because of this view, the Soviet phenomenon, although part of the history of socialist ideology, is not part of the history of socialism as an eventual system, which should not have developed in Russia according to tenets of the doctrine itself.[4] I shall return to this point in a later chapter.

My argument though, at this stage, rejects the validity of the ahistorical "rejections" of the whole post-1917 period, which are very popular in Russia today. This is an ideological, not a scholarly, stand. In many ways, the past is still meaningfully shaping the historical agenda and the available alternatives, although the environment has changed and many older ideas have been reformulated.

Let us now resume the theme of the larger social trends that either defined or transformed the key features of the historical agenda, but from a somewhat different angle. "Pre-urbanized" Russia, which lasted until the late 1950s or even the early 1960s, was still part of the worldwide "grand narrative" of our times—that is, the transformation of deeply rural civilizations into urban-industrial societies.[5] There are different types of such transitions, but they do have some features in common, at least initially.

Attention to social and political change helped us discern in Soviet history much more mobility and many more transitional forms than

---

4. Socialists could still take power, without aiming at an immediate adoption of or transition to socialism. They do just this when, hoping to make a difference, they form governments in capitalist countries. Mensheviks and Soviet Russians did not want to take this road—i.e., form a purely socialist government through the Soviet network that might later have been confirmed by the Constituent Assembly. Lenin's sobering up after the Civil War implied this kind of potential: a socialist government running something much less than a socialist system.

5. Cf. John Thompson, *Ideology and Modern Culture* (Cambridge, 1990), p. 75.

would show up if a more static approach was adopted. The system, including its political forms, was constantly in motion, although this mobility was not only "upward" or "downward" but also zigzagging. Pointing to trends such as "mobility" and occasional "flux" does not mean that no transformations into new and different fixities occurred that defined or redefined the flow and direction of sociopolitical and cultural forms.

Instead, crucial for our discussion is the idea of a (changing) social "bedrock," which I also raised in *The Making of the Soviet System.* I proposed there the concept of an "agrarian nexus" that changed its features as it passed through the tsarist, early Soviet and Stalinist stages until it left the stage to a different social system altogether as Russia became urbanized and, today, tries to "reinvent" itself as an urban society and system. Ideas concerning the changing social background also recognized a recurring syndrome in Russian development, "a curse" of sorts haunting this country's history: rapid change and stagnation have alternated or, often, coexisted. Hectic advances in many aspects of life have been overshadowed by painful "accentuations of backwardness" and retreats, which I sketch out in this introductory chapter and elaborate on in the following chapters.

In other words, the country's developmental effort is still the appropriate (even if not original) approach for studying the making of the Soviet system and also of its unmaking. But the whole approach also requires our further complicating of "the narrative." First, the Russian process must be placed in a broader context of world and European history, which generated enormous pressures, especially in the techno-economic sphere but also more broadly in cultural spheres, that even the greatest isolation and autarchy could not eliminate. Next, we must single out the specific process of state building that was involved in organizing and ideologically securing the "social reproduction," a crucial subnarrative.[6]

These initial remarks represent the framework that the essays in this book try to fill out in different ways and from different angles. It would be good to settle for just one "grand narrative" or central theme, but the complexities of history do not allow this. The big themes tend to overlap or to branch out in different directions, which makes it more difficult for

---

6. See Theodor Shanin, *Russia as a Developing Society,* 2 vols. (New Haven, Conn., 1985). Shanin deals with this problem, especially in chapter 4 of volume 1.

an author to handle and for the reader to follow; but a more complex approach is necessary, even if only to raise problems.

The great weight of the social and economic agrarian base in the tsarist period and, equally, in the Soviet period is well known. But what is probably not yet fully grasped is the "system-making" quality of this base as part of a crucial historical equation that actually commanded the character and fate of the evolving Soviet system during and especially after the Civil War. The predominantly muzhik society—with its small-scale horizons and limited productive capacities, three-field system, very modest market orientation, and interesting but parochial village community and culture—in interplay with the state and its agencies (notably, in the state's capacity as the owner of the most important economic assets and the carrier of a modernizing ideology) are the two big partners, each endowed with a different dynamic and perceptions of reality. They belonged, in a way, to incompatible centuries, with little in between to smooth the contacts or the clashes. It is not too difficult to work out, just by using one's imagination, the string of consequences that could— and did—follow from the actions of a state facing a crisis, when its main object of domination is this kind of social base. The transformation of this agrarian landscape into an industrial one is a leading thread of "the big narrative" of Russia's modern history. The switch was occurring almost directly from a stage dominated by a precapitalist peasantry to some other stage that is today considered defunct. We say "precapitalist" because the Russian peasants, despite the inroad of a market economy, were not yet even "petty bourgeois," that is, a group that was composed of producers of merchandise—not just of objects of direct use. Russian peasants of the 1920s were moving toward this, but only barely.

The extent to which the capitalist market economy managed to transform the peasant economy in tsarist Russia is an interesting but still understudied problem. It is well known that this was happening on some scale, under the impact of railroads, state taxation, the growth of industrial centers, the development of suburban, highly commercialized (export-oriented) farms in the south and the southeast. But had these trends been very powerfully developed, Stolypin's reforms would have been an aberration. The question would not have been "Did his reforms succeed?" but rather "What were they for?" This being the case, the task consists in ascertaining what actually did happen to the bulk of the peasantry in the main overpopulated agricultural regions. If they continued to act, primarily as household economies, with little to spare for the market (because of the weakness of their tradeable surpluses), or if the surpluses were artificially created, negative ones squeezed from the peasants by taxation and vodka, then one would understand the continuing impoverishment and growing surpluses of the rural population. Some interesting signs of progress in selected areas and sectors would not yet change the picture.

Answering the question of the peasantry's fate would help in answering a related one: Was the crisis of old Russia due to too much or too little capitalist development? This would also help us determine, however figuratively, the century to which the prerevolutionary peasantry really belonged. The same question comes into an even sharper focus after the Civil War, during which the peasantry crawled deeper into its protective shell of a naturalized, self-centered economy, becoming a huge social layer (almost a whole nation) of an inward-looking, prebourgeois society that still needed to learn or relearn the ways of a marketing producer. Such a backsliding would not have been possible if the involvement in a market economy had been deeper before.

We can now see that the problem raised in relation to the end of tsarism resurfaces again in 1921 but concerns, equally, the situation in 1928–29, toward the end of the New Economic Policy (NEP), when the overall marketability of the rural economy was still inferior to even the prewar standards.

Hence, dwelling on the essence of this peasantry continues to be important for answering the larger question of how Russia's historical development has occurred, because the state of the *muzhiki* defined the starting base when the violent switchover to an industrial age was undertaken and, therefore, was crucial in shaping the outcome. Corresponding to the noncommodity (or weak commodity) production, was a huge social stratum that was poorly integrated in the national (and international) entity. To a large extent, this stratum comprised a very localized, fragmented mass of "small rural worlds" that did not directly partake of the entity because of their limited experience and horizons. In practical terms, this means that, unlike in a developed rural marketing system, there were not enough resources to educate children properly, especially not in the higher-level schools; the overall literacy level was extremely low, especially among women; the technological orientation was weak; and the reliance on—even addiction to—old ways in life and work remained powerful. Change did take place, but it was blocked; and unblocking it by "direct means," as was tried, brought momentous results for the outlook of the whole polity. Thus, the idea of relatively little mobility is crucial for understanding the turmoil induced in this social stratum and is an important background feature of Soviet development during the 1930s.

Dwelling on the narrow horizons of the peasants means comparing them with contemporaries who partake of broader horizons of their time. But in doing so, the intent is to examine facts, and not to demean or accuse the peasantry. The historical role of the peasantry in Russian history cannot be denied, although they themselves could not glorify this role in history books. The colossal efforts of peasants in mastering the Russian territory—with their axes and scythes, and sometimes even their bare hands, over the immense stretches of taigas and steppes, as they faced many enemies ahead of them and were pursued by the state and its servants, the lords, who were coming to reap the fruits and enserf them—are well-known facts of the Russian (or Slav) historical epic. But it is far from being a joyful story. The image of *burlaki* hauling immense barges on the Volga is a fitting symbol for the fate of the peasantry then and later—but also for much of the heavy thread of Russian history in general.

Parallel to the colonizing toil of the peasants went the expansion and growth of the state, well exemplified by the rule of Ivan the Terrible, with its twin prongs of a centralized state and an absolutist, powerful tsar (who used a terroristic police force in his personal service and who was a crazed individual). Our thumbnail survey can legitimately mention here also Peter the Great, with his impetuous effort of transplanting industrial and administrative forms from abroad while simultaneously reinforcing the chains of serfdom. He was, no doubt, an interesting historical figure, not known to be crazy; but he was an heir, nevertheless, to Grozny's absolutism, since he ran his vast empire like a private domain. (He also practiced a personal brand of hands-on politics: he learned to show his underlings how to find things, and, with sword or axe in hand, he also liked to personally execute rebels.)

Emancipation of the peasants in 1861 was another milestone, an effort to undo much of the work of the previous centuries of enserfment. This momentous event nevertheless reproduced an agrarian problem in a new garb and transformed the muzhik again into a political powder keg, although he was believed to be the system's mainstay.

Famines, wars, and revolutions have to be mentioned in which peasants played a key role, though mainly as victims and as the ones who bore the costs. The same applied to the hectic capitalist development—an important economic upward movement that, nevertheless, contributed to a growing crisis of tsarism that burst to the surface in the 1905 revolution, which looked like a wasted one that dashed the hopes of the peasants and of the by then sizeable middle classes.

From this perspective, the Bolshevik thinking and fears about the petty bourgeoisie *stikhia* (spontaneity) take on a new dimension: it may well be that what Soviet Russia needed, at the minimum, was in fact a transformation of the peasantry into a market-oriented petty bourgeoisie, even though this very need tended to be seen in many party circles (though not at all by everyone in the party leadership) as a grave danger on politico-ideological grounds. The suspicions and the furor of some earlier, but mainly later, Stalinist policies went in part against the emerging marketing sectors, but finally and mostly against the bulk of the peasantry.

Deeply miscontrued and poorly used class distinctions, seeing in the peasants either "breeders of capitalism" or "a petty bourgeoisie spontaneity," only masked the profound reality of the Stalinist revolution. That revolution in fact claimed a special status for itself in Marxist terms but was not and could not have been an anticapitalist revolution (as misrepresented by propaganda), and not even an anti–petty bourgeoisie one, so that it was neither socialist nor capitalist. *What,* then, was it? The terms used seem to engage us in a futile search for an elusive reality. And yet the study of the peasantry brings us nearer to working out a definition, though not without the introduction of additional dimensions.

As my chapter on "Taking Grain" in *The Making of the Soviet System* showed,[7] the state's dealings with the peasantry under Stalin became a

---

7. Lewin, *The Making of the Soviet System.* This essay was initially published in the Festschrift for E. H. Carr.

matter of direct appropriation of surpluses—not unlike in some ancient kingdoms (whether feudal or Asiatic is beyond the point here)—without remuneration. This was accompanied by and resulted in a noneconomic industrialization (of the countryside and of cities) as well. Party, *Komsomol,* propaganda, and accelerated schooling, tried to replace the impact and stimuli that the economic activity in the "collectivized" framework did not provide, and they managed to replace some of the missing links. But they had to do it from scratch, as well as from outside, whereas a highy stimulating economic activity would have generated change from inside, as it were.

Hence, the idea comes to mind that Stalinism recreated in Russia, although just provisonally, the last model of a *sui generis* "agrarian kingdom." But it was a particularly vicious one, in which the stimuli inherent in a free economic activity were replaced with a squeezing of producers by state-coercive means, transforming their status into a replica of serfdom. Against this background, it is easier to grasp also the contradictory policy during Stalin's rule—and in different forms later, too—toward the new social layers that emerged in industrialization: some of them were getting ready to rejoin the spirit of the century and of "modernization" and hence, at least potentially, were becoming critical of the basic premises of the system, even as they were learning to extract from it privileges and power. The appearance of layers that would, sooner or later, press for expanding their autonomy was constantly creating cracks in the Stalinist system, which was based on mass control and ample application of violence, first in the countryside and then in the industrial and bureaucratic workplaces, in an effort to counteract the effects of poor labor incentives and lax attitudes toward productivity. Stalinism therefore was grounded in a fear of the unavoidable results of its own action; hence, perverse and destructive mass terror reigned. The paradox here was that the same "attitude" applied also toward Stalinism's creature and mainstay—bureaucracy, a social stratum that created interests of its own and powerful levers to take care of them.

In this way, the whole frame of reference made a system reappear in the 1930s that was endowed with features of an agrarian despotism. What had stemmed initially and largely from coercion applied to the rural world was perpetuated and applied to the growing nonrural social strata. We explore later in this chapter the extent to which such features were still in place after Stalin's death.

Yet another excursion into Russian history may confirm the recurrence of some features that various observers and thinkers perceived and dubbed differently, but whose substance remained the same: the past kept weighing heavily on the present over centuries and skewed or distorted new developments, policies, and hopes. If this is true, we have to be atuned to the presence of continuities between the prerevolutionary past and the different stages of the Soviet period, including the very latest. This will offer additional ideas for the deeper understanding not only of Stalinism but also of the post-Stalinist era. Examples of what we have in mind abound. Peter the Great developed ("modernized") the country by importing models of economic and administrative institutions, but he also spread and strengthened serfdom. And as long as serfdom lasted, it undermined many of the positive effects of his and anybody else's "modernizations."

Reading Marc Raeff's "The Style of Russian Imperial Policy and Prince G. A. Potemkin"[8] gives more weight to such observations for the post-Petrine period. We learn how Prince Potemkin, the most outstanding statesman in Catherine the Great's service, reproduced, in different forms, the same syndrome: this "last great statesman" of pre-1917 Russia engaged in a large-scale expansion into the south (and Crimea, with beginnings of penetration into the Caucasus, and so on), experimenting with and introducing in the new areas interesting administrative and educational innovations. But, here again, the "modernization" (Raeff knows the reservations about the term but finds it useful in the Russian context—and rightly so) was marred by the spread of serfdom into the new areas, or rather by the combination of serfdom and the constraints of the rigid centralized (bureaucratic-militaristic) regime that existed in Russia itself. The energies, initiatives, and activities of the local, often ethnic, populations—badly needed for the economic and cultural growth of the new territories—were nipped in the bud.

This was the manifestation of a dualism that Raeff discerned—a grand policy that nevertheless undermined itself by its internal contradictions. We can expand the argument by maintaining that the same

---

8. Marc Raeff, "The Style of Russian Imperial Policy and Prince G. A. Potemkin," in G. N. Grob, ed., *Statesmen and Statescraft of the Modern West: Essays in Honor of Dwight E. Lee and H. Donaldson Jordan* (Barre, Mass., 1967), pp. 1–51.

contradictory twin effects (others would call it "effects of combined development") that kept creating in Russia proper a huge social question reproduced themselves in the new territories, populated by ethnically different peoples, in the form of exacerbated ethnic contradictions that would pop up later in the form of numerous "national questions."

Raeff described the Russian ruling class's policy of accepting nobilities of the different "natives" (including Cossacks) into the ranks of its own nobility and gentry, and thus accelerating their assimilation (Russification). This made Russia's ruling class practically multiethnic, which was not seen as much of a problem until a similar phenomenon reappeared in the ethnic composition of the revolutionary parties and regime. But I would point to an additional "dual outcome" again: the policy of incorporating elites of non-Russians into Russia's nobility had a potential of increasing the sources of national strife because the local lower classes, in addition to reacting to Moscow's centralism and serfdom, would also incorporate into the politico-ideological knot the battle against their nobility, whether Russified or local agents of the tsars. The potential for strife and sharpened national feelings could thereby become even more explosive.

This kind of "burden of Russian history," the syndrome of the Russian predicament that afflicted the previous generations, returned after the revolution and took on the form of recurring big thrusts forward, accompanied or followed by the disheartening sight of abused and wasted chances. Deeper layers of history, still smoldering, were at work, and they either induced immobility or skewed the results of dynamic thrusts and envenomed crises that punctuated the history of the country.

I survey the post-1917 period in several essays, pointing to the crashing backsliding during the Civil War. Such backsliding comes as no surprise if one recognizes that during the Civil War many branches, especially industry, saw a precipitous backward movement, in some cases even to the preemancipation level—a catastrophe of major proportions, especially when one adds demography and other vital aspects of human existence. The heavy load of the war and Civil War periods forced the country to move quickly during the NEP toward a target, only to find itself more backward after restoration than in 1913. Hence, an achievement that compared with the pre-1928 boom years in the West amounted to a new "accentuated retardation" of Russia, although the

NEP was a peaceful and relatively relaxed period. Yet another version of the same syndrome, on a huge scale this time, appeared under Stalin. Despite its dynamism, Stalinism itself was another version of the same syndrome of the past—namely, the coupling of a rather backward, strongly controlled society and an overgrown state. Stalinism also represents another example of the "regressive movements" that, through vicious and mendacious oppression, can cause severe sociopsychological damage to the youth, to the intelligentsia, to the broader populace, and to the leadership itself. Stalin made a bold and violent move to handle the problems of a backward country, but he ended up repeating the Peter the Great syndrome: a gigantic industrialization effort coupled with a loss of freedom, a cultural and political counterrevolution, and the making of a barbaric system built on the ruins of a great emancipatory ideal. A few years later came the glorious, but so terribly costly, victory in World War II, followed by a further relapse into the last chapter of Stalinism, this time with a page taken from Grozny rather than from Peter: the half-crazed Stalin, surrounded by security guards whom he did not trust, hid in a bunker and plotted ever more phantasmagoric purges, which he obviously considered to have been his greatest political invention.

Yet another version of the same evolution occurred thereafter. The cold war, on top of the victory in World War II, appeared to be a victory—the Soviet Union gained superpower status, expanded its empire, and experienced an enormous boost for its bureaucratic and other elites. Such changes seemed to be a historical seal of approval for the Soviet methods and, unfortunately, also a powerful anaesthetic. Under the cover of the seemingly glorious status of being a leader "of the peace camp," pernicious forces were at work but were stubbornly overlooked by self-satisfied leaders; these forces made for a repeating of the accentuated, hopeless lagging. Hence, the nation's stride forward to an unprecedented position as a superpower would soon be transformed into dust.

The agrarian past of tsarism and the relative weakness of insufficient strength of capitalist development were important features that could account for the wholesale and, visibly, "premature" nationalization of economic assets under the Soviets. But the idea of "premature" may be misleading: the wholesale takeover by the state, especially in the 1930s, was still something emanating from the depths of the Russian political tradition, not necessarily and not only from the wrong—that is, "premature"—application of a supposedly socialist principle. Whatever the ideological underpinning, this process strengthened and expanded the role of the state; and in this increased power of the state versus the constrained and dominated countryside lies the secret of the backslides that kept recurring, at an enormous cost to society, especially to its culture and moral fiber.

And yet the dual character of, say, Stalinism should not make us miss other important features in Russia's development. A regime does not easily respond to a double-ledger accounting system; it is part of a broader social landscape, with many factors working inside and outside the system of government and escaping its control. Theories that such a regime does manage to control everything miss the other factors, both open and hidden, that powerfully shaped the presumed monopolistic shaper himself. One of the important contributions of social history in studying the Soviet Union was recognition of the processes resulting from what millions of people did or did not want to do in order to go on living as they learned to play the system. The ensuing process—including activities of the state, often chaotic and contradictory themselves, and the reactions of millions—gave to historical evolution the character of spontaneity that was much richer than regime studies alone would afford us. Spontaneous developments were at work in subverting Stalinism, in changing the whole social landscape of the country and the rules of the game, and, finally, in undermining the regime's capacity to act and bringing its downfall. Obviously, a spontaneous development, certainly neither planned nor willed, was (and is) at work; and such a development transcends the narrower confines of the political regime and, finally, makes it or breaks it.

Observing deep structural shifts over the historical period in question allows us to understand better the changing stages and landscapes, crises, and dynamic thrusts that brought us to the most complicated contemporary situation of the 1980s: an urban society getting ever more complex and a political system trying to retain a relatively primitive configuration of power inherited from the 1930s. (In contrast, during the 1920s, the social base was slow-moving, and the state was action-oriented and impatient.) We thus witness a reversal of "the vectors of historical movement." It was now the urban social system that became complex and required a more modern political system, whereas the existing state was now playing the role of the passive and backward-looking factor.

So the shift from a predominantly rural to a predominantly urban society was again a powerful crisis maker, and it is this crisis in which Russia (and the whole surrounding area) is plunged today. Nevertheless, even if it is right to point to the "burden of history" expressed in recurrent backslidings, it still is not true that all there is to Russia is reforms and counterreforms. In the recent changes something quite momentous was also occurring—a point not to be missed.

THE RUSSIAN AND SOVIET STATISM

We are probably in agreement by now that comparisons with Russia's own past—"modernization" of the eighteenth century, reinforced by the imperial expansion of the nineteenth—are useful for understanding key features in Stalinism and not a few features of the system thereafter. Yet it is in fact difficult to find an "age" in the Russian past that can be compared with the post-Stalinist stage in Soviet history, because Russia never had a system so thoroughly bureaucratized. One has to go elsewhere for examples. Despite this, broader comparative elements of the common historical hurdle should focus on the persistence of "statism," whatever the actual form it takes. This "principle" was perfected under Catherine and Potemkin, then got severely weakened toward the end of the next century, only to be recreated by the revolution, in several versions. Statism—a deeply bureaucratized "command-administrative system" that not even the Catholic Church could match (as a historical precedent). The Peter-Potemkin version of capricious authoritarians-autocrats was still continued under Stalin, but it was replaced by the supposedly more collective "bureaucratic absolutism" (a term we explore in the chapter on bureaucracy). If in some earlier stages the party played a leading role in this statism, this role was seriously curtailed and maimed under Stalin, then recovered under Khrushchev—but it got fully "etatized" in the process itself. So it is "etatization"—or rather its full-fledged result, "statism"—to which we should now turn.

Statism needs a thorough theoretical and historical inquiry. Here, we can briefly explain that we mean not just the centrality of the state in the country's life but an ideology extolling its superiority as the highest principle of social organization, for which Hegel's "absolutization" of the state, having Prussia as an implicit and explicit model, would serve here as a fitting descriptor. Incidentally, even though much has been said about the influence of Byzantium on the tsarist state, the impact of Prussia seems to be less known or realized. When we come to Stalin's Russia, we are aware that building a powerful state became the official aim, and the centrality of monopolistic state power, its ubiquity and monopoly on leadership in most, if not all, spheres of life, was especially emphasized through designation of the secret police as representing the highest form of state service. In addition to these features of "statism," an orientation toward bureaucracy—both as the key social force in itself and as the provider of leadership and values—is another crucial component of the whole equation. A preference for cadres of low social origin was characteristic of the regime's revolutionary roots, but this fact was not relevant to the statist phenomenon as such, once remnants of previous privileged classes had left the stage. It is relevant, though, for understanding the support that the regime got from below and the cultural climate inside the power grid. Bukharin's bewildered accusation of his fellow Politburo members in early 1929 that they were erecting "a Leviathan state" proved more than just a suspicion.

After Stalin, the terroristic elements were contained, but the key ideological tenet of the regime—namely, the supremacy of the state and the bureaucratic character of its practices—grew stronger as the state's capacity to rule was diminishing. Obviously, this was the opposite of what a socialist ideology would require. The Soviet development overturned the original aspirations, because the social carrier and ruler became somebody else—namely, the bureaucracy that formed the substratum of the state and of Soviet statism.

Why the world and the Soviets themselves—especially their intellectuals—agreed to consider this system "socialist," and either defended or hated it for this presumed feature, is not a small puzzle.

In any case, statism-as-ideology became the main plank in the platform and in the self-image of the powerful bureaucracy that ran it all; it overshadowed all other aspects that were still lingering from previous ideologies. *Gosudarstvo* became more important than any social principle. The party that in earlier stages had represented the working classes as their vanguard now became the vanguard of the state—which, basically, amounted to the party being the coordinating committee and the representative of, first and foremost, the bureaucracy. In fact, this is not the whole story yet. The bureaucratized party stopped being an independent political party; it was one apparatus among many, and even if very central, it was "coopted." The very fact that all leading positions were taken up by party members (the *nomenklatura*) allowed the bureaucratic interests to become, ipso facto, politically neutralized: they became exempt from the accusation of being antiparty deviations. In an overwhelmingly bureaucratic ethos of Soviet statism, serving bureaucratic interests could easily be presented as acting "in the general interest." Thus, party membership of all the top bosses became largely irrelevant, or it served as a common alibi for the powerful state administrations that kept fighting among themselves for power and means—and, finally, blocked the system from going anywhere. The presumably soothing, even democratic-sounding process of *soglasovyvanie,* or coordination, became a system of discordance. The Russian term *rassoglasovannost'* is more ironic and difficult to translate. In fact, this was a governmental process that was undermined by its agencies turning into powerful lobbies. As the party became subsumed in the bureaucracy, the *rassoglaso-vannost'* paralyzed it, too.

It is this bundle of features and factors that contains the "secret" of the overcentralization that made the center impotent and the regime crumbly. Obviously, any system is bound to change, and some self-destructive features must be present in it, but there also are sources of renovation, a capacity to mend things. In the Soviet case, the self-destructive elements became very strong, while the forces for renovation and alternative models to switch over to became weak. This fact manifested itself in the behavior of the ruling stratum, whose members seemed ready to keep sinking the system, as long as all their own routines and their privileges and power continued. This stratum thus lost any active historical role and sense of identity.

The power of a state constantly recovering and growing in response to the frailty of the body social is one of the "burdens" that afflicted the population in the course of Russian history. Immensely powerful, on one hand, yet under pressure and in danger of decomposition, on the other, the Russian state gyrated at different moments in history, including several times during the Soviet period alone: in revolution and civil war; in the flux of the Stalin years; during World War II; in the uncontrolled, often traumatizing, and poorly mastered urbanization of the last thirty years; and today, again as the fragile nation fights for survival and for regaining control of its fate by restoring a viable state—a big theme in Russian-Soviet history and a very costly challenge for its people.

There were stages and turning points in this process that have to be pinpointed by more research. Chapter 13, called "Autopsy Report," will cast more light on the "self-destructive mechanism" that nagged the system until it was shut tight but that made the "burden of history" into a weighty theme again. I return to this and other points in Chapter 15, although we will have to abstain from too hastily promising firm and unambiguous statements, given the uncertainties, fluidity, and anxieties that mark the current scene.

However, we can retain here, as one provisional conclusion, that the modernizing state system, anticapitalist in its ideology, departed from a basically precapitalist mode and moved forcefully into another mode that was neither capitalist nor postcapitalist. But since such measures of historical change have a baffling relativity to them, it may well be that the whole dynamic and upward thrust of the regime made it move, in many ways, backward (and it runs the risk of backsliding again right now). As noted earlier, in somewhat different terms, this happened several times over in Russian history.

POSTSCRIPT

Reflections about the "burden of history" and "recurrent backslidings" are inspired by, among others, Kliuchevski, most notably in his book on Peter the Great, and by his broadly formulated diagnosis of the Russian system (and syndrome) as a rich and powerful state facing a poor and powerless society. Trotsky's idea about "combined development" was also influential, but in his short introduction to his history of the revolution, he gave no sources.[9] Trotsky may have drawn from Marx himself, who spoke about "uneven development," which Ernest Bloch called "die Gleichzeitigkeit der Ungleichzeitigen."[10] In another version, Alexander Yanov refers to something like a law of history: every reform always ends up in counterreforms. He does not see any end to this "cyclical recurrence" without help (or maybe interference) from the West.[11]

The different aspects of the "burden of history" or "curse of his-

---

9. Leon Trotsky, *The History of the Russian Revolution* (1932; reprint, New York, 1980).

10. See David Blackbourn and Geoff Eley, *The Peculiarities of German History* (New York, 1987), pp. 238–41.

11. Alexander Yanov, *The Russian Challenge and the Year 2000* (New York, 1987).

tory"—namely, the spasms of "recurrent retardation"—are actually different versions and manifestations of a basic historical dilemma. The "strong state, weak society" syndrome and another version of it, a "strong state, weak society, inadequate economic base" syndrome, are interconnected. The dual feature in the Peter the Great syndrome, as repeated in Stalinism, can also be represented by the concept of "combined development," which points to the intermingling of the most advanced with the most archaic features in the political systems of backward countries that attempt a speedy modernization. If this particular type of correlation softened after Stalin, it did not disappear, whereas other versions of the "Russian curse" continued their manifestations, especially in the renewed "accentuated retardation" (accentuated, that is, relative to the indicators of the developed countries) that finally brought down the wasteful state. Some more ideas about this subject are proposed in the conclusion to the chapter on Stalin.

CHAPTER 2: THE VILLAGE AND

THE COMMUNITY

"Molecular Energy" in Rural Societies

THERE IS STILL A LOT THAT IS UNCLEAR ABOUT THE COM-
plexities of the *obshchina,* though much has become known
recently thanks, notably, to the growing amount of work done
by Soviet researchers. This chapter will try to explore some additional
dimensions that will, initially, complicate the picture, in the belief that,
sometimes, things must be further obscured before they get clearer.

But first let me point to a number of confusing terminological and
practical problems that students of this field stumble into.

The first hurdle is the *obshchestvo* and the *obshchina* mix-up. It should
not have been one, because the former was supposed to relate to the official administrative unit established in 1861—*sel'skoe obshchestvo*—the
latter to the unit of land-use called *pozemel'naia obshchina.* Yet in the
later nineteenth century even Russian lawmakers themselves, and many
authors, interchanged the two, probably because they often overlapped if
the territory involved concerned just one village. And this case allows us
to introduce yet another source of problems.

We are aware of three types of commune (the term we adopt, sometimes,
in English to denote an *obshchina*), depending, as Kuchumova explored it,
on their village-related (*poderevenskaia*) structure: the simple one, when we
find one commune representing one village; the "split" one (*razdel'naia*),
when there were two or more communes in one village.[1] The reasons for
such situations lay in the preemancipation mode of ownership of villages by
landowners (*pomeshchiki*). Or else, as V. V. (Vorontsov) explained, a complex commune would also emerge during the colonization of, say, the
southern steppe, when a group of peasants would branch out from the
main village, create a hamlet, and develop it into a village—but stay in the

---

1. L. K. Kuchumova, "Sel'skaia pozemel'naia obshchina Evropeiskoj Rossii v 60–70
gody XIX–go veka," *Istoricheskie Zapiski,* 106 (Moscow, 1981), pp. 333–35.

framework of the same land-use unit.[2] It might also, in such cases, be called *obshchestvo* as long as it served as a police and tax-raising agency for the government, but so far as the function of communal land-tenure was concerned, an important and simplifying factor would set in which is crucial for our argument. The *obshchestvo,* which often, especially in the northern and northwestern parts of the country, included several communes and villages, was obscuring the deeper underlying reality—namely, the single village—that would assert its weight in due course, whatever the categories. P. N. Pershin, in his work published in 1928, showed that in the Central Industrial Region there were 15 percent of "split" communes and only 0.4 percent of the "complex" variety, but an overwhelming majority were "simple"—one commune equaled one village.[3]

The same was attested earlier by Vorontsov for the whole black earth belt: "As numbers go, it is the simple communes that prevail; next come the split ones, whereas the complex ones occur rather rarely."[4]

We will draw more conclusions from these statements later. In the meantime, another phenomenon should be cited: the importance of the commune as an object of research and controversy caused writers to subsume many aspects of rural life under the commune label. The role of the elders, concepts of justice, problems of the family, ethical and aesthetic views, education of youth and children, attitudes toward women—all are sometimes described as characterizing "the commune," happening "in the commune" or deriving from it;[5] the real carrier of such phenomena, the village (*derevnia*), is somehow overlooked by these procedures. On the other hand, numerous titles promising to deal with *derevnia kak ona est', sovremennaia derevnia* ("the village as it is," "the contemporary village") and such, doing a very useful job of it, nevertheless actually do describe an administrative unit, like the *volost'* or even larger areas, without studying in depth the primary cell of rural life. *Derevnia* became coterminous with "peasantry" or

---

2. V. V. (Vorontsov), "Krest'ianskaia obshchina" in *Itogi ekonomicheskogo issledovaniia Rossii po dannym zemskoj statistiki* (Moscow, 1892), pp. 539–75.

3. P. N. Pershin, *Zemel'noe ustrojstvo dorevoliutsionnoj Rossii,* vol. 1 (Moscow-Voronezh, 1928), p. 18.

4. V. V., "Krest'ianskaia obshchina," p. 535.

5. See, for example, N. A. Minenko, "Stariki v russkoi krest'ianskoij obshchine Zapadnoi Sibiri" in L. M. Rusakova and N. A. Minenko, eds., *Kul'turno-bytovye protsessy u russkikh Sibiri XVII–nach. XX–go veka* (Novosibirsk, 1985), pp. 89–104. The title itself points to the problem. The elders played quite similar roles in many, if not all, traditional peasant societies, and Minenko's article lumps together indiscriminately the role of the older peasant in *obshchina skhody* with many other functions inside the village that do not have much to do with the *obshchina.*

"country" on a macrolevel, the micro-level being left to travelers, ethnographers, or memoirs written by people of rural origin. Reading those, incidentally, it is obvious that the autobiographies, whether fondly or with bitterness, speak about their native *village,* never their native *obshchina.* No one was ever born *v obshchine* but rather *v derevne.* (The *derevnia* versus *selo* problem can happily be omitted here. Initially *selo* was a bigger settlement that also had a church—but in time the terms became interchangeable, except in the Ukraine, where *selo* is the accepted term.)

We are now aware that most communes were "simple," but we will also see later that even in cases where this was not so, two versions can be mentioned. Sources say that whenever the *obshchina* was complex or when the *obshchestvo* comprised several villages, those villages would often have little in common (in the case of an *obshchestvo*) in matters concerning land tenure—they just handled their land and its redistributions inside their own compound and deferred to the bigger unit for police and other administrative matters. When the broader unit was termed *obshchina* and had its business debated by the "big gathering" (*bol'shoi skhod*), a similar phenomenon would often take place: for redistribution of land each village would convene its *malyi skhod*—the same pattern, again, of returning to basics. The essential problem of land use and tenure would revert to the unit where it could be handled best.[6]

It is now time to discover yet another angle in our argument. There were different landholding and tenure patterns in the villages. In addition to the communal landholding there also existed villages with a farmstead (*podvornoe*) land tenure, and their land would not undergo redistribution, even though those villages still had a communal organization.[7] Such facts remind us that although there were different communal arrangements in different areas and at different times, which could even fluctuate inside the villages, the communal forms did come and go—but the village stayed.

Now, another intriguing element: according to Kaufman and others, the villagers themselves did not use the term *commune* (*obshchina*)— they knew only the term *mir*[8] (as in "the *mir* decided"—*mir poreshil,* and

---

6. Kuchumova, "Sel'skaia pozemel'naia obshchina," p. 336; V. E. Postnikov, *Iuzhno-russkoe krest'ianskoe khoziajstvo* (Moscow, 1891), pp. 76–78.

7. A. M. Anfimov, *Krest'ianskoe khoziajstvo Evropeiskoi Rossii 1881–1904* (Moscow, 1981), p. 86, gives data showing 2,787,447 homesteads in 1905 (16.6 percent of the total) holding their land in homestead ownership. The book contains a wealth of material on many aspects of rural society and economy in prerevolutionary Russia.

8. A. A. Kaufman, "Pozemel'naia obshchina," in *Entsiklopedicheskij Slovar',* Brokgauz-Efron, T. XXIV (St. Petersburg, 1898), p. 215.

so on). As we realize that there could be different forms of communal organization, we should also avoid, as V. P. Danilov suggested, identifying the commune with its redistributive functions.[9] The farmstead landholding system did not eliminate either the mixed-strip field layout (*chrespolositsa*), nor, as just stated, did communal life disappear there. Obviously, different terms should have been coined for the commune that does not repartition arables anymore and for the one that does.

The latter case was, in fact, sufficiently important to be distinguished; but we must not forget that we have just referred to another term—the *mir*—and it is important to place this rural concept—not at all recognized by official statistics or legislation—among the competing terms and realities. Even very seasoned authors do switch from *obshchina* to *mir* indiscriminately although some, like Vorontsov and, in a contemporary text, Danilov, actually distinguish between the two—without, to my knowledge, elaborating upon the reason for doing so.[10]

But this may be the crux of the matter: the *mir* and its assembly (*mirskii skhod* or *skhodka*) are, to my mind, the genuine and ancient rural feature, a kind of village *veche* that expressed village interests, carried its customary laws, and voted on the form of land use they wanted—unless, of course, an external force prevented them from doing this. Through its *mir,* the village chose its organizational forms and its preferred *obshchinnye poriadki* (communal arrangements) of one sort or another, as institutions of the village. It was not the *obshchina* that made the village—it was the other way around.

The settlements in the countryside that became, in due course, villages were mostly relatively small and relatively isolated from each other and from much of the outside world. How could such settlements produce a rather uniform, cohesive, and persistent culture and quite similar ways of social life, over enormous stretches of territory inhabited by millions of people? The culture we are talking about is often called "the traditional, rural" and it is still a question—and a marvel—how it survived, in Russia and elsewhere, well into the twentieth century. Obviously, there are good reasons to go on deciphering rural social and cultural phe-

9. V. P. Danilov, "Ob istoricheskikh sud'bakh krest'ianskoj obshchiny v Rossii" in *Ezhegodnik po agrarnoj istorii,* vyp. VI (Problemy istorii russkoj obshchiny) (Vologda, 1976), p. 106.

10. Ibid., p. 108; V. V. "Krest'ianskaia obshchina," p. 132.

nomena, in view of the key role the peasants and agriculture played in Russian history, including in the Soviet period—even today migrants of rural origin take several generations to shed their rural outlook and mentality, which continue to affect urban populations and the whole nation in many ways.

A good point to start reflecting upon the phenomenon of the "traditional," following the Polish author Dobrowolski, is to define such a culture as one that depends basically on oral communications for its propagation and maintenance[11]—hence the role of "living memory" or the role of the elders, the importance of popular sayings and proverbs in mastering wisdom and practical advice on ways of handling and doing things, the importance of rites and images, and the general propensity to stick to the old ways and mores. Obviously, one should add, the spread of some literacy and schooling in the twentieth century weakens the validity of the formula. Still, much in rural life depends on oral communication as long as the written word does not become the prevailing way of getting knowledge and transmitting it. A degree of schooling that does not go further than a few years of elementary classes and does not produce a widespread dependence on the written word in professional activity and in social life is not yet enough to transform the previous pattern and to introduce the peasants into a faster-moving and quite different urban cultural world. Cities and ruling classes have tended, all through known history, to influence and affect rural life, often deeply, and to "export" to the countryside patterns and models to be imitated; but the compact traditional defenses were not thereby easily exploded. On the contrary, the peasantry adopted the borrowed elements, selectively, and assimilated them so thoroughly that the overall framework of cultural life was preserved, and the new "products" could even return to the cities and to the upper social layers and be taken there for original popular contributions. There are many examples of this type in the sphere of popular art and folklore, but the subject is too broad for the scope of this chapter.

One has to look for the deeper factors in the life of the peasantry that provided the mainsprings for the creation and survival of the whole stubborn framework. Three interconnected "mechanisms" can be cited (without exhausting all the key factors involved): first, the land-and-

---

11. Kazimierz Dobrowolski, *Studja nad zyciem spolecznym i kultura* (Warsaw, 1961), p. 71.

labor complex; second, the family-kinship systems; and third, the cultural sphere with its underlying importance, specific to the traditional outlook, of the magico-mythical layers in culture and mentality.

That land and tilling are crucial to the very definition of an agricultural population is obvious. But they have to be connected to a labor process based on rather primitive and slowly changing tools, on human and animal power that kept the peasants very directly dependent for their livelihood and survival on the mercies of nature and the vagaries of the climate.

Land, and availability and level of the technology used, were responsible for the difficulty the rural world had, in most cases, in producing very large agriculture-based settlements. The large units, when they did emerge, would be more brittle and less viable than smaller settlements, some of the inhabitants often being forced to leave and produce elsewhere a new village, with its own identity and combativity toward the others. The same conditions of a primitive technology, insufficiency of land, and strong population growth began producing, especially during the second part of the nineteenth century, huge areas suffering from overpopulation. Hence, a growing pressure to emigrate (there were also other reasons for peasants wanting not just to emigrate but also to run away—this is a separate question) and to found new settlements arose. On the whole, oversize villages had great difficulties in handling their affairs, especially where the distributive commune was the prevailing form;[12] traditional rural society and economy tended to prefer narrow confines and dispersal, rather than concentration, intensification, and differentiation. In short, extensive agriculture could handle an intensive social network only on the rather small territory of a self-contained village with jealously protected boundaries.

The family-kinship system to which Soviet ethnographers and demographers have dedicated much attention in recent works is extremely important in understanding rural society. The proverbial "patriarchalism," the important role of the elders, the solidarity of the villagers, the very cohesion of the village society—all were grounded in family-kinship and matrimony relations, especially in the extended fam-

---

12. Postnikov, *Iuzhno-russkoe*, p. 82; Pershin, *Zemel'noe ustrojstvo*, p. 10. According to Pershin, a big settlement is too difficult for the *obshchina* to handle. Other data and sources show that big villages where the main income comes from agriculture tended to be poorer (at the existing technological level) than smaller ones. (Ibid., pp. 10–12).

ily of the earlier stages when often one or two such families would be the
founders of the settlement and later accept—or join—others, transforming a largely "biological" base for rural society into the mixed, family-
and-neighborhood network that became more characteristic of village
structures in later stages.

The cultural sphere and the strong elements of magico-mythical
beliefs in it are another key factor. This is a rich subject which accounts
for many features that keep the rural world apart and specific. In con-
junction with the family aspect (to be treated further below—we will
have to define it as the "family-*dvor*" aspect) a tradition could be sustained and grounded, as it were, in an almost direct link and identification with the previous generations, mediated by a cult of ancestors that
was strongly adhered to.[13]

It is the interaction of the three "mechanisms" that accounts for the
tight social organization that was the village, and that allowed it to sur-
mount internal strife and defend itself, as long as feasible, against external powers. It also made the village into *an effective primary socializer of
the rural population,* through the irresistible pressure of its public opinion, the family and the elders, and through the all-encompassing impact
of the *mir.*

It is in the first, the land-and-labor sphere, that the redistributive commune has its roots and from which it derived its power to influence some
other spheres of life. But much in rural and village life cannot be
accounted for under the heading of "*obshchina.*" The role of the elders is
a feature of rural life that does not depend on how land is used; the position of women in family and society, internal family life and conflicts,
youth and children, many moral attitudes, relations with the church,
artistic and cultural traits—all are broader themes than the commune,
and it is the *derevnia* that holds them together.

It is interesting to note, in this context, the similarities between rural
life and culture in Russia and in many, if not most, other countries. The
Polish peasantry, for example, at the turn of the century (including those
under Austrian rule) and still in the interwar period, exhibited an astonishing number of traits common with Russians, even if they did not know
the Russian-style partitioning commune. Private ownership of land, or

---

13. On this problem, see M. Lewin, "Popular Religion in 20th-Century Russia," in *The
Making of the Soviet System: Essays in the Social History of Interwar Russia* (1985; reprint,
New York, 1994), pp. 57–71.

coveting of it, was the rule, but it did not prevent the Polish village from producing intense social bonds, a strong patriarchal family, a similar position of women in society, a three-field system with compulsory crop rotation and work schedules, common pastures on fallow and stubble, and an intricate locked-in maze of strips not unlike that in Russia. There was also a similar collective ownership system inside the family, despite the enormous power of the head of the household, some rights to personal property, and a set of cultural traits—an agro-religious work calendar, cult of ancestors, veneration (of relics) of *ziemia-matka,* the equivalent, almost verbatim, of the Russian *mat'-syra-zemlia*[14]—and the list is far from exhausted. It is here, of course, the case that the Polish *wieś* shared a lot, in its social essence, with the *derevnia,* including its considerable stability and longevity, sometimes spanning centuries.

But the same stubborn adherence to the once-established patterns applied equally to the spatial configuration of the village and to the social and spiritual habits that emerged in it. The thick and rich web of relations—family, neighbors, elders, festivals, meeting places, common beliefs, helping a relative or neighbor to build his house (*pomochi*), a host of other institutions and mores—united the village against others, including against neighboring villages, in a spirit of, sometimes, fierce distrust of strangers and a propensity for self-seclusion, especially in remote areas. V. A. Lipinskaia reported settlements in Siberia, in the nineteenth century, that preserved the ethnic or cultural singularity acquired in their places of origin even if they were separated from other settlements by no more than a brook. Cossacks, Old Believers of different denominations, Orthodox peasants from the Tambov area—all created their own villages and avoided dealings with each other, and especially intermarriage.[15] Except for the Orthodox who searched rather freely around for brides in other villages, thus engaging in some additional and meaningful contacts with neighbors, the others preferred their different seclusion and endogamy.[16] The old rural glue worked, sometimes better than needed, as long as the basic social and cultural coagulants still functioned.

One would guess that in the case of a "split" commune, that is, with

---

14. Dobrowolski, *Studia,* has ample material on this subject.

15. V. A. Lipinskaia, "Semejno-brachnye sviazi u russkikh krest'ian zapadnoj Sibiri v kontse XIX–go-nach. XX–go veka," in *Kul'turno-bytovye protsessy,* pp. 66–67.

16. Ibid., p. 71.

more than one *obshchina* in one village, especially if the latter was not too big, village life must have taken the upper hand in things other than land affairs—though the point needs testing on concrete examples.

The fact of correcting the unduly expansive use of the term *obshchina* and trying to place it in a broader village context does not mean that the importance of the commune is doubted. But the institution or the phenomenon of the *obshchina,* as already hinted, has to be seen in its different manifestations. Villages with consolidated homestead ownership of land still had a communal organization, although not of the "classic" redistributory variety. Arable land was not redistributed any more in this case, but other usable land and forests, ponds, and mills were often held in common ownership, not to mention the adminstrative and social functions that a commune might have performed. But the flexibility of the communal forms and their versatility do not end here. Numerous cases were reported from the heartland of *obshchiny* that had never redistributed their land since the emancipation. Government officials often considered them to have switched to individual ownership, and such communes were actually declared, during the Stolypin reforms, to have become "consolidated" automatically without requiring any decision by the village gathering. Actually, many of these may still have been "unextinguished" communes, their propensity to equalize holdings just in abeyance. When inequalities in conditions of land hunger and growth of mouths to feed became unbearable to the poorer inhabitants of the village, a prolonged battle would take place between opponents and proponents of the communal regimen; and if the proponents won, the juridical definitions of external observers would be proven false.

The flexibility of those communal arrangements becomes even more remarkable when we consider what Vorontsov, Kaufman, Kachorovskii, and many others reported, on the basis of field studies and excellent *zemstvo* publications, from Siberia as well as from central and southern Russia. We are talking mainly about Russia's huge *okrainy,* then still in the process of colonization. Settlers would come here from their native villages and, enjoying a plentitude of available land, would begin by ploughing up freely as much as each family could, without much interference from the *mir.* It is clear that they would immediately, or over the same period of time, found settlements; hence, some kind of *mir* and village life, and their prerogatives, would emerge automatically, by virtue of the logic of village life or by just continuing the arrangements and habits acquired in the villages of origin. The agricultural system in the new territories consisted basically of a one-field-cum-fallow (*perelog*), and no redistributions of any kind were necessary. But in due course, sooner or later, by the *mir*'s decision, they resorted to redistributions.

In many cases even this would not be the end of the story. In the next stage, a tendency toward individual ownership could emerge, and reversals in this or another direction could be observed. We should remind the reader that we are talking about the second half of the nineteenth century, and the common opinion of the writers cited was that the prevailing trend all over those immense territories of the *okrainy* showed a transition to the partitional commune, leading some of the authors to the conclusion that this form of handling land problems by villages was not necessarily, in itself, an ancient institution, as others often maintained, but a response to the needs of the population and to changing circumstances. Vorontsov, in particular, insisted that ethical considerations were an important factor in the decisions of the *miry* to go for redistribution,[17] and Kachorovskii, as is well known, elaborating upon an idea borrowed from A. Efimenko, proposed a broader version of a two-prong principle operating in rural life: the right to labor and labor right. All this, supposedly, evolved independently of whether these peasants knew or did not know redistribution before.[18]

The versatility of the commune's different arrangements made it into a particularly important institution—or, rather, a set of changing institutional forms—that served the village rather well not only in dealing with administrative problems (many of which interested the state more than the villagers) but primarily with the complex task of handling the problems of land use and many of the labor problems, too. In its redistributory functions, the commune took care of the needs of a growing population (and a clearly growing surplus of mouths to feed), organized the village for the defense of its interests, including, sometimes, the expression of dissent; tried to satisfy the villagers' demands for social justice; and endeavored to contain the disaggregating effects of social strife and economic differentiation. In its fullest and most significant manifestation—that is, when practicing repartitions, partial or integral—

---

17. V. V. "Krest'ianskaia obshchina," pp. 137–38.

18. K. R. Kachorovskij, *Narodnoe pravo* (Moscow, 1906), pp. 134–47 and passim.

the commune got involved in dealing with different social security matters, conflict resolutions, and, to some extent, judicial functions. As M. M. Gromyko stated, the commune became the carrier of the customary law concepts of the peasants.[19] There is no doubt that such communal functions also prevented the villagers from developing a strong commitment to private property, despite their all-consuming interest in land.[20]

The flexibility of the institution was the result of its obvious dual character, an equilibrium between a collective village interest and the *dvor* (household, family unit) as the main social cell of the village and its basic economic unit. Most of the farming was by family units (*dvory*), and this could not but reflect itself in the way the *mir* functioned. Its *skhod* was composed of the heads of *dvory,* and it was their unanimity, or majority, that made up the common will and decided how land use and other matters would be handled. Here is, therefore, the formula of some kind of dyarchy of the communal and the familial principles, and of their equilibrium that was, at times, not too stable. Those excluded from the deliberations—women and youth—still weighed heavily on how different *dvory* would perceive their interests and how, in the final analysis, they would vote: for or against redistributions, for or against the *obshchina* itself, including also for or against the dissolution even of the village itself, through the adoption of isolated farms (*khutora*). Not unnaturally, the very props of the system were also carriers of different propensities toward maintaining, changing, or abolishing it.

The two actual or potential claimants to land ownership that we have just described, finding themselves sometimes in collusion, eventually in collision, were the most important, but not the only, sources of property rights in rural life, with a potential for conflict and with different social realities behind them. In addition, therefore, to the communal and the farmstead rights that puzzled, if not bedeviled, the jurists, other property rights and ownership claims should be mentioned briefly. The

---

19. M. M. Gromyko, *Trudovye traditsii sibir'skikh krest'ian* (Novosibirsk, 1975), p. 307.

20. V. P. Danilov in his articles on the *obshchina* explains that they were instrumental, from this point of view, in preparing the ground or facilitating the transition of peasants to collectivized farms. In his *Sovetskaia dokolkhoznaia derevnia: naselenie, zemleustrojstvo, khoziajstvo* [(Moscow, 1977), p. 222], he states that the *obshchina* has to be credited with "the absence of a deep attachment [in the Russian peasant], consecrated by the ages, to his private patch of land."

largest in importance, after the two main categories, was *the collective ownership right of* dvor *members* to the whole farm, except the arable and pasture if those were in communal jurisdiction. This was astonishing in a patriarchal order known for the power of the head of the family, but most sources maintain that the latter, the *bol'shak,* even if he himself did not like to acknowledge it, was head of the family and manager of the farm—but he could not bequeath it to anyone because it belonged to no one but those persons (relatives and *primaki*) who lived and worked on it. It was supposedly an old tradition that the government tried to abolish during the Stolypin reform by declaring the *bol'shak* sole proprietor of the farm. Until then (and maybe even for some time thereafter), the *dvor* was common property without any specified shares for its members; these would be determined only when the *dvor* came up for subdivision.

An interesting intermediate category was the land on which the farm buildings were located, including the small garden-and-vegetable plot. This was the *usad'ba* to which every *dvor* was entitled, and it could be subdivided by family members but not by the general communal redistributions. The status of such land could probably be seen as a condominium: the commune had to supply *usad'ba* land to new members who did not have it, and this would revert to the commune if the family died out—otherwise, the *usad'ba* was firmly in family use and jurisdiction.[21]

Next came *outside earnings* of family members controlled by the *bol'shak* as part of the common family kitty although these revenues could easily, in part, be concealed or become the subject of dispute or compromises. If those who earned something on the side, especially during a regular *otkhod* activity, acquired *personal belongings,* these entered the realm of yet another category of fully accepted private property which could be freely disposed of and bequeathed.

There was also the so-called *kladka*—a personal kitty, so to speak, that belonged to women. It was composed of the personal belongings and gifts that a woman brought from her parents' house, and also some earnings to which she was entitled from outside work. She could bequeath it to her daughter, who would then begin to gather a small "treasure" of her own. It certainly played some role in the life of women, who were otherwise denied rights to household property equal with men.

All these different components, and their definitions, often shaky and

---

21. D. A. Khauke, *Krest'ianskoe zemel'noe pravo* (Moscow, 1914), is an excellent source on categories of property rights among the peasants.

changing over time and space, would be handled according to precepts of customary law and would come to be tested for their reality and value when some part of the *dvor*—for example, a young family—would demand and be granted the right to leave (*vydel*) or, mainly, when the *bol'shak* died and members would demand a full subdivision (*razdel*). This would often become a complex and lengthy procedure that had to be handled either by the commune through its representatives (*poveren-nye*), or by a less formal group of elders, or even just by neighbors, and sometimes by family members themselves; especially when the *razdel* was "illegal," the commune was not asked for permission and looked the other way because it did not care, or would not be able, to enforce government regulations.

All this is a good illustration of the complexity of rural institutions that were more numerous than the strictly communal arrangements, even in affairs concerning important economic issues. The eyes of the students and polemicists dealing with the commune (though not those of the ethnographers) were riveted to the repartitional commune, or to the question of communal versus *dvor* ownership (sometimes for ideological reasons), whereas a more detailed survey points to different, often old, institutions—in the sphere of property rights among many other spheres of rural relations—that reflected the social realitites. Obviously, each form of ownership was a source of claims and of conflicts, potentially damaging to the *dvor,* to the *obshchina,* even to the village. A potential for conflict was already alluded to in the case of the commune-versus-*dvor* dichotomy. Common-versus-*bol'shak* ownership of the *dvor* is another such source of tensions that the government tried to use in order to accelerate the change of the rural ownership system. Personal belongings and outside earnings, especially in areas of widespread *otkhod,* provide another source of conflict inside the *dvor,* reinforced, as I surmised recently, by the small seed-money that the young wife's *kladka* could offer to a younger son who had his own dreams.[22] All these troublesome tensions were kept at bay under the stern control of a patriarchal family, the rural commune and other institutions, and a strong, conservative public opinion in the village. Obviously, under the pressure of cities, railways, technology, schools, and markets, the hidden seams of village society would turn into

---

22. Some material and sources on intrafamily relations can be found in M. Lewin, "Customary Law and Rural Society in the Postreform Era," *Russian Review* 44 (1985), pp. 1–19.

cracks; but the structure would not collapse immediately, nor would it succumb easily.

The previous sections dealt with the structures of village society and its culture. But it is also relevant to dwell, as will become clear in what follows, on the physical and spatial shape and layout of the villages. It turns out that these configurations were numerous; that there were historical, geographical, and economic reasons for the forms they took; and that they had a capacity to last for centuries. The Soviet Union, as sources attest, inherited and had to live with the types and shapes of those *derevni i sela* during the 1920s; and there was not too much of a change later, despite the otherwise momentous results of collectivization. By 1939 most *kolkhozy* were small and based on the preexisting villages.[23] But even nearer to our time (our source dates from 1962),

> the overwhelming majority of kolkhoz settlements in the areas of old colonisation of the country exist in the same spots where they were founded initially and were registered by census books of the XV–XVII centuries, preserving in essence the same pattern of settlement. Historic documents testify to the presence of hundreds of villages in the northern regions, on banks of lakes and rivers, on the same locations where the villages remain till today quite small in size, not unlike what they were then.[24]

That in itself is quite remarkable, and it did not concern just the north or the center. We cannot undertake here an evaluation of the different typologies of rural settlements that geographers have studied and developed. It is sufficient for our purpose to underscore the great variety of those forms, sizes, and shapes that the villages took on according to the topography and climate of the respective regions. A village contained, on the average, some 11.6 homesteads in the *guberniia* of Pskov, but 547.9 homesteads in the *guberniia* of Stavropol', according to A. N. Chelintsev.[25] These figures already signal a characteristic trend from north to south: the farther south, the bigger the settlements became. In the Central Industrial region (Pershin reported) villages contained between 12 and

---

23. S. A. Kovalev, *Sel'skoe rasselenie* (Moscow, 1963), p. 123.

24. S. I. Riazantsev, ed., *Tsentral'nyj raion, ekonomiko-geograficheskaia kharakteristika* (Moscow, 1962), p. 142. The statement applies not just to this particular region but to many other areas of the USSR.

25. A. N. Chelintsev, *Sel'sko-khoziajstvennaia geografiia Rossii* (Berlin, 1923), p. 37.

135 homesteads, with an average of 35. Again, the more to the south of this region, the bigger the settlement.[26] In the Northern Caucasus in 1926, 105 rural settlements had a population of over 10,000 each—most of them the famous cossack *stanitsy*; another 185 settlements had a population of 5,000 to 10,000. These big settlements together comprised over half of the population of the region. The rest of the population lived in 15,000 small villages (one would guess that these were mostly *inogorodtsy*).[27] Siberian peasants also tended to live in rather big settlements, and so did the population of the southern steppes of European Russia, where huge villages, in conditions of scarce water resources, spread their houses in rows along riverbanks.[28]

The national picture in 1926 (taken again from Kovalev) looks like this: European Russia alone (without the Caucasus) had 431,900 villages, 45 percent of them small—only up to 50 inhabitants; 22 percent had over 200 people; 33 percent had 50 to 200 inhabitants[29]—and we know already that such averages conceal enormous differences in size and character. Settlers adapted their dwellings to marshy and broken landscapes in the north, to forests and hilly areas, creating what Russian geographers called *redkoochagovye* ("scattered-dwelling") settlements in the far north, *gnezdovye* ("nested") in the forests, *skuchennye* ("clustered") in the agricultural areas of the Center, *riadovye* or *lineinye* ("ribbon") in the forest-steppe and the steppe, ribbonlike along rivers of the south, one-row or two-row (streetlike) layouts where the landscape allowed or compelled it.[30]

Our inquiry, of course, cannot stop at the geographers' contributions

---

26. Pershin, *Zemel'noe ustroistvo,* pp. 4–7.

27. D. A. Konstantinov (sost.), *SSSR po raionam: Severnyj Kavkaz* (Moscow-Leningrad, 1928), pp. 38–39. *Inogorodtsy* were peasants other than Cossacks who came to the region later.

28. N. Ia. Gushchin, ed., *Krest'ianstvo Sibiri v period stroitel'stva sotsializma* (1917–1937 gg.) (Novosibirsk, 1983), pp. 114–15; for the villages in the Southeast, see Tulaikov, speech at the Congress of Soviets, *Deviatyi Vsesoiuznyi S'ezd Sovetov, sten. otchet, 22–27 dekabria 1921 g.* (Moscow, 1922), pp. 110–11.

29. Kovalev, *Sel'skoe rasselenie,* p. 11. A. Vyltsan, in *Istoriia SSSR* (no. 6 [1967], pp. 49–50), quotes results of population censuses showing 613,000 rural settlements in 1926 and 573,000 in 1939. By 1959 not much change had occurred; and still 70.1 percent of the rural settlements had fewer than 100 inhabitants, and about 300,000 settlements had fewer than 50 inhabitants. Vyltsan mentions that such dispersal of villages and rural populations is one of the serious problems of servicing social and cultural needs in the countryside.

30. This information and these terms are taken from the *Entsiklopedicheskij Slovar'* article explaining the term *derevnia*. I cite them only as examples of an effort to express the varieties of settlement—not as the last word in geographic scholarship.

that explain how and why villages use bays, lakes, rivers, valleys, or mountains and how they adapt ingeniously to the configuration of different terrains. It cannot be satisfied (though this is an indispensable step) with descriptions of single villages, or *volosti,* or macrolevel studies of the rural economy or culture. If rural society and culture was and still is one of the key factors in national development almost everywhere, especially in Russia and the USSR, then a different, more elaborate typology should emerge on the basis of the contributions of geographers, with the cooperation of cultural geographers, ethnographers, sociologists, and historians. The question would be: How does this enormous variety in configuration and layout of villages, as well as their different economic environments, relate to the type of society and culture that was created in them?

The problem also arises of how self-contained and isolated the villages actually were. In the immensity of Russia there were many thousands of settlements, often small and so dispersed that many of them come near to a state of isolation. Such isolation and dispersal, which still weigh heavily on the former Soviet Union today, must have produced truncated, if not semidegenerative, nonviable communities.

But in most other areas, when settlements were dispersed, the population was at least quite large, or if the settlements were small, they were much more concentrated.[31] To take an example: in the *uezd* Belozero, Cherepovets *guberniia,* the villages had 15 to 60 homesteads, and the average distance between villages was 2 to 5 *versts*—which means walking distance. A distance of 10 to 15 *versts* was rare.[32] In such a region— and there were many more like this, especially in central Russia—contacts between villages, not to mention conflict, could be quite frequent and relatively intense. One of the most crucial types of contact was matrimony. Villages that were not precluded from doing so by ethnic or religious reasons looked for brides and grooms in nearby villages, thereby enlarging their family and neighborhood relations and, obviously, attenuating their self-containment.

We should therefore consider the fact that villages had a certain radius in which they maintained some valid outside contacts. We learn from

---

31. Pershin, *Zemel'noe ustroistvo,* pp. 147–49.

32. G. Dement'ev, *Derevnia Pal'tsevo: ekonomicheskij i sotsial'no-bytovoj ocherk* (Leningrad, 1926), p. 10.

V. A. Lipinskaia that Siberian Orthodox villages maintained an area of basic matrimonial relations with other villages within a distance of no more than 10 to 20 km.[33] Data from the turn of the century in European Russia, Moscow *guberniia,* show a radius of matrimonial relations of no more than ten kilometers, and 80 percent of the new families were created inside this confine (years 1861–1901).[34]

So contacts existed that cannot be underrated, including neighborhood, commerce, mutual help, and feuds. But the perimeter was narrow and so was the cultural horizon of villages. Yet additional, larger contact areas existed and should be mentioned. They were created by the nearest market or regional center, or an industry planted in the rural milieu; by railways, big cities, and their impact, which reached the villages whether they wanted it or not; and by the state. Therefore, the study of the social and cultural activity and potential of villages has to consider these three fields of interaction: (a) the nearest contact area with neighboring villages, (b) the nearest centers of gravitation, and (c) the larger zones created by the pull of external forces coming often from very remote centers. To sum up, the villages that fashioned the peasantry and provided them with their distinctive social, cultural, and psychological traits must be seen in all their diversity. Peasant "uniformity," despite those numerous common traits, is a misleading impression. Was it immaterial whether the village was big or small, in the forest or the steppe? Near some cities that allowed a sizeable *otkhod* or somewhere in a forlorn spot, far from any center or railway station? In a cossack *stanitsa,* a bustling trading and *kustar selo,* a flax-producing village in Smolensk or a beet-root supplier somewhere in the Ukraine?

The validity of these questions seems self-evident. We can now add the need to show the impact of different systems of land tenure. What kind of difference did it make to the attitudes and mentality of the peasants to have a redistributory commune in their village, a family ownership system, or a network of *khutora* (that is, no real village anymore)?

Such a question can be answered in the framework of a broader sociocultural typology of villages that would start, as already mentioned, with the schemes produced by geographers and complete them with data pro-

---

33. Lipinskaia, 'Semeijno-brachnye sviazi', passim.

34. Ibid., p. 72.

vided by ethnographers, sociologists, and historians to include the main features of society, culture, and institutions.[35]

Much would become clearer thanks to such a correlation. A richer matrix of village and intervillage relations, a firmer grasp of the role of the *obshchina* as one of the internal mechanisms that preserved the "little worlds" from powerful pressures—these will help to explain why the metaphor "sphinx of Russian history" has been used when talking about peasants. Obviously, there was always some change going on in their midst, especially around the turn of our century and thereafter. And yet our "mechanisms"—the land-labor complex, the *dvor*-family structure, the cultural sphere (and its magico-mythical undercurrent)—did not change enough or crack; and so they kept village societies on their ancient, even archaic, subsoil, on layers of mores, beliefs, ways of doing things and settling their affairs, that made it so difficult to define them sociologically and predict their political behavior. Clearly a hard nut for both the scholar and the politician!

The difficulty was compounded not by the apparent immobility of rural societies—this was an illusion—but by a relation of incompatible motions: the strong cohesion of the rural world crumbling all too slowly in a world that was then changing feverishly. The "traditional" rural world, widespread and stubborn but ever more incongruous, could not act predictably in an environment it was not equipped to understand. Hence, outbursts, submission, disaggregation, dispersal, demoralization, and resilience—all were equally possible; and hence also the sphinx metaphor.

---

35. In addition to works cited above, the following have also been consulted during preparation of the present study: V. A. Aleksandrov, "Obshchina v krepostnoj Rossii (XVIII–nach. XIX v.)," *Istoricheskie zapiski* 89 (Moscow, 1972), pp. 231–91: id., *Sel'skaia obshchina v Rossii (XVII–nach. XIX v.)* (Moscow, 1976); A. N. Anfimov and P. N. Zyr'ianov, "Nekotorye cherty evoliutsii krest'ianskoj obshchiny v poreformennyj period (1861–1914)," *Istoriia SSSR,* 1980, no. 4, pp. 26–41; L. A. Anokhina and M. N. Shmeleva, *Kul'tura i byt kolkhoznikov Kalininskoj oblasti* (Moscow, 1964); P. G. Arkhangel'skii, *Ocherki po istorii zemel'nogo stroia Rossii* (Kazan', 1920); A. Bol'shakov, *Derevnia 1917–1927* (Leningrad,1927); B. D. Brutskus, *Agrarnyj vopros i agrarnaia politika* (Petrograd, 1922); Michael Bunce, *Rural Settlements in the Urban World* (New York, 1982); E. P. Busygin, *Russkoe naselenie Srednego Povolzh'ia: istoriko-etnograficheskoe issledovanie material'noj kul'tury (seredina XIX–nach. XX veka)* (Kazan', 1973); I. V. Chernyshev, *Agrarno-krest'ianskaia politika Rossii za 100 let* (Petrograd, 1918); V. P. Danilov, "K voprosu o kharaktere i znachenii krest'ianskoj pozemel'noi obshchiny v Rossii," in L. M. Ivanov et al., eds., *Problemy sotsial'no-ekonomicheskoj istorii Rossii, sb. statei* (Moscow, 1971); N. D. Druzhinin, *Pravo i lichnost' krest'ianina* (Iaroslavl', 1912); S. M. Dubrovskii, *Sel'skoe khoziajstvo i krest'ianstvo v Rossii v period imperializma* (Moscow, 1975); L. Grigorov,

Ocherki sovremennoj derevnj (Moscow, 1924); N. Gushchin and V. Chizhov, *Derevnia segodnia* (Moscow, 1928); K. R. Kachorovskii, *Russkaia obshchina,* 2oe izd. (Moscow, 1906); A. A. Kaufman, *Russkaia obshchina v protsesse ee zarozhdeniia i rosta* (Moscow, 1908); F. Kretov, *Derevnia posle revoliutsii (Iaropoletskaia volost')* (Moscow, 1925); Stefan Inglot, ed., *Historia Chlopów Polskich,* T. II (Wroclaw, 1972); B. Mironov, "The Russian Peasant Commune after the Reform of 1861," *Slavic Review* 44, no. 3 (Fall 1985), pp. 438–67; B. V. Mironov, "Traditsionnoe demograficheskoe povedenie krest'ian v XIX–nach. XX v.," in A. G. Vishnevskii, ed., *Brachnost', rozhdaemost', smertnost' v Rossii i v SSSR* (Moscow, 1977); N. P. Oganovskii, *Ocherki po ekonomicheskoj geografii SSSR,* izd. 2oe (Moscow, 1934); Iu. A. Poliakov, *Perekhod k NEPu i sovetskoe krest'ianstvo* (Moscow, 1967); M. L. Saburova, *Kul'tura i byt russkogo naseleniia Priangar'ia, XIX–XX v.* (Leningrad, 1967); N. Sazonova, *Kuda idet derevnia* (Moscow, 1928); N. Sukhanov, a discussion on new land-use policies and the role of the *obshchina* in *Na Agrarnom fronte* 11–12 (Moscow, 1926); P. A. Sorokin et al., *A Systematic Source Book in Rural Sociology,* vol. 1–3 (Minneapolis, 1930–32); P. A. Sorokin and C. C. Zimmerman, *Rural Sociology* (New York, 1929); V. A. Zverev, "Brachnyi vozrast i kolichestvo detei u russkikh krest'ian Sibiri XIX–nach. XXgo v.," in L. M. Rusakova and N. A. Minenko, eds., *Kul'-turno-bytovye protsessy u russkikh Sibiri XVII–nach. XX–go veka* (Novosibirsk, 1985).

CHAPTER 3: THE CIVIL WAR

Dynamics and Legacy

THE CIVIL WAR WAS, NO DOUBT, A CRUCIAL PERIOD IN THE history of the new Soviet regime. The demarcation of this period is a matter for debate. It may be argued that it began in November 1917 and ended in the middle of 1922. These dates encompass all the most important trends and traits that produced the flavor and substance of the period, the particular ways of acting, and the specific culture of the emerging system and its leaders. By mid-1922, almost all the military operations of importance, including those directed against the widespread bands of guerrillas and bandits, had ceased; the first reasonably abundant harvest had begun to supply enough food to start healing the country's terrible wounds, particularly the consequences of the atrocious famine of 1921; and the war economy was returning to more normal, peacetime functioning.

We are dealing therefore with a time-span of about four years, marked by upheavals, battles, slaughter—a protracted national agony during which the new system was created and took shape. For historians and for other students of social and political systems, it was not simply an important period but also a very exciting one. It seems easier to grasp the essential features of a regime at its inception rather than to try to extract them from the numerous accretions that accumulated at later stages of development.

The system we are studying was not built methodically according to some preestablished blueprint. It was, rather, improvised under the pressure of constant emergencies, although ideologies and programs of the previous era did play their role. This is visible, notably, in some policy preferences such as distaste for markets and a special relation with the working class, to take just a few examples. But these ideological preferences produced more than just facts. They also engendered illusions that are best illustrated by the policies subsumed under the term *War Communism*. An "illusion in action" or, to use a better term, "utopia" is a powerful mobilizer, and yet its results can be—and were—quite different from what was hoped for. In any case, utopias of different kinds are often an important part of historical events and present an intricate subject for study.

We can state further that, although improvised, the key institution of the new system, the party—its only preexisting feature—was created or recreated in the course of the events under consideration, in a new garb, quite different from what it had been at the start. Party cadres, during their short history before October, had trained themselves to be leaders in a revolution that was not even supposed to be socialist. During this period they produced an ideology and a small number of dedicated cadres who, after October, engaged in activities and events, notably a bloody civil war, during which they organized and ran armies, built a state apparatus, and presided over a new state. As they became rulers of the improvised regime, they recreated themselves and acquired a new identity, even if initially this process was not self-apparent. Nevertheless, the transformation went on speedily in all facets of party life and in many of its principles, such as ties with the masses, organizational structure, modus operandi, social composition, ways of ruling, and style of life.

All this was not the main concern of the participants in the events, proponents or foes of the new regime. They, and observers abroad, were still absorbed by the novelties introduced by this newcomer into the family of world systems. Whether a separate peace with Germany, land to the peasants, workers' control, nationalization of banks and key industries, or less formalized but sharper and more frightening notions such as "rob from the robbers" (*grab' nagrablennoe*)—all of these developments were an outrage to domestic opponents and an insult to the Western world. Forced labor for the bourgeoisie did not improve matters. Under these conditions a civil war was inevitable. What was puzzling was the considerable calm that prevailed during the regime's first months in power. Some would explain it as a power vacuum that the Bolsheviks skillfully filled. But with the crumbling of the Provisional Government the power vacuum was filled, at least partly, by the networks of soviets that had helped the Bolsheviks into power and given them strong initial backing. As for the forces of the old regime and many who were undecided, they needed some time to regroup, to recover from the initial shock, and to reap the benefits of the new regime's predictable difficulties and errors—errors that did not fail to appear.

That civil war was likely can be hypothesized on grounds other than the sole challenge of the Bolshevik program. We know how deeply the Whites hated the forces that stood behind the Kerenskii government. Social Revolutionaries, Mensheviks, and later also the Liberals were considered by monarchists and nationalists, especially by the officers, to have been the main culprits of the Bolshevik takeover. It is therefore not an idle speculation to contend that a Constituent Assembly dominated by the SRs would have been dispersed; indeed, the SRs gave ample proof that they were incapable of mounting an effective defense. They did little when told to disperse by the Bolshevik sailors, and later, in their Samara stronghold, they failed again to produce a military force capable of sustaining them. They depended fully on the Czechoslovak units. Their own forces were commanded by White officers who were just waiting for the chance to eliminate them,[1] which is what happened somewhat later in Siberia, where White officers eliminated SR leaders, making clear how unwelcome they were in the White camp.

The basic reality of those years was that the battle was being waged not between democracy and authoritarianism but between two different authoritarian political camps that could field big armies and fight it out. Supporters of the Constituent Assembly could not do the same—and they were eliminated from the historical arena.

We are next faced with another riddle: Why did the Bolsheviks, whom we just described as unprepared for the job of ruling a huge country, nevertheless become victors in the Civil War? An easy answer comes to mind—which has a grain of truth in it: Their success owed mainly to the ineptitude of their opponents. Victor Shklovskii, in his riveting *Sentimental Journey,* said that it was not a matter of who was the stronger but, rather, who was less weak.[2]

But such an explanation will not do. The Bolsheviks worked feverishly to create a central government as well as important civilian services and local authorities; at the same time they organized a war machine, complete with an armament industry. To sum it all up, they created a state. This achievement testified to a dynamism that the other side

---

1. Cf. David Footman, *Civil War in Russia* (London, 1961), pp. 85–135, for a description of the ineptitude and full dependence of the Samara government on the Czechoslovaks. There is enough evidence to confirm the statement that the White officers who commanded Samara's own forces were more a threat than a shield to the SRs.

2. Victor Skhlovsky, *Sentimental Journey* (Ithaca, N.Y., 1970), p. 187.

clearly lacked. Neither of the main White territories—the Siberian or the southern—managed to produce a credible state administration, despite their claim to superior experience in "statehood" (*gosudarstvennost'*). Numerous documents, notably memoirs of White officers written during and after the events, attested to the sad state of affairs in the different central and local administrations of the White areas.[3] One officer described the administration of the Stavropol region under the Whites as the rule of *pompadury,* corrupt and arbitrary little despots.[4] The evidence from Kolchak country was not more cheerful. In the battle between the *pompadury* and the *komissary,* the latter certainly deserved to win. They turned out to have had a knack for state building that representatives of previously privileged classes lacked or lost. The deeper cause of this deficiency lay in their inability to convince their previously faithful subjects, especially the peasants, that they still had something to offer them. Their demise in October was not really an accident.

It is worth noting that the Bolsheviks were entrenched in the very heart of historical Muscovy, where they drew most of their support. Russia's heartland, and the resources of the nation and the state accumulated by history in this area, served them well in winning the war and, later, in reuniting the country. The huge border areas (*okrainy*) where the Whites operated, although well provided with raw materials, grain, and an excellent military resource—the Cossacks—did not give them the hoped-for chance to surround and take Moscow. The *okrainy* proved, on the contrary, too diversified, too distant from each other. Instead of being a base for victory, they turned into a morass that engulfed them.

The sociohistorical study of this period, focusing on classes, nationalities, bureaucracies, and parties, as well as on the social composition of the armies, is an indispensable tool, although this kind of study is still in its infancy. Yet it is particularly noteworthy to the historian to learn that not just the Bolsheviks but also the key figures of the opposite camp, notably Paul Miliukov and General Denikin, looked to the social factors, including the class composition of the contending camps and of the country as a

3. References to memoirs by White officers are to the useful multivolume collection of excerpts and unabridged texts in S. A. Alekseev, comp., *Revoliutsiia i grazhdanskaia vojna v opisaniiakh belogvardeitsev* (Moscow-Leningrad, 1925–27).

4. V. M. Krasnov, "Dobrovol'tsy na Severnom Kavkaze," *Arkhiv russkoj revoliutsii,* vol. 11, reprinted in N. M. Meshcheriakov, *Nachalo grazhdanskoj voiny* (Moscow, 1927), pp. 248–74.

whole, in order to explain the victories and defeats. The nefarious role of backward-looking *pomeshchiki,* the actions of the bourgeoisie, their policies in relation to the peasantry, the behavior and attitudes of workers—such were the factors Miliukov cited in his postmortem analysis of the Whites. And Denikin, although he denied that his side had a class character, admitted and regretted that it never managed to shed its class image in the eyes of the population, a derogatory image at that. Denikin also resented the duplicity and stinginess of the bourgeoisie who did not want to come up with the necessary means to save what they themselves declared to be their cause.[5]

Such explanations are, in fact, indispensable, provided they are used flexibly and are based on good research. Both camps were coalitions, not neat, clearcut classes. Each side had an obvious, although not entirely monolithic, core, around which coalesced broader layers of the population that often hesitated, changed sides, returned to the fold again, or created a camp of their own. It was this flux that made the Civil War so unpredictable for its participants at the time and so complicated for the analyst today. Such a fluid state of affairs applied equally to both sides. We can cite many examples of military or partisan units, armed with red banners and commissars, turning against the Communists, even killing them, and going over to the other side, continuing on their own—or even staying...with the Reds.[6]

We know that there was a nucleus of workers, poor peasants, and *raznochintsy* on the side of the Reds and a core of members of the formerly privileged classes, richer peasants, and, especially, military officers on the side of the Whites. The problem was who would emerge as the better social and political strategist, who could mobilize the support of large circles of the urban population and, more importantly, the small-scale peasant farmers. In this crucial task of social strategy the Bolsheviks proved superior. The Whites, on the other hand, who much of the time were stronger militarily, found themselves in

5. Paul N. Miliukov, *Russia Today and Tommorow* (London, 1922). These were lectures given in the United States soon after the Civil War. For examples of A. I. Denikin's assessments, see his "Kak nachalas' bor'ba s bol'shevikami...," in *Nachalo grazhdanskoj-vojny,* p. 31, and passim.

6. For an example of a partisan unit from Antonov-Ovseenko's Red Army in the Ukraine that called themselves "Soviet" but that persecuted Communists, or, at best, prevented them from organizing cells in the unit, see V. I. Nevskii, ed., *Za sem' let* (Leningrad, 1921). There were many partisan, even regular, military units of this kind.

trouble the moment they turned to the forceful drafting of peasants. According to Lenin, that was their undoing.[7] Their basic force became hopelessly diluted.

But social analysis makes us aware of yet another complexity and strain in the social environment of each side. The heat generated by the Civil War was such that the nucleus of both sides showed cracks at different moments, especially in the later stages of war. Dissension and decomposition settled into the White camp first, but neither were the Bolsheviks spared. Confusion, exhaustion, and signs of fragmentation finally hit the party—the tool that the Whites could not match—but luckily for the Reds, this occurred after the Whites' defeat.

What it all means is that the Reds were tested in the crucible as cruelly as anybody. The Civil War marked them as deeply as it marked the whole nation.

This was a time of incredible suffering, cruelty, and destruction. Terms like *time on the cross* and *via dolorosa* were evocative of the age for many deeply religious people. Writers used such terms in their works about the period. The symbolists even posed the question of whose side Christ was on. The church, though, was quite firmly on the side of the Whites.

The human suffering resulted not only from the direct cruelties of the Civil War but also from its broader aspect: the widespread dislocation; destruction; decomposition of groups, classes, and parties—briefly a deeply morbid state of the whole social fabric. Shklovskii, again, in his strangely titled work written soon after the events, was particularly impressed, even fascinated, by the phenomena of morbidity—cruelty, the dissolution of social and human bonds, the sickening sight of a society in a state of disaggregation.

These important—and fatal—characteristics of the period have to be studied attentively. Without them, the problem of the aftermath and the legacy of the Civil War will remain unintelligible. We have emphasized that social strategy was a key aspect in the outcome of the war. But we have also mentioned one other aspect of the big game in which the Bolsheviks bested the Whites, namely, the domain of state building. Once the tsarist state collapsed and the Provisional Government was unable to

---

7. V. I. Lenin, in *Deviataia konferentsiia VKP(b), sentiabr' 1920, protokoly* (Moscow, 1972), p. 12. He stated: "We defeated Kolchak and Denikin only . . . after their main, solid cadres were diluted in the mobilized mass of peasants."

shore it up or build a new one, the stage was set for the social forces in attendance to try their hand at recreating a new political organization. There is no need to repeat the well-known story about who tried and failed. The country was going to be reunited and the sociopolitical system would be established by the camp that could produce a state. In abstract terms, one can imagine situations where a large movement of the masses could win and could subsequently create a state. Historically, such seems to have been the case during "the time of troubles" (*smutnoe vremia*) in Russia at the beginning of the seventeenth century. During the no less tragic *smuta* of the twentieth century the (Bolshevik-run) state was produced, at first, hand-in-hand with a social movement, and soon ever more independently of it, or at least independently of the shifting moods of the sympathetic, neutral, or even hostile masses. An important feature of this process, to which we will return, was that the new state was being erected amidst a disintegrating economy and a decomposing social fabric, at a catastrophic time for the whole country. Indeed, the state was emerging on the basis of a social development in reverse. The Bolsheviks were little aware at that time of this aspect of their achievement, but at the very moment of their triumph, the shadow of Pyrrhus was certainly present.

THE ORDEAL

Studying the demographic trends, cities, social classes, economy, and parties will allow us to distinguish such shadowy aspects of the emerging regime. These factors are "system makers" in any conditions, and we shall try to pull together these themes, after a survey of the different components. In addition to hunger, breakdown of communications, and demographic losses endured by the population, I would like to draw particular attention to the collapse of the two capitals. The capitals were the centers and main bases of the revolutionary movements, in particular for the Bolsheviks. But both Petrograd and Moscow suffered the biggest losses. Neither was ever conquered, but the enemy was at times nearby, and the social and economic situation was particularly severe in the capitals. In 1917 the two cities had a combined population of four million inhabitants. In 1920 only 1,674,000 remained. Almost the entire industrial workforce of Petrograd was lost through migration, mobilization, and death. Existing data show that 380,000 industrial workers left production, and only some 80,000 remained.[8] Calamity is certainly an appropriate characterization.

But the weakening of the social mainstay of the regime was occurring not just in the capitals. The population of all the big cities shrank to different degrees: the more developed and dynamic the city, the more it suffered. Smaller and less industrialized cities declined less, and some might even have grown. Branches of large-scale industry that did not come to a full standstill declined drastically. Finally, the national industrial labor force decreased by half and was strongly "diluted" or "declassed" by black-market activities, idleness, and flight to the villages.[9] The term *deindustrialization* is fully legitimate here. Only armament industries working for the Red Army were kept alive. By the end of the Civil War many key industries, absolutely vital for the functioning of the country, had reverted to their pre-1861 levels.[10] Cities and industries became parasites on the rural economy, not unlike the armies of those days that lived "off the land." As long as such a situation prevailed, an ever-deepening economic crisis, coupled with the continued tearing apart of the social fabric, was inevitable. There were, in addition, other corrosive and destructive factors, such as the onerous duty of raising and equipping, let alone enduring, so many armies, their activities, iniquities, and casualties.

The Reds alone had an army of over four million toward the end of the Civil War and suffered some 1.2 million casualties. Kolchak, at his

---

8. V. P. Naumov, *Letopis' geroicheskoj bor'by. Sovetskaia istoriografiia grazhdanskoj voiny* (Moscow, 1972), p. 424. According to his data, Leningrad had 2.3 million inhabitants in 1917. In 1919 only 900,000 remained. Industrial workers, 418,700 strong in 1917, numbered only 87,900 in 1920.

The figures on the combined losses of inhabitants in both capitals are from V. Z. Drobizhev et. al., *Izmeneniia sotsial'noj struktury sovetskogo obshchestva, 1917–1920* (Moscow, 1976), p. 62. Iu. A. Poliakov's *Sovetskaia strana posle okonchaniia grazhdanskoj voiny: territoriia i naselenie* (Moscow, 1986), which contains a mass of data relevant to our theme, was not available to me when writing this article.

9. I. A. Gladkov, ed., *Istoriia sotsialisticheskoi ekonomiki*, 7 vols. (Moscow, 1976–1981), vol. 1, *1917–1920 gg.* (Moscow, 1976), p. 354.

10. An overall statistical evaluation shows a decline, for 1919–20, to just 13.4 percent of the base year. See I. A. Gladkov, ed., pp. 262–63. More revealing data can be found in *Istoriia Kommunisticheskoj Partii Sovetskogo Soiuza*, vol. 4, book 1 (Moscow, 1970), p. 10, where it is stated that in terms of industrial development "Russia was thrown back by whole decades." The so-called census industry produced five times less than in 1913. The output of iron was half of the 1862 output, and output of cotton fabrics stood at the level of 1857.

peak, mobilized some half-million people. Denikin began his dashing northbound drive in mid-1919 with some 300,000 under his banners, but as his offensive developed, he mobilized several hundred thousand more, mainly peasants.[11] His army seemed to have stumbled badly with these draftees.

The casualties of the Whites are not known, but we have different assessments of the general population losses from war, epidemics, and famine.[12] A figure of eight million people, including the unborn, is sometimes quoted in Soviet sources as the sum total of direct losses from the Civil War. But all assessments must be tentative. On the other hand, the whole problem of mobilizations and of armies and their numbers urgently needs further study. Let us take, for example, the problem of deserters. The figures quoted for the Red camp alone are staggering. Some talk about 1.5 million, others of 1 million. With such disparate figures, no data on the size of the armies can be reliable. Many joined at the induction centers, even enrolled in units, and then melted away. Many others, who did not present themselves at all, stayed in their villages or headed immediately for the forests. They also, at some stage, returned in considerable numbers,[13] an event of great significance for the outcome of the war. The riffraff quality of the Red Army, especially

---

11. For the overall losses of Russia during the Civil War, see V. Z. Drobizhev, *Izmeneniia*, p. 333.

12. V.Z. Drobizhev (*Izmeneniia*, p. 332) quotes an official Soviet publication that assessed the loss of population between 1913 and 1919 at 5.1 million, excluding the unborn. But it is known that the following two years, 1920 and 1921, were particularly devastating for the population. Nevertheless, even 5.1 million looks too small. In his most recent book Iu. A. Poliakov assesses at about 13 milion the direct loss of population through war, revolution, and civil war, while another 12 million were indirect losses (unborn) (Iu. A. Poliakov, *Sovetskaia strana posle okonchaniia grazhdanskoj voiny*, pp. 127–28).

13. L. M. Spirin, *Klassy i partii v grazhdanskoj vojne* (Moscow, 1968), p. 347, maintains that between June and the end of December 1919, 775,000 deserters returned to the ranks of the Red Army. It is believable that a movement of this magnitude did result from a change of attitude among the peasants and helped clinch the victory. But the basis of this figure is not known.

The number of soldiers in the Red Army is often given as 5 million toward the end of military operations against the Whites. See G. V. Sharapov, ed., *Istoriia sovetskogo krest'ianstva*, vol. 1, 1917–1927 (Moscow, 1986), p. 81. But Iu. A. Poliakov in *Perekhod k Nepu i sovetskoe krest'ianstvo* (Moscow, 1967), quoting different sources, speaks of about 4 million Reds and up to 2 million Whites.

The social composition of the Red Army is given by G. V. Sharapov, ed., *Istoriia sovet-skogo krest'ianstva*: peasants, 77 percent; workers, 14.8 percent; others, 8.2 percent. The commanders of all ranks were: peasant, 67 percent; intelligentsia, 20.7 percent; workers, 12 percent; 20 percent of all commanders were party members. It is obvious that the peasin the early stages, was predictable in these conditions, and the shiftiness and unreliability of the recruits instilled considerable paranoia in the Red camp. So many of those recruits could easily find their way to and swell the ranks of all kinds of "greens"—Makhno, Grigoriev, Antonov—and of the opposite camp. But the other side faced a similar problem.

The story of the deserters is, of course, a story of peasants. It does reflect, quite faithfully, their moods and attitudes toward both camps. The figures given for the numbers of deserters who began to return in mid-1919 and later are significant not only for their impact on the rout of the Whites in the autumn of the same year but also for the hint they give us about the predominantly peasant character of the Red Army. When the Reds were recruiting volunteers only, the majoity of the soldiers were workers. After compulsory drafting was instituted, the Red Army became 80 percent peasant. Its NCOs (noncommissioned officers) were at this time 60 percent peasant, but the peasant component diminished drastically in the middle and higher ranks.[14]

Such a huge peasant participation in the ranks of the army at a time when the peasantry was not only supporting but also deserting, "hesitating," and changing sides underscores both the complexity of the tasks the Reds were facing and the degree of their achievement in transforming rather unruly bands into something resembling an army and in learning to execute serious strategic and tactical moves amidst the chaotic conditions of those years. All this attested to the talent of the leadership and their growing military know-how.

Until recently, modern Soviet writers still stuck, officially, to the version that all the achievements were due to the leadership of Lenin and

---

ants constituted the majority of the lower ranks, especially of the NCOs. The higher ranks had a majority of ex-tsarist officers (see note 14).

It is highly significant that the units in the field, the actual fighters, had at the same time just 337,879 infantry (bayonets) and 72,374 cavalry (sabers). The figures are from N. N. Azovtsev, ed., *Istoriia grazhdanskoj voiny v SSSR, v dvukh tomakh,* vol. 2 (Moscow, 1986), p. 46. This book by military historians and the one edited by Sharapov contain a wealth of data that allow us to reconstitute the making and composition of the Red Army through consecutive mobilizations. N. N. Azovtsev also includes detailed figures of the field units facing each other on the different fronts during the main battles of the Civil War.

14. The number of ex-tsarist officers who volunteered or were, mostly, drafted into the Red Army reached 48,000; this is the figure most often cited. It is less well known that the number of NCOs from the tsarist army who fought with the Reds, also mostly drafted, reached the substantial figure of 200,000. This was, no doubt, an important factor leading to victory. See also note 13. It is possible that the number of ex-tsarist officers that worked with the Red Army was much higher than what is commonly thought.

the party. Trotsky was mentioned mainly for his real or imaginary errors, although some writings in the mid-1980s managed not to mention him at all, or to mention him occasionally but without the usual virulence. Finally, the days of *glasnost'* saw the beginning of a reassessment and "creeping rehabilitation" of Trotsky that is still inconclusive.[15]

Memoirs of the Whites, among others, are an inestimable source for the assessment of the Red Army, the Whites themselves, and the behavior of different groups in the population toward them. We read often in generals' memoirs about how industrial settlements or even quite peaceful-looking villages could suddenly open fire at the approaching Whites. They prided themselves that their hundreds could easily rout thousands of Reds, but they also noticed, with growing disillusionment, that the Reds kept coming at them as their supporters never dried up. The quality of the Red Army kept improving, and the memoirists consoled themselves that it was all because of the good work of their own kind who deserted to the Reds or were forced to serve them.

In fact, the Reds had their own problems with numbers, especially where "bayonets and sabers" were concerned. When it came to fielding armies, they were often outnumbered by the Whites, who almost always had a superior cavalry—the Cossacks—at their disposal. A measure of the difficulty of wrenching out fighting units from the mobilized mass of recruits is that in an army about four million strong (by the end of 1920), no more than 400,000 "bayonets and sabers" could be fielded. But the same figures (see note 13) make clear why the Whites believed the Reds were "inexhaustible." The latter managed to build up reserves that the Whites could not even dream of. Support for the Reds—enthusiastic, lukewarm, or even nonhostile neutrality—is confirmed by these figures. But this is certainly not the whole story. The picture of social decomposition we are sketching suggests convincingly why the support for the Reds was weakening and had actually begun drying up toward the end of the war.

In our inventory of destructive and decomposing forces we should next mention terror. For some, of course, this was an indispensable tool of war,

---

15. S. S. Khromov, ed., *Grazhdanskaia voina i inostrannaia interventsiia v SSSR: Entsiklopediia* (Moscow, 1983). For an example of rethinking Trotsky in conditions of glasnost', see V. P. Danilov in "Kruglyi stol," *Voprosy Istorii,* no. 9 (1988), pp. 5, 8. Danilov calls the expulsion of the left from the party in 1928 "a tragic error."

notably as a means of paralyzing actual and potential enemies by spreading fear among them. But at the same time, terror is a physical and psychological source of all kinds of pathologies and an important factor of demoralization for all involved. The existing literature in the West has paid attention mainly to the Cheka. In fact, even on the Red side alone there were all kinds of other security units, as well as a special security army to deal with security problems in the rear of the fighting forces.

But the depth and scope of the destructive effects of terror cannot be understood without realizing that terror was not a monopoly of the Reds. It is less known that the different White armies had intelligence and security units of all kinds, special antisubversive and punitive squads. All of them applied individual and mass terror against the population, chased after Communists or members of soviets, engaged in executions or mass flogging of whole villages. All this is well described, sometimes with glee, sometimes with disgust, by White memoirists. There were so many armies, each with its own *karateli,* that villages, or cities, were not always sure who was marching in, assembling the population, and engaging in exactions and executions. Such killings and atrocities were widespread—and the existence of illegal networks of sympathizers, spies, and saboteurs on both sides of enemy lines ensured that a "rationale" for terror and counterterror was not lacking. In the conditions of moral decay, so ripe in those days, terror easily gained its own momentum and acquired a special attraction for psychological perverts of all kinds. The chaos and arbitrariness of those times offered considerable scope for destructive urges in the human psyche.

Among the casualties the country suffered—through terror, starvation, migration, demoralization, or death—we should mention the loss of a considerable number of professionals and intellectuals. This important pool of talent—Kendall E. Bailes showed that it was not that big in the first place—was greatly diminished by the ordeals of the war. The damage caused by casualties of this type has been directly acknowledged in Soviet writings only recently. No quantitative assessment has been offered as yet, to my knowledge. What was never acknowledged as constituting a regrettable loss was the dispersal or destruction of the cadres and leaders of the multiparty system that emerged about the time of the Revolution of 1905. Only Bolsheviks and some remnants from other parties were preserved by either joining the Bolsheviks or being employed by them as "bourgeois specialists."[16] It is worth discussing whether, how, and to what extent the loss of at least certain parts of the political class contributed to the political and intellectual impoverishment of the country.

Whatever the cost, presumed unavoidable, of a revolutionary upheaval, Lenin must have known the extent of such damage. We have an indirect inkling of his thinking from Lunacharsky's *Revolutionary Silhouettes,* written in 1919 and published just after Lenin's death. Lunacharsky reveals, among many other important things, that Lenin did regret that it was not possible to attract a man like Martov to the Bolshevik party. He might have made, Lenin said, an excellent leader for the party's right wing.[17]

If the problem of a political class is sufficiently tricky, the loss of a different group of opponents—the owners and captains of industry—most of the country's entrepreneurial talent—is certainly an obvious and straightforward debit. Such a "commodity" takes time and effort to be recreated. After all, if there were parasitic sectors in the Russian economy and society which had to be removed, the dynamic capitalist sector was not one of them. Lenin's awareness of this problem is reflected in his hope that the country would become "state capitalist," albeit under the aegis of a socialist government. This meant not just employment of bourgeoisie technicians and specialists but cooperation with big and smaller owners of capitalist enterprises in a regime of co-ownership. Whatever the merits and realism of this idea, it proves our point that the loss of the entrepreneurs was a deep tear in the social fabric—one that has to be included here in the "decomposition" column.

Demographic losses and other forms of social decay struck all the classes, groups, and caucuses in different ways and degrees—except, probably, the criminal underworld, which should have actually thrived in such conditions. The peasantry, the sturdiest and least vulnerable of all classes because of its closeness to the essential means of biological survival, also endured its share of calamities, deaths, casualties, and loss, at least temporarily, of a great mass of able-bodied men through mobilizations, desertions, and participation in guerrilla groups.[18] The worst dis-

---

16. By 1921 about 7 percent of all party members came from other parties. *Istoriia KPSS,* vol. 4, p. 85. During the NEP this percentage increased considerably.

17. A. Lunacharskij, *Revoliutsionnye siluety* (Kiev, 1924).

18. Rykov maintained that during the Civil War the countryside lost 30 percent of its able-bodied men; see *Vtoraia sessiia TsIK 4-go sozyva, stenograficheskii otchet* (Leningrad, 1925), p. 24. He did not specify in what way these losses occurred. A similar figure is quoted by N. Oganovskij, *Ekonomicheskoe obozrenie* 12, p. 60. Many of them were temporarily absent.

asters struck millions of peasants just after the Whites were defeated: the famine that resulted from a poor crop in 1920 was followed by an even worse crop and famine in 1921. These same years saw the most furious and widespread uprisings of peasants against the Reds, under the slogans "down with the *prodrazverstka*" (compulsory grain requisitions) and "Soviets without Bolsheviks." Finally, workers in industrial centers—or what was left of them—engaged in waves of strikes, making it clear that they, too, had had enough. The whole system looked like a phantom. A rickety state faced emaciated masses who seethed with unrest but were so enfeebled that even the weakened state could put them down.

The turmoil and general exhaustion finally caught up with the ruling—and now victorious—party, until now almost indefatigable. Leaders and the rank and file in different ways showed symptoms of strain. This was most obvious at the moment of transition to the New Economic Policy (NEP), when the "trade-union debate" revealed a party splintering into groups and grouplets, disoriented, and, according to Lenin, "shivering" badly. "*Partiiu likhoradit,*" he declared, and decided to take drastic measures.

But even before the decision to forbid factions, which effected a fundamental change in the party's inner life, keeping the party in a state of permanent alert and high morale was not easy. Even in the highest echelons of leadership, cliques and personal infighting were rife. Intrigue reached particularly dangerous proportions in mid-1919, when it began to weaken the very top, until then the party's main asset. It revolved around the powerful yet vulnerable figure of Trotsky, whose strength derived in part from his talents but also from the crucial support of Lenin. The cooperation and mutual trust between these two leaders were an important source of strength for the Reds, but the intriguers, whatever their reasons, were working hard to break up this duumvirate, as the party, the country, and the world conceived it.

During these years, Lenin, working at a superhuman pace, suffered debilitating headaches. One can surmise that some of his chief lieutenants' relentless efforts to discredit Trotsky must have made him waver. A crisis was reached in early July 1919. During a meeting of the Politburo on July 3–4, Lenin abandoned Trotsky and voted with his critics on all points in dispute. Outraged, Trotsky resigned from all his posts and stormed out of the room. Members of the Politburo, first among them Stalin, ran after him and implored him to stay on, notably in his capacity of war overlord. The vote was reversed, and Trotsky was, officially, given satisfaction on points of interest to him.[19]

It would be worthwhile to see whether the protocols verify this story. But it is clear that at this point the intriguers overplayed their hand. They would be back at work later. Relations between Lenin and Trotsky remained strained during the next year and a half. Another crisis was the trade-union debate, when the two fought each other over issues that would soon become irrelevant. In 1922, however, there were signs of a new rapprochement.

These events illustrate, among other things, the ravages and the difficult legacies of the Civil War. The war certainly undermined Lenin's health and soon removed him from effective leadership. Iakov Sverdlov died from an illness in early 1919. Trotsky emerged from the war apparently basking in glory, but was in fact isolated within the party, having provoked an alliance against him that would bring about his undoing. In short, not all was well with the victorious party and its leaders at the end of the Civil War.

THE INTELLIGENTSIA

The complicated and tortured saga of the new regime's relations with the intelligentsia, related to the crisis and dislocation of the Civil War, also illuminates the problems of state building, with many important implications for the future. Although both sides had good reasons to distrust each other, they had equally good reasons to cooperate. But the intelligentsia, along with the mass of elementary school teachers, responded to the new government with a wave of strikes and hostility. This attitude, widespread among intellectuals of all kinds, was shared by yet another large literate group—the state officials.

The strikes, though of short duration, taught Bolsheviks a bitter and unexpected lesson: The professional segments of the population, however small their relative numbers, were strategically important. It was impossible to build and run a state and an economy without them. Even the army could not be built and run without ex-tsarist officers. Commu-

---

19. Some of these events are described briefly by Jan M. Meijer, ed., *The Trotsky Papers, 1917–1922* (The Hague, 1964), vol. 1, pp. 592–94. The Politburo decision is on pp. 590–92.

nism, intended as the creation of the liberated popular masses and a rev-olutionary party, had to be constructed, as Lenin said, "with foreign hands." But restoring members of the previous ruling class to positions of privilege and power smacked of treason. Even if flanked by commis-sars, the presence of "bourgeois specialists" in the government, and espe-cially in the army, was offensive to most party members and to many working people.

The new regime's policy of enlisting the services of experts tended to reinforce antibourgeois and anti-intellectual feelings among the popular classes that supported the revolution. Uncontrolled, such attitudes could cause a reaction against the party, especially against many of its leaders, themselves intellectuals. Keeping an alien body in sensitive positions was a dangerous strategy that did not augur well for the smooth functioning of the new system. Distaste for the privileged bourgeoisie experts, expressed in "specialist baiting" (*spetseedstvo*), was widespread not only among the rank and file but also among activists in the middle and upper levels of the party and the state. A powerful "military opposition," for example, resented and fought bitterly against the employment of such experts in high places.

With the end of the Civil War, the situation became calmer, but noth-ing was simple as yet in this vexed domain. The expert, even if ready now to shed some or most of his previous hostility, remained at best skep-tical and eager, in any case, to end his subservience to politically appointed superiors. Party bosses in commissariats and factories resented their own dependence on the "bourgeois," with his expertise and accompanying air of superiority. The regime defended the bour-geoisie experts but proclaimed that its aim was to produce, as soon as fea-sible, "its own" experts endowed with the right ideology and class origin.

But soon a new dimension entered—imperceptibly at the start, ever more visibly later—into the complicated partnership. As long as revolu-tion was the aim, the party's orientation toward the masses took prece-dence. This was true, as well, during the Civil War, when the moods, interests, and reactions of the masses were decisive for the outcome of the struggle. But as the task of ruling began to assume the first priority, the party's emphasis switched to "the cadres." This tendency was to blossom a decade later, but many militants or just attentive observers perceived the buds with increasing anxiety. To assuage such anxieties, the party argued, often quite sincerely, that there was no danger involved in cadres of popular extraction. As for the experts of alien origin, their expertise was being used without conceding any power to them. Such arguments sounded plausible as long as the experts were openly hostile, making clear that they remained on the job just because there was no other employer.

The situation began to change when, during the NEP, many specialists got used to and accepted the regime and even found more positive reasons for continuing to work for it. Their party bosses also learned to live and work with them, came to trust many of them, and defended them from detractors. During the NEP a partnership, and here and there even a co-rulership, began to emerge. This, though, was just a beginning. A status revolution would take place in the 1930s and would then involve a larger sector than just those old specialists. Although this process would be marred by tragic setbacks, it would not be reversed. The co-rulership, in conditions of the dictatorship of those days, would turn out to be easier to preserve than the wholehearted loyalty of the popular masses—and that much could already be perceived by perspicacious observers during the NEP and even during the Civil War.[20]

It should become clear to the reader how many problems, lessons, and legacies were rooted in the party's relations with the professional classes that were trained in the tsarist period. Out of this maze emerged a certain "Bolshevik art of governing" that the leaders presented often, especially in the 1930s, as the quintessential wisdom for governing and motivating cadres. When charging people to do what was asked of them, they were to be told, "If you do not know, we will teach you; if you refuse, we will force you." This prescription seems to have emerged during the Civil War. The first part of the slogan applied to those who were not professionally prepared for the jobs to which they were being promoted. It sounded paternalistic and was certainly a mass phenomenon in those years. The other half of the slogan was applied to those who did not wish to serve, notably the professionals of the previous regime. The term *art* implied some fine balancing between persuasion and coercion, but in fact the whole prescription was sternly dictatorial. The fact that so many experts helped build the Soviet system was not the result of coercion alone. A relaxed

---

20. N. N. Azovtsev, *Istoriia grazhdanskoj,* vol. 2, p. 397, shows that by mid-1919 the Peoples' Commissariats of the RSFSR alone employed 28,000 experienced staffers who had worked for the tsarist regime. In the factories, 35 percent of the administrators and technicians were from the same category.

interpretation of the "art" was possible, but in the absence of clear rules for restraint, the ingredient of force had ominous implications. The force aspect prevailed during the Civil War, subsided during the NEP, and prevailed again, full blast, under Stalin. Yet during the Great Purges the "art" was applied much more leniently to the "bourgeois" intelligentsia than to the huge numbers of newly created cadres of immaculate social origin and ideology. This is one of the enigmas of Stalinism.

THE PARTY

It is time to turn our attention to the ruling party—an agency without precedent in the history of political systems before 1917. The opponents of the regime during the Civil War did not have at their disposal any equivalent to it.

The party certainly was a versatile agency. It helped produce a central and local government, raised and organized an army, sustained the fighting military by an influx of dedicated party members, responded to mobilizations for all kind of tasks, and, finally, effectively carried out clandestine activities behind enemy lines.

Not unexpectedly, a tendency appeared among party leaders, with the exception of Lenin, to glorify, later even to "mythologize," the party. This certainly did not attest to its continuing good health. A political party has to be submitted to all the stringencies of sociohistorical and political analysis—and the tendency to turn the Bolshevik Party into some sort of superhistorical tool hindered analysis from early in the party's development. We know that the party went through rough times and acted in ever more complicated and changing situations. The impression given by Soviet and many Western presentations of an immutable "essence" called "the Communist Party" has to be dispelled. First, as we know, the party consisted of a network of clandestine committees, not more than 24,000 strong, at the beginning of 1917. During its short history, the number of its adherents had fluctuated widely. It was led, from abroad mostly, by its founder, Lenin. There also was leadership inside Russia, but it was often decimated by arrests.

Was the party before 1917 really the disciplined and centralized squad of "professional revolutionaries" who did as told by the top leader? Would this "classical" Leninist model withstand the scrutiny of a good monograph? The party represented more than just professional revolutionaries. There were elections, conferences, congresses, debates. As is often the case, a closer look may change many preconceived ideas. It is clear, though, that the Bolshevik Party was an unusual organization. It was not bracing itself to take power directly, because its leaders did not expect the coming revolution to be immediately socialist; at least, they were not at all sure what its character would be.

Dramatic changes occurred in this party in 1917. It became at the very least a different genus of the same species, if not an entirely different species. It was now a legal organization operating in a multiparty system; it grew in size to perhaps more than 250,000 members, and it operated as a democratic political party, under a strong authoritative leadership. Lenin was at the helm, but he was flanked at the apex by a group of leaders, below whom were influential networks of lower cadres who participated actively in policy making. If his colleagues accepted Lenin's line, it was mostly after lively debates and having sounded out the moods and opinions of the rank and file. Factions existed and were fully acknowledged as the party's normal way of doing business. At this stage, under Lenin's proddings, the party was aiming at power, but, again, not without serious differences of opinion about the modalities of taking and exercising it.

Once the party was in power, in conditions of a civil war, another, deep transformation took place: the party became militarized and highly centralized, in a state of almost permanent mobilization and disciplined action. Its cadres were moved around where necessary by a newly created department, the *uchraspred*. Elections to secretarial positions ended, not to reappear in any meaningful way until Gorbachev's efforts to reintroduce them. The center became all powerful, even if this development was often regretted as an unavoidable event in the circumstances of war. The situation did, in fact, demand it. Still, factionalism and intraparty debates continued, and conferences and congresses were regularly convened.

During the Civil War there was no sign of any "religious" reverence toward Lenin in the party caucuses. His prestige was enormous, but criticisms of party policies and of Lenin personally were often sharp. This aspect of the party tradition was unextinguished. There was hardly a leader or activist of any standing who did not engage in a polemic or even a serious challenge to Lenin's policies at one time or another.

Another important factor for change in the party was the fluctuating membership and shifting social composition characteristic of those years. We learned from one good source that there were 350,000 members between October 1917 and mid-1918; this figure subsequently dropped to 150,000 and then began to climb again, reaching 600,000 in the spring of 1921.[21] Whatever the accuracy of such figures, one interesting phenomenon becomes obvious: the party entered a period of hectic growth at a time when mass support for the regime was at its lowest—in 1920 and 1921. Was this an aberration? Probably not.

By the end of the Civil War many would-be members and cadres perceived that the regime was here to stay. The growth of the party reflected the fact that no alternative was visible or possible anymore, despite the incredible furies of the uprisings. It also indicated the party's growing concern with the need of ruling and running things. Nobody spoke seriously anymore about "every cook" being able to run the state. Hence the influx into the party, including numbers of careerists and crooks, who would soon be removed by a powerful purge of unsavory elements, if such a feat was at all possible.

Toward the spring of 1921, party statistics showed that 90 percent of the membership was now of Civil War vintage.[22] Prerevolutionary cadres, even those who joined in 1917, were drowned in a mass of new entrants, many of them active participants in military and security operations and, quite naturally, imbued with a military, if not militaristic, political culture. The new recruits carried this attitude into the party, where it persisted, in different forms, for decades.

After the 1921 purge that discarded, probably, one-third of the membership, a new, powerful influx occurred, and during the next five years the membership reached the one million mark. The majority would

---

21. L. M. Spirin, *Klassy i partii,* pp. 29–30. The party had few peasants in its ranks: N. N. Azovtsev, *Istoriia grazhdanskoj,* vol. 1 (Moscow, 1986), p. 397, shows just 4,000 peasants at the beginning of 1918 and 12,000 at the end of the same year. From G. V. Sharapov *(Istoriia sovetskogo,* p. 176) we get the figure of 55,000 peasants in the party by January 1918 in 40 gubernias of European Russia, followed by a big increase toward the end of the year. Yet another source gives the figure of 16,700 peasant members in 1918, increasing to 165,000 in 1921. All this shows that exact figures were difficult to come by in those years and that, whatever it was, the number of peasants in the party was small. In addition, in 1921 there were 138,000 members classified as "officials" *(sluzhashchie),* only slightly less than the number of peasants.

For the global numbers of party membership we can turn to the computations of S. G. Strumilin based on the 1922 census, quoted in *Rabochij klass v Oktiabr'skoj revoliutsii i na zashchite ee zavoevanii* (Moscow, 1984), p. 348: in 1918, 115,000; in 1919, 251,000; in 1920, 431,400; in 1921, 585,600. A serious purge followed in 1921 that expelled almost one-third of the total, but during the next few years hundreds of thousands of new members were recruited.

22. *Istoriia KPSS,* vol. 4, no. 2, p. 70, states that 90 percent of the membership at the beginning of 1921 joined in 1918–20. Thus, it is plausible to hypoothesize that the party was built anew in those years and from a different human material.

now be made up of entrants who joined during the NEP, bringing to the party their own political culture and culture *tout court*. In the wake of these massive changes in social composition, the "old guard" was still at the top and running the show, but their numbers, stamina, even their health, were slackening. Could they assimilate, reeducate in their own image, the enormous mass of "crude" newcomers? If not, what would stop this mass from having a pervasive impact on the party and from transforming it in *its* own image?

There is evidence that many of the "old guard" despaired, overwhelmed and besieged as they were by huge numbers of people whose culture and mentality differed from their own. The Civil War entrants had brought to the party a military culture, whereas the culture of the newer entrants reflected the values of the NEP society. At the same time, the top layer, continuing an earlier Bolshevik tradition, still fought among themselves using terms and arguments that the bulk of the rank and file did not understand. It can be said that the "old guard" came to constitute a separate party within the larger party being formed around them. Finally, the new membership created a new model of a party run differently, and politically and ideologically transformed.

THE PEASANT REVOLUTION

The role of the peasantry in these events was multifaceted, and relations between them, the Reds, and the Whites were rich in momentous meanders and turns. Always a heavy factor in Russian history, the peasants' weight, if anything, increased considerably during the Civil War. For one thing, in 1917–18 they produced a genuine agrarian revolution of their own with specific aims and methods. In addition, whether they realized it or not, they became the underwriters of the Bolshevik revolution and the regime it engendered. Without their concurrence, the Bolshevik revolution would not have been possible. A good witness on this score was Trotsky, the presumed antimuzhik accused of "underestimating the peasantry."[23] Yet the peasants not only made Bolshevik power possible but also saddled themselves and the new regime with endless problems.

---

23. L. Troskii, *Istoriia russkoj revoliutsii*, vol. 1 (Berlin, 1931), p. 73: "Had the bourgeoisie solved the agrarian problem, had it been possible to solve it, the Russian proletariat could not have conquered power in 1917." And, "The agrarian problem constituted the subsoil of the revolution" (p. 429)—we do not know whether the pun was intended.

The support given by the peasants was unpredictable, extended here, withdrawn there, given back again here. Each time the peasants hesitated, as one Soviet author suggested, armies swept to and from Moscow, over the endless stretches of Russian territory.[24] The peasants' support was no more than a marriage of convenience related to the possession of land. This aspect of the revolution—the redistribution among themselves of privately owned land—was irreversible in the eyes of the peasants. The Whites were blind to this crucial point and paid the price for it. Once they were defeated, the peasants turned against the Bolsheviks, to repay them, in turn, for their iniquities and errors.[25]

The threat of the landlords' returning was gone, but the Bolsheviks were enforcing the policy of *prodrazverstka,* forceful requisitions of grain from the peasants, with the help of a special "food army." The rationale for this policy is still debatable. On one hand, there were ideological motivations, namely the elimination of the markets that had provided the underpinning for the policies of "War Communism." On the other hand, it cannot be denied that, in the prevailing conditions, it was necessary for the regime to acquire some grain from the peasants in ways other than through market transactions. But from this combination of utopia and perceived necessity grew a policy that virtually swept clean the peasants' granaries.[26] The claim that there was no alternative is dubious. It is also reasonable to ask whether a change of strategy similar to the NEP should not have been tried earlier than in the spring of 1921. Some Soviet authors have, cautiously, raised this question themselves.[27]

Two other policies, less often described in the literature, were straightforward blunders that whipped up the ire of the peasants. First, a policy of collectivization proclaimed in 1919 was, at least initially, implemented with considerable zeal and coercive pressure. Although Lenin soon realized the trouble it was causing and tried to apply the brakes, the responsibility for this policy was his. Peasants hated the

---

24. L. Kritsman, *Geroicheskij period russkoj revoliutsii* (Moscow, 1925), p. 226.

25. On the widespread and massive peasant uprisings and guerrilla movements, see Iu. A. Poliakov, p. 194, and more details in Sharapov, pp. 214–17, and Azovtsev, *Istoriia grazhedanskoj,* vol. 2, pp. 322–27.

26. Iu. A. Poliakov, *Oktiabr'i grazhdanskaia voiny* (Moscow, 1966), p. 367, quoting a letter to Lenin from a rural party member.

27. Iu. A. Poliakov, *Perekhod k Nepu,* pp. 198–99 and 235–36. Although Poliakov dismissed this possibility, he nevertheless raised it.

kommuniia, as they called it, as much as they hated the *prodrazverstka,* and it was doubly offensive that the collectivization policy was launched just at a time when the agrarian revolution had whetted their aspirations to become independent farmers on their own land. This was true for the peasants who were better off as well as for the poorer ones. It is puzzling that such a policy could have been launched right after the disbanding of the *Kombedy* and the official adoption of a new pro–middle-peasant line.[28]

The collectivization policy failed and was abandoned, only to be replaced by another grand scheme, also of "War Communist" inspiration, namely, the "statization" (*ogosudarstvlenie*) of agricultural production. The aim of this plan, of course, was to cope somehow with the desperate food situation.[29] According to this scheme, the peasant household and land were to be left alone but would be subject to a state plan—a sowing plan, to begin with—in which every household would receive its pre-scribed target of what, how much, even where and how to sow. A national network of "sowing committees" was decreed, to supervise the imple-mentation of the whole scheme and to enforce the quotas. The work of the peasants, well in line with the ideology of the day, was declared to con-stitute "a state duty" (*gosudarstvennaia povinnost*), and penalties were to be meted out for noncompliance.

---

28. Ibid., pp. 73–74, stated: "The party's programmatic orientation on transition to col-lectivization was immediately perceived as an orientation on a broad, large-scale forced movement." A noted agrarian specialist and participant in the events of those years, P. Pershin, remarked in his article in *O zemle,* vyp. 1 (Moscow, 1921), pp. 73–74, that col-lectivization was launched (in the beginning of 1919) just when the peasants aspired predominantly to family farming on their own land. The authorities were blocking ini-tiatives of peasants to move onto separate (*uchastkovye*) lots, and numerous troubles with the peasants followed. V. Osinskii, the chief architect of the new agricultural policy of "statization," stated unambiguously: "The countryside turned out to be indifferent toward socialism. It rejected the *kommuniia* categorically" (Osinskii, brochure published in 1920 and reproduced in O. S. Rozenblium, *Zemel'nyj kodeks RSFSR,* 3rd ed. [Moscow, 1929], p. 96.)

29. E. G. Gimpelson, *Voennyj kommunizm* (Moscow, 1973), pp. 84–85, describes how the policy of collectivization was rejected and replaced by the one of "statization" (*ogosu-darstvlenie*). A contemporary author, I. A. Kirillov, *Ocherki zemleustrojstva za tri goda revoliutsii* (Petrograd, 1922), p. 10, stated that it was the catastrophic situation in agricul-ture that caused the switch to a new policy toward the end of 1920. This policy, as explained by V. Osinskii in *Pravda* (September 5, 1920, p. 2), consisted in essence in "a decisive, coercive intervention of the government" in running the agricultural sector.

For a good brief survey of Soviet agricultural policies during the Civil War, see the speech by Sviderskii, *XI Vserossiiskij s'ezd sovetov, stenograficheskij otchet* (Moscow, 1924), pp. 17–19.

Soviet authors today write about this episode with barely concealed embarrassment and point to the fact that this policy was no more than the last gasp of War Communism. The NEP was, in fact, only a few months away. But for the peasants this plan was just the last drop in a bucketful of exactions—labor duties, grain requisitions, collectivization—and they erupted like a chain of volcanos in numerous uprisings and guerrilla movements. They fought against a force they now perceived as a foreign conqueror. Antonov-Ovseenko, in his report to Lenin about the causes of the dangerous uprising in the Tambov areas, used the term *military-confiscatory raiders* to describe Soviet officials and the military as seen by the peasants. In this remarkable document Antonov-Ovseenko, himself one of those "raiders" (*naezdniki*), talks with great lucidity about the Soviet power as "military occupants." His opinion may have been instrumental in deepening the NEP policies that were being tried out, initially timidly, from March 1921.[30]

Shedding this kind of image was certainly on Lenin's mind when, two years later, he wrote, "Better Less but Better." His "testament" condemned "War Communist" policies, past and future, and offered an alternative strategy. But other, earlier texts of Lenin's supported quite different policies. The "testament" would be entirely forgotten when, some years later, policies were launched that would surpass what "War Communism" only adumbrated. This time the collectivization and statization of agriculture would be applied simultaneously.

But the problem is not in the ideological aspects of these precedents for Stalin's policies. It is more important to point out that the seeds of the future fateful turn were sown, to a large extent, by the agrarian revolution of 1918. By forcefully taking and redistributing the land of the *pomeshchiki,* the peasants initiated important changes in their own economy and society. Many poor peasants got land, while many of the richer lost not a little of theirs. Social stratification and differentiation in the countryside were narrowed considerably, and it is legitimate to speak about a certain "equalization" (*poravnenie*) among the peasants. It expressed itself in a new predominance of the middle peasants—the *seredniaki*—in rural society. The peasants' revolution transformed Russia into an ocean of small family farms, mostly oriented toward family consumption, with little left for marketing. Before this equalization

---

30. Antonov-Ovseenko's memorandum to Lenin is in Jan M. Meijer, ed., *The Trotsky Papers,* vol. 2 (The Hague, 1971), pp. 494–95.

there existed sectors of petty bourgeoisie producers and large-scale entrepreneurs in agriculture. The term *petite bourgeoisie,* used in relation to most peasants, did not make much sense at this stage. A petty bourgeois, by definition, worked for the market. This not being the case, the term did not apply to the peasants of the early NEP, in a situation where the landlords' estates and the larger-scale peasant producers—that is, any remnants of capitalism—were gone.

There was not too much capitalism in Russian agriculture even before the revolution; otherwise, the events we are studying would not have happened. The Stolypin reforms would have been pointless, too, as there would have been no need to turn the countryside upside down in order to create a class of "sturdy producers."

In the meantime, it can be stated that the agrarian revolution wiped out almost all the effects of the Stolypin reforms. Most of the consolidated homesteads (*khutora*), Stolypin's main plank, were reintegrated into the villages except in the western region, which had not had much of a peasant commune (*obshchina*) in the first place. After the revolution, the *obshchina* itself—the traditional agrarian community that was the main target of the reforms—reemerged, on a larger scale than before, to become the prevailing form of land use in most of the country. Property rights within the household, which the Stolypin reform had declared the household elder's private property, reverted to the former, ambiguous collective family ownership.

The Russian peasant now became not just more "traditional," more muzhik, than before. Because of the widespread ruin, agriculture and the peasantry now loomed larger in Russian society than ever before in modern times. Along with this "ruralization" of a rural country, the peasant even "ruralized" himself by retreating economically and culturally, at least for some time to come, into his age-old shell, charactertistic of much more primitive times. The whole country, willy-nilly, was drawn backward to a considerable extent by this retreat. The agrarian revolution in Russia—an event of great consequence and drama—turned out to be sterile, if not actually wasted, at least from the vantage point of its immediate results.[31]

---

31. The problem needs a special treatment, but we can point to the opinion of a number of Bolsheviks for whom the agrarian revolution was a political success because it enabled the party to conquer power but also constituted a serious economic setback for the coun-

CONCLUSION

This idea of a "wasted agrarian revolution," a subject for further thought, brings us to our conclusion. It is extremely important to keep in mind phenomena of social disintegration discussed above as we now try to pull the threads together. The sufferings endured by the peasant population did not lead it to the same state of decomposition that afflicted other social groups. Peasant society survived much better, but it recreated or reacquired traits that had been on the wane in the prerevolutionary period and that ran counter to the developmental path of the times. The post–Civil War village hardened into a sturdy system that did not respond easily to change, in particular as long as the urban sectors were still recovering from their own misfortunes. What we described as the "archaization" of the rural world was paralleled by the destruction or weakening of vulnerable modern sectors of society. We can therefore speak of a more generalized "primitivization" of the whole social system.[32] The main legacy of the Civil War can be stated simply: When the new regime finally got the chance to lead the country toward its declared goals, the point of departure turned out to be more backward than it would have been in 1917, let alone 1914.[33]

As the peasantry loomed larger and urban society grew weaker, the other side of the legacy became clearer, too. The democratic components

---

try. In fact, the 32 or 35 million *desiatins* the peasants received in the RSFSR at the expense of the *pomeshchiki* diminished the number of *bedniaki* (without eliminating them altogether) but did not raise sufficiently the average size of the farms, did not absorb the notorious overpopulation of the countryside, and did worsen considerably the supply of agricultural output to the markets.

For a contemporary evaluation, see B. Knipovich, *O zemle,* vol. 1 (Moscow 1921); also two leading Narkomzem officials, Latsis and Sviderskii, in *XI Vserossiiskii,* pp. 63, 80.

Seen from the peasants' side, there certainly were important advantages for many of them in reaching the status of independent *khoziaeva* and in some improvements in the economic situation of many of them, except for the richer ones. But for such a stormy and shattering revolution that was not followed by any serious advance in productivity and way of life, the achievement is problematic, whereas the negative consequences were quite palpable, especially on the national scale.

32. I raised the problem briefly in *The Making of the Soviet System* (New York, 1985). See the introduction and the last chapter. The whole subject still needs to be explored in greater depth.

33. The opinion that the countryside moved some centuries backward was expressed by the noted ethnographer Tan-Bogoraz, *Revoliutsiia v derevne* (Moscow-Leningrad, 1924), p. 7. During the Civil War he said, "The Russian village looked as if it was reliving again the seventeenth and eighteenth centuries." It seemed to be sliding back "a century per year."

of the revolutionary regime that were initially important in this system—trade unions, workers' committees, soviets—were all weakened, atrophied, or eliminated. The bureaucratic and coercive features of the state became, on the contrary, much more potent and, finally, predominant. The democratic aspects of the party itself underwent a metamorphosis in the same direction. Although the militarization of the Civil War subsided, the party was well on its way toward becoming an administrative machine dominated by its top leaders and, increasingly, by its *apparaty,* with little or no say left for the rank and file.

The interaction of the two processes engendered by the Civil War—"archaization" and deep "statization"—created, in due course, most of the sequels that are part of the "legacy" we are trying to establish. The second of the two processes warrants some further remarks. The strain and decomposition caused by the ordeals of the Civil War made the extensive use of administrative and coercive methods look almost natural, and, often, they were the only ones available. The fact that state agencies were staffed, to a large extent, by revolutionaries and people of popular origin helped mask the ever-deepening trend toward a pervasive authoritarianism: the revolutionary masses were being eased out as meaningful actors and partners in power, whereas bureaucrats and commissars of the new, still-rudimentary state were becoming the mainstay of the system. More ominously, the coercive measures that were initially devised mainly for the bourgeoisie—labor conscription and forced labor—soon began to be applied to other groups and, finally, to the principal backers of the regime themselves. The militarization drive was all-consuming, whereas the shiftiness of social support, including that of the industrial workers, especially in the later stages of the war, instilled a profound anxiety in the system, which required an ever-present vigilance. And again, the decay of any autonomous social activity—the sources inform us[34]—along with the pressures of the prevailing methods of *udarnost'* (shock methods), mobilizational by definition, all worked in the same direction. The constant exactions of "state duties," the unceremonious shuffling of cadres by the *uchraspred,* were all features that had come to stay and, later, even to flourish.

The Civil War dealt a severe blow to the libertarian aspirations of the

---

34. "Local life came to a full standstill (*sovershenno zamerla*)," wrote V. S. Nemchinov about the Civil War years in his *Izbrannye proizvedeniia,* vol. 3 (Moscow, 1967), p. 31. The quote is from a text written in 1926.

makers of the 1917 revolutions. By causing an enormous "geological" shift backward in society, it made the historical process change rails, as it were. It created parameters in the social system and political environment that narrowed severely the available choices and made some of the nastier prospects still ahead look more like an inevitable outcome than an alternative. Because of the destruction of so many previous cultural, political, and economic advances, the country and the new state became more open and vulnerable to some of the more archaic features of the Russian historico-political tradition and less open to the deployment of its forward-looking and progressive features.

The peasantry and the state, although shaped by the same circumstances, were, nevertheless, moving in different directions. They lived on different historical floors; that was yet another legacy for the future, portending clashes and crises still to come. The mentality of the rural mass, reared in the communal, relatively isolated, and mostly small villages, was deeply patriarchal, and the culture, naturally, was parochial. The state, however, was authoritarian. It was a dictatorship by its own definition, and its vistas and horizons were of a grand scale. The complicated crisscrossing of these traditions and cultures contributed to the mixture of attitudes and outlooks of the people entering the ruling party in great numbers and of the bureaucracies in party and state that were composed of such heterogeneous elements. Authoritarianism was an unavoidable feature in these conditions—the question was, What type of authoritarianism was it going to be? What kind of socialism, if any, was, obviously, a related question. It would be a "backward socialism," said Bukharin sometime during the NEP.

In this context it may be appropriate to single out the readiness during the Civil War, among leaders and cadres alike, because of ideology and circumstances, to believe in the instant feasibility of socialism, even communism, despite the prevailing massive disruptions. The well-known caveats that a transitional period would be necessary, especially in a backward country, could be disregarded all too easily. It was understood by some, then and later, that without the creation of indispensable preconditions "instant communism" could not be attempted without massive coercion. In fact, as we know, such coercion was already as characteristic of War Communism as was its other trait—extreme egalitarianism—or the aversion to markets and the preference for a "natural," planned economy. Lenin himself spread enough of the War Communist illusions, and maybe he came to believe in some of them himself. Trotsky, as is well known, stumbled on the War Communist identification of militarization with socialism, and many party cadres accepted the practices of the Civil War as the right policies leading directly to the final goal.[35]

All these developments have a direct bearing on our quest for the legacy of the Civil War. Notwithstanding the unpopularity, during the NEP, of terms like *War Communist methods* or *spirit,* and the dying Lenin's warnings against such methods, one trait of the temporarily discarded policy proved durable, namely the identification of statization with socialism—a longstanding Soviet ideological plank that has now begun to lose some of its potency, hesitantly, in the most recent perestroika. One of the upshots of this kind of legacy was excessive centralization of power and the stifling of the autonomous initiatives and actions that are indispensable for the healthy development of any modern system. For a time, such action became deeply suspect and was castigated as "spontaneity," the enemy, supposedly, of planning. Instead, there were to be endless agencies of control and others to control the controllers—all embodying the germs of stagnation, at least in the longer run, and in some walks of life, almost immediately.

The way the Civil War evolved and was won carried some concrete, albeit not necessarily openly acknowledged or even consciously perceived lessons that supported, nevertheless, the future version of Stalinist despotism.

Any proponent of realpolitik—and there were some among the party leaders—would hardly be taken aback by the following political lessons

---

35. We do not know of any serious testimony that Lenin did *not* share some or most of War Communism's illusions. The quotes we are offering here do not exclude Lenin from the general assessment. War Communist policies found a deep response among cadres in the highest positions and this was the reason Lenin, once he went over to a different strategy, had to devote a lot of energy to prove to the party that he was not reneging on principles.

"Things moved at such speed," reminisced Pokrovsky in 1922, "that we imagined we really were near to Communism, a Communism being produced by our own means without awaiting the victory of a proletarian revolution in the West." Lunacharsky, in the mid-twenties, concurred. It was necessary, he said, to adopt the War Communist road, but "we got used to it, we almost came to like it, and when the times demanded to reject it, we hesitated and stalled." (E. G. Gimpelson, *Voennyj kommunizm,* pp. 196 and 220, respectively.) Lunacharsky's statement can be applied to the year 1920, not just to the first months of 1921.

that the hard-nosed politicians, to my mind, perceived as the Legacy of the Civil War:

1. That there is no class that can be fully trusted in conditions of adversity;
2. That alliances, on the contrary, can be struck with social groups that are not necessarily friendly and that support can be gained from such unreliable forces or even from past or potential foes;
3. That stick-and-carrot policies can be applied successfully to whole social groups, even large ones;
4. That when popular support is waning or absent, the state, if it wields its power ruthlessly enough, can hold out in relative isolation;
5. That the condition for holding out in such circumstances is the absence of any real political alternative in the social system;
6. That, finally, the bureaucracy, even when of alien social origin and ideologically inimical, can become a reliable and even massive social base—not to mention the more favorable situation that occurs when it is staffed by socially more reliable cadres. In this case, such cadres can offer, at least, a surrogate of social support.

All these situations actually did occur during the Civil War, and appropriate policies were implemented, although without much grounding in any experience. They became a legacy, even if dormant for a short period, but certainly remained available for future use.

In brief, the Civil War legated a whole tradition—a knot of problems to handle and some rather grim advice for handling them. The "archaization-cum-statization" with which the Civil War saddled the Soviet system will weigh heavily on the whole course of Soviet history.

CHAPTER 4:

RUSSIA/USSR IN HISTORICAL MOTION

An Essay in Interpretation

LOOKING AT THE ENTIRE SPAN OF SOVIET HISTORY, ACTUALLY no longer than a modern man's life, one can observe two distinct time segments that differ considerably in the intensity and direction of their historical development.[1] The first, from the revolution to the end of Stalin's rule, was characterized by enormous volatility and huge doses of coercion and dislocation, either of sheer destructiveness (wars, famine, purges) or of the intense tempo of construction (industrial, educational, and related efforts). In fact, one can more appropriately date this period not from October 1917, but from August 1914, which triggered a chain reaction, piling up ever-new calamities on the already enfeebled body social. The second period, inaugurated by Khrushchev, was by contrast reasonably peaceful, stable, and gradual on the internal fronts.

Although the first, "catastrophic" leg was interrupted by the relatively idyllic New Economic Policy (NEP) interlude, this did not seriously modify the basic features of the period as a whole, which with each successive upheaval narrowed the range of freedom to choose and act, and the options for future development. The historical agenda was increasingly dominated by a powerful, oppressive, and ubiquitous state. To be sure, the NEP was a promising alternative, but the political framework of the time did not allow the formation of political constituencies powerful enough to exploit the NEP's possibilities for a viable developmental strategy, as Lenin seemed to have bequested. The concentration of institutionalized power in the Communist Party, and inside the party at its narrow apex, by the same token depoliticized first the country and subsequently the party itself. When the time approached for important new strategic decisions, the assessment of the current economic and social crisis, the

1. This paper was written during a study leave supported by the National Endowment for the Humanities. It was initially presented to the Shelby Cullom David Center for Historical Studies at Princeton University on April 6, 1990.

choice of strategy, and the power to make decisions (even the definition of "reality" itself) depended on a very small group of people who controlled the apparatus. These decision makers, partisans of a strong-armed developmental policy and Stalinists of Stalin's line of 1928, were not all to become Stalinists with a capital *S*; that development was still ahead.

This happened despite the fact that the NEP, unlike the Weimar Republic, did not have powerful enemies during this period, especially not in the population at large. However, by the time the NEP was rejected "from above" and replaced by a different policy, there was no Bolshevik Party anymore, and one could even say, *no political party at all.* And this is not just a problem of semantics—the Bolsheviks before this time *were* a political party. But by the time the last opposition was evicted, the organization still bearing the Bolshevik name was already a bureaucratic-hierarchical administrative body in which the rank and file simply obeyed orders or, at least, were expected to do so.

The post-Stalinist period of stability, by contrast, exhibited a more complicated and even contradictory set of features. To be sure, a modest but still significant sphere of liberty began to open up, and pure Stalinism was replaced by a much less virulent breed of authoritarianism. But beyond this, a certain pronounced bifurcation of trends set in. On one hand, the "command-administrative system"—that is, the Soviet-style bureaucratic organization and domination, twisted in its "natural development" by Stalin's whimsical despotism—reached its apogee after his death (not before, as some versions would have it) and flourished as never before in Russian or Soviet history. Yet this deceptive blossoming of bureaucratic rule was all too soon beset by signs of stagnation and decay. On the other hand, the larger societal sphere, unlike the bureaucracy, exhibited considerable dynamism: urbanization proceeded at a hectic pace; the whole social structure, including the educational and professional profiles of nearly all population groups, changed quite dramatically; and the rural Russia that served as the social backdrop to Stalinism (as well as to its bureaucratic successor) was replaced by a very different social structure and system. The political system remained state-dominated, hence "statist," but society kept steadily evolving into a diverse and restive "civil society." Against this rapidly changing social landscape, the "command-administrative system"—created essentially in the 1930s to push a rural nation into factories, *kolkhozy,* schools, and camps—kept losing its capacity to solve problems, and hence to rule.

This applied above all to the economic sphere, where the "primitive accumulation" stage of industrialization, seemingly well served by administrative and coercive methods, had long since been superseded by the demands of a more modern, techno-scientific stage, requiring deep changes in the patterns of economic management and the functioning of the polity. This applied above all to urban society, which by now was enormous and had outgrown the system's ability to respond to its needs. The gap "between society and the state," in the classic formulation, kept widening. An interesting effort at reform initiated primarily by Premier Alexei Kosygin in 1965 came to nothing a few years later. Fifteen more years were wasted until the sclerosis became almost deadly. A new, fateful crossroad was approaching, again not unlike that of the late NEP, which now loomed larger than life and beckoned would-be reformers. Though not as yet visible to outsiders, such reformers were lodged in the heart of the sclerotic apparatus itself, biding their time.

This bird's-eye view of the Soviet historical experience calls for a study of the "moving forces" that produced all these crises, revolutions, and alternative waves of dynamism and stagnation, and such a study cannot confine itself to the new regime alone. One must also examine the prerevolutionary period and reflect on the circumstances that brought about the fall of tsardom. This pertains particularly to that huge social class with ancient roots that was to dominate the nation (and the nationalities within) sociologically into the 1960s and 1970s, namely, the peasantry. The fact that this "domination" lasted until very recently is crucial to the whole analysis: precisely because of its recent memory, the carryover in mental attitudes among the newly minted city dwellers is still at work—indeed, quite markedly so—in the contemporary psychology of the Soviet citizenry.

THE AGRARIAN NEXUS IN THREE VERSIONS

It is fitting that the examinations of a deeply rural country like Russia, the proverbial land of *muzhiki,* should begin from that perspective. But the problem or riddle of Russia's tribulations is not just that of the muzhik, as is so often maintained, but of the agrarian system as a whole, with its complex social scaffolding. Furthermore, that scaffolding, to a large extent, though in different forms and circumstances, was imported from tsarist Russia into the Russia of Lenin and Stalin, so that no period of Russian history can be understood without examining these agrarian and rural features. Our treatment here can only be a shorthand essay, presenting complex relations of modern Russian history in abbreviated form.

The tsarist social system can be demonstrated to have been held together by a triad composed of the peasantry, the landowning nobility or gentry (also a largely rural class), and, broadly speaking, the tsarist court, the pivotal institution of tsardom, where many of the most crucial political and administrative decisions were made. The tsar, in fact, did call himself, and actually was, *"pomeshchik number one,"* and the court, as well as the upper layers of the central and provincial bureaucracies, were dominated by actual or aspiring landowners.

Of course, many changes had occurred in this system since the time of Peter the Great. But in the early twentieth century, despite the array of complex changes and the fading image of traditional despotism, it is still possible to think of Russia as, in essence, an old agrarian kingdom. The bulk of the taxpaying population and of the army was composed of peasants, while the main ruling sectors in the polity were likewise agrarians, and most of the national income was still generated by agriculture.

To be sure, the mainstays of the system continued to evolve and erode—nobles high and low were losing much of their land and economic significance in society. The peasants were overburdened with taxes, crowded into overpopulated villages, and starved for land. The court proved over and over again that it was not equal to the imperatives of empire, particularly as validated in warfare. The menacing prospect of losing the crucial support of peasants' bayonets to keep the internal peace was grossly underestimated, despite very clear warning signals.

The "triad," though dominant, did not completely immobilize the system, which had to come to terms with the powerful dynamic force epitomized by the term *capitalism.* (A fourth component in the system— the bureaucracy—is omitted here, as it requires a different kind of analysis.) We can lay aside the learned arguments over the depth and consequences of capitalism, and allow the observation to suffice that the intrusion of this dynamic force underscored the weaknesses of the "agrarian kingdom," deepened its internal imbalances, and exposed its archaic traits.

Lenin was not too far from the truth when he contended that the fast-moving forms of the modern capitalist economy still ensnared all kinds of "remnants" of the primitive, slow-changing agriculture from the pre-reform system, and that this disparity was at the root of Russia's structural vulnerabilities. Capitalism in Russia was not given enough time and ran into too many obstacles to be able—forgive the pun—to "plow up" agricultural Russia, muzhik and *pomeshchik* alike, and overcome the glaring gap. The historic distances between different social, economic, and political sectors of the system were too great, and this hampered the system's ability to resist shocks, especially one as powerful as a world war. (An infinitely smaller shock—the Russo-Japanese War—triggered the Revolution of 1905!)

The extent to which the peasantry continued to be stuck in an older socioeconomic mold is crucial for the arguments presented here for postrevolutionary events. But the problem is more complex, for it is not merely the peasantry but also the whole political system, still welded to the agrarian nexus, that was hopelessly "stuck" and could not handle the challenges of economic and social development created by capitalism. Capitalism on this scale was still a rather new phenomenon, vindicating for Russia Fernand Braudel's view that modern, large-scale capitalism historically descended on a primitive, though already market-oriented, society from above. In Russia's case, the technological level tended to be from the very beginning supermodern and large-scale, transplanted from a foreign-made model onto a basically different, still-agrarian society, and consequently was dependent on the state for support and political backing. The result was the wholesale alienation of the working classes, which lacked social standing within the industrial system, while the industrial system failed to penetrate and transform the country's rural world (or even the political system, as just pointed out).

That agriculture did experience in many ways the impact of the market economy and its capitalist drive can easily be demonstrated. The main problem, however, was that this agriculture was plied almost exclusively by traditional peasant technology: the three-field system, few machines and fertilizers, and a ridiculously small amount of iron per household (Russia remained a timber country—*Rus' dereviannaia*). Despite improvements, yields and marketability were low, production served primarily direct family needs, rural overpopulation vastly exceeded the capacity of cities to absorb it, and progress in popular education remained slow.

Foreign trade is an excellent index for the points under consideration.

Products of the newly developed industries could not yet compete on world markets and still needed heavy state protection for internal markets, while imports remained primarily industrial goods. Russia continued to carry the classic imprint of underdevelopment, in that 80 percent of its exports consisted of agricultural products of the bulky, extensive variety—not only cereal grains but, even worse, fodder, so badly needed internally. Paradoxically, Russia's export economy served to intensify foreign agriculture while freezing its own on a preindustrial level.

The *pomeshchiki* did not fare much better on their private domains. Some managed to modernize their agricultural enterprises, but most availed themselves of the abundant and cheap peasant labor (and their primitive tools), mostly through leasing and sharecropping arrangements rather than wage labor. These practices undermined the economy and even the social role of the *pomeshchiki* as a class; that the latter could not avoid this trap is a problem worthy of further analysis, but here we just state it as a fact.

The factors cited thus far certainly have much to do with the persistence of an acute agrarian problem and its side effect of a politically unreliable peasantry. The road from the wooden plow to the airplane was bound to be rough, whatever the strategy, but alternatives certainly existed. The problem for development lay not in a presumed inherent incapacity for change in Russian peasants—indeed, frequent, almost perpetual changes affected many aspects of their lives. It was the pace of such change relative to other sectors that often strained the adaptive abilities of peasants and induced deep crises in their midst. "Change" can also run in the reverse direction, as noted later, with incalculable results for the development of the country, a characteristic inherent to an unfinished or unsuccessful developmental transplant. An additional concept, quite useful for deciphering the preceding reasoning, is the one of "combined development" that played an important role in Trotsky's thinking about Russia. In this conceptualization, the dynamic elements of a new, not yet prevailing system tend to exacerbate the internal incoherences of the old one, whose considerable staying power and inertia weaken and disfigure the modernizing factors (as measured by their Western prototypes), resulting in a system combining the most modern with the most barbaric. Trotsky applied his concept only to tsarist Russia and somehow failed to see that it fits Stalin's Russia even better.

THE RURAL NEXUS, LENIN'S VERSION

Both the relatively weak implantation of capitalism in the rural economy and the potential for deep backsliding are crucial for understanding the fate of Lenin's Russia and of Leninism as an ideology. The short period from the beginning of World War I to the end of the Civil War is pivotal, yet seldom properly understood in interpreting Soviet Russia. This short period comprised in rapid succession the collapse of tsarism, the failure to implant a Western-style democratic political system, and, finally, the unexpected triumph of a new state and regime led by the Bolsheviks. The weakness of the democratic forces, the radicalization of the urban and rural masses, and the policies of the Bolsheviks all contributed in the first instance to a dangerous decomposition of the state and to a debilitating civil war. The outcome of the latter, raging for nearly three years over Russia's immense territory, hinged on who was to recreate or restore Russia's statehood. While neither the democratic nor the counter-revolutionary forces proved capable of achieving this end, the Bolsheviks were successful first on the territory they controlled, and subsequently on nearly the entire territory of the former Empire.

How and why these newcomers to power politics could pull this off is an interesting problem, but for the moment we are concerned primarily with the circumstances. By 1921 the cumulative effect of the tremors that began in 1914 threw Russia many decades backward. Temporarily, at least, Russia was considerably deindustrialized, partly de-urbanized, and purged not only of both "feudal" and "capitalist" elites and technicians but also of most of its urban working class—the mainstay of the new regime! Against this background of enfeebled cities, the peasantry, though in very poor shape itself, assumed a much larger specific weight than before in the economy and society of the new Soviet order. Furthermore, it was no longer the same peasantry that had existed on the eve of the war and the revolution. As a result of their own agrarian revolution, the peasants eliminated many of the inroads of markets and capitalism, as well as the modest achievements of the Stolypin reforms, and recreated a mode of existence resembling the distant past (as did, to some extent, the social order as a whole). The market- and export-oriented sectors of agriculture were destroyed or considerably weakened, and the already fading *mir,* the rural distributive commune, was restored over an immense territory—except in the regions where it had never existed—

and took back into its fold many of the enclosed farms of recent and not-so-recent origin. The *muzhiki* turned inward, transforming themselves into a family-consumption-oriented ocean of microfundia—institutions that calculated "mouths to feed" rather than productivity and market opportunities. This was, of course, a strategy of self-defense and survival, but it harbored a deeply anti-urban bias (never lacking among Russian peasants) that worried, even frightened, many intellectuals and politicians who saw in this rural self-enclosure a dangerously destructive potential.

The proper term for this relapse of the peasantry into a precapitalist, even pre–petty bourgeoisie mode (that is, no market orientation whatsoever) is *archaization*. The market orientation of Russian peasants, weakly developed before the revolution, now shrank even more and remained low well into the NEP. Archaization, as it affected not just the peasants but the whole system, needs to be further explored. The term, of course, should not be used to signify paranoid accusations of frightened intellectuals against peasants—it should be axiologically neutral, to describe a phenomenon for which there is no better term. This kind of "geological" shift of a society "backward" does not occur very often, yet in this case it profoundly affected the further development of the new regime: the next few years had to be spent restoring the economy to the prewar level, which was not too impressive in the first place, and the seeds of a future crisis were inherent in this very restoration.

From the Bolshevik perspective, this momentous retreat of *muzhiki* into themselves constituted "an accursed problem." Peasant aspirations, once seriously at odds with the aims of the tsarist government, were now even more distant, socially, economically, and ideologically, from the aims, and even language, of the new regime. At a time when the state's leaders perceived themselves as the carriers of the century's most grandiose visions, there seemed to be nothing ahead but a deadly clash, since here, as elsewhere, only the peasants would bear the brunt (that is, the human costs) of realizing these visions.

The hurdle to be surmounted, however, was not of the peasants' making alone: the new state was born in the heat of a deadly battle with the economy and society in a state of advanced decomposition. The Bolsheviks found themselves responsible not only for preserving the state's territorial integrity, but also for recreating the state in a new garb. Given these deadly conditions, coercive and bureaucratic traits became ingrained in the system and in the mentality of many of its cadres. Though a few of the state's leaders (Lenin among them) were ready to support other strategies once peace was restored, the coercive inclination remained powerfully present, biding its time. The New Economic Policy, by dismantling key mechanisms of War Communism, showed that there were alternative variants within the ideology of Leninism. As the new Leninist variant, the NEP continued to be a self-proclaimed dictatorship but, though not to be trifled with, became in reality a kind of paradoxical "pluralist authoritarianism." This amounted to a mixed plan-and-market economic system, with clearly implied "social compacts" or deals with the technical specialists, the administrative elite, the artistic intelligentsia, and the peasants. It allowed a considerable flow of information in the press, reasonable freedom for research (even in the humanities), and a fair amount of economic and cultural traffic with the West. The scope of police interference and state terror was modest, especially by standards of the previous and the following periods, and the prospects for law and due process appeared to be quite promising. Finally, a powerful political battle with opposition groups was still raging inside the party, despite the ban on organized factions introduced by Lenin in 1921. After some years of intense infighting, the various opposition groups were successively eliminated, and the party was moving in a direction opposite to that of the broader NEP system. The party was becoming ever more bureaucratized, centralized, and depoliticized (that is, none but the select few engaged in decision making). In fact, the liquidation of the last party opposition also tolled the bell for the NEP.

Why so? Though archaization was the pervasive background phenomenon, a few other causes were at work. In the party-state system, the party served mainly as a source of cadres to resolve endless emergencies and to staff and supervise the state machinery. The internal organization of the party was relatively neglected. As of 1921, it had an astonishingly small apparatus and was very modestly differentiated by function. The Civil War "trained" it to be a top-heavy party, not so much by design as under the pressure of the wartime conditions of a military camp. The endemic militarization of the Civil War destroyed the formerly autonomous system of soviets, as well as the internal political life of the party. The outcry "send us cadres," reaching Moscow from all corners of the land, expressed a genuine need at a time of a high rate of attrition in Civil War circumstances. In practice this meant that any candidate for secretary sent from the center would immediately be elected. The center, of course, obliged as best it could. However, only during the NEP, in response to a growing need, was a party apparatus hastily built up by Uchraspred, the organ responsible for locating and distributing cadres.

Another crucial factor was the massive influx into the party from the lower orders of society. Their low level of literacy prevented them from directly participating in intraparty politics and ideological debates. Seen from above, the influx was deemed necessary to meet the requirements of ruling the country (while also conveniently flushing out the oppositionists). Seen from below, it was a crucial new avenue to social promotion or, more simply, to jobs. This was not merely "conformism" or "careerism"—though both were present—but a result of the more elemental social need in poor, "archaized" Russia for advancing new social groups to positions of responsibility, and thereby advancing the country. The keys to advancement, especially in urban Russia, were now in the hands of the party. The leadership of the party kept developing its apparatus, the "secretarial machinery," as the most expeditious way of coping with the pressing problems of assimilating, educating, activating, and controlling the enormous mass of new members. Recruiting and deploying cadres for pressing tasks became the key function of the apparatus, which, in the first place, was required to instill elementary discipline. Training for serious participation in the formulation of policies, however, ceased to be a priority. No matter how much consecutive opposition groups kept clamoring for more meaningful participation by the rank and file, blind execution, military style, became the order of the day.

All these trends were powerful facts of life, but whether they had to lead to "Stalinism" is another matter; certainly, at a later stage, they facilitated it. *Later* should be underlined, because this party, though the first of its kind, was to be followed in the coming decades by many more party-states, left and right, in other countries, enduring the process of revolutionary battles, civil wars, or wars against foreign domination, each having its own "style" of authoritarian rule. The fact that not all of them imitated, or showed tendencies toward "Stalinism" should introduce some caution in attributing to the phenomenon a single predetermined causal chain.

However this may be, during the NEP the party came under the domination of the *apparat,* or, rather, of a narrow group of leaders working *through* the *apparat* (the making of *apparatchiki* itself requires additional clarification) who fought for internal unity and discipline by methods soon to be called *apparatnye* and to whom "Leninist traditions of party life" were reduced to ritual phrase making. Bolshevism soon originated from, and for most of its political life had been a variant of, European and Russian Social-Democracy, but by now it had been eradicated and replaced by an adminstrative organization geared toward running the new system. During the next decade these systemic tendencies were to become mightily reinforced and "enriched" by further innovations.

It was precisely this party with these characteristics that had to face the NEP's complexities and difficult problems, as the mixed economy revealed its troublesome side effects as well as its benefits. The official objective was to "restore" the country's economic performance by the yardstick of 1914. The industry that recovered, however, was mostly the old tsarist one, with its equipment now worn out and ever more obsolete. As the West (until 1929) was rushing ahead, Soviet Russia, despite her recovery, seemed relatively more backward than before.

The party debates over industrialization and other key problems during the 1920s represented meaningful efforts to find solutions and chart the future, but by the time of the so-called procurement crisis during the winter of 1927–28, only a narrow circle of leaders—specifically, Stalinists and Bukharinists—remained to diagnose the crisis and to determine a course of action. A battle ensued, and the Stalinist victors decided that the crisis was severe and that NEP policies should be drastically reversed. The strategy chosen at this juncture by leaders grouped around Stalin greatly stimulated the full blossoming of Stalinism, although, as we said above, the preconditions had already been created earlier for a power pattern heavily skewed toward the top.

AN AGRARIAN DESPOTISM

Stalinism was the third and final embodiment of the agrarian nexus. By 1939, 67 percent of the population were still peasants. Although this means that 33 percent—a record figure for Russia—were city dwellers, the majority were recent arrivals from the countryside, and in this sense the cities were heavily "ruralized." Therefore, the population base on which the social structure of Stalinism rested was composed of poorly "collectivized" peasants in the countryside and poorly urbanized ones in the cities. The considerable social flux set in motion by rapid industrialization and other measures thrust millions of people into new social positions, and inaugurated a period of extreme upheaval and tension. These features were to become the hallmark of the social landscape for some time to come, and are indispensable for the understanding of this epoch.

Sociologically and culturally, Russia was still a rural country, but unlike the previous, "Leninist" stage—a state system constructed against the background of deep regression in socioeconomic life followed by modest recovery—the newer state edifice was built (not unlike certain phases of tsarist Russia) by imposing on a slow-moving social system a violent industrialization drive. Whereas the tsarist experiments failed to pass the test, the Stalinist system of the 1930s succeeded—but at the price of a malignant growth *pas comme les autres*. This system combined spectacular development with massive oppression, and it carried in its bosom the mechanisms of its ultimate self-destruction—some of them self-evident in its malfunctions, other still invisible, buried in the entrails of the institutions bequeathed to its successors.

Accelerated development probably imposed disruptive tendencies throughout the system, but those were intertwined with sources of strength, trailing the shadows behind, even when moving forward; the overall results for the human condition differ according to the sources and type of the developmental dynamics. The above applies not just to economic dimensions but to political, cultural, and ethical ones as well, and this is why the term *human condition* is appropriate.

The party is a case in point. Vibrant when it came to power, transformed by civil war, in the ensuing peaceful years the party continuously reaped the fruits of those victories because, fundamentally, the popular masses recognized its achievements as legitimate. They now flocked to the party in their hundreds of thousands, a sociologically inevitable process in a backward country with low standards of living and high expectations. Precisely for such masses the party became an immense school and clearinghouse for cadres for the whole nation, a role it had assumed earlier, albeit on a much smaller scale. Although key functions in the new system had to be filled by specialists—mostly remnants of the old regime—the bulk of the political and administrative jobs, high and low, went to people of plebeian social origin who constituted the overwhelming majority of the population. The socialist ideology was perceived by such cadres as both justifying and legitimizing the process. It also bred in the new class of rulers and administrators a sense of entitlement to be where they were, by virtue of their social origin, their historical mission, and their proven reliability. Though a social and cultural phenomenon of great historical importance, the massive promotion lent itself to acting as an aesthetic and provided ideological camouflage for the making of a new breed of authoritarian, even despotic bosses.

The party was likewise the gatekeeper to technical and professional careers, controlling entrance to schools, placement, and promotion, and hence served as a "smithy"—a favorite metaphor—for the modernization of the country. Even for members of the rank and file who did not ascend these occupational ladders, party membership offered the prospect of advancement or, at the very least, the sense of a role in national development denied to people of other social origin under the previous regime.

These "side effects" of the massive influx into the party—the more sudden and massive, the deeper and more dangerous—were precisely the above-noted decline in educational and political standards, bureaucratization, and the displacement of the original Bolshevik Party by one quite different in its way of functioning, social composition, and ideology. Such phenomena were to repeat themselves several times over on an ever-larger scale during the "big drive." Party membership reached three million by 1933, and the number of jobs and cadres needed in state administration, security, the army, and schooling kept pace accordingly—not to mention the growth of the working and employee classes in the national economy. The party now became deeply "economized," that is, most of its cadres, functions, and apparatus were now applied to handling the rapidly expanding economy. Its monopoly over all the important spheres of life meant that "economistic" blueprints, methods, and routines were grafted onto the handling of other spheres, including culture. Hence, already an administrative monolith rather than a political party by the end of the NEP, in the 1930s; it bestowed on this "monolithism" an ideological status in its own right, destined to guide not only its own behavior but that of the whole society.

Three important policy drives contributed to forging the new monolithism into a different type of state system: forced "collectivization," forced industrialization and, finally, the social spinoff of both these drives, which amounted to a permanent social crisis. "Collectivization" is a misnomer, hence the quotation marks. Collectives, in theory, were supposed to be self-governing cooperatives; in fact, driving the peasants into *kolkhozy* forcibly amounted to the etatization of agriculture (that is, its complete domination by local bureaucracies whose exclusive role was to extract maximum deliveries to the state without remuneration). The result was an agrarian system that forced people to accept a mode of life and economic activity that offered few incentives to work. Consequently, administrative pressure became the sole method of exacting labor from a reluctant population.

Initially these policies actually led to a *decline* of agriculture, complicating the drive for industrialization, since shortages of food could scarcely be conducive to a healthy productivity of labor. The so-called planned industrialization—yet another misnomer, if not a plain myth— was purely *administrative* in character, that is, it rested exclusively on the initiatives and wishes of the state, a system later to be called, quite appropriately, the "command-economy." The enormous drive and economic spurt (which could not have been achieved by any other strategy in such a short time) was launched from the center, which maintained control of the process. Centralism reached unprecedented heights, giving birth to a peculiar dialectic: abrogating markets, denying any autonomy to producers, dictating from above targets and working conditions in minute detail. All this actually imposed heavy new burdens on the state. There were few built-in incentives for productivity and creativity throughout the economic system, and this had to be compensated for by devising ever-new pressures from above. But however ingenious the methods, they were inevitably top-heavy. The more complex the system grew, the more concentrated the main driving force became at the narrow apex, and the larger and more unwieldy became the bureaucratic mechanisms indispensable for control and supervision in a centralized system.

Such methods can scarcely be characterized as "planning." The ever-more-minute supervision and target setting were mainly an exercise in administrative, not economic, activity: deprived of measures of cost and price determination, the economy, even if growing, could not but develop all kinds of bottlenecks and deep imbalances. The planner was sucked into the maze he himself created and lost control over the economy's total performance and coherence. As I argue in the next chapter, the overadministered economy was actually drifting. An economy with an overenergetic top and a sluggish base, even if capable of considerable growth for a time, carried along with it, and inside it, the baggage that would sooner or later block its performance.

An analysis of the social changes involved in the restructuring of the nation's life in those years worked in the same direction. The situation of flux induced in the social organism by the rapid changes created, for a time, a "quicksand society." This was, of course, a short-term phenomenon, but all was "short-term" in this period. Immense waves of social and spatial mobility had to induce, in the first years, various phenomena of social disintegration and disorientation that would subside in due course, in conditions more propitious for stabilization. Such conditions, though, were still missing in the 1930s. The entry of millions of people, mostly of rural origin, into institutions of higher education, into new professions, and into positions of power on the different social and politico-administrative ladders can be seen as offering new prospects and expectations to great numbers of people, thus buttressing the existing regime. Nevertheless, it did so at the cost of creating new strains and stresses of a contradictory nature. One contradictory effect of the massive feat of social uplifting, other than the depression of the standard of living everywhere, was the watering down of culture in the cities and urban-industrial institutions, which engendered the widespread phenomenon of inadequate professional preparation of people in all occupations. The hurried training and schooling could only lag behind the needs of the hectic modernization, where the massive imports of new machinery could not be matched by improvements in the level of workers' technical proficiency or even by an adequate supply of engineers and administrators. An enormous mass of *praktiki*—workers appointed from the bench to jobs of responsibility with little training—was to become the hallmark of this stage of social and cultural development.

The same contradictions were evident in the political sphere. The widespread discrepancy between job and qualification that pervaded the system, combined with the fallout from social flux and the "ruralization" of cities, set the stage for the "cultural counterrevolution," which can be seen in many ways as the central feature of the Stalinist political system. The combination of rapidly promoted but inadequately trained ex-workers and peasants thrown into positions of technical, administrative, or political responsibility could not yet produce cohesive social or interest groups—such integration demands time, experience, and leadership in countless informal ways, as well as a sense of self-importance and mastery of the environment. New to their jobs, the rank and file and the bosses in factories, offices, and institutions were socially insecure, frangible, and in most cases still grateful to the system and its leaders for having promoted them. In short, they were followers and clients rather than responsible co-definers of the system's parameters.

Stalinism can only be understood against this background of social flux, its climate of newness and insecurity on the job, as at once thriving on it and perpetuating it. The proliferation of the bureaucracies, of networks of bosses and watchdogs, has to be related to the regime's efforts to master this flux, caused by the immense feats of "social engineering" such as collectivization and massive industrialization. The first of these feats is the most crucial, as it destroyed an economic system based on the peasantry's largely autonomous activity and replaced it with one in which bureaucratized and coercive elements prevailed and economic incentives were weak. The application to agricultural production of this administrative, etatized system strongly reinforced the idea (held equally by outside observers and the peasants themselves) that this was some new form of serfdom. However, this understanding is softened by the fact that the parallel industrialization drive made it impossible to attach the peasants to the soil, though efforts to this effect were not entirely absent. Peasant views to the contrary, this was not exactly serfdom, because many could take up industrial occupations in the growing towns and at building sites, where the need for additional labor was enormous. Still, for those who remained, it was not much different than forced labor. Such a state domination of labor was unthinkable under the NEP, where peasants worked the land they considered their own, planted whatever crops they wished, functioned as real *khoziaeva* on their farms, and disposed of their produce as they pleased. In short, collectivization deprived them of their status as free producers. The other plank in this strategy, accelerated industrialization, though promoting mobility and weakening the bondage features in the *kolkhoz* system, strengthened immensely the administrative-coercive character of the system overall and reintroduced through the back door something even more "peppery" than bondage, namely, the slave labor of the Gulag (where the majority of inmates were again peasants).

One important feature of Russian historical development that continued to shape the character of Soviet industrialization was its extensive orientation, its centuries-long expansion over wide stretches of territory, comprising first of all agriculture, but also determining the quantity-based strategy of industrialization from Peter to Stalin and beyond. This system was based, to a large extent, on a combination of a surfeit of underqualified physical labor and vast quantities of large-scale, advanced machinery, a combination sufficient for the achievement of breakthroughs in production, but creating enormous obstacles to a further conversion to an intensive, quality- and efficiency-oriented phase. Although the latter did occur, it could only be achieved in certain priority sectors, while the rest of the system vegetated in a low-intensity regimen, even more wasteful of human than physical resources. All the characteristics cited above fit together into a picture of a *sui generis* "agrarian despotism"—agrarian by virtue of the character of its population (including the recent arrivals to the towns and industry), but also by virtue of the preservation of the space-dominated thrust of the earlier agrarian despotisms of Russian history. Soviet-accelerated industrialization shared the extensive thrust of the past, as well as the features of hectic tempo and spectacular goals. Thus, it is no wonder that in the process Stalin's regime rediscovered the legacy of the tsarist empire builders and incorprated it into its own policies. They still had in common a rural-peasant social base along with a coercive-bureaucratic apparatus. Yet all these powerful features of agrarian despotism were preparing its demise and a future of quite a different order.

THE "IMPOSSIBLE" STALINISM

The observations above help us to discern the transitional stages from stalinism to Stalinism, and later, from Stalinism to something else. The unifying concept I would like to propose in interpreting Stalinism is that of *institutional paranoia,* the by-product of the social tensions of the 1930s, the mushrooming administrative economy, and the fettered agricultural system. The groundwork, as we observed, was laid during the NEP—the concentration of enormous power in the hands of a narrow group of party leaders, the Civil War legacy, and the social influx into party and state institutions. The pressures of hypercentralization, the penchant (even necessity) to control literally everything from above, the severe dislocations, the monumental tasks, and perpetual crisis phenomena all created enormous pressures to preseve this pattern and not relinquish any power to other bodies of the citizenry. The consequence was an ever-present sense of danger and fear of losing control. Such worries were not unwarranted, as the bewildering realization set in that the greater the concentration of power, the more difficult control became, and the more inefficiently the entire mechanism functioned. And yet the only answer to the situation created by the overconcentration of power seemed to be the application of sharper and heavier doses of the same medicine. This desperation and anxiety over the loss of control is what we mean by institutional paranoia.

It seems clear (though documentary evidence is thin) that by 1933 some in the leadership realized that matters had gotten too far out of hand and that a reformulation of the current policies was in order. This was the first attempt by the inner circle of Stalinists to shake this institutional paranoia. They apparently felt overwhelmed by the results of their own policies and were frustrated with the difficulties of coping, experiencing a growing sense of powerlessness despite the fact that they had concentrated so much power in their hands. Thus, a number of leaders were looking for a way to escape this trap. But hesitations and vacillations within the very narrow circle of power brokers created favorable conditions for the seizure of absolute power by one who already had more of it than his co-rulers (and maybe even more than he himself realized). Under the NEP, Stalin had been a powerful but vulnerable leader, and in the struggle with the Bukharin Triumvirate (Bukharin, Rykov, and Tomsky) he had been elevated to the top player and strategist by his Stalinist cohorts, who preferred him to the opposition. This stage ended with the death of Kirov, however, which inaugurated the full-scale despotism of "High Stalinism," as some authors have dubbed it. If previously the leadership was composed of people who viewed themselves as leaders in their own right (or, at the very least, junior co-rulers), the new stage was to have but a single leader.

If the institutional paranoia that afflicted a small group of leaders because of their self-induced power glut proved to be unbearable to them, the elevation of one man to supreme leadership meant that this kind of paranoia changed its character and dimension: it now vested itself with enormous force in a leader who was, evidently, endowed with a paranoid personality and, quite probably, suffered from recurrent paranoiac delusions. Thus, paranoid fear and anxiety pervaded both the political environment and the psyche of the figure who was the pivot of power. A collective leadership in this situation might compensate for this structural weakness with a change of policy or mutual self-control by other means. But the welding of a structural insecurity with a personal-psychological insecurity allowed a whimsical despot to play out his deliria and to do so on a broad historical stage.

Personal despotism, is, of course, an "overcentralized" system by definition. And from this point of view, the growingly complex business of ruling an enormous country in the throes of hectic transformations renders such a despotism "impossible," also by definition. Personal control is an absolute must for the despot, but in order to rule effectively he must delegate. Nevertheless, he cannot do both at once. Many institutions are needed to accomplish complex tasks, and for this they need autonomy. But autonomy is precisely what an autocrat or despot of the Stalinist type cannot allow. Partners are needed to run the country effectively, and this means genuine leaders in their own right. But true partnership was inconceivable to Stalin. In fact, his direct subordinates resembled a coterie of slaves. Though it was stated above, for instance, that the Soviet *kolkhozniki* were not actually serfs but rather under "some kind of bondage," with respect to members of Stalin's entourage the term *slave* is proper: Stalin could remove, arrest, and execute any of them, persecute their families, forbid them to attend meetings of bodies of which they were members, or simply rage against them uncontrollably. This inbuilt arbitrariness of "High Stalinism" belongs equally to the domains of political science and psychiatry. Since his collaborators knew him to be capable of killing them, Stalin could never know whether they were really faithful to him or merely feigning loyalty out of fear. Though some (Poskrebyshev, Stalin's personal secretary, for example) might have been blindly faithful and therefore trusted, Stalin's morbid and pervasive suspiciousness toward his entourage was a permanent condition. His unique position of power, therefore, was not just a conquest but also a trap into which he had allowed himself to fall.

At its highest stage, Stalinism was consequently already a historical anachronism, capable of hanging on for a time through various artificial devices, but incapable of arresting its eventual removal from the stage.

SOME CONCLUDING IDEAS

This chapter set out by positing two fundamental phases or segments of Soviet history—the "catastrophic" and the "gradual" or evolutionary. During the gradual period, Stalinism *sensu stricto* was eliminated. This distinction is crucial because so many find it difficult to grasp. The intensity of historical changes is the key to the whole distinction. The bone-breaking social changes in a highly compressed period of time, the bellicose complexion of events, the "big drive" launching a new wave of large-scale mutations and disruptions, again tearing apart social bonds and sparing little of former cultural traditions and political patterns, the destructiveness of the plan period—all indelibly impressed themselves on the character of the state and the ways it was run; in fact, in many ways, the five-year plans resumed key traits of the Civil War methods and mentality (besides adding quite a few of their own).

The later, post-Stalinist years were, by contrast, "gradual," but one must be careful to characterize them properly. Nearly gone were the coercive pushing and shoving, the terroristic herding of people into new occuaptions, and the massive displacement through mobilizations. People and institutions settled into predictable routines and careers, especially in the *apparat*. This was precisely what the vast bureaucracy so dearly wanted and did in fact achieve. Some have theorized that the dreaded bureaucracy was the very basis of Stalinism and continued to be its custodian. Bureaucracy and bureaucratism did indeed develop under Stalin prodigiously, but, in the conditions of those times, bureaucrats could not constitute a serious ruling stratum. For this they were too fragmented and insecure, too new to their jobs, and too inadequate for their tasks. Exposed to permanent danger from above, they could not—as a true ruling stratum must—conduct their offices with self-confidence, defend their collective and individual interests, and fashion their role in the polity according to their own rationally devised formulations.

After Stalin's death the upper layers of the bureaucracy systematically eliminated those elements of the previous period that had made their life and work so difficult and had inhibited their exercise of power. "Collective leadership," an expanded environment of "legality," and a curbing of police arbitrariness transformed the bureaucracy from one of the most frangible into the most tenured in the industrialized world. But similar transformations were extended to a much broader social base. The elements of bondage in the life of the *kolkhozniki* were diminished, and—a novelty—peasants were soon actually to be paid for their work; security, freedom of choice, and other rights in the workplace were extended to both city workers and those on the *sovkhozy*; and, finally, the vast Gulag empire was considerably transformed.

Such changes in the bureaucracy and in the position of workers and people in other walks of life negated the very essence of Stalinism. There were still plenty of Stalinists around and many vestiges of the system remained (since the memory or knowledge of viable alternatives was weak), but the result was a very different version of authoritarianism that came to be known as the *command-administrative system*. The latter system must be analyzed on its own terms. The chief characteristic of this system's historical evolution was the fact that even while it flourished (under Brezhnev, after the Khrushchev interlude) and seemed fully insured against change, the bacilli of stagnation and decline worked mightily to guarantee its ultimate demise.

Our claim of gradualism should at this point, however, be modified in one important respect, already noted in the introduction. Though coercive, violent social restructuring was gone, the body social was subjected to yet another deep restructuring. During the years of bureaucratic immobility and apparent bliss, a hectic urbanization again brought tens of millions of peasants into the cities on a scale and at a pace that surpassed the ability of the existing institutions to assure their successful integration into the urban infrastructure and culture. The transformation of a rural country and sociology into a predominantly urban one occurred in a matter of three decades—a new historical restructuring bringing its own strains, traumas, and social disorientation, and the further fragmentation of ideological, national, and cultural identities.

On one plane, over the entire span of seventy years, transformed and shattered social layers were superimposed on one another in rapid succession, intermingled and juxtaposed, and not allowed time to solidify new common bonds or cultural identities before facing a new wave. The effect was much like grafting new tissue onto the old before the latter had properly healed. On another plane, following Stalin's death, the institutional framework of a directed economy and society, the bureaucracy and party, steadily evolved stable features that contrasted sharply with the complicated and rapidly changing social system. The more recent social flux, unlike the one of the 1930s (the "peasantization" of the cities that was conducive to the solidification of "agrarian despotism," Stalinist style), produced an urban society in quest of a new civil order made possible by the elimination of many of the forms of agrarian-despotic bondage. The emergence of a new "civil society"—this is the name of the real novelty—continually undermined the all-too-stable command-administrative system.

When passing judgment on the achievements and failures of pere-stroika, it is helpful to keep in mind our oft-repeated theme: the legacy of the past waves of deep restructuring that were inimical to social consolidation and to stable, widely shared values, at least among the different elites. The life experience of the elites and of the different broad social layers—of the party-state and the emerging civil society—were still poles apart, both having been thoroughly "depoliticized," or rather "depolitized," by the previous period. A parallel phenomenon obtained in the economy, where economic forces were replaced by administrative ones. The result was an economic system without economics and a political system without politics.

The historical development of the Russian-Soviet state was a mix of these two powerful trends, each of them profoundly influenced by the other and between them shaping the social and political system: the centuries-long experience of extensive development had its corollary in a peculiar state system, alternately thriving and vegetating on this prevailing pattern of history. The ways of the old agrarian despotism were perpetuated even when the state finally, under Stalin, became the initiator and promoter of industrialization. This new industrialization retained the extensive character of the agrarian society, transposing the underproductive physical labor of rural Russia to the still-not-too-productive industrial setting. The various social upheavals, different in their origins but coinciding in time, became "system makers" (that is, they all affected the tasks and character of the state.)

The historical legacy, as described above, is essential for the interpretation of Russian-Soviet history in our century; and Stalinism, a unique agrarian despotism reemerging in the twentieth century, is certainly a very Russian phenomenon. But this statement does not preclude the need to examine other factors, notably the impact of the international scene, which this essay has left out. Still, it is important to remind ourselves that the twentieth century was replete with "Orwellian" dictatorships, some inspired or installed by Stalin, but others, quite original, often preceding Stalinism. The existence of some transnational features in the historical environment of, at least, Central and Eastern Europe is a dimension that has to be examined in order to reach a more satisfactory interpretation.

The stage Russia is living through these days no longer features an "agrarian nexus" of importance. It was, rather, profoundly shaped by the powerful urbanization of, notably, the last forty years, which was bound to come into conflict with the stagnating superstructure inherited from the 1930s. The new social realities forced the issue of a fundamental shake-up. What we are witnessing just now is yet another recasting of the political, social, and economic institutions, but this time, quite probably, with, over an unpredictable time span, the potential to switch to very different historical rails and to produce a renewed and viable urban-industrial polity.

PROMETHEUS UNBOUND— AND CHAINED AGAIN

CHAPTER 5: THE DISAPPEARANCE OF PLANNING IN THE PLAN

C OMMENTING ON AN INFEASIBLE PLAN MEANS REOPENING a set of issues that were in the center of heated controversies of those years. In the hectic and tense days of 1928 and the first months of 1929 when the first five-year plan was officially approved, academic and scholarly issues easily turned into ideological and political ones; the political ones very soon became the basis for criminal prosecution; finally, the executioner was brought in to resolve the controversies. An opinion on rates of growth uttered at that time was likely to lead to a degrading trial and prison sentence in 1930, to become "commuted," formally or informally, into a death sentence from 1935 on. Thus, the cool reevaluation by a mathematical economist of the set of figures that was triumphantly presented to the world in April–May 1929 as the text of the plan conjures up not merely specters of the past but burning political issues of the 1960s and 1970s, which the Soviet leadership did not like to face.

At that time many Soviet experts and politicians argued heatedly that the version of the plan as officially adopted was unrealistic. Such was the opinion of Gosplan's majority of specialists, especially the top nonparty men. But Bukharin, Rykov, and Tomsky, Politburo members, claimed the same. They disapproved of the more ambitious "optimal" version of the plan and preferred the more modest "minimal" (*otpravnoi*) version of it.[1] They also proposed working out a special "two-year plan" for agri-

---

1. Bukharin, Rykov, and Tomsky voted against the optimal plan and fought for the "minimal" (says an official source), though formally they abstained. See *Voprosy Istorii KPSS,* 1960, no. 4, p. 76. Rykov spoke openly against most of the targets of the optimum version, in *Pravda,* April 6, 1929.

culture to straighten things out in this field as the condition for the success of the whole plan.

But it is quite clear that even dedicated and ardent party spokesmen in Gosplan, like Krzhizhanovsky and Strumilin, were aware of the plan's excessive rigidity. They were competent people and could not have missed the point that the whole set of "qualitative indicators" (labor productivity, costs, yields)—the plan, quite officially, rested on those—were impossible targets if simultaneously the rate of accumulation in the national income was to be sharply increased. Perhaps justice should be done to those planners by recalculating the targets of the "minimum" version, too, because there is enough evidence to believe that this was the one that the planners really trusted. To realize this, it is sufficient to remind the reader that the planners officially presented four conditions under which the tougher version would be possible in subsequent years: (1) five good consecutive crops, (2) more external trade and help than in 1928, (3) a "sharp improvement" in the quality indicators, and (4) a smaller ratio than before of military expenditure in the state's total expenditures.[2]

Could they seriously have envisaged such serene prospects without smiling? Nobody in Russia would hope for five consecutive good crops. This alone can be taken as proof that Krzhizhanovsky did not mean it seriously. The same is true of such qualitative targets as a 110 percent rise in labor productivity, a 35 percent drop in industrial costs, and a 35 percent improvement of agricultural yields, not to mention the rosy assumptions about international relations, which, had they been true, would have undermined the very rationale for breakneck speed.

Other glaring inconsistencies were quite visible, too, such as stepping up investments steeply and simultaneously promising substantial raises in the standard of living of the masses in only five years. Bazarov, for example, pointed to another source of the plan's infeasibility—lack of cadres—and warned the Presidium of Gosplan, in February 1929: "If you plan simultaneously a series of undertakings on such a gigantic scale without knowing in advance the organizational forms, without having cadres and without knowing what they should be taught, then you get a chaos guaranteed in advance; difficulties will arise which will not only slow down the execution of the program of the *piatiletka,* which will take

2. G. F. Grin'ko, "Plan velikikh rabot," *Planovoe khoziaistvo,* 1929, no. 2, pp. 9–10.

seven if not ten years to achieve, but results even worse than that may occur: here such a blatantly irrational squandering of means could happen which would discredit the whole idea of industrialization."[3]

We know enough about the history of Soviet industrialization to realize what a brilliant prophecy this was;[4] but party planners also were subjected to pressures that made them write into the plan figures in which they did not believe. It was Strumilin who told us how his planners finally preferred to "stand for higher tempos rather than sit [in prison] for lower ones,"[5] and he himself was not very far from "sitting" when he was removed from Gosplan, together with Krzhizhanovsky, in 1930. It was obviously the political pressure from the Politburo that forced the planners to comply. They had to balance out their plan somehow, to make ends meet; and as the targets for output and investment soared, they had to be balanced, on paper, by raising the targets for productivity, costs, and yields, and by placing the resources in rubles "gotten" in this way directly into balance sheets.

There is an illuminating document showing how this was done. V. V. Kuibyshev, the leader of VSNK at that time, who is credited with introducing "rising curves" into his plans instead of the "dwindling curves" in which his experts believed, wrote the following comment in a letter to his wife, in fall 1928, when his maximalist version of the industrial plan was being prepared: "Here is what worried me yesterday and today: I am unable to tie up the balance, and as I cannot go for contracting the capital outlays—contracting the tempo—there will be no other way but to take upon myself an almost unmanageable task in the realm of lowering costs."[6]

Trying to balance the deeply imbalanced figures, Kuibyshev knew well—he heard enough about this from his experts—that he would not get his cost slashes (he eventually must have known that costs would climb instead). How did he expect to get resources for his rates and targets without those costs falling?

---

3. Quoted from Gosplan Archives in I. Gladkov, *Planovoe khoziaistvo,* 1935, no. 4, p. 136.

4. See the studies by Naum Jasny, *Soviet Industrialization, 1928–1952* (Chicago, 1961); Eugène Zaleski, *Planification de la croissance et fluctuations économiques en U.R.S.S.,* vol. 1: 1918–1932 (Paris, 1962); and Alexander Erlich, "Development Strategy and Planning: The Soviet Experience," in Max F. Millikan, ed., *National Economic Planning* (New York, 1967).

5. S. G. Strumilin, in *Planovoe khoziaistvo,* 1929, no. 1, p. 109.

6. G. V. Kujbysheva et al., *V. V. Kujbyshev: Biografia* (Moscow, 1966).

We don't know what he believed in matters of economics, but we know where he stood politically. He was Stalin's protégé and owed his Politburo post to him. Incidentally, although he, too, was a member of the Politburo, Kuibyshev could not freely propose plans that he believed feasible. Ordzhonikidze, probably an even more impetuous industrializer, and nearer to Stalin at that time, was there to tell him that he did not push hard enough. However upset Kuibyshev was by figures coming from above making nonsense of his laborious calculations, he was not ready to fight back vigorously enough. To do so would have meant, in fact, to lend support to Rykov, the political enemy of that period.[7] Instead, by that time, at least in public, Kuibyshev was developing themes about tempos that amounted to the end of the whole five-year plan.

Subsequent events attest to the lack of realism of the plan's figures. When, at the beginning of 1933, the government announced the fulfillment of the first five-year plan in four years and three months, even its own figures contradicted the claim. Industry, so ran the claim, reached 93.7 percent of the planned target—which would have been superb. But this figure was not only unreliable but also meaningless. The plan had other targets, too—for national income, transportation, building, investments, agriculture, costs, real wages, and consumption. And in all these essentials, and many others, the results were a big failure in terms of the plan. To mention only costs, for the trouble they caused to the conscientious Kuibyshev, they went up instead of falling by the planned 35 percent. Productivity of labor rose officially by 41 percent instead of 110 percent, real wages fell instead of the promised rise of 69 percent, agriculture for a time was reduced to a shambles, and the costs of the whole operation went up beyond any expectation. Although 22 billion rubles were to be invested in industry, transportation, and building, 41.6 billion were spent. Not unexpectedly, the money in circulation, which was supposed to grow by only 1.25 billion rubles, had swollen by 5.7 billion rubles in 1933.[8]

There is no ambiguity in this verdict on the results, even when only official figures are used. But there is a second aspect to this problem: in

7. For more on the trouble Ordzhonikidze kept creating for Kuibyshev see S. N. Ikonnikov, *Sozdanie i deiatel'nost' ob'edinennykh organov TsKK-RKI v 1923–1934 gg.* (Moscow, 1971), p. 344; and about more trouble, after Ordzhonikidze attacked VSNKh during the Sixteenth Congress, see Kujbyshev et al., *V. V. Kujbyshev,* pp. 299–300.

8. V. I. Kuz'min, *Istoricheskii opyt sovetskoj industrializatsii* (Moscow, 1969), pp. 71–72.

fact, the text of the five-year plan was shelved almost as soon as it was adopted. The control figures compiled for 1929–30 marked the defini- tive divorce from the perspective framework. By adopting such figures as 17 million tons of pig iron for 1933 (instead of the proposed 10 mil- lion), or the new target of 32 percent of industrial growth in 1930, by stepping up the previously anticipated figure of investments by addi- tional staggering amounts, to mention but a few of the new objectives, whatever coherence and consistency the old plan might have had was disrupted. The wholesale collectivization of the peasants that was decreed at the time of launching those control figures was followed by Molotov's frank declaration that, in this field, talking about five-year plans was nonsense.[9]

The planners were by now in a state of complete disarray. The five- year plan—the indispensable framework without which they did not know how to compile their yearly figures—was dead. This was frankly stated by one of the top planners in February 1930. There is talk, he said, about such figures as 17–20 million tons of pig iron, 120–150 million tons of coal (instead of 75 million), or 450,000 tractors (instead of 55,000) for the last year of the quinquennium. The planners had, of course, to accept the figures prescribed when preparing their blueprint for 1929–30, but—said the planners—"insofar as these targets were not always con- sistent among themselves, insofar as they were not put together in a uni- fied, national-economic program, we were facing extremely great diffi- culties in considering these directives of party and government during the preparation of control figures for the year 1929–30." But then new control figures had to be prepared for 1930–31. "What happens now to the *piatiletka*?" Something at least roughly resembling a five-year frame- work had to be quickly compiled, only internally, "for us," so as to have something to be guided by.[10] But a new plan would never be compiled, not only because two years were needed to prepare a *piatiletka,* but because the leadership did not believe in this anymore.

The main motive now became speed. The "tempos decide every- thing" slogan was more than just a slogan; it was policy. Plans were here to be overfulfilled, and targets (whatever they were) became not really

9. Talking about five-year plans in agriculture now is a "useless affair," said Molotova, *Bolshevik* (1922), p. 22.

10. V. A. Levin, *Planovoe khoziajstvo,* 1930, no. 2, p. 32.

targets but challenges. The overwhelming majority of planners did not believe in such an approach. They probably viewed the whole drumbeating planning with bewilderment. This was why the old Gosplan, "with all its old-fashioned planners," was swept away, as Molotov proudly asserted to the December 1929 Central Committee Plenum; and, he said, "we are now founding a new Gosplan,"[11] which would exclude Krzhizhanovsky, Strumilin, and other party men.

With the shelving of the first five-year plan, only yearly figures remained as valid blueprints for economic activities, and the even-thinner volumes presented later as *piatiletki* were no more than a facade, as Naum Jasny put it. In fact, as "Bacchanalian planning" took over with targets like 45 percent a year for industrial output, and since the five-year plan had been declared finished in four, it was a meaningless operation, indeed, to return at the end of the period, with a touch of modesty, to the deceased old text (prepared "by wreckers") and to claim a seemingly honorable underfulfillment. This procedure was devised in order to gloss over what the *piatiletka* years really looked like.

It is true that those years presented a sight which was extolled by many—a huge country transformed quite suddenly into an impressive building site. But it would be a distortion to leave things at that, since those were also years of a national catastrophe of major proportions—of a "severe disruption of economic life," to use the more careful wording of a Soviet author.[12] Agriculture was utterly disorganized, and huge rural areas plunged into a severe famine; there were inflation, black markets, and a drop in the nation's standard of living, unheard of in conditions of peace. The whole social fabric was shattered, and to keep the kettle from blowing up, the powers of dictatorship were enhanced to an extent that probably could match the extremes of the Civil War period. Mass coercion, a set of terroristic laws, persecution of whole categories of the population, fake trials, mass shootings, and a witch hunt swept the country. For the first time, still several years before the Great Purge, dozens of top government officials, party members themselves, were shot for alleged sabotage.

It was clear that things on the economic front were out of hand. To

---

11. *Bol'shevik,* 1931, no. 3, p. 24.

12. S. P. Pervushin, in V. G. Venzher et al., *Proizvodstvo, nakoplenie, potreblenie* (Moscow, 1965), p. 20.

save the situation, the device of "shock-construction-sites" was resorted to—a list of top-priority constructions to be taken care of, with all the rest left to their own devices, in an effort to clear the investment jam and to make the frozen resources move. But so much was invested that even more was needed to keep the pace, and toward the end of the quinquennium a dearth of investment means was added to the strains of a crisis-ridden economy.

Overinvestment in and overexpansion of the industrial construction front—these were the traits of industrialization conceived as a rush. Economists, managers, and party people were certainly unanimous about the diagnosis of the disease: because too many means were glutted in the *stroiki,* they failed to supply in time the indispensable returns to the economy. Haste in such matters, ironically, slowed down development. New enterprises cost much more than expected and emerged with painful slowness. The government, trying to embrace too much in almost all spheres of the economy at one stroke, was saddled with functions it was utterly unprepared to handle. It was not ready to cope with the task of running agriculture, with its numerous and inept *kolkhozy* and *sovkhozy,* and it had no way of replacing the private merchants and artisans it suddenly evicted or discouraged. "Commercial deserts," to quote a Soviet source, were the penalty for such policies. It was incapable of tackling competently the huge labor force now expanding by additional millions, well above anything anticipated. As disproportions caused emergencies, and bottlenecks endangered the whole structure, the government, presiding over this sort of chaos, resorted to levers it best knew how to apply. When the economic process threatened to get entirely out of control, and masses of peasants and workers roamed the country in search of better conditions, thereby wrecking productivity and raising costs, the "extraeconomic" factors came forcibly to the fore.

These "extraeconomic" factors have to be stressed; without them the Soviet industrialization drive cannot be understood. But they also explain the character of the political system that emerged in the process. The key factors here are, once more, those impossible targets and haste. They made any planning impossible, too. It was the unplanned character of the whole process that forced on the state ever more "planning," meaning simply the need to enlarge the scope of administrative controls, and the takeover of the whole of the national economy by state apparatus. The more bottlenecks and crisis areas that appeared, the greater the urge to close loopholes by putting the hand on more levers. In other words, this is the process through which a fully nationalized "command economy" emerged—in a short span of time—with internal mechanisms pushing to a very centralized pyramid-shaped power structure. Economic and other factors at work were inextricably enmeshed and contributed also to the shaping of the political system. Economic administrations, ministries, and supply agencies were not all that was needed. Strong incentives had to be discovered to make people fulfill their tasks, and such incentives were not easily improvised. A search for them continued; in the meantime a new stratification policy had to be enacted, and exhortation-cum-coercion had to make good what other stimuli failed to produce.

Party leaders contended that they were quite legitimately resorting to tools from an ideologically consecreated arsenal. It was always fashionable among party politicians to boast of their capacity to employ a blend of "persuasion and coercion" as a token of political wisdom. But in the reality of those years, even ideological exhortation and appeal to the spirit of self-sacrifice and patriotism tended to take on terroristic forms. In addition, the fewer results exhortation yielded, the more reliance was put on coercion, mass terror, and the swelling "punitive organs." It becomes clear by now that the abrupt suppression of the NEP and the concomitant severe curtailment of the market economy caused a great increase in the state's direct economic responsibility. The larger its scope, the larger the scope of "extraeconomic" tools the state used. The party was unable to find the correct mixture of "persuasion and coercion." The balance was certainly—and suddenly—disturbed. In a situation where forced labor and an economic empire of the secret police based on it were growing, where workers were disciplined by allowing administrations to deprive them of food rations or throw them out of factory dwellings, where *khozraschet* became a business of procurators and criminal prosecutions, the party itself could no longer remain the same political agency it had been and still claimed to be. In fact, it became totally transformed, together with the whole political system. We stress this fact, because the change occurred precisely during the few years of the so-called five-year plan. The new state system that emerged in Russia in those years became the most important product of the *piatiletka,* more important even than economic planning itself. It had entirely changed its leadership structure; it discarded a mixed economy and replaced it with a "command economy"; it imposed cultural uniformity on what previously had been and still was a plurality of cultures; it eliminated all political and ideological activity from the ruling party and changed it into a *sui generis* politico-administrative bureaucracy; it introduced coercion on a scale that made the term *police state* applicable. This is why it is essential to talk about the five-year plan not only in terms of rate of growth but in terms of political system-building as well.

We can now turn to the question "Why?" which Professor Holland Hunter asks after having shown the overly optimistic character of the plan's targets. He lists several factors that could account for the sudden drive to achieve the impossible. All are illuminating—and one can do no more than elaborate on his arguments. Scholars keep returning to the same question because the available records do not yet allow for definitive answers. We do not know enough, from internal sources, about the state of mind of the leaders, their arguments and considerations, held in private or among themselves in secret meetings.

Nevertheless, what is already known allows some advance in solving our riddle. One thing is clear: only part of the decisions and actions were "strategy" or decisions made with some degree of interrelation between moves and anticipated results. Much was also pure—sometimes bewildered—improvisation, in reaction to unexpected consequences of reasonable steps and sheer blunders. All this still awaits a further detailed history of the period. But a better insight can be gained if we replace our question with two, and ask first "Why did they accelerate?" and next "Why the supertempos?" This way we will better distinguish between two separate stages, the first beginning in 1926 and continuing through part of 1928, and the next extending from sometime in 1928 until the summer of 1929, when a new stage ended in those far-reaching decisions about which we are inquiring.

The decision to take more firmly to the road of industrialization resulted from progress accomplished in the NEP years. Agriculture and industry were nearing prewar capacities, and it was obvious to all factions in the party that the "restoration period" was ending and a new era had to begin. What the new policy should be was at the center of the intraparty debate (nonparty experts contributed to it substantially), and the heat of the debate grew as two big snags became apparent: one was the "goods famine" (the shortage of industrial goods); the second was the relatively weak marketability of the predominantly small peasant farms. Preobrazhensky was the man who quite precisely prophesied that this situation would soon lead to a crisis, which would be all the more acute the longer the industrial capacities remained inadequate to match the needs.[13] More investment was going into industry from 1926 on, and the new orientations in this and other crucial spheres were epitomized by the decisions of the Fifteenth Congress, which responded in fact—whatever the actual fate of this or other opposition in the intraparty struggle—to the demands of everybody. Decisions to launch a five-year plan, to engage in the serious work of creating *kolkhozes,* to do so with all the necessary precautions and brakes applied, and specifically in the framework of the NEP, expressed the existing wisdom of the main Politburo groups inside the party. Or so it looked.

But what took place soon after the congress—we refer to the grain crisis of 1927–28—triggered the chain of events that made the year 1928 a real turning point in Soviet history. During that year Stalin's faction gained full domination inside the party, whereas the crisis phenomena engendered by the acceleration spurred them to launch the all-out drive of 1929.

In order to understand better the events of 1928, three factors should be singled out. First, industry still benefited from unused capacities inherited from the old regime and kept rushing ahead by impressive percentage figures. Second, agriculture, too, was still moving forward, mainly in cattle raising and technical crops, although not in grain production; and food and money reserves in the hands of peasants improved during the last NEP years. But agriculture suffered from unfavorable terms of exchange with industry. Third, the party, then in the throes of an intraparty struggle with the Bukharin faction—partly in response to external factors, partly according to its internal dynamics—was undergoing important internal changes.

The grain crisis of winter and spring 1928 brought the leadership to a new crossroads. Inside the party, once more, all protagonists knew that a turning point of tremendous importance was nearing. Trotsky, in Alma-Ata, recommended an "offensive" against hostile class forces, especially

13. For Preobrazhensky's forecast of a nearing crisis similar to the one of autumn 1923, see *Bol'shevik,* 1927, no. 6, p. 61, written in March 1927. But he had been analyzing and anticipating this kind of difficulty in exchanges with the peasants since his "Economic Notes," *Pravda,* December 5, 1925.

in the countryside, and he was not displeased by the left turn Stalin was just taking in the direction of precisely some sort of offensive. Trotsky did not yet see what this turn might lead to, but Bukharin already realized that Stalin's faction was considering plans of quite a new dimension. Trotsky, in fact, came to the same conclusion very soon and declared that he had in mind nothing that ruthless.[14] The Bukharinites by then had changed not a few of their ideas on industrialization, accumulation methods, and so forth. A serious effort in the field of investment in industry, with the appropriate tightening of the screws, was accepted by them. But their effort concentrated on avoiding a strategy of "military-feudal exploitation of the peasantry" and industrial tempos of "madmen" that would lead to a policy exclusively based on "extraordinary measures"—namely, mass coercion. These are some of the accusations they launched against the majority group.

While Stalin was fighting these "agents of kulaks," his ideas emerged and crystallized during this same crucial year, including all the elements that would soon merge into a full-fledged new strategy. He adopted the "tribute" argument (tribute to be exacted from peasants), launched his famous "catch up and overtake" slogan as a leitmotiv for industrialization policies, and announced another of his "firsts" of that year, saying that the class struggle would grow fiercer as socialism was winning. To illustrate his point, he initiated (or let be initiated) the first of the big sabotage trials, against the Shakhty engineers, which was to become the trademark of Stalinist policies. Two other themes appeared at the same time: the appeal to launch an offensive against all the "capitalist classes," and a new reliance on *kolkhozy* and *sovkhozy* as basic prescriptions for solving the agricultural tangle—though there was yet no sign that the medicine was to be applied all at once. These points, and a few more that we will soon mention, were the key pieces of Stalin's new program. It was so different from what they understood to have been the spirit of the Fifteenth Congress that the Bukharinites could rightly conclude that the leading group was going to shed the NEP framework.

This is a crucial point. As long as Stalin's group did not make up their

---

14. Trotsky recommended "an offensive" in "What Now?" (July 12, 1928), *Third International after Lenin* (New York, 1957); but he advised his followers in Agusut 1928 that he did not mean at all the same thing that Stalin was doing. This is discussed in Isaac Deutscher, *The Prophet Unarmed* (London and New York, 1959), p. 447.

minds about the fate of the NEP, the new big drive was not ready. But it was maturing, as a combination of successes and failures of those days sharpened the situation and the issues in debate. Force applied to extract grain in 1928 gave a measure of success, but boded ill for the results of the next agricultural and procurement campaign; and rationing was going to be introduced very soon to meet the food-supply stringencies. "Extra-ordinary measures" in grain procurement had the capacity to help prophecies come true about the limitations inherent in the family-run agriculture, with its natural antipathy to low grain prices and high industrial ones. Temporary coercive measures would soon become per-manent, and Stalin did say in the Central Committee that he was ready for such a course. But this was incompatible with the NEP and, in any case, seemed more appropriate for a total change of rural structures than the continuing, year-after-year drudgery of extracting grain quotas from twenty-five million homesteads.

Another new argument appeared to back up the need for a deep over-haul of the rural world: the country "cannot march on two different legs," a socialist industry and a nonsocialist agriculture. This formula meant a divorce from Lenin's "better less but better." Toward the sum-mer of 1929 this idea was to become a firm conviction and a guide for decisive action. And it harmonized with another one dealing with the debate on industrial growth. The "productivity first" approach—mean-ing industrial growth first, socialist measures in the countryside next (an idea that was widely shared in the party and among "bourgeois special-ists")—was now declared a "kulak" idea. A different course, Bazarov warned—and Rykov fully agreed—would mean mass coercion and eco-nomic disaster. "Revolutionary force" was nothing new for any Bolshe-vik, but it had to serve the purpose of advancing socialism; and this last formula introduced restraints in the thinking of some of them.

But the leaders who now took full control of the party and state dif-fered from other leaders on precisely these points. This majority of lead-ers were committed to state action as their main tool, on military lines, and were therefore ready to use as much force as necessary, ignoring checks and restraining devices. The responsibility was now fully in the hands of Stalin and the people he was ready to work with, and the accu-mulating difficulties convinced them of the uselessness of the NEP framework. The elimination of the last opposition in the name of "monolithism"—itself not exactly a traditional party term—removed the last obstacle. Readiness to use massive force could be justified, for the Stalinists, too, only in terms of socialist transformations.

This group of tough ex–Civil War leaders, mainly action-oriented bosses, who probably were quite impatient with theories and scruples, now looked at the reports on results of the economic year 1928–29, which piled up on their desks in the summer of 1929, and could easily see that industrial growth was impressive but productivity of labor was lagging and costs were going up, and that agriculture was not going to deliver its goods if the procurement went on by force and without economic incentives. It was not difficult to conclude that if very decisive changes in the countryside did not take place during the winter and spring of 1930, the industrial growth of the country would stop by 1931.

Kolkhozes and *sovkhozes* looked to them now very much like the structures that obtained in industry, with the additional advantage of promising a tamed peasantry and a more productive agriculture. Such seems to have been the reasoning. There was enough power to eliminate, brutally if necessary, any other way of viewing things. In the summer of 1929 the rightists were silenced for all practical purposes, and the leadership was now ready to attack simultaneously both weak links in the economic and social setting: the insufficient industrial basis and the insufficiently productive and socially unreliable agriculture. A massive influx of investments into the first and a massive collectivization of the second were the two bold decisions. In these conditions not only the NEP had to go but also the original five-year plan, which was based—it is worth stressing—on the premise of the continuing existence of private sectors.

It may be added that the fight against Bukharin's group certainly pushed the majority to formulate aims and methods leaning to the extreme opposite pole. This is the normal "logic" of a fierce factional fight. But the genuine belief that the new strategy actually would work if decisively and boldly applied and a sort of utopian mood quite understandable in such circumstances were also factors necessary to understanding the new strategy. Metal, machinery, fuel, *kolkhozes* and *sovkhozes*—this seemed a clear, relatively simple program based on the "leading links" approach. These things had the power to haul the whole chain (an instance of metaphoric thinking tending to replace some harder reasoning), and it was worth launching an all-out offensive if it held the promise of quick benefits for a higher, more productive social system: socialism.

*

The turmoil and results of the first five-year plan were on everybody's mind during 1933 and 1934, when a kind of lull was declared and a tenuous fight went on, mainly behind the scenes, for the strategies to be adopted next. All the protagonists of the predrive debate were still alive (though some were in prison), and they were free to draw their conclusions, at least for themselves if not openly. Surveying the events of 1928–33, the critics felt that their warnings had been vindicated and that what they had feared had come about. To be sure, those who had opposed any acceleration of industrial growth—there were some—would have had to admit that an impressive industrial development had taken place, and that this was not only possible but highly desirable. By now Hitler was in power in Germany, and national defense needs appeared quite clearly and dramatically to everyone.

But what about the "supertempos" attempted from the end of 1929 on? Bukharin clamored in 1928 against the "madmen" who suddenly wanted to double the already speedy rate of growth. So did many economists. And the outcome, for everyone to see, attested to the unsoundness—in fact, collapse—of the tempo-pathology and the thoughtless speed. The official figures tell us that industrial output grew in 1928–29 by 20 percent, somewhat below the planned mark, and this result was taken as justification to aim for 32 percent the next year—but only 22 percent could be attained. For 1931 the percentage was 20 instead of the incredible 45, and for 1932 it was 15 instead of 36 percent. In 1933, which was to be the last year of the original five-year plan, the percentage was 5 (compared with the modest 16.5 percent of the control figures), though according to Jasny there was no growth at all.[15] The official figures are not sufficiently reliable. They certainly fail, for instance, to account for the deterioration in the quality of the products, which at times reached alarming proportions. But it is even more important to note that industry was not all there was in the plan. If figures for transportation and power plants were added, and when agriculture is considered with its drop of production and loss of cattle, the overall results certainly did not warrant wild jubilation—not to mention the enormous waste, which

---

15. The figures are from *Narodnoe khoziajstvo SSSR v 1970 g.* (Moscow, 1971), p. 131; E. P. Gorbunov, *Sotsialisticheskaia industrializatsiia SSSR i ee burzhuaznye kritiki* (Moscow, 1962), p. 37; and S. P. Pervushin, in Venzher, *Proizvodstvo, nakoplenie, potreblenie,* p. 20. For Jasny, see note 4.

Bazarov predicted, and the grave problem of the cost of the whole operation. Bukharin, Rykov, and Tomsky, who pressed for the more modest "minimum" version, could claim that their approach was fully vindicated by events.

The debate on "dwindling curves" could also be said to have been settled by events in favor of the much-maligned planners, especially when longer-term results are considered. All of them, up to August 1928, kept turning out plans with dwindling curves of investment and growth. Soon only the opposite view was allowed to exist, and it reached its apogee with Kuibyshev's announcement before the Sixteenth Party Congress that the target was "doubling from year to year the investments in capital construction, and reaching 30 percent of output growth every year."[16] Most of the experts involved sensed correctly the limits of such growth, whatever the pressures and efforts deployed, and the results of just the first five years amply vindicated them. The underlying economic realities and limitations find an ever-clearer expression in today's official figures for the three five-year plans: 19.2 percent for the first, 17.1 percent for the second, 13.2 percent for the three and a half years of the third. This was a dwindling curve indeed. The opponents were right, and they had to be punished.

The average for the years 1930–40 is worth retaining. It was officially 16.5 percent, certainly an impressive figure (and not much less impressive even if smaller assessments by Western economists are preferred).[17] But a question comes to mind: If the government had listened to its experts and minority leaders and had agreed to aim at some 20–22 percent at the beginning, letting the figure drop over the years so that the average would oscillate around 16 percent (these certainly were figures

---

16. Quoted from *Saratovskaia partijnaia organizatsiia v period nastupleniia sotsializma po vsemu frontu* (Saratov, 1961), p. 155. Bukharin's critique against "madmen" who dreamed of doubling the tempos is quoted by Bogushevsky in *God vosemnadsatyi: Almanakh vos'moi* (1935), p. 473.

It may be worth quoting Rykov's opinion on tempos and investment, which he put forward to the November 1928 plenum of the Central Committee: "One should not think that there is some law for the whole transition period according to which tempos must contantly grow, or at least be kept steady from year to year." The demand to increase industrial investments every year is no more than "naked arithmetic" (*golaia aritmetika*), which is economically unfounded; it is quite plausible "to lower the curve of investments," and in any case, "it is by no means permissible to make a fetish out of tempos" (Quoted from Party Archives—disapprovingly, of course—by F. M. Vaganov, *Pravyjuklon v VKP [b] i ego razgrom [1928–1930]* [Moscow, 1970], pp. 97–98).

17. These figures are from Gorbunov, *Sotsialisticheskaia industrializatsiia*, p. 37.

acceptable to many of the discussants), what would the debate have been like in those years? We remember that the Politburo minority called for fixing more balanced targets—instead of doubling them—against a majority in the leadership who wanted precisely to double the efforts and were ready to silence any other view.

The rights and wrongs in the respective positions on *kolkhozes* are more difficult to assess, because hindsight offers only half of the answer. The catastrophic results of forced collectivization can be taken as vindicating the views of those who opposed such a course. After a period of failing output, agriculture began to recover somewhat, but not enough to convince anyone that the shattering experience was worthwhile. Before the war, nothing more than the level of the NEP period was reached for gross agricultural output, and the animal foodstuffs still did not match even the 1916 level. But some 20 million more people had to be fed compared to 1928, and even more compared to 1916.

Such considerations alone did not tell the whole story. The stagnating agriculture, though it kept providing labor for industry, was nevertheless weighing heavily on the economic development of the country. One has only to think about the loss in terms of foregone growth of national income through the failure of agriculture to contribute an adequate part to such growth; or to consider the resources that had to be diverted from industrial uses and poured, in an emergency, into agriculture to replace the slaughtered horses; or else the damage to productivity of labor because of queues, weakened labor discipline, and an immense labor turnover— all caused to a great degree by food and goods shortages. The critics and skeptics had therefore enough ammunition with which to charge. But the supposition that privately run agriculture, with the support of a sector of cooperatives and some *sovkhozes*, would have allowed for the same 16 percent of growth is more difficult to prove, simply because such agriculture was not allowed to exist. The decisive proof that only events can offer is missing, and the answers can only be hypothetical.

Professor Hunter, reflecting on the whole economic performance, believes that alternative paths existed and that the same, if not better, results could have been achieved "with far less turbulence, waste, destruction, and sacrifice." But he does not specifically speak about agriculture, and a few words can be added to sustain his opinion in that sector, too.

It is obvious that the countryside would have had much more food in its barns if the cattle had survived. The problem is whether it would have been willing to offer that food for sale. The government had a problem here, but the same approach of "better less..." was equally preferable. The government still would have needed to search for forms of larger and more-productive units—besides helping the family-farmers to improve their methods—and here less haste and somewhat more time for trial and error could have yielded good results. More diversified forms of cooperative undertakings, including *kolkhozes, sovkhozes,* tractor stations, both state-operated and cooperative (and especially many fewer at a time of each of them), would certainly have secured a greater measure of success to these forms. It would have been easier to supply them with good managers, capital, and technicians. It would have been a much more manageable task for these people—peasants and organizers from the cities—to operate smaller units and to take their time learning the job. As a result, good grain would soon have come from them to help out the government.

One could also envisage a larger-scale operation of collectivization— but never of a wholesale character—in which only the extensive grain production was collectivized and mechanized, leaving the cattle in the hands of the families. There were enough chances for a program of this more limited character to succeed and prove beneficial to both branches—grain and stock—and therefore convince the peasants. In such a case the experience could snowball, and no amount of "kulak agitation" would stop the movement.

On the other hand, regarding the period of search for new forms, the dangers of a full "supply strike" are often exaggerated. It is not proven that peasants in Russia really could withdraw into a "natural economy" for a long period. Nothing diminished the power of government to tax in order to generate a need for cash, and nothing diminished the desire of peasants to acquire industrial goods. The government had only to moderate its industrializing zeal and to stick, at least, to its initial plans in order to find more resources for the countryside. It also had to be more realistic about what agriculture had to do and could do. It was an aberration to claim that agriculture had to develop at the same pace as industry. If the leaders had sought some modest growth of 3 percent per year, which would have made all things manageable—with or without any rationing—the drive to collectivize en masse, and to compromise thereby both output and the very idea of collectivization, would have been less urgent. In an emergency, for a few years if necessary, who could doubt the capacity of the

Soviet government to reimpose a tax-in-kind on the richer producer?
Didn't it prove powerful enough to do much more and much worse?

This leads us to another theme in the debate that loomed large in the
background—namely, the very essence of the system that would result
from these or other policies. All participants realized either dimly or
quite clearly the link between industrialization—in town and countryside—and the institutional setting to emerge in this process. Bukharin
was especially alert to this problem, and this alertness was epitomized in
his fight against the building of socialism through "extraordinary measures," meaning mass terror. He insistently opposed the idea of a "third
revolution" in regard to the peasantry, and echoed the same theme that
appears in the last of Lenin's writings. His idea that peasants were not a
"capitalist class" implied that he denied the justification of an onslaught
against the peasants through the ideological consecration of an "anticapitalist" (hence "socialist") revolution. This is how the "big drive" was presented, claiming the great honor of being more important than the October Revolution. In this regard, the test of historical experience is clear.
Stalin's antipeasant drive was an attack against the popular masses. It
required coercion on such a large scale that the whole state had to be
transformed into a huge, oppressive machine.

The first *piatiletka* period had, as is obvious, a tremendous impact on the
fate of Russia. Especially interesting is the interrelation between the
methods of industrializing and the character of the political system. It is
amusing to read Stalin's words, in May 1928, deriding those who wanted
to plan "everything and anything" (*vse i vsia*) before conditions were
right. But soon his government was doing precisely that: engaging in a
rapidly growing amount of planning—or, rather, as we prefer to say,
administering. During the first quinquennium all the essentials of the
system for running the economy were ready; and the methods that
evolved could only be considered what Soviet economists today call
"administrative methods," which persisted at least until the early 1950s.
During this period the system, as Czeslaw Bobrowski, the Polish economist, put it, learned better the art of controlling the masses than the art of
managing efficiently its resources,[18] including human resources. It was
the "overextension" and "overambitiousness" of the initial period that

18. Czeslaw Bobrowski, *U źródel planowania socjalistycznego: Analiza doświadceń radziec-
kich* (Warsaw, 1967), p. 157.

accounted, to a large degree, for the fact that the economy was "administered" but not really "planned."

Too much power, unlimited and unchecked, in the hands of the state leadership is the other side of the coin. It permitted the very existence—and persistence—of the pattern. The state could nationalize as much as it wanted and remove private and cooperative elements at will. It could decide to put to the task as many officials as it felt it needed, and to allocate resources and impose its will on economic agents—all state employees. By so doing, it engaged itself in an enormous task of running, directly and in detail, the whole economy, including many spheres it had not previously taken over. The economy became the central effort, and methods applied there spilled over into all other walks of life, since it was the same central apparatus and the same leadership dealing with economy and culture alike. The state, and this leadership, had by now so much to control that it had to adapt itself to this task and build an appropriate machinery, in which "repressive organs" loomed very large. Such a setting became a pattern, and soon any attempt to weaken such controls or the scope of centralized power became *lèse-majesté*.

Such a course of hardening the practices of the initial drive into the regular functions of a leviathan state was mightily helped by the absence of any countervailing forces, the last vestiges of which disappeared with the last opposition. In this situation no noticeable influence of planners and economists could be tolerated. The existence of a long-term economic plan, with its internal consistency, coordination of ends and means, and balanced structure, could not be acceptable to a despotic government; it would have become a very serious check on the leadership. It is not astonishing that the science of economics went into a quarter-century period of decay, for it was not needed under these conditions.

The first plan had thus produced a kind of self-perpetuating mechanism in which uncoordinated and quite arbitrary economic targets served to enlarge the scope of "planning." The larger the scope of such state intervention, the greater the power of the state. When in the late 1950s and early 1960s, in a considerably changed climate, economists were asked to come forth and propose remedies for the troubles of the economy, they discovered the whole range of amazing dysfunctions and imbalances—including the capacity of the government not only to build but also to wreck and squander—with which the first *piatiletka* had saddled the national economy.

CHAPTER 6:

ON SOVIET INDUSTRIALIZATION

C HANGE IS DEMONIC," DAVID LANDES MAINTAINED IN THE
epigraph to his book on industrialization[1]—and during the years
we are studying, change was certainly more demonic than at most
other times.[2] The 1930s were a brief period, but a period crammed with
shifting, intermingling social processes that moved in a chaotic and intense
historical development. These processes produced, simultaneously, the
most advanced and most archaic features, which permeated and actually
defined the whole period.[3] On the face of it, the period looked as if it had
been neatly packaged into five-year installments, planned and executed by
a strong, forward-looking state and led by a towering leader. As historical
research advanced, the tidiness of this picture began to crack, revealing
contradictions and pathologies. What was transitional in this system, and
what was bequeathed to its heirs, also began to emerge.

One of the key features of the whole industrialization process was the
role of the state and of the will of top Soviet leaders in the country's
developmental strategy (although there was also plenty of spontaneity—
the obverse side of the coin—which I will deal with later). About 8,000
huge and presumably modern enterprises were built during the twelve
"planned" years (1928–41) under state-imposed tempos and the more or
less unlimited priority accorded to heavy industry. The special circumstances of the period added stringency and intensity to the process, especially the dwindling performance of agriculture and the menace of a war

---

1. David S. Landes, *The Unbound Prometheus* (London, 1969), p. 7.

2. This paper was written during a leave that was supported by a grant from the National
Endowment for the Humanities.

3. This is really the idea Trotsky expressed in his *History of the Russian Revolution,* ch. 1,
entitled "The Peculiarities of Russia's Historical Development," which he clearly developed under the influence of other historians and thinkers. Interestingly, Trotsky did not
apply this idea to Stalin's time, probably because he believed a "workers' state" still persisted under Stalin.

looming on the horizon. In particular, the fear of having to fight on two fronts—west and east (Japan)—must have played an important role in the "pushing" and pressurizing style that was adopted by the leaders on the economic "front." There were other issues as well, as we will see.

First, however, it is worth a brief flashback to the late 1920s and the period that triggered the "big drive" from 1928 on. The late 1920s were a watershed. Modern anti-Stalinists in the Soviet Union exaggerate the economic achievements of the New Economic Policy (NEP). They fail to see that much of what the NEP accomplished consisted in "restoring" unused or poorly used plants to full production. Restoration could be presented as a success—it certainly was one—but it had its pitfalls. The marking point for the restoration effort was the level of 1913, and attempting to reach this point in Russia's past involved particular difficulties. First, industrial equipment, already old, was aging further at a dangerous pace. Second, despite the successes of restoration, the shadows of backwardness were also lengthening.

"Backwardness" is an idea that comes "from abroad." The level of the most developed countries determines who is backward and to what degree. In the late 1920s, the industrially advanced countries were moving ahead in science, technology, and the rationalization of management; they crested, actually, just before the big crash of the 1930s; and from this point of view, Soviet Russia was actually crawling backward. In practical terms, this meant that Russia needed more capital to acquire the most advanced technology, not as a whim but as an economic necessity. The same was true for technical and administrative cadres.

Another difficult problem was the so-called goods famine. Industry was not supplying enough goods at sufficiently cheap prices for the population, most notably for the agricultural majority, including what peasants needed to improve their productivity.

On the government's agenda there thus emerged the vital problem of formulating a strategy for industrialization. The need was to improve and accelerate industrial production and to innovate—and it had to be done on some significant scale, not simply "incrementally." It was not just a matter of whether to do it but also of where to find the necessary means. By the same token, an industrialization strategy had to devise social policies, attend to relations with the peasants, and reflect on the role and methods of planning; in actuality, it affected the shape of the regime itself.

If change is demonic, then speedy economic and industrial change is particularly so, as events in Russia would prove. Those who thought that all that was needed was to go slowly, "on the peasant cart," "on the rails of the NEP"—as Bukharin believed around 1925 (but understood better a few years later)—were wrong. The NEP, in practice, showed signs of not coping, perhaps even in the throes of a crisis. Rethinking its ways was urgent. Whatever the uses to which the general NEP framework could still be put, the NEP economy itself was too weak a base to assure the safe survival of the Soviet state. Its "restoration," important per se, consisted basically in "catching up" with the prerevolutionary past. This was a historical handicap, emphasized, as we have said, by the continuing advances of the West.

Consequently, 1928 was a real, not a contrived, crossroads, which Stalin seized upon and interpreted in his own way. Does this mean that the policies Stalin and his supporters adopted were justified and that the NEP should have been discarded? Was Stalin's interpretation and response at this moment the only one possible, or was it even correct at all? Was everything Preobrazhensky said during "the industrialization debate" necessarily wrong? Or was the NEP itself, so to speak, "guilty" of Russia's difficulties?

To point to the difficulties or even the crisis of the NEP is not, in itself, to prejudge the problem of its viability; nor do we imply that there was only one way of dealing with the difficulties. Any student of the Stalinist five-year plans knows that the story of Stalin's industrial and agricultural policies offers plenty of arguments to its critics. At least it requires that very serious consideration be accorded to all and any of the protagonists in the debate, before and during the plans. This is so because the history of industrialization in the 1930s is not just a story of what was done but also a long list of things that should not have been done, or planned. In fact, when studying the economic history of the period, it makes no sense at all to use the plan sequences as markers for periodization. The first five-year plan, which was supposedly fulfilled in four years, landed the country in such chaos that it took at least two years to straighten things out. One of the causes was the constant augmenting of different plan targets by the center. This deprived the plan itself of whatever coherence it might have had and nipped its very essence in the bud. The second plan was certainly a fictitious product, because it was launched two years after it was supposed to have begun. A look at the printed volumes of those plans, notably the third, in comparison with the impressive (on paper) first plan, tells the story. So it is time to put to rest the myth that the economy during the plans was planned. It was at best administered, but this begins to touch on questions that belong to an altogether different book.

The problems at the end of the 1920s were very serious indeed, and good leadership would have responded to the complexity of the situation with an appropriately formulated, thoughtful strategy. What the country got instead was industrialization, not as an economic activity or even an administrative-economic one but as an "onslaught," a civil war cavalry charge, a quasi-military operation, in which military terms themselves became the language of the day, used profusely and with good reason. Why did it get this strategy, rather than a different one?

Before we address this question, we should briefly account for the fact that Stalinist policies in the 1930s and later enjoyed considerable support in the party and the population at large. The degree of this support and its social map varied at different times, but there was enough support to ensure the whole policy a high degree of success. The sources of support for the policies can be sketched out as follows.

First, one should mention the tactical weakness of the opponents of the line adopted by Stalin. This in itself is related to the character and development of the party at the time the fateful decisions were being taken. Its centralized and "depoliticized" features were reinforced in the battles against the oppositions, and this process occurred against the background of a massive influx into the party of ordinary Russians (and other sociological trends to be explained briefly) who, almost by definition, could not be a factor in these debates. These people mostly just followed the *apparat*. This is one of the facets of "depoliticization"—the exclusion, in fact, of party members from involvement in politics.

The narrowness of the ruling apex, the other face of the same process, is crucial; it allowed a small number of people to define the historical situation and the strategy to adopt—and it was this small number that decided that the NEP should be discarded. More precisely, this narrowness of the apex in a depoliticized party allowed for very crucial decisions to be taken by only a part of the leading group, its majority (in a system where even a strong minority did not have any statutory way of preserving at least the possibility of regaining power once the policy in question failed).

Obviously, chance also had a role to play in these events (the skill of a leader, accidental elements in the making of the majority, and, notably, simply the lack of intelligence or stamina in one or two people at the top). But whatever the explanation, a line of action emerged with incalculable consequences. (The same combination of trend and chance occurred in the transformation of the obvious first fiddle into a personal tyrant— which was just a few years ahead, in conditions that were also part of those "incalculable consequences.")

Our inquiry into the "sources of success" must now consider the large social restructuring that took place—prominent among them the massive promotion of millions of people into new, often socially more prestigious jobs. In view of the low social status of most of the population, this was rather easily done. The process was already under way during the big recruitments into the party during the 1920s, notably, during the "Lenin enrollment," as well as in later recruitment campaigns. In the 1930s, the policy of advancement acquired a much broader dimension. The phenomenon of the so-called *praktiki* was the epitome of the process. We must pay attention to the feat of massive schooling that industrialization entailed. But schooling could not supply the necessary cadres quickly enough. The answer was found by promoting people from lowly backgrounds into positions of importance—technical, administrative, and political—in most cases without the proper education and professional training. Such cadres constituted the majority in political, administrative, and even engineering jobs. One would expect on the part of the cadres "gratitude" toward the regime, a feeling of insecurity on the job, and a dependence on patronage.

A further impetus to success was provided by the powerful appeal of the "backwardness" thesis and by the need to overcome "backwardness" in a single leap. Stalin's "manifesto" about Russia being perennially beaten by foreigners and now having to catch up in ten years to what others had taken a century to achieve became the official ethos of the building effort. Identification of this policy and this leadership with the greatest of national and patriotic tasks, and with the only strategy available, dazzling by its daring and range and without precedent in Russian and world history—all of this struck a chord in many hearts. This has to be remembered and understood.

Here one can see some of the sources for the acceptance of Stalin's leadership by the cadres, and probably by many, if not most, of the people. Even his resoluteness and ruthlessness in pursuing these aims and their supposed enemies made a big impression, providing the appropriate psychological underpinnings for "the cult" and much of what went with it. But this was also notably so because the "big drive" itself was capable of going a long way toward actually industrializing the country and, by the same token, strengthening its defense.

But locating these supports for the policies of industrialization is not in itself an assessment of what it was and, especially, what it produced. What it produced was *a system*—and this is what counts most for our purpose. The achievements of the early state were of enormous importance, but it was equally important that this sytem, which developed early on, contained within itself the mechanisms of its own exhaustion or self-destruction.

Once applied, the industrialization and other political strategies of those years caused a massive and multifarious restructuring. The system now had to live with and endure its results, which were many and quite complex. The economic sphere lashed back at the political system by "economizing" it, notably, by transforming the party into an economic-administrative agency. In return, the party "exported" its ways of running the economy to all other spheres of its activities.

The social sphere, stirred up by enormous changes and the ensuing social flux, entered into a state of permanent tension and crisis, which the state tried to control and master, most often by hardening its repressive methods and urges. The effects of the forceful collectivization of the peasants added enormous complications, throwing millions of peasants into the cities but supplying quite insufficient amounts of food. The famine of 1932–33 that took millions of lives has to be attributed to the ensemble of policies rather than to vagaries of nature.

As the big drive unfolded, planning and administration became oriented toward quantitative targets and measures of performance. Such an orientation underscores the extensive character of the policies and of the whole endeavor, with its insistence on tons, units, and percentages imposed from above on economic actors, thereby reverting, as it were, to an old historical tradition. Because the ruling agency was the same, a similar tendency prevailed in many other spheres of life.

The period cannot be understood without considering the cost of eliminating the NEP. Markets and market categories, considered to be breeders par excellence of capitalism, became of residual economic importance.

On the other hand, the scope of economic nationalization by state agencies surpassed by far the statization that occurred during the Civil War. As prices, profits, and costs lost their guiding function, the economy (except for its illicit sectors) no longer worked for profits, but neither did it work for consumers. It worked "for the plan." And this meant, again, that the whole setting built in the primacy of the political-administrative institutions and principles over the economy and economic ones.

It also promoted a partially illusory independence of those institutions (and of the officials who populated them) from economic realities. The bureaucratic grid and methods that grew immensely during those years managed to arrogate for themselves, for a time, a set of shelters guaranteed by the political will—but no shelter from the political will itself, again, just for a certain period.

A very steep concentration of power at the top—already considerable at the end of the NEP—was also built into the "planning" of those years. A bureaucracy that is allowed to operate independently of economic criteria and results, and that lacks a concept of cost, looks for criteria and reference points that are, in its view, natural and manageable, that is, quantitative targets. Unfortunately, the complexity of real processes, and notably the behavior of economic actors and agents, highly skilled in finding a host of evasive subterfuges, made such targets ineffective. Thus, instead of saving resources, the factories hoarded them; instead of using labor sparingly and training it well, they overemployed; instead of working well, they tried to look good.

The list of malfunctions is long and well known. They were countered by more targets and even more controllers to watch over their fulfillment. A quantity-oriented management, with its multiple-target planning, requires a bureaucracy oriented toward control and a growing army of officials. Here was an additional stimulus toward the centralization of power in circumstances that already showed increasing signs of suffering from "overcentralization."

Grounded in dysfuntions, the command system was a dysfunctional factor itself. The history of the five-year plans was one of the deep-seated arhythmia, of "storming" at the end of each quarter, of spasmodic campaigning, of constant jolting of individuals and masses of people, of cascades of emergencies dealt with by "shock methods." No wonder that the system tended to be characterized as "mobilizational" by some, as a "command economy" by others. But obviously it was also a system plagued by perpetual imbalanaces. Bottlenecks were treated by shock methods, and shock methods created imbalances: production was surging ahead, but transportation was lagging; workers were massed on a building site, but there was no housing for them and not enough engineers; heavy industry was promoted, but agriculture was in terrible shape; labor productivity was demanded, but not enough food, spare parts, or material ever arrived on time, causing endless production stoppages (*prostoi*).

It conforms to the logic of the situation that mastering such a whirlwind pushed the controlling needs and appetites of the center to new heights. And the personal despot who emerged in those years was the incarnation of supercentralization—one could not go farther than that on this road.

Accompanying this situation was a sense of omnipotence that was real in many ways, even if illusory in many others: a power over the fate of many people, but actual powerlessness in regard to the process in general.

Again, the unplanned character of Soviet industrialization has to be emphasized to make the previous remarks more explicit.[4] Actually, economic activity conducted as a set of pressurized waves of investment for growth and at an imposed pace could not be planned. Hence, despite so many controls and controlling agencies, the mastery of the process itself eluded the state. The economic process as a whole was not obeying the commands, although the planners were drowning in endless details. The system was losing its sense of direction, and the much-vaunted tempos, the heart of the strategy, had to be manipulated by the statisticians to look better than they actually were.

No wonder that this latest version of the age-old tradition of "extensive" methods was showing its limits. It suffered from a penchant to destroy (or a failure to create) incentives and mechanisms indispensable for qualitative improvements and technological change.

The deep bureaucratization of the economy, coupled with the special features of the Soviet polity, produced a mix of contradictory driving forces deriving from bureaucratic self-interest, on one hand, and arbitrary politi-

---

4. I argued this in my contribution to the debate on the feasibility of the first five-year plan, initiated by a pioneering piece by Holland Hunter, with comments by Robert Campbell, Stephen F. Cohen, and myself.

cal will, on the other. As whole branches of industry were built, some entirely new to the country, one certainly could speak of a new industrial power emerging in Europe—a fact that cannot be taken away from those years. But this new power was endowed with disquieting features. We have alluded to a built-in tendency to produce damaging imbalances that, if left unchecked, were an economic time bomb for the longer run. Initial successes therefore had their Achilles heel: their cost—the cost, that is, of not heeding cost, of not being able, actually, to heed it.

This peculiarly "uneconomical" quality was an important factor that fed growth during the "big drive," but later, not unexpectedly, it turned into a phenomenon of waste. And here again, costs could not be calculated. The system came to be hooked on waste—it could not work without it, and it built up huge constituencies that thrived on it. Much of what was done was actually unneeded! One day the absurdity simply became overwhelming.

All of this followed from the basic premises of the initial action. In the absence of market mechanisms that could supply feedback to correct problems, the emerging system produced elaborate ways to hide them. On the face of it, the ubiquitous party, the trade unions, the secret police, the procuracy—this is not the whole list—should have "seen" the problems, should have signaled and mended malfunctions. Instead, the proliferation of such agencies, mostly irrelevant to economic activity, was itself part of the problem.

The waste that was exposed in Gorbachev's USSR with such vehemence and bewilderment was also embedded in the mode of operation introduced in the 1930s. The big building sites (*strojki*) of industrial giants were the pride of those years and the heartbeat of the big drive, but they were also an illustration of the waste that had come to stay. These sites were the biggest recipients of the investment splurge of the plan era—*splurge,* because too many of them were initiated simultaneously, without enough experience, cadres, or builders, and all ended up taking much more time to build than planned, cost much more, and went through extremely painful startup periods. Construction began before the design work was ready; machines arrived from abroad but often rusted in the snow because the factory was not ready to house them or nobody knew how to install or operate them. Such *stroiki* thus became great consumers of capital, tying up for many years badly needed resources and forcing still further efforts and more investment—all to keep the economy moving. Waste was written all over these methods and, curiously but symptomatically, it remained a permanent part of the system in the form of a large *front* of new *stroiki*, seemingly never finished and increasingly obsolete, morally or otherwise, well before they could produce anything.

Pressure for quantity as the main criterion of controllable success led toward the overextension of resources, an overextension that could only be overcome by pouring still more investment, which had an ever more difficult task of overcoming the accumulating mechanisms of slowdown. The Hungarian economist Janos Kornai, who studied the already mature result of the 1930s in the 1970s, defined the system as basically driven by an orientation on investment, but it was still a mechanism plagued by permanent and widespread shortages.[5]

Kornai stated correctly that such a system can and does function, but he did not ask how long it could last. The resources of a huge and rich country could allow some time to pass, and another internal mechanism—the illegitimate but widely practiced hoarding and concealing of reserves inside the plants—helped to cushion production against stringencies of the plans and thereby afford, unwittingly, some more breathing space for the whole system. But eventually the system had to come to a grinding halt, after years of stagnation, or *zastoj,* as Soviet writers call it. A *zatratnyi* system, that is, one oriented on spending, was inefficient by definition. It produced enormous amounts of *brak* (waste) and useless items, almost deliberately *na sklad* (for the storerooms), that is, for no one in fact. But such production still earned reimbursement by the state, as if it were normally useful output. Enormous numbers of people, workers and officials alike of different standing, were reared on inefficiency, poor workmanship, and, basically, economic parasitism. The lack of interest in technological innovation in these circumstances goes without saying. Technological progress was selectively introduced by pressure from the state, but primary production units had no use for it or interest in it. It was actually a nuisance to them and even to the planners.

---

5. Janos Kornai, *Growth, Shortage and Efficiency: A Microdynamic Model of the Socialist Economy* (Berkeley and Los Angeles, 1982).

Here was a powerful trap for the not-too-distant future. The constant attempt to motivate people, to provide them with stimuli to exert themselves or to engage in creative initiatives, did not yield results. Working "for the plan" was not the same thing as an activity exercised in conditions of sufficient autonomy that depended on self-interest and results. In the 1930s the system was still dynamic; in the late 1970s it was barely moving under the impact of sclerotic sediments accumulated over the decades.

It is of interest to the whole question of Soviet industrialization to mention here, briefly, the anticipations of some Bolsheviks in regard to bureaucratization. Trotsky, for example, in the 1923–24 *Pravda* articles that were collected and published as *The New Course*,[6] observed and analyzed the making of a party apparatus, the concomitant loss by the party of its initial political essence, and its transformation into a different type of organization. The party, a supervisor and direct "guide" of the state apparatus, was being contaminated, as it were, by the object of its supervision. In later years Bukharin, once he turned in 1928 against Stalin's policies, warned equally emphatically against the bureaucratic danger. In his "Notes of an Economist," he forecast that the elimination of markets and small-scale private sectors and reliance on an administrative type of planning would lead to the creation of a colossal and costly apparatus.[7]

Together, the observations and premonitions of these two very different Bolsheviks anticipated correctly some of the facets of the coming administrative system, and there were many more such insights and reflections in those years. What they could not yet envisage was the virtual engulfing of the party by the state system at some later stage and its transformation, essentially, into the mouthpiece for the upper layers of the state bureaucracy.

Obviously, industrialization was not the only impetus to bureaucratic state building of the 1930s, but it was a crucial one; and this time the phenomenon surpassed in scope anything tsarist or NEP Russia had seen. Commissariats and other agencies began to proliferate, especially in the later part of the decade, and acquired a momentum of their own. As they were, in many ways, producers themselves of incoherences and, of

---

6. There are numerous editions. See L. Trotsky, *The Challenge of the Left Opposition (1924–1925)* (New York, 1975), a useful compendium of different texts, "The New Course" among them.

7. "Zametki Ekonomista," *Pravda,* September 30, 1928.

course, red tape, the practice of the 1930s consisted in dispatching powerful troubleshooters—a Kaganovich, Ordzhonikidze, Postyshev, or
Kirov—to make things move, notably, by forceful and energetic pressure (*nazhat'*), which sought the solution of problems "by any means" (*vo
chto by to ne stalo*). It is symptomatic to hear these powerful bosses complain in the 1930s about the bureaucratism and red tape that by now had
become painfully widespread in the system over which they were presiding. They were constantly trying to shake the bureaucracy up—and yet
they remained quite impotent, in substance, in the face of the system they
had to rely on.

One term used to characterize the "creature" is *vedomstvennost'*,
denoting a way and style of behavior by the *vedomstva*—a collective term
for all kinds of bureaucracies, from ministries to other governmental
agencies. Expansion of the economy, urbanization, education, and the
growth of different spheres of government activities were all predictably
sources of bureaucratic employment. But there were other propellants
for the growth of officialdom and its power, as well as for the development of skills to defend vested interests. Imbalances and shortcomings
that marred the developmental thrust of the 1930s demanded more
agencies to deal with the growing waves of spontaneous social reaction to
the tensions and strains of the times. *Vedomstva* were thus becoming the
system's entrepreneurs, its controllers, and, for all practical purposes, the
owners of the branch that each of them was entrusted with. The *vedomstva* quickly became power greedy and investment hungry. They learned
to fight tooth and nail for resources, and they could get their way, as the
main vehicles for economic action.

Moreover, the party itself, now deeply involved in economic construction and, as noted, thoroughly "economized," at a later stage became
hooked on the bureaucratized system and became part and parcel of it.
Under Stalin, as we know, a real war was conducted against cadres and
against the whole growing administrative class through the process of
the purges. This was a key strategy in the making of a despotic personal
rule, but it also exposed its inherent weakness in coping with the crisis
phenomena of those years. The accumulation of malfunctions, deviance,
sluggishness, and social disorders did not abate. Authorities berated the
very phenomenon they called *stikhiinost'*—spontaneity—and as the system was not yet really solid and most people could not yet cope with their
new jobs, lines of responsibility were blurred and incompetence was rife.

Such conditions were propitious for inducing paranoia in leaders, or in some of them, and hence also for a large-scale criminalization of a whole range of usually normal human behaviors. As most people and institutions worked poorly, the outcry against "sabotage" was heard ever more stridently; and although no one in particular was actually responsible, anyone could be declared guilty. The gates of arbitrariness and terror were thus thrust wide open. They had yet another social underpinning, stemming from the same "developmental" rush of the regime that added more ferocity to the regime's repressive bent.

The *stroiki,* or building sites, have now to be brought up again. The living conditions of workers on these *stroiki* were appalling, especially at the beginning. Even in the more settled conditions of older cities, this was a time of barracks and crammed rooms for the *rabsila*—which was neither a class nor an assortment of individuals, but simply a mass. Towering over its members was a growing class of *nachalstvo* that tended often to mistreat them, except when there was a labor shortage. Workers were supposed to partake of the much-vaunted *chuvstvo khoziaina*—the feeling of ownership—but very soon it was quite clear who the *khoziain* was.[8]

This attitude toward labor as a cheap and formless *rabsila* is one of the key features of industrialization in the Stalin era—and of Stalinism at large—notably, because the crude treatment it represented in the initial stages carried within it the seeds of a further step downward, into the atrocious mistreatment of labor in the camps. Despite the official emphasis on heroics in those *stroiki,* the Gulag was their obverse and their shadow.

The road from the *rabsila* into *zeki* was strengthened by a paradox. The ethos of economic development that dominated the era under consideration took on a perverse direction when the secret police were allowed to become an agency for industrial and other construction. Security agencies usually engage in surveillance, investigation, and punishment. But in Stalin's Russia they knew by the 1930s that the road to more prestige and resources led through the economic function of construction, especially of projects to which a normal force would not be

8. This meant that workers were supposed to share this feeling as members of the "ruling class." It was one of the most damaging red herrings of official propaganda.

attracted or would have to be highly paid. Once granted this function, the NKVD would act like other agencies with plans and quotas for "recruitment" of camp inmates in huge numbers. The sprawling Gulag system was produced by a confluence of all these factors.

The whole industrialization story is therefore one of an economy launched and run "from above" that frustrated and undermined initiative from below—without being able to prevent the self-defensive, informal, or illegal (*levye*) initiatives that proved to be unbeatable and shadowed the system constantly. An inability to motivate, a low propensity for innovation, the creation of deep systemic imbalances, the low or falling productivity of labor and capital—all were exacting prices that had to be paid for the strategy chosen at the 1928–29 turning point.

State intervention in priority sectors managed to mend things here and there, but overall most targets imposed by "the planning system" were met by techniques of dodging that, in this economy, operated almost like a "law." If technological innovation was translated into targets, it met the same fate. The system did better with motivating in emergencies like war, but this is what it actually was—"a permanent emergency" system, even in peace. The hierarchical bureaucratic model lent itself relatively well to this kind of activity—hence the term *command economy*. But economic activity, already extremely intense, cannot be permanently mobilized from above. Constant mobilizations—an important and irritating feature of the 1930s—had to end up producing an enormous sluggishness. The economy could not be stimulated in the longer run to efficient use of resources and effective action without some leeway for autonomous activity from below conducted with a sense of self-interest, as understood and clearly perceived by the producers themselves.

Unfortunately for these producers, there were layers of decision makers alongside and above them with different self-interests. Hence yet another paradox of this economic system: although called *khoziaistven-niki,* the economic bureaucrats were an administrative, not an economic, class, situated not within but above the economy, as far as their interests were concerned. They were also, for all practical purposes, the owners of their respective branches. The well-known fact that they had to spend enormous amounts of time on "coordination" (the notorious and endless *soglasovyvanie*) showed that despite their monopolistic power, their ability to act and solve problems kept dwindling, reflecting the process of growing cumbersomeness and immobility—without the resources to cut through red tape that were still available to an omnipotent despot.

So long as its main features were not yet fully in place, the system still offered some economic growth and, especially after Stalin's death, improvements in standards of living. Some would even say that in the early Brezhnev period, both butter and cannons could be provided.

But once the main features hardened they quickly begen to coagulate into a mechanism of self-destruction. There were limits to incoherences the economy could stand, limits to resources that could be wasted, and limits to the credibility of the political institutions that were so tightly seated on this particular way of running the economy (as well as in other spheres of life).

CHAPTER 7:

WORKERS IN SEARCH OF A CLASS

BETWEEN "PERSONALITY" AND "CLASS"

THE "BIOGRAPHICAL METHOD" PROPOSED BY REGINALD ZELNIK raises many important questions about appropriate analytical approaches.[1] There is a hint here of problems and, eventually, tension between the sociological method—which prefers broad, impersonal agglomerations and trends—and the "biographical" method—which begins from concrete persons and lives that the "broader" method overlooks. The clash that is implied here between two theories of reality, and between two ways of approaching it, can be formulated somewhat differently: the deterministic-structural approach and the personalistic one both tend to claim the whole field, each to the exclusion of the other. Thus, two exclusive approaches, verging partly on different ideologies—namely, methodological collectivism versus methodological individualism—compete with each other. Interested readers may find a sample of this problematique in Jon Elster's book on Marx.[2]

The personalistic approach claims that there is no society except as it works in individual minds, and therefore the study has to begin and end with the reading of individual minds. Elster saw Marx as partially redeemed from irrelevance—a conclusion Elster arrived at because he applied the (erroneous) structural approach inconsistently and was at least aware of the (correct) personalistic one. In the supposedly more correct conception, however, collective bodies have no reality themselves.

---

1. This essay was presented as a comment on the papers delivered at a conference on Russia's working class held at Michigan State University, October 9–11, 1990. Because references to authors concern for the most part the work they presented at the same conference, they are not footnoted. The proceedings of this conference are scheduled to be published as Lewis H. Siegelbaum and Ronald Grigor Suny, eds., *Making Workers Soviet: Power, Class, and Identity* (Ithaca, N.Y.: Cornell University Press, 1994).

2. John Elster, *Making Sense of Marx* (Cambridge, 1985).

The contradiction between the supposed antipodes is, to my mind, an artificial rift between aspects that belong together. The macrodimension is indispensable and is the final objective. The quest for dissolving social entities in individual beings amounts to denying the fact that without a social web there is no "individual" and that individuals must to some extent be "social." On the other hand, the sociological approach, if it refuses or is unable to incorporate the lessons from studying the personally specific (thus excluding human psychology and individuality from the processes), is equally at fault. The big theoretical battle should be about how to relate and merge the two, not simply to counterpose them; and such a task, however difficult, is the real one.

Thus, the discovery Zelnik makes of the importance of the individual's biographic memory—such as how Gerasimov's experience of being a pupil in an orphanage (*pitomets*) was a shaping force in his political activism—enriches and complicates the task of the generalizer, but it does not contradict the fact that there was a factory system with its class realities. Many of our conference papers, as expected, try to grapple with "class," but most seem to doubt the validity of this concept and the related one of "class consciousness." But class consciousness as studied in the papers, whether from the standpoint of the role of ethical concepts (Steinberg), or the empirical reconstruction of the actual making of such a consciousness (Hogan), or in connection with dependency relations with immediate supervisors (Smith), must be recognized as historically real, on the following conditions:

1. "Class" itself has a historical reality.
2. Such a consciousness is time- and context-bound, meaning that it can form itself and reform itself into something else.
3. Context influences the formation of class consciousness, meaning that it does depend on the existence, reactions, and self-consciousness of other cofactors such as factory owners, other layers in the plants, the state, social origins of the workers themselves, and the political situation (e.g., revolutions, reforms). The list is longer, but clearly there is no class consciousness without such context.
4. Marx's concept of class *an sich* is important. There must already exist a commonality of situation, position, and income in the economy (or in noneconomic spheres, as with state bureaucracies) for masses of people across the board, facing others around or above them, in order for a

consciousness of this situation to take root. *Above* does not always mean direct exploitation, because there are classes that exploit somebody, but not each other.

Domination, which Steve Smith prefers to *exploitation* and which refers to workers in factories or other employment where there are bosses, is, to my mind, the overarching category: there can be no exploitation without the presence of domination (except for "suckers," or psychological weaklings, in interpersonal relations, but this also implies domination). Still, there may be different concepts of exploitation. It is often not acknowledged when expressed in the usual Marxist terms, but it is broadly recognized in all cases when the working conditions are below the usual, normally acceptable standards or when there is harsh treatment.

On the other hand, when certain classes are in a position of being dominated, one would assume that they pay some price for this—whether they agree to or not, whether they accept the concept of exploitation or keep saying that Marx is dead; and this "something" will come back and will have to be explored—in whatever terms—when somebody wants to win an argument at any price. So classes do exist, whether they know it or not. The latter is less frequent, and many would reject the idea of a class that did not recognize itself as such. But one only has to think of well-known examples when large circles of revolutionary movements (the Bolsheviks in their leather coats, among them), after gaining power, took some time to realize and admit that they were a ruling class, not a popular or a working class anymore. Accusations of their being exploiters and oppressors were met with the most sincere denials, at least for a while. In the early stages of the system, they saw themselves as authentic, full-fledged revolutionaries. But others were already telling them, with good reason, that they were a ruling class, at least *an sich,* if not yet *für sich.* A switch from one state of self-consciousness to another, from *an sich* to *für sich,* can be triggered by different events or circumstances, a classic example of which was the salvo of the tsar's guard against a religious procession of workers during Bloody Sunday in 1905 when the *an sich* state of things suddenly became a *für sich* class consciousness.

There can be a flare-up of solidarities in other groups, but if they are quite heterogeneous in character, the ties may disappear once a particular irritant or problem is removed. Thus, a category like *obshchestvo* (society), known to us from tsarist history (and elsewhere), or "the intelligentsia" could, quite often, share opinions and lines of action but would rarely produce something akin to a stable trade union, unless something like a more solid infrastructure developed that would maintain a capacity to defend clearly perceived interests, as trade unions do.

CONSCIOUSNESS COMING AND GOING

The consciousness of a class *für sich*—that is, the appearance of a self-awareness with an ideology and accompanying political programs—does not mean, as the Bolsheviks often tried to make us believe, the adoption of some particular program or party. We have to accept a consciousness as it is, including, say, the "trade unionist" one, or the fact of adopting several political programs. One can even speak of a "false consciousness" in cases when a class, or large strata of it, experiences rude awakenings after its members let themselves be led by politicians and ideologies that do them a lot of harm. This happened quite often to different popular classes and layers, but upper classes, too, pay a heavy price for similar false routes.

All these phenomena related to politico-ideological self-awareness are changing as circumstances change, and we therefore often see both parts of the equation (not just the "consciousness" but also the underlying social structure) undergo sometimes quite uncorrelated, or seemingly uncorrelated, transformations. For me, it should be obvious, the two *are* related, although they are autonomous. We can reconstitute a social history of each class that undergoes transformations under the impact of social, technological, educational, and political circumstances, as it goes through transitional stages, as it keeps evolving groups that are new and different, and as, at times, a class just ceases to exist—sometimes for good, sometimes temporarily, when it needs time to reconstitute itself. So if one drops any explicit or implicit claims of the ironclad reality of a class, or a concretelike quality of "structure," if one understands that social realities can be, and often are, very fluid, then the concept of class becomes real and useful. But the study becomes more intricate because we do not take class and class consciousness for granted anymore. We have to find them, rediscover them empirically (and conceptually); and when we do locate them, we do not expect them to have a predictable appearance and "consciousness." There is also the need to learn how to live either without them or, in general, with fluidity or situations that are as often "in transit" as they are firm and fixed.

It seems relevant to propose a parenthesis at this juncture: The tsarist regime after 1905, whenever it calculated and plotted its electoral policies, operated already, partly at least, with class terms, despite the preference for using *sosloviia* (estate). The idea of a workers' curia recognized them as a distinct reality par excellence, and neither side had to read Lenin for this. Later, when reading the memoirs of Denikin and Miliukov written after the Civil War, we find that both analyze the problems in clearcut class terms—workers, bourgeoisie, peasantry (including kulaks as a category separate from other peasants) and *pomeshchiki* (landowners). And they too made errors in using this kind of terminology. This usage of class terms was not necessarily a result of a Marxist influence, but of an advancing new stage in economic development in which more clearcut class formations kept emerging, making obsolete and irrelevant the officially used categorization by *sosloviia*.

On the other hand, during later stages of development, as observed in countries we are living in now, the more rigid and massive configuration of class is replaced by a more complex differentiation. Classes become less prominent and coexist with a variety of social groups and layers that acquire ever more weight and importance in the social system but do not respond to terms that connote broader sociopolitical entities. If we subscribe to the aforementioned conditions, we are, I believe, in business. We find constantly in Russian history—as well as elsewhere—examples of the metamorphoses and transitions just described.

Let us add that the conference papers very appropriately address additional dimensions of social reality: gender, family, different forms of contact and coping (clientele, patronage, patriarchalism), a variety of cultural factors, ethnic identities, and different systems of ethics (communal, religious-orthodox, religious-sectarian, etc.). They are all indispensable, as are, of course, internal social differentiations and networking of all kinds. They constitute the texture of any social aggregate, without which such an aggregate is just "void."

It is interesting why one should underline, as Steinberg did when speaking about ethical ideals, that "this is morals," not class. Why, if the evoked phenomena pertain to "culture" or "ethics," should "class" be evicted? The demand for just treatment and for justice more broadly, stemming from the reality of an oppressive environment and system in the labor process, is easily about class; and it is not important whether this class arose somewhere else, is new, or does not ask for anything in class terms. How is *nas za liudej ne schitaiut* ("they don't consider us people") not an expression of a class reality, though not just of one particular class?

All these aspects of social reality have nothing to do with bursting asunder the overarching concept. Doing that might land us in an unenviable situation of having the working class or classes "disappear" when they are all over the place—in factories, workshops, and construction sites—clearly visible to everyone who wants to see them, and different from their bosses, *chinovniki* (officials), and everyone else. This does not mean, as I said, that classes do not occasionally disappear. Yes, a working class, but also a state, a party, institutions, and systems can evaporate, even before this is realized, exactly as they may already be in existence without being noticed. That is inherent in the very character of changing and shifting social realities. Such is the character of this historical field, and such is the power of illusions and myths that accompany any human reality and are responsible for the masqueradelike aspects of it. Still, it is mostly a nondivine comedy, which means that it does exist whether the curtain is up or down.

Thus, from paper to paper, the squads of workers described change in their composition, attitudes, politics, and ideology: Zelnik's 1870s versus the 1890s; Hogan's *metalisty* before and during the revolution; Kuromiya's miners, a nonclass group par excellence and yet a political powder keg; Koenker's printers, highly articulate and ready for socialism, entering into a battle for sheer survival against the Communists (as they probably would against anyone else) in certain conditions, and accepting the same Communists in other circumstances. Let us add Gabor Rittersporn's supposition about his working class becoming "an urban laboring mass"—disputable, no doubt, but part of this same group of nations.

Others, too, have described the fluidity of classes. Dan Orlovsky has discovered even a whole "hidden class" where there was not supposed to be one—the white-collar employees. Other authors, as soon as they go into details, invariably become aware that the preferred group is layered, even multilayered, and, before long, something initially perceived as class begins to crumble. Peasants are an entity taken for granted as long as we know little about them. When we undertake microstudies of local varieties, we have our hands full of social layering again. The peasants suddenly become something tricky and almost vanishing. A version of such a sociological disappearing act comes up also every time we deal with uprooting and re-uprooting, as in the case of the massive influx of people of a different background, even civilization—the highly "traditional" peasants—engulfed by massive industrialization, urbanization, and other speedy and widespread waves of change. Can it be said that a reality is "vanishing"? It could be, but only as a stage in the course of research. After the process of uprooting, when *deconstruction* is certainly a good term to use, reconstruction and the striking of roots will follow. The only problem is that in the language of some writers it looks as if "somebody," maybe even the writers themselves, are doing the reconstructing. If so, this would be a nice case of megalomania. The real thing, being a multitude of acts by a multitude of individuals, is therefore a *process*—that is, is constructing and reconstructing itself—and that is why, if we work well and come across vanishing or reappearing realities, we can grasp them *because* they are processes. The shiftier and more variable quality of social reality does not invalidate concepts like class; they just cannot claim to be more real than life, to be there before they emerge, or to still be there as they move from stage to stage until, ultimately, like the peasantry in most industrialized countries—and social structures overall—they actually do make their exit from history. Finally, another caveat is still in order: a reality in flux that does dissolve our concepts continues to be a reality, potent and active in shaping historical outcomes.

HIDDEN CLASSES, HIDING CLASSES

When reading about Orlovsky's "hidden class," one could object that officials have been barely hidden during the New Economic Policy (NEP), despite the proletarian mantle they were offered in some speeches and statistical tables. Incidentally, it would be good to ascertain when the term *proletariat* was first used for workers *and* employees and when this usage was discontinued. The reason, though, for such a "mislabeling," to put it mildly, is clear. It stems from the ideological assumption that the state is proletarian; therefore, all those it employs, except for the obvious "bourgeois specialists," should be included in the "proletariat." By the same token, the small proletariat came to look bigger, and it was easier to show its growth. Here already is an example that points to the tendency to use class terminology as a strategy of mystification, leading at a later stage to an even broader one of a full-blown "mythological sociology." This became a key trait of the Stalinist period, making social theory entirely devoid of any relation to life and thereby destroying the social sciences altogether. Stalin's "two friendly classes and one layer" (*proslojka*), or the quite unsuccessful effort to drape the poorly schooled mass of Soviet employees of the 1930s in the toga of the supposedly massive "intelligentsia" (instead of their previous inclusion in the proletariat), are examples of such a mythical sociology. Another is the category of *byvshie liudi* (former people), those who really became, if not hidden, then at least a hiding class. They, as well as numerous "alien elements" who fled dekulakization, became an object of a frantic chase in the early 1930s and a ruthless rooting out from factories, *sovkhozy,* offices, and academic institutions, more often than not because of what the person, or just the person's father, did or owned before the revolution.

But there is another way in which the idea of something "hidden" about employees can be revealing: they were or they became an important support of the regime. Early on, this fact was "hidden" because the employees themselves did not immediately acknowledge this, and the regime was not happy about such unwanted support. It remains a key fact in the social and political history of the Soviet system, not only that this support was finally accepted on both sides, but that the bureaucracy, especially its upper layers, supplanted the working class as the mainstay and powerholder. This fact actually was made almost official, though not without some ideological manipulations. Ideological makeup still continued to be used, but it was fading away as quickly as the "workers' state" itself. An unwanted ruling class, if you will, took over. As long as that class still consisted of old tsarist employees, they were a support *malgré soi,* because they depended on their employer, the state, however, many ended up becoming quite loyal toward it. But they were, mostly and traditionally, inimical to the working class, and there is no reason to assume that this attitude changed very much.

The story is more complicated with employees and cadres of popular extraction; but social origin, although important, did not block the process of the "status revolution"—or counterrevolution, if one prefers—in Soviet state building in the 1930s. The leaders and the main groups of servants of this state had to emerge, sooner or later, into the open as the real powerholders that they actually were. In this context, the term *administrators*—even *administrative class,* as part of a broader category known as the bureaucracy—should be mentioned. Whether called in Soviet parlance *vysshij komandnyj sostav, otvet-rabotniki, otvet-politrabotniki,* or even just *rabotniki,* they had to emerge, quite logically, as superior to and ruling over the popular strata, be they workers or low-level employees. These *rabotniki* also urgently need their historian. When talking about the Soviet phenomenon of "mythical sociology," we should be reminded that the reality of classes gives rise to a lot of trafficking, posturing, and manipulating in every society.

A whole politico-sociological choreography on the themes of class and power can be observed everywhere because deep interests are involved and much is at stake. What are the realities behind the terms? Who wants to present or misrepresent? Such things have to be discovered and rediscovered in every country over and over again. What was it that the Soviet system, our topic here, tried to hide at different times, notably by making impossible any serious sociological study and an honest class analysis? Quite a lot, no doubt. Yet it can be summed up very simply: the realities of power and of rule. This is what it is always about. Grappling with class therefore should be a bona fide scholarly endeavor, but it is rarely if ever a politically innocent exercise. It becomes easily offensive to power relations and thus deeply enmeshed in ideology, whatever the system.

A PROLETARIAT WITHOUT CAPITALISTS?

I will not dwell on the precise stages in the formation of the working class; some work has been done, but much more is still needed. But it is worth reiterating that the key trait of most of those years were waves of migration, of varying intensity, into (and sometimes out of) the cities and their different social strata. Hence, there was a process of decomposition and recomposition of social groups on a large scale.

A lot of attention has been paid to the making of a tsarist working class and its recreation in the postrevolutionary period as a proletariat again, instead of as a hoped-for liberated working class. This disappointment engendered quite a lot of ideological propagandist "fiddling" with the class reality, notably the use of the already quoted formula of "two nonantagonistic classes plus one *proslojka*" (the latter referring to the intelligentsia) at a time when somebody else was actually ruling over the economy, the state, the culture, and "the two nonantagonistic classes" themselves. The latter were provided on average with no more than three to four years of elementary schooling and were thus barely literate, literally as well as politically. The fact that the statist system did not have a classical bourgeoisie and ruling class to match the term *proletariat* is important. Without a capitalist class, one cannot speak of capitalism.

This presents a hurdle: a working class reminiscent of the old capitalist system, but the ruling stratum (later, class) reminiscent of what—an even older, precapitalist system? There is no doubt that these forms were indicative of a stage and of a continuity that has to be considered and explained. But continuity of what?

In the search for answers, it may be useful to turn to, say, 1905 and then to skip directly to the 1930s and later, too. It is not surprising and is worth noting that so much of what our papers show us about the prerevolutionary period would still be alive and well in the Soviet period. Sexual harassment and exploitation of women were still very widespread. So was the fawning before *mastera* (shop-floor superintendents) or the rebelling against them. But the role of *master* was changing in different periods, and this can be reconstituted only by empirical study.[3] Material cited by Hogan on poor incentive systems, obsolete machinery, and so on in the Russia of 1905 sounds so similar to what could be observed in 1975 or 1985, and the parallels point, no doubt, to a system in decline in both cases.

The industrial system in its early stages is a deeply authoritarian, if not despotic one everywhere, and its essence is about owners commanding labor. This statement encourages one to look at the Stalinist system as being the outcome of a "marriage" between a deeply patriarchal social reality of rural Russia, still powerful in the 1920s, with the despotic traits of a smokestack industry of the day. The situation of workers during these years, the type of environment in which they lived, and the social vortex from which they came and which they faced illustrate with greater intensity than before the validity of the aforementioned heuristic formula. It is also possible to expand the discussion of Stalinism to include the uneasy symbiosis between a bureaucratic system and the Stalinist despotism that occurred against the broader social framework alluded to by this formula.

And so, even where there are no private owners, we still hear the demand for respect that is due *nashemu bratu* (to our brothers) but is not to be found. Many of the bosses are from working-class origins, and we do know that many of the most despotic foremen and superintendents in tsarist Russia and later were of this origin. What does this mean, sociologically and politically? As alluded to, we may be dealing with a situa-

---

3. See Lewis H. Siegelbaum, "Masters of the Shop Floor: Foremen and Soviet Industrialization," in William G. Rosenberg and Lewis H. Siegelbaum, eds., *Social Dimensions of Soviet Industrialization* (Bloomington, Ind., 1993).

tion that has, externally, some similarities with an older imperial combination of despotism and bureaucracy, except that, in fact, the current
situation belongs to the twentieth century. It is an industrial or industry-
oriented bureaucracy, implanted on a bedrock of a patriarchal peasantry, leading to the phenomenon of the "economization" of the political system, including the monopolistic party, the economy having
become its main function and raison d'être.

But it is important that the bedrock was changing, too, and, with it,
the very constitutive parts of a new intelligentsia, which was a novelty in
character and scope. At the same time, we cannot overlook the enormous
numbers of *chernorabochie* (unskilled laborers)—officially, not less than
65 percent in 1940, and still about 35 percent in 1985. Actually, these figures concern only the *osnovnye,* or basic jobs. Among the auxiliary workers, the rate was 95 percent. So, for a time, the social base of the country
consisted of the physical labor of the peasants, who worked mostly with
their hands, despite the tractors, and the mostly physical industrial labor,
whose members also worked *rukami, bez mashin* (mostly with their bare
hands, without machines). If there was a certain reintegration of the
labor force, as Ken Straus puts it, it happened inside this sociological base
at the bottom of the industrial system in the form of an enormous, still
poorly differentiated, unqualified industrial labor force.

The transformation of the factory into a provider, into actually a
replica of Western company towns, fits this primitive stage of industrial
development, as does the existence of a powerful controlling and constraining system, which a primitive and poor labor force needed, maybe,
but for which it paid heavily with accrued dependence. The low initial
standards of living allowed for these arrangements to produce an
improvement, in certain respects; but we are also aware that those standards, low as they were, were constantly under a downward pressure.

During, and for a few years after, the Civil War, authors spoke of the
physical and biological menace to the workers caused by undernourish-
ment. Housing was also a tough problem, becoming catastrophic in the
1930s. The food situation and standards of living improved during the
1920s (not lodging, though), but they deteriorated from 1928 onward.
Some Soviet calculations, taking 1928 as 100, show a drop to 80 by 1932, a
slight improvement to 90 in 1937, and a new deterioration by 1938.
Worse, the purchasing power of an average salary of a worker or
employee did not go above the 1928 level until the mid-1950s. This is

why, from the rationing of 1928–29 on, food and some other supplies could be used as a deliberate policy tool for disciplining and rewarding. Lodging, too, when it was more than just a *zemlianka* (dugout) became a reward that factory administrators could dangle before workers. This was yet another side of Soviet factory-town practice, where not just disciplining but simply retaining the labor force was the aim, a problem that cannot detain us here. The low cost of labor favored keeping labor surpluses, the surpluses hindered raising professional standards, and low standards meant low labor productivity. All these factors together contributed to the appearance of the phenomenon I call *rabsila*—a crude labor force, rather than working class, that the managers treated as such unless labor shortages forced them to act differently. Workers resisted in many ways, including "voting with their feet" and by other means, but that topic goes beyond our discussion.

The aforementioned developments have to be supplemented by at least some basic data on "culture" and, in the first place, on schooling and levels of skill. The existence of the mass of *chernorabochie* is already a testimony to the low professional level of most workers, and it goes with an education that does not exceed, say, three years of elementary schooling in the 1920s and probably less than four in the late 1930s (with only about 8 percent having gone through seven years or more). Interestingly enough, the 1926 census did not yet ask a worker about his or her *obrazovanie* (education), only about *gramotnost'* (literacy).

Could a "ruling class" be so poorly literate or partly illiterate? Yes, in the entourage of Charlemagne in the eighth century A.D. In the twentieth century, however, the requirements were different. Nevertheless, swearing was still all-powerful among the population, but not only and not necessarily at somebody. It was often a way of speaking, almost a way of life. I have even heard of competitions in swearing where the swearer was not allowed to repeat himself and the arbiter had a timer in his hands. It was, I think, developed in the tsarist fleet, and continued, to my knowledge, well into the 1930s, if not later.

"COMRADE NACHAL'NIK, SIR"?

One of the general trends, for the 1930s and for some time thereafter, consists, as said, in the following: the bulk of the industrial working population switched from one type of a mainly physical labor—in agriculture—to another type of physical labor—in industry. The difference is significant because the industrial system was a new and different stage of development, but not yet good enough for making this social base powerful and able to force the top leaders and institutions into changing the pyramid of status and power. The index of the standards of education is crucial here: averages may hide improvements and a layer of better-educated and better-qualified labor, but they also reflect the effects of the influx from rural areas, where standards were still very low.

Whatever our opinion of the deskilling process, the fact remains that, at times, the method of adapting to low levels of worker competence by oversimplifying tasks was tried out; but this was found to be excessive, and psychologically and culturally damaging to labor. Whatever the methods or solutions actually adopted, the sociological key feature remained: the bulk of the labor force were *chernorabochie* (hired on an as-needed basis)—a fact that remains even when one calls them "semi-skilled."

The other problem raised, the one of socialization by the system and acceptance of it by the workers, is tricky. We have not yet fully charted periods of worker alienation versus periods of, more or less, acceptance. We know well about the period ending in 1922, during which Zinoviev told the Twelfth Party Congress, "We really reconquered this time the working class and its faith in us," making it clear that it was lost for a time. We can also document waves of strikes in 1927–28. Later again, in 1932, we hear Postyshev saying that the moods of the workers are *ochen' skvernye* (very ugly). The better-known campaigns for labor discipline can also be read politically. There certainly was much acceptance or identification with the regime at different times, but, still, seen by the party, it was not as good or as positive on its own terms. Otherwise, why whould they have constantly bewailed the "petty bourgeoisie *stikhiia*" (chaos) that kept swamping workers from inside and outside? Why would they constantly cleanse the factories of "alien elements," or fight those numerous categories of *letuny* (rolling stones), *rvachi* (self-seekers), and so on as varieties of shirkers? The acceptance is political, and even political indifference has a political meaning. But the opposition to norm raising or to Stakhanovism (which was actually tamed, I suggest, by a united front of management, technicians, and workers themselves) and the resentment toward rude bosses and the privileges that they reserved for themselves were widespread and recurring. And that resentment could also, at any time, turn political in a direction unwanted by the regime, especially when workers (as I myself witnessed during my factory spell in the Urals) tended to develop a clear conscience of "them" (the *nachal'niki*) and "us" (*nash brat*) as two separate entities that could harden into a dangerous polarization. And if it was there in 1941–42 when I witnessed this phenomenon, there must have been enough of it before or after. We should therefore try to identify stages of the workers' perception of *nachal'stvo,* yes, as a class, and of the system at large.

During the NEP this might have been partly obfuscated by the division of bosses into "red" directors and "bourgeois specialists." Maybe so, but later it was different. Remember also that in the 1930s supplies were differentiated by status, and top administrators (like higher-ranking personnel in the army) never took meals in the same factory cafeterias as the laborers; the administrators had their own, much better ones. This also occurred on the level of the shop floor, not just of the central management (*zavodoupravlenie*). The joke of those years about the ORS is telling.[4]

The continuation of the *Vy* and *Ty* well into the postwar period is no less revealing about the reality of status. *Ty i Vy* was still a theme for a social psychologists writing in the 1970s. Some ambiguity existed, at first because a worker's addressing of the director in the *Ty* mode could still be a relic of the revolutionary period and its egalitarianism, at least inside the party. But *Vy* reappeared in official circles, and, at the same time, *Ty* became the way a boss talked to a worker or other lower-rank people, while the boss was addressed respectfully by them as *Vy*. These terms are no trifle: they are expressions not only of relative status and power, but also of authoritarianism in a civilization that did not depart enough from the culture of crude domination, wielded directly and potently so that there be no misunderstanding about who is the boss and who the underling.

And the reaction "from below" was equally characteristic: on the one hand, an acceptance of the right and of the position of the boss, including his crude attitude; on the other, quite often, also a sense of indignation for lack of respect implicit in the way of *tykat'* (jabbing) the workers, while they had to remain deferential. There is no need for pompous and ceremonial titles from medieval courts, like *vashe vysokoblagorodie* or

---

4. The initials of *Otdel Rabochego Snabzheniia* (Department for Workers' Supplies) were read, in a widespread joke, as *Obespech' Ran'she Sebia* and then reread as *Ostal'noe Rabochim i Sluzhashchim* ("Take care first of all of yourself; what remains, give to the workers and employees").

even *velichestvo,* to express social chasms. Simpler words can be equally discriminating and telling of subordination and social distance. I do not know whether it is realized that the term *tovarishch* can do just as well, when a subordinate is not allowed to approach a superior directly and personally as *Ivan Ivanovich* but *must* precede it by *tovarishch,* which becomes a title denoting a higher status.

So this *Ty* problem is a meaningful indicator of the culture of power relations and of its substance. Formally polite address may still hide, even accentuate, the actual power gap between the interlocutors, but there is a difference of historical system between a *Vy* to *Ty* and a *Vy* versus *Vy.* A feudal lord did not have to be polite, because polite address was reserved by definition only for equals, or at least for "the free." It would have been inadmissible to use respectful terms toward a serf.

The crude treatment meted out to workers—here, it is industry we have in mind—points also to a stage in the history of industrialism. As students of American history know, the use of foul language and the beating and abuse of women were common when the workers were recruited "from the gate"—that is, mostly from a poor mass of émigrés. Here, too, the whole gamut of the sociology of industrial and labor relations comes into play, with many features similar to those we find in Russia. The "crudity" and the despotic foremen begin to disappear at later stages in the United States and more slowly in the Soviet Union as well. But the phenomenon is not an exclusively Russian or Soviet one.

In Russia, the rather humble-sounding requests for being treated "like human beings"—based on an ethical self-image that sometimes led to a violent reaction against administrative personnel—is a continuation of a similar outcry that came from peasants who carried it from the depths of serfdom. I do not know to what extent these peasants expressed the same relations to serf owners, or in what terms. But, clearly, the demand for respectful treatment had to become more pronounced, since the emancipation was not followed by an improved status. With their disappointed expectations, the peasants certainly had to emphasize this demand, which expressed their growing self-image of personal value and outrage at others' refusal to recognize their human dignity.

The problem specific to the 1930s was that collectivization reinforced or regenerated, for a historical period, the crude forms of coercion in relation to peasants, their heightened dependence, and the arbitrariness of the behavior of state and party officials. The outcry against the fact that *nas za liudej ne schitaiut* and, similarly, the preference for at least paternalistic forms (which then constituted progress) were very much in evidence in the 1930s and much later, until these features began to fade away, though not universally, with rising educational standards.

To conclude, Stalin's cult was more than just the apotheosis of a person. It was a version of an apotheosis of the state, and when Stalin's cult declined, the broader version remained and blossomed. But workers (as others), under both versions, had to do as told, which meant both assimilating and displaying a *chuvstvo khoziaina* (sense of proprietorship), although the *khoziain* (boss) was somebody else. If they felt, appropriately, that they actually had no say in the business, they were sternly told that this was an erroneous view that stemmed from the petty bourgeoisie residues in them.

But here something baffling can be mentioned, similar to the phenomena we explored when speaking of classes. The superstate, so immensely powerful on the face of it and accepted as such by the world, was itself losing the *chuvstvo khoziaina,* and not just once. Stalin, who seemingly had immense and undisputed power, was displaying clear signs of struggling for the reigns that were constantly eluding him. Some twenty years after his death, the state system at large actually stopped being a real *khoziain:* it presided over a *beskhoziajstvennost'* (proprietorlessness) of monumental proportions until it entered into a stage of full decomposition. It was, or became, an iceberg—not that icebergs are not heavy or powerful, but an iceberg may be melting away even as observers remain impressed by its immensity. So here we have yet another case of the historical game of "hide and seek"—here it is and here it isn't—but when it is, observers and contemporaries often do not know what it is, and when it actually isn't anymore, they tend to think it is still there.

CHAPTER 8: SOVIET SOCIALISM

A Case of "Mislabeling"

THE THEME OF "SOVIET IDEOLOGY AND SOCIALISM" REQUIRES a reflection about the interactions between ideology (intentions, programs) and the type of historical system that actually emerges and uses ideology. Ideological orientations certainly play a role in shaping basic attitudes of revolutionary or nonrevolutionary political actors, some of the actions they take, and the ways they like to present and explain their actions. But the eyes of the observer should be fixed, in the first place, on the "process" and its results—that is, what the system is and how it works. What it says about itself is a factor, but one has to go beyond that. Ideologies are not fixities, not entirely independent factors. They have a fate of their own: they undergo changes, lose some content and acquire some other, and may actually become just an empty shell. They express or relate in many ways to surrounding realities, and what these realities are can be ascertained only through empirical studies. The fact that they influence actions and attitudes does not change our basic contention.

The study of Russia offers ample material for observing just this kind of "fate of ideology." Terms like *Marxism, Marxism-Leninism, socialism,* and even more so *communism* are all legitimate objects of study, but they are not the right departing point for either grasping the system or for understanding those ideologies themselves. The Soviet founding fathers were, no doubt, committed to their ideological principles, but they knew and said quite often that Russia could not produce a socialist system by its own devices. So they did not have a mandate from history, in the terms they were themselves using, to create socialism in Russia. Sooner or later, manipulation of the initial ideology had—and did in fact begin—to account for the fact that the initial diagnosis was the right one. We will therefore be facing a particular case of a broader phenomenon whereby theories or ideologies, whenever they are borrowed or transferred into an environment that is different from their original context, will, unavoidably, lose their original meaning and function, even if they still sound the same. In fact, they actually may come to mean something entirely different and either express or mask a different reality.

These ideas, which are suggested by the study of Soviet ideology, found a strong confirmation from the German scholar Alfons Soellner, who contributed to a 1984 colloquium covened in Paris by Gerard Raulet.[1] Soellner studied left-radical and right-radical concepts in Germany as they have changed places and meaning. The author says: "Concepts and theories are not neutral entities. Once they leave their context and are placed in a different frame of reference, they change their meaning and function."[2] The same certainly applies, as we have suggested, to ideologies. In the case of Weimar Germany, which the colloquium studied, a left-wing ideology—communism—was being borrowed and wandered over to the right to become a radical national-communism not very far from fascism. In the USSR, though in quite different ways, the whole ideological outlook was being reshaped and moved, over the years, into a conservative direction, including ever more of the old right-wing ingredients—as I illustrate later in this chapter.

"IDEOLOGY" MAY NOT BE WHAT IT SAYS

In light of the discussion thus far, it is astonishing to hear comments on the events related, say, to the perestroika as having shown "a sudden collapse of a messianic ideology," as several scholars expressed during a 1990 conference on perestroika.[3] It is difficult to think about the leaders of the Soviet "command-administrative system"—the likes of a Suslov or Brezhnev, for example—as being anything near "messianic." Nor were they championing the doctrine of *The Communist Manifesto*. Theirs was a system dedicated to a status quo that still used some of the terminology of the "founding fathers" but that took good care to geld—actually, destroy—the very essence and content of the original. Moscow was not the place to study Marxist theory or socialist ideology—and certainly not the place to observe them in action.

Moreover, it certainly was not right to talk about anything "sudden" in the collapse of the system and the death of its ideology; the latter, inci-

---

1. Gerard Raulet, ed., *Weimar ou l'explosion de la realité* (Paris, 1984).

2. In Catherine Merridale and Chris Ward, eds., *Perestroika in Historical Perspective* (London, 1992).

dentally, occurred well before the former. This was a process, a whole cascade of transformations, until it reached a point when official lectures on "scientific communism" bored everyone to death. The loss of ideological vigor was the price that the ruling elite or party paid for its systematic indoctrination of the population in terms that had little relation to the reality of everyday life. Obviously, for such a thing to go on for a lengthy period, the population also had to be "depoliticized," that is, deprived of free political expression. But this was to cost the party its very existence.

The other theme, widely in vogue for some time as a test of wisdom and postmodern lucidity, is the critique of any "societal projects" as having to turn totalitarian, supposedly by definition. The notion that any project of social transformation has to have pernicious effects is in itself pernicious. But in the Soviet context it takes on a different tilt: to what projects do such statements refer? Those who espouse this theme do not bother about history and would not be aware that even under Lenin there already were at least three such projects, and the situation changed again under Stalin. In other words, the pre-October, Civil War, NEP, Stalinist, and later periods changed their methods and aims quite meaningfully, sometimes dramatically. Therefore, the supposed sameness or identity of the "totalitarian design" is an ahistorical contention—to put it mildly.

In the heyday of revolutionary ideology, many propagandist themes were willingly and enthusiastically promoted by politicians, educators, and artists, and in popular festivities, paintings, films, and theatrical productions. Dziga Vertov, Pudovkin, Eisenstein, and Meyerhold, writers and artists of the 1920s and 1930s, were not forced to undertake their works, even in the earlier days of Stalin's rule. Kataev's *Times Ahead* was already a "social order," a commissioned work, but it was executed willingly. *Propaganda* was not a dirty word yet; it was seen by artists not as an exercise in manipulation but as an effort to spread enlightenment.

As years went by and the takeover by different kinds of ideologues and bureaucrats became the prevailing reality, painting or otherwise picturing reality had to be done as the political leaders wanted it to be seen. With this change came the routinization of cultural activity as well as its "commandeered" capacity. Cultural life became "planned" by the Agitation and Propaganda Department—an "agitprop" approach to culture—and it reflected the wishes and tastes of the upper layers, but especially Stalin personally or, during the crucial 1946–48 period, Zhdanov. This snowballed into torrents of propagandist verbiage, ever more lifeless in both the "cultural" and the mass-agitational domains. I personally experienced it during World War II when I was working in an Uralian factory. The enthusiasm for some party activities and slogans was by then a thing of the past and was replaced by a very vacuous sloganeering. Mass meetings "decided" to write a letter "to Comrade Stalin," to take on some meaningless "targets," or to "challenge" somebody to overfulfill some plan. Many of the "shock methods" (*udarnichestvo*) and much of the Stakhanovism were conducted in this vein. The system exhibited an amazing propensity to push its ideological machinery into costly campaigns that kept turning within a void. The wasted time of millions of people bred boredom, cynicism (but, happily, also quite a number of good jokes), and, finally, total irrelevance—as in the huge slogans over Moscow's skyline that I observed in 1987 during my first visit since the end of World War II. They claimed triumphantly, "Communism will prevail"—when the whole edifice was crumbling. A 1987 survey conducted by a television crew proved that nobody paid attention to such slogans—and this certainly had not just begun in 1987.

It is true that many ideas and slogans meant a lot to great numbers of people for quite some time, and more detailed study is needed on which ideas meant what to whom and when. Many biographies and autobiographies do attest to various people's shifts in allegiance to and enthusiasm for the regime, followed by spells of disappointment, sometimes renewed hopes, and, finally, disillusionment and outright opposition as expressed through either "internal emigration" or direct political opposition. In such reminiscences offered after the perestroika began, the writers would sometimes be less than frank when speaking about the degree of their commitment, especially at the height of the Stalinist purges, and this fact adds complexity to this painful chapter of many people's lives.

But whatever the degree of past commitments, ideological terms used to define the object of the commitment become rather irrelevant. Whether a Molotov or a Stalin himself sincerely believed in socialism or understood Marxism is somewhat beside the point. Such terms might have been used, but we already know that they could become suffused with other meanings or even replaced by something entirely different. In fact, not only Marxism but even its Soviet version, called "Marxism-Leninism," acquired over time some quite different contents when employed by people such as, say, Suslov, as against another apparatus man such as Yzkovlev (then the interim head of the propaganda department of the Central Committee). Many at the top stopped being Marxist-Leninist altogether. (I discuss these points later, in chapter 12.) And this confirmed a widespread phenomenon, as Soellner probably meant it: Even if a resounding allegiance to the founding fathers is ascertained in many speeches, the old creeds may be as good as dead. Similar phenomena have been observed elsewhere, and there is nothing new per se in the Russian experience.

WHAT IF MARX CAME TO VISIT THE GENERAL SECRETARY?

What was new was the fact that so many observers and students of Russia refused to acknowledge what they saw: Soviet leaders were rediscovering or reinventing a national past to fit their needs; were flirting with nationalism of all kinds; and were producing cults and manipulating eclectic messages custom-made for different layers and mentalities in the bureaucracy and in the burgeoning Soviet multitude of specialists. The regime was using terms like *socialism* or *communism* when they were in fact out of tune with reality and were actually shadowed by more realistic and not necessarily hidden ideological alternatives—and this was the real and, in a sense, normal maneuvering that occurred with ideological materials in a power game. Taking the stock phrases as a depiction of reality was a remarkable failure of judgment.

Did we see in the USSR the accession of the citizenry to democratic ownership of the country's wealth? This would have been a socialist development. What this ideology meant for the prewar German social democracy and for the Second International of Socialist Parties, from which the Bolsheviks got their inspiration, is quite well known. Socialism, including its Marxist version, was about producers' emancipation from the effects of the private property system, which governed the main productive assets of society. In such a system, the huge productive forces get ever more deeply "social," or public even on an international scale, although they remain mostly privately owned, managed, and disposed of. This domination of the social economy by private interests—a key principle in the market economies—causes many distortions in economic and social life.

Although such effects of the market mechanisms were being corrected by state regulation, to some extent, socialists could still show that imbalances and dysfunctions kept growing and that something more might be needed: a more powerful intervention of "society," through the mechanisms of a democratic state, in order to make the private forms of appropriation better serve the social essence of the economy, which cannot be anybody's private property or any group's de jure or de facto. As long as broad social interests were filtered and shaped through private interests and powers, crises and social injustice would inevitably result.

The socialist idea (and ideology) was obviously about more than just overcoming the effects of a form of property; it was also about eliminating the effects of deeply embedded and oppressive structures, including punitive and militaristic states, as well as a constraining class system— the proletariat, even if called "working class," being one of them. The latter is often forgotten: The proletariat is, in itself, not anything ideal; it is a severe impediment to overcome. And in Marx's conception, socialism would lead to the disappearance of the proletariat and its transformation into an educated middle class of the future, though the term *middle class* was not used in this way by socialists. After all, not just a ruling class but economic classes in general, as they were historically known, were constraining—if not directly oppressive—structures.

These were the sources from which the Russian social democrats, including the Bolsheviks, got their socialist inspiration and schooling. This stayed in their language for a long time, as practices strayed from the language early on in the history of the regime. As the deeply bureaucratic, hierarchical, antiegalitarian regime expropriated the material and intellectual producers and excluded them from participation in politics, no twisting of quotes from Marx could justify blaming him for the system. His main plank was "socialization," meaning a massive emancipation of working people from whoever is ruling over them, as well as surmounting their own class position.

The system that claimed—falsely—to be the socialist alternative to capitalism, although not capitalist itself, shared with the latter a mechanism of exclusion from appropriation for the benefit of ruling elites (even if the system's mechanisms were structured differently). The carrier of the monopolistic appropriation—a highly centralized bureaucracy— did not allow a private ownership of means of production, and the personal wealth of the system's grandees was mainly in consumer goods. But their power over the economy and the distribution of national wealth was beyond doubt. The system, however, was designed in a way that made it work toward an exhaustion of resources and of its own historical relevance. More about the causes of this "exhaustion" will be added in chapter 13.

Economic and political democratization was deeply embedded in Marxist or other socialist ideas; and without that, any system—including capitalism—was considered oppressive. What would Marx have said, had he been resurrected by the imagination of a Dostoevsky or Bulgakov, upon seeing Stalin's or Brezhnev's Moscow for himself? One would not need a great author to plagiarize Dostoevsky's "The Grand Inquisitor" and bring Marx, rather than Jesus, to see the Grand Inquisitor, or rather the General Secretary. There are plenty of texts by Marx to construct his reaction. As readers of his correspondence know, Marx was adept at cursing in German, English, and French.

RUSSIAN SOCIALISTS FIRMLY BELIEVED IN . . . CAPITALISM

Another thing to be considered is the interrelation with the outside world. Even when a country practices autarchy and isolationism—as the Soviet Union did, especially under Stalin—the interplay never stops, in either direct or roundabout ways. The initial socialist ideology of the Russian social democracy was, as we said, German-made or, more broadly, shaped by the Second International. There also were contributions and adaptations made in Russia, many of them by Plekhanov, Menshevik leaders, Trotsky, or Lenin; but the socialist ideology was a European product transferred by Russians onto Russian soil.

The idea of an "agrarian nexus," which I proposed in my essay "In Search of Stalinism,"[3] refers to a commanding feature of the social system that was valid for tsarist Russia but also (in modified versions) for both Lenin's and Stalin's regimes. It showed a retarded and retarding complex of sociopolitical and cultural trends and structures that the development of capitalism in Russia could not chew up and that the socialist experiment in Russia also stumbled on. The relevant formula in Marxism was built on the assumption that capitalism replaces feudalism, and that the developing capitalist-urban markets and class systems would explode the feudal relations that blocked development. These

---

3. Moshe Lewin, *The Making of the Soviet System*.

changes were supposed to occur, sooner or later, in Russia and every-where else. The bourgeois-democratic revolution that was to happen in Russia under the pressure of the capitalist dynamics was to eliminate the vestiges of feudalism. This was what Russian disciples of Marx, includ-ing Lenin, believed.

In one version of earlier Marxist schemes concerning Germany in the midcentury, a special case was also envisaged: a government by workers with socialist aspirations could gain power, thanks to the help of peasant masses. Something like that did, in fact, happen, not in Germany but in Russia; and this might have served as a Marxist legitimation for the socialist character of their revolution. But Marx and Engels had another prediction, specifically addressed to Russia of the early 1880s. According to them, a revolution in Russia could occur and trigger a proletarian rev-olution in the West, but the two would have to complement each other for a socialist orientation (based on the Russian land commune) of the Russian revolution to become possible. In other words, the unique, but still primitive, Russian conditions would not carry a socialist revolution on their own. This view can be found in a collection of texts by Marx and Engels relevant to this chapter's themes.[4] Russian Marxists also knew and often debated a dire prediction from Engels, who had studied the case of Thomas Muntzer, the leader of a rebellion of German peasants in 1525. Engels mused about the tragic fate that befalls revolutionary lead-ers who attain power prematurely, that is, before the conditions are ripe for realization of their ideals. Such revolutionary leaders might find themselves "irretrievably lost."[5]

Considerations like these were sufficient for the development of capi-talism in Russia to be closely watched by the Russian Marxists, because it was capitalism that would bring them nearer to their own objectives. No wonder that the eagerness to see these objectives getting closer prompted some Marxists, young Lenin among them, to exaggerate quite consider-ably the level of capitalist development in Russia. But this only illustrates the hopes Marxists pinned precisely on capitalism. Marx's opinion that if a specifically Russian "slippage" into a premature power takeover by socialists occurred, its success would be explicitly conditioned on revolu-tions in the West, was largely shared by Russian Social Democrats. The

---

4. Theodor Shanin, ed., *Late Marx and the Russian Road* (London, 1983), p. 139.
5. Frederic Engels, Preface to *The Peasant War in Germany* (New York, 1966).

West, on the other side (or its most developed countries), was considered more or less ripe or getting ready for such a revolution, but seemed to need a trigger, or so Marx implied in the text I just referred to. This being so, Lenin, well aware of Russia's backwardness but also of its revolutionary potential, could reach the conclusion that the initial revolutionary breakthrough could in fact happen in Russia—precisely because it was underdeveloped and therefore a "weak link" in the world imperialist chain. Still unfit for the real thing, Russia could nevertheless serve as the trigger Marx and Engels were talking about for the higher-placed Western models to step into the revolutionary wave and transform it into a socialist reality. This was a precondition for the survival in Russia of its revolutionary potential.

These reflections were actually hypothetical projections. On the eve of the February revolution, Lenin did not yet know whether he would live to see anything revolutionary at all—West or East. The most realistic scenario for Russia, thought Lenin, was for that country to replicate, first, a version of the "bourgeois democratic revolution" that had brought or was pushing developed countries into a democratic era. Without this stage, there was no way into a socialist future. The socialist society had to be a postcapitalist development—certainly not the other way around.

So this was not just the Menshevik approach. Lenin shared it fully, and it made sense—whether Marxist or not—for a country that still had enough trouble in becoming capitalist. But Lenin's analysis faced a warning light, triggered by the experiences of the revolution in 1905. It made him doubt the ability and will of Russian liberals to lead such a revolution. Here was the beginning of a further deepening of his conflict—both immediately and, even more so, potentially—with the Mensheviks. The events of 1917 actually looked to Lenin like a confirmation of his misgivings: the bourgeoisie democratic revolution had arrived but was already fading because of the absence of a resolute carrier.

LENIN'S TURNABOUT:
BUILDING SOCIALISM WITH CAPITALIST HANDS

With Lenin enduring today, in Russia and elsewhere, a fate probably worse than Marx's, many may not care about his views; but we will still ask the same question about him that we did in regard to Marx: What would he have said if he could, miraculously, return to Russia and see all the changes there? In fact, he was saying quite a lot already in 1922. I argued elsewhere that more than one Leninism existed, and, as far as testaments go, the only valid one is the last. I dealt with this in *Lenin's Last Struggle,*[6] but the essence of the testament could be heard quite clearly already during the Eleventh Party Congress, the last Lenin attended. His speech there on March 27, 1922, was somewhat repetitive, which was uncharacteristic for a meticulous preparer such as he. Lenin himself mentioned to the listeners that he was not well.

His message in this and some earlier speeches was as follows: First, learn to run the economy; notably, learn from the international and local private capitalists, even from the lowly employees in a commercial firm, even from former "white guardsmen" if they performed well—all in order to prove to the peasants that the new masters know how to run things to the peasants' advantage. Do this or else. The "or else" note was clearly audible in a lengthy quote in which Lenin said, in substance: "Either we pass the exam of competition with the private sectors, or there will be a *proval*," best translated as "flop." Logically, he raised in the same context the problem of "state capitalism" (an idea he had launched in the spring of 1918), which he clearly favored—if the new state could learn "to keep state capitalism in certain limits." In that same speech, Lenin preached the readiness "to redo things ten times over, if necessary," in order to correct erroneous policies, and those policies; he said, should proceed "infinitely slower than we believed before" and, actually, not faster than the peasants could adapt to and assimilate. It is also entirely forgotten that the same congress—and Lenin in his speech—raised the problem of getting the party out of administration and primarily into political leadership—implying that administration should be left to professional bureaucrats, to the forces of "state capitalism," to the cooperative organizations.

Such are some essentials of the last version of Leninism, to which should be added the whole crop of ideas that he expressed in his "testament" less than a year later, notably, his powerful warning concerning the nationalities.[7] That it all looked alarming to Lenin and in need of urgent new programs and measures is clear from the state of affairs that

---

6. Moshe Lewin, *Lenin's Last Struggle* (New York, 1968).

7. See *Lenin's Last Struggle,* ibid.

he characterized to the same congress in the following terms: "The car is heading not exactly, sometimes not at all, in the direction the driver who sits at the wheel imagines it to be."[8]

The fact that Lenin quite clearly said no to much of the future policy cannot be wiped out from historical recollection. The same applies to the ideas expressed by other leaders—all of whom, paradoxically, came initially from the party's left wing—about democratizing the party. The most elaborate was the project by Ossinski,[9] published in *Pravda* under the title "What Has to Be Done for the Realization of Proletarian Democracy"—which simply meant democracy in the party. He had the foresight to propose rules of a democratic game in the party as a means to saving it as a political organization. The article seems to have been forgotten; I have never seen it quoted. Of course, Lenin's interdiction of factions three months later did not help, but he did not mention this rule anymore when he wrote the testament. Even more, there is a clear sign of his rethinking even of this. During the same Eleventh Congress, Lenin reminded some opponents of debates that, without freedom of political debate, the party would not be able to function.

This was the way a number of leaders, including Lenin, went about executing a change of course for the Soviet Union, until Stalin won his bid for ideological (as well as political) supremacy and did change the formula—but in a quite different direction (maybe the one Lenin suspected "the car was heading in" already). At a time when the historical leader was so alarmed, his unwanted heir was preparing his own version of things to come. For the moment it sounded simple and reassuring, and was meant to be so. Launched at the end of 1924, Stalin's thesis signified that the ideological complexity was over. From then on, it was to be understood that socialism could and would be built in Russia alone. Stalin's revision worked well for him politically, but the system he produced proved the reassuring formula to be false. What actually did happen reflected the failure of the Western patterns or ideology on Russian soil: first, instead of just toppling the backward organization, capitalism itself was nipped in the bud. Development of productive forces was introduced by a different force—a plebeian absolutist state and its bureaucracy. The outcome in the political sphere was, in

---

8. *Protocols,* 11th Party Congress, pp. 18–19.

9. *Pravda,* December 29, 1920, pp. 2–3.

many ways, a cross between older-style absolutism and capitalist indus-trial authoritarianism, culminating—as seen and felt by those in the lower classes—in a regime akin in many ways to an older-style bondage.

Paradoxically, the toppling of the still-weak capitalism left the new regime perched on the most backward parts of the previous agrarian nexus. It was on the predominantly rural-agrarian social and economic base (without *pomeshchiki* and private entrepreneurs) that the new sys-tem—especially Stalin's leg of it—flourished into a very special state system. This system still exhibited features of an agrarian despotism—a traditional way of ruling over rural civilizations. It turned out that this was to be a provisional stage, to be followed by another that could not be called "agrarian despotism" anymore. It became predominantly urban, industrial and was run by a coterie of bureaucrats and experts.

Compared to the previous personal despotism, the latest version was much more advanced. Still, this was a *sui generis* new absolutism, a bureau-cratic one, defying existing theories but still responding to a certain intu-ition in Marx's theoretical effort about the probability of an additional basic formation that he called "Asian despotism," and he agonized end-lessly about its character. But that was based on models from quite ancient history, whereas Russia was firmly committed to the most advanced industrialism and, hence, a social structure that could not fit the ancient models, though it still could have something in common with them. The fervent industrializers skipped stages that they defined in their preferred ideological terms. They did make a thrust into the industrial age, but what they "skipped over" was democracy—and they did not seem bothered by this. Democracy is not always available, even when more usual forms of capitalism prevail. But without democracy and without a market econ-omy, we were in a bureau-industrial absolutist phase, which the officially adopted ideological definition was clearly and inappropriately misplacing on the ladder of commonly known social organizations.

We can therefore return again to the contention, initially shared by most Russian social democrats, that socialism in Russia could not suc-ceed without a successful revolution somewhere in the West. This turned out to be basically correct; therefore, there is no need to fault the Marxist conception that saw "maturity" as a precondition for socialist aspirations or, conversely, to doubt the conception of "prematurity" as a warning against precipitous actions.

Now, Lenin's revolutionary takeover can certainly be seen as "premature" in this perspective—leading to the conclusion that he, Lenin, "should not have done this" and he was guilty of "a catastrophe" because "he did this." There is some logic to that argument—but no relation to what was happening in 1917. The situation in Russia was characterized by a downfall of, first, tsarism, almost of its own weight; next came the downfall of political democracy, again, more of its own weight than under Bolshevik pressure. A catastrophe was therefore already in the making—and very plausibly a civil war, which the Provisional Government and the forces behind it would not have won.

Once the Bolsheviks were in power—especially after the Civil War—Russian "reality" caught up with them, too. First, Lenin himself began reworking and readapting his conceptions and programs, and, next, Russia actually responded in a Russian way to the Russian syndrome by reviving and developing a powerful state. Consequently, ideology was not just readapted but subsequently manipulated to fit realities of power and to express them in some ways, by using different ideological constructs. To put it succinctly, the socialist ideology was increasingly used as camouflage for the nationalist and statist ideologies, which were the real credos. The noncapitalist character of the system seemed to be expressed by the socialist ideas; but with "nationalization"—not "socialization"—having been the basis of the system's power, it was the bureaucracy, not the producers, that got the upper hand (even as speeches about "Soviet democracy" eventually stopped producing even good jokes).

So if there actually was more than one "flop" (*proval*), then a later one was caused by the leaders' disregarding of the wishes of the founder, who wanted the revolution to be a radical one, while it was occurring, and then insistently demanded to moderate it quite profoundly, in order for it to last. "No third revolution," "no communism in the countryside," "no shooting from the hip," "better less but better," and "learn to trade"—these are quotes that tell much of the story, which amounts to Lenin having delivered a clear message that after the revolution there should be neither "leaping" nor "skipping." It will take some time for today's Russians to erect a monument for Lenin in "de-Leninized" St. Petersburg—and, of course, they should not rush. But this may still happen.

ONE IDEOLOGY WAS NOT ENOUGH
TO HIDE THE TRUTH

Growing tensions between the initial ideology and the realities of the country and of the power configuration provided the source for constant shifts of political and ideological battle lines; drove people to opposing stances; and commanded, as we saw, much of Lenin's reflections, as he perceived more clearly than most the dilemmas and menaces involved. Trying to keep power and remain faithful to ideological premises demanded the discovery of an appropriate political strategy to bridge the gap between the two. The sketch of Lenin's growing unease after the Civil War and the evolving new outlook and program showed his way of dealing with the dilemmas. Ideology had to be trimmed of what the country was not ready for—and this was what he was doing. He thereby tried to stem the powerful trend of "statization" that constantly narrowed the choices and kept forcing a reorientation of the whole system to and around state power and its mainstays. The growing role of this "mechanism" of sheer power was represented by important elements inside the party who were less interested in the original creed and more so in the new possibilities afforded by the tools of power. For them, the tools were becoming the very aim of their action. That is one of the main features to which I return often in other chapters.

Another theme of interest for the whole of the Soviet period was the character of the state's economic policies. Those were widely accepted and believed to be socialist in inspiration, but they landed the country in an obviously low-productivity economy—one can even say a low-productivity–high-waste system—and not just in the economy. It was, in many ways, particularly wasteful of human resources. Lenin often stated that only an economic system with a higher productivity of labor could claim to be "superior"; he could not see a low-productivity system as being socialist at all. I have already discussed the idea that Stalin's system—despite, or maybe because of, its furious building tempos—perpetuated a historical Russian pattern of large-scale action with an extensive and prodigal, rather than thrifty, use (and abuse) of resources, not just in agriculture but even in the industrial sectors. The leaders repeated in speeches the hope to achieve their ambitious goals by combining "the Russian revolutionary sweep (*razmakh*) with the American business acumen (*delovitost*)"; they got the *razmakh,* all right.

Despite achievements, in particular in producing a highly competent scientific establishment, much of which was wasted on the needs of the military, the "extensive" features were not overcome after Stalin, even when Russia astonished the world with its *Sputnik* spacecraft and reached the status of a superpower. The scientists could build an excellent prototype of a supercomputer, but industry could not make it into an available industrial product. This feature is just a hint of problems we already dealt with and will return to, especially in chapter 13.

In light of the reasoning presented thus far, we realize that the study of the Soviet system presents us with an interesting phenomenon of *mislabeling*—a rather gentle term for what was a rather large-scale mystification. The ideological packaging was so effective that the system successfully "evaded" being seen in terms and concepts adequate to reality and managed to induce many people to stick instead to the labels. It was not difficult, for instance, to show that the system was not "Soviet"—had it been Soviet, it would have been a form of democracy, as "promised" in slogans and depicted in propaganda. It was perhaps more difficult to see through the claim of "planning," although the economy was not "planned," and this is not too difficult to prove: A system that tried to fix a million or more prices on arbitrary grounds, which led constantly not just to one or another imbalance but to a damaging wholesale *system of imbalances,* is not a planner. Actually, research shows that the bureaucratic maze was skillfully distorting and evading the planning targets, and that the targets themselves could not but stay in each other's way. The widely used term *nationalization* is also imprecise, because what we observed is much better rendered by *statization* (and *bureaucratization*), given that the nation would not and could not be in the driver's seat. Pursuing this argument, one must discard, once again, also the broader concept of socialism quite categorically—the system being a case of a massive dispossession of the producers of rights in politics and the economy, instead of the massive empowering that the ideology aimed at. The system of more or less complete "nationalization" meant that it was the state that "employed society" in its service, instead of the process being the other way around. Here, the often-used concept of "state socialism" as applied to Russia does not fit the bill; a state behaving as if it owned its own society belongs to a different, much earlier age. The "classically" subjugated role of most producers and consumers is as antithetical to socialism as is the political domination by any group. Dragging Marx into this is a case of disturbing the peace of a defunct thinker by irresponsible quoting. The continuing popularity of the phenomenal mislabeling (leading to so many wrong conclusions) is a puzzle worth pondering, but this is a separate problem.

The Russians who enlighten us today with an eager anti-Leninism and anticommunism that is so pleasing to some Western conservative ears are engaging in a very interesting exercise of juggling myths: from a regime they knew to have been mendacious they take its myths and its lies and then declare themselves opponents of what never really existed. They saw socialism and it did not work, so they now want capitalism because it is more advanced. Capitalism is certainly more advanced than what they got—but more advanced than what? The Soviet regime, created in the historical conditions of Russia, could not fare well when put in the mirror of Western capitalism—except maybe during the Great Depression. But it was during the same Great Depression in the West that the initial ideals and ideologies of the prerevolutionary and the revolutionary eras were already being eradicated or "frozen" into clichés beyond any recognition. No wonder. The system that was emerging there would have been gravely endangered if those ideologies and their spokesmen had been allowed freedom of expression, let alone organizational forms. On the other hand, as the founding ideology did not respond to the needs of reality, other ideological props had to be found and put to use.

THE PARTY AS IDEOLOGICAL "SAFEKEEPER"

We should now reexamine the historical stage when it turned out that capitalism "did not oblige" and did not collapse in the West after World War I. A set of consequences, mostly well known, began to flow from that fact. It would not be right to say that most of the leaders just "dumped" or "betrayed" the ideal in order to retain power, although a growing number did. They still had enough of a message for their people, but it had to be achieved now through a more complex strategy of transition and searching for original ways to preserve intact the initial goals and continue to pursue them. With the mass of the population still belonging in "another age," the party seemed the only, but appropriate, politico-ideological agency that could be entrusted with "safekeeping" the initial message for a transitional period, notably, by controlling the main sources of power—especially the state machinery. It should be remembered that the party's functions, as initially conceived, were of a quite different character—a fact that was lost on the leaders and forgotten by many students of this organization and regime. There were no grounds for ascribing to this party any kind of a predetermined trajectory that it did not really possess, but the safekeeping function turned out to be an illusion. A political party, soon to be better characterized as a politico-administrative one, was no shrine but a historical product— and, by definition, a powerhouse. It could not but end in formulating and representing interests, notably, of the ruling groups; and it had to change, adapt, or jettison ideologies that did not serve this purpose (except for enshrining some personality or tenets, which is precisely what it did in the most literal sense). There were alternative courses of action, but even the available alternatives were still in the framework of an authoritarian polity—not from some democratic dreamland. Still, *authoritarian,* like the term *democratic,* covers many different realities, which actually can make quite a difference.

The fact remains that the sociology of political power produces disquieting effects anywhere, and Bolsheviks could be and often were aware of and worried by phenomena like etatization, bureaucratization, and despotization, to name a few. This is why such Bolsheviks, such Marxists, and Marxism itself had to be destroyed by the effects of this "safekeeping"—quite logically, to a large extent—when instead of "socializing" the bureaucracy, the latter kept etatizing the system and themselves, and these effects had to be camouflaged at any price. Whatever the terms used—including those from a truncated initial evangel— what had to come in this situation was an "ideology" in one of its classical definitions: a veil. But these are all condensed versions of a process that took some time, although not really too long.

The transition to the NEP is an interesting illustration of the fact that the party was then still a potent political organization of considerable resolve and potential for action. This transition was executed in atrocious conditions, was an incredibly difficult strategy to conceive and put into action, and for some was even unthinkable. Yet there were debates, decisions, experimentation, flexibility, and, finally, the transition and the discovery of means and ways, whereas the switch to the industrialization stage and the collectivization of the peasants was already decreed, rather than voted in after reflection and deliberations.

Out came a full-fledged usurper bureaucratic colossus, hierarchical and monopolistic, a new type of usuper of social power for the benefit of the new ruling model and vision—in fact, for the benefit of a new incarnation of a group interest that, although not private, still exercised quasi-proprietary rights for the whole national economy.

Opposition to this course of events was real, from Lenin himself, many party cadres, and different layers in the population. The maintenance of sufficiently independent economic and intellectual sectors, a continuation of political life in the party, and a more real respect for science (experts) were all there to some degree during the NEP. As a real system, the NEP was endowed with enough features that differentiated it from what preceded and from what was to come. The deep turn that occurred in the late 1920s toward such dramatically different policies should make clear that the new line saw itself as poles apart from anything and everything the NEP period stood for. The decisions taken then were fatal and drastic, but one should not mistake them for the only or the best available. That important new measures *had* to be taken in 1928–29 and that this was a real turning point can be argued very plausibly. There also were, no doubt, favorable conditions for the exclusion of markets from the economic model and of society from politics, but the particular strategies that were selected were anything but fatalistically inscribed in some "original sin."

The famous French novelist André Gide was one of the quite numerous foreigners who believed in the validity and progressiveness of the widely accepted principles, but his case can also serve as a good illustration of the images that the Soviet experience was beaming to the rest of the world and of the way some foreign intellectuals received these images. Gide's "visit to the USSR" in 1934 was dominated by his impression of the uplifting of a huge country "from darkness to light"—a seeming epic. But already his "Retours de l'USSR" a few years later attested to the emergence of something else: indoctrination and domination of the masses—the supposed object of enlightenment and emancipation—now became the prevailing reality of the system.[10]

As in any kind of sociopolitical development, observers have to ask and

---

10. André Gide spoke to the first congress of the Soviet writers on December 1, 1934; see his *Retours de l'USSR* (Paris, 1936).

answer several questions: Who is in power? In whose interests? How do they rule? If Gide or others could not see clearly earlier and therefore did not ask or answer such questions earlier, several years later answers could be provided: The power base was the state machinery that grew by leaps in numbers and power as the industrial building was surging ahead. The question of whose interests were being served demands a more discerning answer: There was, in the longer run, a measure of emancipation there, in many ways and for many people, but it occurred in relation to a largely illiterate baseline, and most of it happened after Stalin's death. Even so, the chief benefactor of the emancipation from Stalin's rule was the bureaucracy for whom the road to full domination of the state, previously blocked by Stalin's power, was now largely open. The making of the "Soviet bureaucratic absolutism" is a convenient way to characterize the process. It was, in the first place, the shifting of power of the upper layers, with not much of it left—especially not of the political type—to the lower ranks. Yet even lower down, amidst at least some of the lowly officials, a compensatory effect was at work: Very often, the lowly official acquired over the years something like a proprietory right to his office—which gave him an irritating but tangible power over customers, especially the power of not serving them properly, or of using the power over scarce goods for all kinds of scams. It was a result, as the party economist Preobrazhenski anticipated, of "primitive accumulation," but it was not to be an accumulation of means for socialism. Paradoxically, not only was socialism omitted but the interests of the ruling system were also badly served by this accumulation, as recent events proved quite conclusively. It was, by any criterion, a failed accumulation, although certainly a very primitive one.

SOVIET SOCIALISM AND THE RUSSIAN PAST

As we reflect about the metamorphoses of Soviet ideology, it is worth exploring the extent to which the Russian historical tradition, certainly an influence in the making of the Soviet system, also "participated" in suffusing its socialist concepts with some national flavors, or had its own historical practices clad in a socialist garment. The principle and practice of "nationalization"—making the state into the owner of the main productive assets of the country—is a good example of the continuity of historical practices and the osmosis of different, even hostile, ideological products. On the face of it, nationalization belongs to the revolutionary creed, although in fact the takeover of assets by the state was considered in socialist theory to be a bourgeois-democratic principle—a fact that is often overlooked. But this clarification is beyond the point here. The main point is that the Soviet system made state ownership into its basic principle and proof of its socialist character.

This interplay with the past does not concern only ideology. Naturally, a whole social structure actually wandered over—how else?—to the new regime: peasants, officials, experts, intellectuals—carrying in their minds powerful cultural and political traditions. Many of the unsolved problems of the previous era emerged in Bolshevik Russia, and some of the factors that brought the tsarist state down continued to weigh on the destinies of the new regime. When in crisis—as during World War I—both the tsarist and the Provisional governments used forceful methods in trying to overcome social fragmentation, economic disintegration, peasant inertia, and unrest. They centralized, etatized, controlled, and suppressed market forces. The new regime had even more troubles to cope with, not only during the Civil War but well beyond it. They continued a similar line of state controls, but now with a different ideological justification and ambition.

Nevertheless, this reflection prompts us to attenuate the weight of ideological motivations and the otherwise undeniable role of "socialism" and "Marxism-Leninism" in the shaping of the Soviet system and to reemphasize the role of continuities with different "chunks" of Russian history. This would mean that the "Great Retreat" that Nicholas Timashev observed and placed in the mid-1930s was already at work much earlier.[11] This becomes apparent not only when dealing with the problem of nationalities and the creation of the USSR in 1922–24 (as explored in chapter 12) but also through the channel of Stalin's new ideological canon about the feasibility of "socialism in one country," which made its first, initially almost unnoticed appearance at the end of 1924. Both cases, especially when viewed in tandem, carried the unmistakable seal of the readoption of a centralized-statehood tradition. With it came rather easily a Russia-oriented nationalism.

The fairly self-evident thesis about the pervasive presence of "the past" should not be mistaken for the rewriting of tsarist history (rather fashionable these days in Russia) that ascribes to the tsarist past some

---

11. Nicholas S. Timashev, *The Great Retreat: The Growth and Decline of Communism in Russia* (New York, 1946).

mythical vitality undermined by pernicious forces. As far as the old regime is concerned, this myth will keep us on a false trail. The inept tsarist government, a rotten imperial court, a flawed army, the decomposing and backward-looking ruling class, an atrociously neglected peasantry, the weakness of democratic traditions and forces, the backward economy—all of these were structural deficiencies, not mere errors.

It is true that a hectic capitalist development was proceeding, often impressively, in Russia. But, as comparison with Germany can show, there was a peculiar twist to this dynamism. In the case of Germany, capitalism was developing powerfully, but it grew into and merged with the previous conservative political structure, "modernized" its economic policies, and actually strengthened it. In the case of Russia, "the market forces"—including entrepreneurs, merchants, and other constituents of the capitalist sector—were actually much weaker and much more dependent on foreigners, and although these forces were not antitsarist in a direct sense and were ready to cooperate with the changing economic climate, they did not "grow into" the semifeudal structures and did not manage to "modernize" them. Hence, the market forces actually weakened the old regime—an outcome entirely different from the German story. The lack of credibility of Soviet propagandist claims and their denial of many achievements of prerevolutionary Russia cannot be used to reverse the fact that the edifice was rotten and that no "pernicious force" toppled it; it fell of its own weight.

Enter a very new player: the revolutionary ideology. Its initial impact was powerful, and the message of "a new era" was believed by many friends and foes. But after the Civil War the initial ideological framework found itself confronted with Russian circumstances. A process of readaptation began and then bifurcated. The thinking of Lenin produced a version of readaptation and strategies to go with it. So first, already before the Civil War, came Lenin's vague idea of "state capitalism," replaced during the NEP by a whole complex of measures best summed up by an article entitled "Better Less but Better." Bukharin followed up with his message of "we are already overplanning too much" and, in a secret meeting, "you are going to produce a Leviathan state."[12] This other version was also taking shape, inspired by the Civil War. The Stalinist strategies grew out of the anti-Leninist line on the national

---

12. See *Lenin's Last Struggle,* pp. 134–41; for Bukharin's quote, see L. Kaganovich, *Sovetskoe Gosudarstvo i Revoliutsiia Prava* I, 1930, pp. 29–30.

question and the emphasis on a unitary, highly centralized state. The dynamic unleashed by his regime was impressive and could still appear socialist in its inspiration.

A degree of bureaucratization was unavoidable here, and this bureaucratization initially had a considerable dynamic potential of its own. But the refusal of market mechanisms (the admission of small-scale "kolkhoz markets" was important for consumers but only marginally important in the economy) contributed to the depth and scope of the bureaucratization process. The interests of this growing layer of bureaucrats and their monopolistic power were served, as well as justified ideologically, by the ongoing overall nationalization, widely accepted and legitimized as being a socialist concept par excellence. The absence of competing autonomous forces (civil society, economic agencies, and market mechanisms) allowed the type of development we know of, and in the longer run it gave the bureaucracy in the USSR a position unheard of in the twentieth century.

Obviously, no one will deny that transforming the population from lzpti-wearing *muzhiki* into a modern, educated population (however unhappy nowadays with its situation) was achieved under this aegis. The achievements were, at least officially, ascribed to "socialism," and this was rendered more credible inasmuch as anticapitalism (if not necessarily socialism per se) was a deeply seated and widespread attitude in the popular and ruling strata already in tsarist Russia. Such attitudes can be traced in part to the widespread communal land ownership in the peasantry; to the opposition among many of the nobility-gentry to market forces, which undermined their landownership and kept pushing the owners into debt; and to the traditional conceptions in the tsarist court and in influential parts of the tsarist bureaucracy.

Of particular interest is the fact that ownership of all lands by the prince was the source of absolutist power in Russia. The latest tsar and emperor still continued, in many ways, to wield the putative ownership of all real estate and other riches of the country, as it was done, in a very real sense, in earlier stages of history. In other words, a conception of property ownership of the capitalist stage did not yet penetrate the population at large, the rulers, or the bureaucracy. The prince as owner—meaning also the state as the owner of the national wealth—was still present, or at least was far from being washed out of the national conscience. The reverence for, or readiness to defer to, the tsar's authority has, as its central ingredient, the deference to the ruler as owner. An example can help us to follow this line of argument: Prime Minister Kokovtsev addressed to Tsar Nicholas II a memorandum in which he criticized the tsar's unwillingness to adapt to the spirit of new times and phenomena. The tsar's opposition to the Duma was visceral because it "undermined the erstwhile prestige of the Moscovite tsar governing Russia as his own patrimony."[13] Although this conception looked dated to Kokovtsev, the tsar's behavior as an autocrat (*samoderzhets*) was real— even if not realistic—because the base of it, in Nicholas's eyes, was still the *svoia votchina* (his own estate) concept, which he could cling to for another historical moment that would last as long as this idea was not contradicted by a different view of reality widely accepted by the general populace.

State ownership in socialism was to be only a stage in the process leading to "socialization," but, as we saw, the ruling bureaucracy definitely wanted to freeze it in this position—no wonder, since it was the base of their power.[14] In sum, we are facing here an ideological "product" of some complexity. A basically precapitalist (feudal) tenet of sovereign ownership of all state wealth—that capitalist development usually kept breaking down and deeply changing whenever it had the time to do so—became suffused after the revolution with elements of a modern ideology, in service of a hierarchical pyramid of power that was itself reminiscent in many ways of an ancient political structure with a peculiarly Oriental bent to it. At least, this held true insofar as Stalin's period was concerned: The initial imprinting of a development-oriented ideology on an almost precapitalist country ended up in a reversal of ideological tonalities, in favor of a version of statism that stood nearer to the traditional state of affairs, even if the latter was already seriously corroded. The historical frame kept working behind whatever ideological discourse was used by the new regime, and it permeated the whole system and its ideological emanations.

So, in this sense, state ownership in Soviet Russia can be seen as a continuation of an older noncapitalist Russian political tradition, with its concept of a tsar "owning" a whole state that grew out of a princely

---

13. Quoted from Kokovtsev's memoirs by P. Miliukov, *Vospominaniia, 1859–1971*, vol. 2 (New York, 1955), p. 103.

14. For a discussion of the whole knot of problems related to socialist ownership, as viewed by a Polish-born economist, see W. Brus, *Socialist Ownership and Political System* (London, 1975).

estate—exactly as the Moscow princes actually built it. One could understand why Tsar Nicholas II insisted on this notion: It was for him the only base for a credible autocracy.

Bourgeois development in the West (and, to a lesser degree, already in Russia, too) broke the feudal concepts down, but it developed new "public" forms and state-owned sectors, in pace with the trends of "socialization" of the productive assets, as foretold by Marx (one of his best predictions). The different trends transforming the character of ownership in capitalism grew from its own dynamics. The movement of these forms in the Soviet system was different: it went in a direction contrary not only to the trends prevalent in capitalism but also to the ideas and expectations of socialist thinking. The Soviet system embraced state ownership of a deeper and larger scope, but it did not accept the private, public, and mixed forms already available in capitalism. This was due, I suggest, to this system having grown from a different social base—namely, tsarist Russia—and having been aggravated by the retardation and archaization caused by the Civil War. These were the conditions that enabled the "big drive" by the state under Stalin's leadership, during which markets (and the NEP) went overboard and a big leap from a still precapitalist into another noncapitalist system was engineered.

THE PRICE OF HYPOCRISY

The conditions described thus far account for the political and ideological circumstances in which the concept of socialism was losing, in substance, any relation to the reality of the Soviet Union, if ever there was one. But the term *socialist* was widely used, left and right, East and West, in speaking about the USSR. Why? Maybe because this was an excellent argument against socialism. The label *socialist* in relation to Russia took on an ideological character of its own that was both perverse and abusive. It might have been convenient for the West to accept this label as a self-defeating feature of the regime.

"Free-market capitalism" in the West survived its crises and deep structural imbalances and inadequacies thanks especially to two crucial "supportive" factors: primarily, the intervention of the state and, secondarily, the phenomenon called "the USSR." The latter played this paradoxical role in two ways. First, at the time when Soviet socialism was still believable and exhibited faith and dynamism, it, together with socialist

movements in the rest of the world, exercised strong pressure on the capitalist states to intervene and regulate their economies. This first period
and its manifestations in Soviet history were replaced by a clearer picture
beginning from the later stages in Stalin's rule, and from that time on the
second way comes into play.

Independently of what it actually was, the system could be presented
as bogus, and its claims could easily be discredited or unmasked. In this
garb it became an easy target, as did the idea of socialism. With a system
like that, obstinately claiming for itself the credentials of an alternative
and better system, capitalism could remain reassured: the USSR was the
most effective argument against any socialist ideology. Moreover, even
many of the democratic institutions that actually tended to rust and were
in need of constant, vigilant repair seemed to be constantly shining in the
mirror of the "evil empire." With a competitor like that, it was a pleasure
to champion capitalism and easy to keep one's own left sterilized and
one's own liberals tamed.

In the USSR itself the insistence on its socialist credentials instilled a
state of "permanent hypocrisy" as a way of functioning. Proposing irrelevant formal goals when it actually was moving elsewhere eventually led
to a discrediting of both the real and the putative ideological framework.
As the leaders later looked to other, either hidden or open supportive
ideologies, without parting openly with the older creed, it caused the
regime to exhaust its own ability to lie. Any system needs some reserve of
this "resource," but when it dried up, no one would believe the leaders,
even when they finally tried to say a word of truth. Behind this loss of
realism in the ideology, one could discern not only a loss of vitality in the
regime but also powerful internal ailments and imbalances—actually, a
whole system of those—that would, in due course, spread cynicism and
produce an ideological vacuum and a calamitous crisis of values.
Hypocrisy can work, but it does not pay.

There was also a price of ignorance to be paid by both East and West.
Ideology can and often does camouflage reality, but terms used to hide
rather than inform cannot serve as a tool of study. "Ideologically loaded"
terms had a face value for a time; but as the system underwent numerous
and deep transformations (a key idea on which we insist), the original
terms acquired different meanings, including a total loss of substance in
changing circumstances. This is something that scholars and other analysts cannot afford to miss. The powerful propaganda battle during the

cold war detracted from the West's ability to see what the Soviet system's character actually was or was not, and to work out better theories and see more clearly where Russia was heading.

This is why we continue to be saddled with an interesting puzzle: If it was neither capitalist nor socialist, what was the Soviet system after all? This question was already raised in reflecting on what the character of Stalin's social wars was, against whom they were conducted, and with what results. Paraphrasing an old saying, one can embroider: "Tell me whom you are reining in and I will tell who you are!"

If we experience some difficulty in defining what the Soviet system was, there is no doubt about what it was not and could not have been. This is why the widespread, if by now already somewhat muted, slogans about "the demise of socialism and Marxism" that the Soviet collapse was supposed to have heralded are in themselves "pure" ideology and therefore misleading. Socialism as an ideal that aspired to more democracy and higher social ethics never existed anywhere as a system. The rather backward Soviet system had none of socialism's basic attributes. The so-called Soviet, or Communist, regime should be seen as belonging to the class of historical phenomena that combine "underdevelopment" with "statism"—a genus of the bureaucratic species. In the minds of the actors involved, stopping the movement toward market mechanisms in the economy might have had a socialist ring, but in fact it just put the system into a precapitalist stage, operating—when compared to Western countries—a *sui generis* detour, which it is still trying to overcome today.

If and when a more stable market economy emerges in the former USSR, we will be able to conclude that the role of the Soviet period consisted in doing what Russian capitalism initially failed to do: bring about an industrialized, educated urban society ready to switch straight into the more advanced stage of contemporary economic systems. This would represent the closing of a circle rather than the opening of a new phase in the history of humanity—as ideology claimed. It remains, of course, to be seen what version of the contemporary market systems Russia will be able to produce.

THE FACES OF
LEVIATHAN

CHAPTER 9: BUKHARIN'S BUREAUCRATIC
NIGHTMARE

ALTHOUGH BUKHARIN WAS INTERESTED IN THE PROBLEM OF the state early on in his politico-intellectual life—the capitalist state, to be sure—he did not devote any thought to the problem of bureaucracy. Like all the other Bolshevik leaders, he had very little to say on the subject that was going to become, once the Bolsheviks were in power, the real Bolshevik nemesis. After the revolution, Lenin realized quite soon that he had a problem on his hands. He even demanded a census of officials, at least in Moscow, to get some data indispensable for analysis, but such an analysis never really materialized. This theoretical omission cannot be discussed here in depth, but its main ideological roots are quite well known. The "dictatorship of the proletariat" was supposed to end up in the withering away of the state. Bureaucracy, a service layer of the state and of the ruling class, wasn't supposed to represent much of a problem. It would become apparent in just a few years that, far from being some auxiliary and easily mastered factor, it was rather complicated, almost opaque, and totally misunderstood. Bukharin, sometime in 1929 or earlier, was one of those who called for the creation of a whole new administrative science, in order to understand both the arcana of government and the essence of bureaucracy. Its obvious staying power and ability to frustrate the intentions of the leaders of the new regime also kept blurring ever more the previously unclouded vision of the new state as a working class in power and in arms, a sole carrier of statehood. A growing unease kept emerging among some thinkers at the thought that somebody other than the proletariat might serve as the carrier or substitute itself for the legitimate sovereign.

For some time, at least, leaders could shrug off the worry by ascribing the malfunctions of bureaucracy to the habits of the prerevolutionary officialdom that dominated the offices of the new state well into the 1920s. The well-known placebo called *perezhitki* (leftovers) thereby made its appearance. Trotsky was probably the first to question the validity of such a theoretical copout when he raised the problem of bureaucratization in the party in 1923, during the "New Course" debate. He raised quite strongly and provocatively the specter of a political takeover of the party by its apparat—the so-called secretarial array. And it was quite clear that the party, at least, which did not have much of an apparatus of its own, either before the revolution or even during the Civil War, could not have inherited such a phenomenon from the tsarist past. There were, obviously, elements of a carryover, but only in terms of the general historical conditions of the country. The secretarial party machine was a genuine Soviet postrevolutionary product destined for an even more spectacular expansion during the years of forced industrialization.

Bukharin's deep apprehension about the oppressive potential of the modern superstate—as he observed it in the West during World War I —was to remain an important streak in his thinking, as documented by his biographer Stephen F. Cohen. But the revolutionary hopes and War Communist illusions (and some other factors, too, as we shall see, in the early 1920s)[1]—managed to dim his theoretical alertness to produce this almost incredible oversight. In his Civil War writings, he glorified the moves of the Soviet power structure as it paved the way to a new socialist order by adopting the supposedly superior model of a "proletarian-natural," or nonmarket, economy—an important plank in the War Communist ideology. It did not occur to the young theorist that a non-mediated system of direct production-cum-distribution *in natura* would inexorably breed a huge administrative apparatus. This omission could not have been ascribed to his poor understanding of dialectics; the master of dialectics himself shared the same blinkers.

The advent of New Economic Policy (NEP) opened his eyes to the

---

1. For the necessary background material and further elaborations, see Stephen F. Cohen, *Bukharin and the Bolshevik Revolution* (New York, 1973); Moshe Lewin, *Political Undercurrents in Soviet Economic Debates* (Princeton, N.J., 1974); and Moshe Lewin, "Bukharin's Ideas on the Soviet Road to Socialism," *Annali* (Milan, 1973), pp. 914–37.

evil of the *glavki*—the Civil War bureaucratic fortresses that now became an object of negation and opprobrium, as an unacceptable foretaste of a purely bureaucratic system. Still, the phenomenon continued to evade him, although he kept bumping into it through different avenues. Anxiety for the fate of the revolution, in the Russian conditions that did not fit any prepackaged theoretical model, coupled with the skepticism that is the privilege and handicap of any genuine political intellectual, led Bukharin quite early in the Soviet experience to admit the possibility or circumstances that could transform the new elite into a self-closed caste, even class. At this stage, as we know, such thoughts were detached from the problems of bureaucratization. But centralization of power in relatively few hands—yet another pointer in the direction of bureaucracy—was for the moment seen, mainly, as one of the factors causing the hypothetical menace of "sectarization" of the ruling elite.[2]

All those hypothetical stumbling blocks lurking on the historical horizon would come into sharp focus somewhat later and merge with the broad problem of bureaucratism. This would happen when the budding Stalinism would force it on Bukharin's thoughts and sensitivity. But he would have to pass through some not-too-glorious detours, one caused by intoxication with power, another by an all-too-idyllic vision of prospects for the NEP as he formulated them by the mid-1920s. The unglorious chapter in his career of battling Trotsky and the left served as some kind of anaesthetic that blurred his thinking on the chances of the new regime. It was Trotsky who first raised the bureaucratization problem.[3] Unfortunately, as happened also with other problems, if it was Trotsky's theme, it had to be denied at any price.

The left kept going further in its attacks on the regime by raising the vexing theme of "thermidor," or *pererozhdenie*—and for Bukharin, then in the height of his influence, it sounded like a calumny. Degeneration and the need to democratize, as one of the indispensable remedies, were met by Bukharin with emotional and rather demagogic refutations. But

---

2. Bukharin brooded often over the possible "degeneration" of the leading stratum of the party (*pererozhdenie*), although he kept denying it as a reality during his polemics against the left. For his thoughts on the danger of the leading stratum's possible detachment from the masses and transformation into a new "ruling class," see Cohen, *Bukharin*, pp. 143–44; and A. Averbakh, *Revoliutsiia i Kultura*, vol. 2 (Moscow, 1927), p. 176. Averbakh observed that Lenin also had misgivings about the leading stratum.

3. L. Trotsky, *New Course* (New York, 1943).

these battle cries of the left were actually pointing to very real menaces of a different kind of thermidor, first broached more realistically by Rakovsky in his "Letter to Valentinov."[4] Little did both sides understand that these themes—namely, *pererozhdenie* and democratization—should have been unifiers and providers of common ground. Bukharin first realized this in 1928, and when he met Kamenev (clandestinely, he believed), he communicated to Kamenev his disquieting discovery that the differences between left and right were, by now, overshadowed by a new political menace altogether—from inside the party. The left at that moment in time—except for Trotsky, who supposedly had some flash of insight in the same direction—still preferred to stick to the image of the right as "kulak spokesmen," representatives of the rich peasants' interests. They stuck to this bogey until it became irrelevant for both sides.

The other "tranquilizer" that kept Bukharin away from the bureaucratization theme in the mid-1920s was his overly optimistic belief that the correct strategy—the one embodied in the NEP—was finally found. In his programmatic work on "The Road to Socialism and the Worker-Peasant Alliance,"[5] the grand strategy seemed to have been spelled out. With some important corrections made in 1928–29, this program was to remain, in history, as the unrealized alternative strategy to the one adopted by Stalin. Whatever those later corrections concerning accelerated industrialization, among other things, the key remained the same: moving toward socialism "on the rails of the NEP."[6] This necessarily included using the market mechanism in the process of planning and executing the industrialization schemes. The concomitant method and objective was inspired by a vision of socialism (one could even call it a definition) as a pluralist "state-cooperative" agglomerate where state, cooperatives, groups, and individuals dispose of enough rights, which would make a return to any form of War Communism implausible.

With a strategy and vision like that, there didn't seem to be any serious menace of bureaucratism in sight. "The rails of the NEP" seemed, on the contrary, the best insurance against the system—party and state—getting

---

4. Christian Rakovsky, "The Professional Dangers of Power," in *Bolsheviks against Stalin, 1925–1928* (Paris, 1957).

5. *Put' k sotsializmu i raboche-krest'ianskij blok* (Moscow, 1926).

6. The notion of traveling to socialism "through market relations" and "on the rails of the NEP" was postulated in ibid., pp. 64–65, and quoted disapprovingly by F. M. Vaganov, *Pravyjuklon v VKP(b) i ego razgrom, 1928–1930* (Moscow, 1970).

infected with the spirit and foul methods of the *chinovnichestvo*. Viewing things this way, in his halcyon days, Bukharin could, in all naiveté and in his anti-Trotskyite ardor, ask the question aimed at knocking the ground out from under the opponents: From where in the Soviet system can a class suddenly appear that would lead to some thermidor?[7]

Like all the other Bolsheviks who used the "classical" class terms, the *pererozhdenie* (degeneration) could be facilitated by incorrect policies, but it had to be led by some group of the bourgeoisie. The left considered the bureaucratization of the party, as such, a facilitating factor already— but they did not imagine that bureaucracy per se could become such a class. Even in Rakovsky's text, where functionaries of working-class extraction were undergoing a process of embourgeoisement through the impact of factors like power and the "car-and-harem" syndrome (as he put it), they themselves were not becoming a property-owning class and therefore some hope still remained. Thus, Bukharin was not alone in failing to realize, during the NEP years and even later, that the Soviet system could become an administrative organization, thoroughly dominated by a bureaucracy capable of pervading all spheres of life and finally even confiscating for its own benefit the very concept of socialism.

If Bukharin did not pay attention to this kind of horoscope for the Soviet system, he certainly read authors who did just that. Max Weber, Waclaw Makhaisky, and Alexander Bogdanov did envisage the bureaucratization of socialism and the takeover by either bureaucrats or "the intellectuals" or the professional classes, according to each author's choice. Weber put it simply by saying that under socialism the bureaucrat would devour the proletariat, not the other way around.[8] He was so right, at least for a considerable historical period—whereas all the Bolsheviks were barking up the wrong tree.

Bukharin's moment of lucidity did finally come later when he joined the battle against the emerging Stalinism. It was then that he produced his most insightful ideas on bureaucratization, though not on the essence or internal dynamics of bureaucracy itself—Soviet or otherwise.

The year 1928 was dominated by intraparty battles concerning policies

---

7. This ingenious question is in "O Kharaktere nashej revoliutsii," *Bol'shevik,* 19–20 (October 1926), p. 57.

8. For Max Weber's prediction, see H. H. Gerth and C. Wright Mills, *From Max Weber: Essays in Sociology* (London and Boston, 1974), p. 37.

of planning, industrialization, rates of growth, and another huge strategic plank—attitudes toward the peasantry. The broader strategies presented themselves as two alternatives proposing, mainly, either using market mechanisms or resorting to coercive methods, soon to be called "administrative." During this political infighting, Bukharin clamored against the latter alternative, with its orientation on planning as a command system, supertempos, and infatuation with bigness. The prospect of an equally large array of functionaries now began to look really serious.

Each important aspect of the policies as they were adopted pushed into the same direction. The elimination of markets and of the sectors traditionally active through them—namely, the masses of small-scale urban and rural producers, long the hallmark of Russian economic life and still vitally important—tended to produce, as a replacement, hosts of officials. The supertempo orientation and a one-sided preference for heavy industry were so deeply unbalancing that nothing less than a constant interference by the state could provide some modicum of economic activity. And this meant, again, ever new offices.

As is well known, Bukharin posited more modest targets and assailed what he called "overplanning" that entailed the refusal of "spontaneity" of any kind in economic life and the eviction of any and all private sectors. Such planning, of course, meant the end of the NEP. And it also necessitated, as stated in the "Notes of an Economist," "a colossal state apparatus."9

All these considerations were also intimately related to agrarian policies adopted by the Stalinist faction that Bukharin denounced as amounting to "a military-feudal system of exploitation of the peasantry."10 By *feudal* he had in mind something many peasants began to fear in those years: the advent of a "new serfdom," as peasants often said themselves. If the term *serfdom* could not have meant at that time the return of the landowning aristocracy, it still could apply to central and local surrogate-lords to whom wholesale collectivization delivered the peasants almost gagged and fettered.

The massive so-called collectivization quickly turned into a full-fledged statization that produced a cascade of sequels that were already

9. Most of these ideas are in "Notes of an Economist," *Pravda,* September 12, 1928.

10. The source for Bukharin's accusation about the "military-feudal exploitation of the peasantry" is Rudzutak, *16tyj s'ezd VKP(b), sten.otchet* (Moscow, 1930), p. 200.

amply commented on in a comprehensive literature. The main source of interminable problems caused by the ill-fated collectivization stemmed mainly from one root cause: loss of interest in the land and in farming among the peasants. Hence, a constant battle resulted between the state, which was eager to squeeze resources without paying for them, and the peasants, who were trying to mind their own business, somehow feed their families, or get out of the countryside altogether. This situation brings us back to our problem of local bureaucratic chieftains. Nothing but administrative-bureaucratic pressures and a further increase in the power, often very arbitrary, of the bureaucracy could keep the agrarian system of this kind in one piece.

The counterpart of the whole process reverberated throughout the Soviet system. The powerlessness of the producer and the efforts to keep the economic activity afloat without adequate economic incentives, especially when it concerned the majority of the working population, certainly contributed to the hardening of the overall sociopolitical organization into its Stalinist form. The impulses inherent in the forced industrialization, mightily compounded by the scarcity of agricultural products, worked in the same direction that collectivization did.

Bukharin observed and understood the dangerous linkages even when they were only beginning to be felt. The producers' lack of rights and the suppression of "spontaneities" were equally present in War Communism and in Stalinism, although around 1929 even the most unbridled imagination, when already occasionally using the term *Stalinism,* could not see what this term portended. But one facet of the growing system—the impersonal one—showed already in the early 1930s the workings of an inbuilt mechanism of reproduction and self-perpetuation. Arbitrariness—today much discussed in the Soviet Union as *proizvol*—was, curiously enough, of a dual character. One stemmed from the traits inherent in the growing personal despotism; the other, from the power of the small and big bureaucrats who were facing a citizenry without rights.

The most telling description of the missteps and malfunctions of bureaucratization was offered by Bukharin, in a semi-Aesopian language that was still possible in 1929, in his *Pravda* article, under the heading of "The Theory of Organized Chaos."[11] This was a survey of German sociological and economic literature dealing with modern industrial organiza-

---

11. "Teoriia organizovannoj beskhoziajstvennosti," *Pravda,* June 30, 1929.

tion and its flaws in the West. These flaws amounted to such a long list of malfunctions of modern bureaucratic formations that the Soviet readers certainly asked themselves whether Bukharin talked here about Germany or about the Soviet Union. But one sentence at the end of the article dispelled the idea that the article was even Aesopian at all. Bukharin stated that the phenomena described could be observed in the Soviet Union. The title of the article, taken from a German author, presented the gist of the phenomenon as "organized chaos," and Bukharin's readers who also knew his 1928 *Pravda* article "Notes of an Economist" easily realized that he thought in similar terms about the Soviet planning. Was it not this "planning" that went for targets specifying numbers of factories to be built without providing for the necessary bricks?

Five years later, when Bukharin still had another chance to say something, however general, about what he saw around him, the "organized chaos" was already a system in full blossom and likely to stay, in some form or other. We do not possess enough material about this period in Bukharin's thinking. By then he must have reflected not only about the problem of bureaucracy but, more generally, about the overall system that actually emerged, instead of the "dictatorship of the proletariat" that never materialized. Was he still trying to find excuses, to consider the phenomena he observed just transitional? The dictatorship as it actually unfolded contained so many baffling characteristics—especially for one of the founders of a socialist republic—that the existing conceptual tools were of little help. This concerned not only the Marxist schools, but also most others available in the Western intellectual arsenal. This situation still applies today, in our own times, and we say more about this in chapter 10. In the meantime, we remain in the dark about what was going on in the minds of Soviet Marxist intellectuals as they faced the realities of the *piatiletkas* under Stalin's aegis. (We do know what Trotsky thought about it all, and he did not always cope better with the essence of the problem than the mute insiders.)

The little we do have is still interesting enough. The last and the most eloquent statement by Bukharin—too short and, again, presented in barely camouflaged semi-Aesopian terms—about the political realities and features of the Soviet system appeared in an article he wrote in 1934 in *Izvestiia,* which he still edited at that time.[12] Something could still be

---

12. Bukharin, "Krizis kapitalisticheskoj sistemy i problema kul'tury," *Izvestiia,* March 30, 1934.

said during the enigmatic year 1934, when gathering clouds coexisted with many hopes connected with the presumed—though not at all documented—"Kirov faction." In his piece, Bukharin seems to be praising, even chanting the glories of "the gigantic apparatus of the state" that carried on its shoulders the task of building socialism. But he also engaged, significantly, in pointing to the very gloomy sides of this "marvel." The gigantic apparatus carried with it the great dangers of bureaucratism; it deployed traits and engaged in methods that we translate as "bureau-pathological" (a term borrowed from Victor Thompson), whereas Bukharin uses the Russian terms *kantseliarsko-biurokraticheskie metody,* referring in both cases to a string of malfunctions. Moreover, very ominously in the Soviet case, this apparatus engaged in "planning" all the vital functions of society, strangling in the process the initiatives, groups, and society at large.

If a reader wondered whether Bukharin was exalting or denouncing the state apparatus, Bukharin helped him by referring to a well-known satirical personage from the famous prerevolutionary satirist Saltykov-Shchedrin, who was not tender toward tsarist bureaucrats. The character of Ugrium-Burcheev, which Bukharin borrowed from Saltykov-Shchedrin to characterize the workings and face of "the gigantic state apparatus,"[13] even if only coincidentally, was telling—and through it Bukharin did not intend at all to ascribe the troublesome bureaucratic iniquities to "leftovers" from the tsarist past. In 1928, in fact, he had already blamed "overcentralization" and the new system of planning in his "Notes." It was not difficult to put two and two together: in Bukharin's view in the late 1920s it was "the bureaucratic-centralistic regulation of the economy"—not the tsarist past—that was at the root of "the organized chaos." In later years it became quite obvious that these kinds of methods were contagious: They infected all the public institutions, including those acting in the sphere of culture and, in a grand way, in the sphere of politics. In this latter domain the process was relatively slow, but it certainly began to gather momentum in the party during the NEP. Two interconnected processes worked in tandem to produce the outcome. The first was observed and commented on by Trotsky in 1923, during the "New Course" debate. In essence, his argument ran as follows: The party is a political organization, and the state apparatus is a straightforward

---

13. Ibid.

administrative bureaucracy, hierarchical in its structure. The party should be run on different principles than a hierarchical command structure; but the Communist Party in power, in the process of organizing, running, and controlling the huge state machinery, got "etatized" by this exercise, becoming ever more similar to the administration it was supposed to guide. The party thus became bureaucratized, and Trotsky saw here a dangerous trend that should have been blocked. Five years later, during his (presumably clandestine) conversations with Kamenev, Bukharin added yet another facet of the same process: by now the party and state merged—*slilis'*—and this, he stated, "was the greatest misfortune."[14]

This statement was very short and therefore cryptic, but one of the sequels of this "misfortune" was that the party apparatus and its leaders—or, eventually, leader—reigned supreme over the party and over the state apparatus and could now eliminate not only any criticism but also the critic or whole groups of critics. Many other consequences of the *sliianie* were not yet clear or not spelled out. In the longer run an obverse phenomenon could be observed, in the form of the growing power of the state apparatus in and over the party itself; that is a point for further discussion. Still, the idea that, for example, Stalin was just an emanation of sorts of the apparatus missed some substantial points.

During the mainly behind-the-scenes debates in 1928 and 1929 between the Bukharinists and the Stalinists, the emotions ran high and the verbal stakes were rising, from statements on economic policies to problems concerning the intraparty regime and, finally, to the assessment of the whole Soviet system. The battle against the "right," later to be coupled in a curious but quite meaningful way with the "left" and combated by Stalinism as its central battle cry against the "Trotskyist-Bukharinist bloc," produced accusations that seemed to have haunted at least some Stalinists. Thanks to the fact that Kaganovich quoted from the proceedings in print, their words were not buried in the archives for decades. Thus, Bukharin's pluralistic conception of the Soviet state, as expressed in "Notes of an Economist" was attacked by the Kaganovich as a program leading to a "bourgeois-democratic state." Bukharin's

---

14. These conversations, from notes taken by Kamenev, were published in *Sotsialistich-eskij Vestnik* 6 (1929), pp. 10–11; and *Sotsialisticheskij Vestnik* 9 (1929), pp. 9–11.

entreaties about the need to make at least some steps toward "a commune-state" were repulsed as a slur on "the Soviet state."

He was right, to a point. The "commune-state" Bukharin was proposing was not a countermodel to some Soviet state, but to what seemed to him a "Leviathan state"—a term he used during the shouting matches in the Politburo, as Kaganovich's quote allows us to surmise.[15] This term must have greatly irked Politburo members—though we do not know how they understood this term, nor what Bukharin had in mind when using it. But we are allowed to guess.

Bukharin's thinking did reflect correctly the unfolding reality of a broad process of bureaucratization and its roots in Soviet reality. No in-depth theory of bureaucracy could be produced by the Bolsheviks, although different empirical data began to be collected and the Commissariat of Inspection (disbanded in 1934) did engage in serious studies of administration, management, and organization. Still, the hectic zigzags of history kept the attention riveted to real class enemies; and after the dismantling of the Civil War *glavki* proved feasible, the main problem with bureaucracy and its worrying malfunctions seemed, during the NEP and some years thereafter, mainly connected to the presence of transplanted tsarist bureaucrats and other remnants of formerly privileged, hence alien classes.

At the sharp turnabout of accelerated industrialization, when all those "alien" elements were drowned in the growing mass of incoming functionaries of the Soviets' own minting, the party's thinking, unprepared for the sudden surge of bureaucratic agencies, still clung to social origin as the culprit of inefficiencies or graft. Inasmuch as this thesis became ever less tenable, the regime turned toward mythical "enemies of the people," whose hostile intentions were not necessarily dependent on class origin.

Industrialization as practiced—Bukharin, as we know, did not miss this point—was one of the key factors that fed the trend. Modern studies in the West (Blau) allow us to discern further sequels of the same origin.[16] As the adopted tempos, being unfeasible, became detrimental,

---

15. The revealing quotes from confidential Politburo meetings are in L. Kaganovich, *Sovetskoe Gosudarstvo i Revoliutsiia Prava* 1, 1930 pp. 29–30.
16. Peter Blau, *On the Nature of Organizations* (New York and London, 1979), esp. pp. 243–62.

and different leaders, at different times (Kuibyshev, Kirov, Ord-zonikidze), became disillusioned, the pressure against tempos deemed *neposilnye* (untenable) kept mounting. It had some success at times, but not enough to change the extensive character of the effort that could cope with the required tempos mainly through concentration on quantity in most walks of life. The main victim of such a tendency was quality. An emphasis on quantity means not just poor quality of products but also poor or mediocre quality of the labor force, whether technicians or managers. At the same time, economic life suffered from endless bottlenecks and breaking points. Here a food crisis, there a transportation or fuel shortage, a labor discipline problem, trouble stemming from overextensions of investments, flight of engineers from shop-floors to offices, flight of peasants from kolkhoz production—the list is long.

This is the right juncture for a reminder about one more special feature of the times, or rather a double feature. On one hand, we witness a "status revolution" operating in favor of professionals and bureaucrats, although ideology still maintained the fiction of the worker-king. On the other, together with the elevation of these layers, "purges" or mass slaughter of the same cadres were in progress, pointing to a contradictory process at work under Stalin's rule—the erection of a superbureaucratic state and a simultaneous antibureaucratic fury.

This was an anomaly and it would not outlast Stalin. It is therefore fitting now to turn our attention to the question of what was passing and what was enduring in all those phenomena that Bukharin observed and that we elaborated on further. A host of enigmas persist, and much research and many new disclosures are necessary before anyone can answer the very numerous questions of Soviet history. Still, an attentive student can conclude already that the phenomenon of Stalinism, if properly defined, was a passing one. It was a product of its time, but one can venture a hypothesis that the same period that produced Stalinism also produced its gravedigger. Some writers hoped that this job would be done by the working class, but this was not to be. It was the much-maligned bureaucracy itself that eliminated most of the features of Stalinism, once Stalin was out of the way. The normal—and even the abnormal—growth of the bureaucracy and of its privileges that occurred under Stalin went on in conditions of considerable social upheaval; and the bureaucracy, still new and quite shaky, had to endure the despotism as long as it was not yet solid enough to cause significant changes in the functioning of the system. One of the functions of the purges, whether intended or not, consisted in preventing such a solidification of the bureaucratic layers. But this solidification was going on anyway. It is the contention here that a stable bureaucratic system and a whimsical autocracy are incompatible in our times, and certainly in the longer run. We will say more about this in the next chapter.

When reflecting recently on the Soviet "administrative system"—this is the term widely used today in the former Soviet Union to denote a regime many are now loathing—the economist G. Popov thought that Stalin and Beria were indispensable features of it. Stalin was the autocrat and carrier of a cultlike despotic power, and Beria was the indispensable terroristic provider of the element of fear.[17]

We believe that the "administrative system" became its real self only *after* these two, and most of what they represented was eliminated. For example, mass terror was gone, and the slaughter of cadres and arbitrariness in relation to an officialdom in its routine activites were stopped. Many institutions of the state were rearranged to fit the preferences of the bureaucracy—at least, of its top layers. In this process, not a few advantages accrued to the citizenry at large. But once settled into its routine, unhindered by fear, the bureaucratic system acquired its shape after Stalin's death, mainly during the 1960s. In this process it began losing its dynamism and, another decade later, the ability to run the country effectively. Stagnation ensued.

Much and many were, in fact, devoured; and yet the worst, as expected by some writers, either did not happen or did not become permanent. Huxley's *Brave New World* did not really materialize; Orwell's *Animal Farm* did occur, but *1984*, finally, did not. Tvardovsky's Vasilii Terkin thought that the celestial bureaucracy was pretty awful, and he preferred to return to the one on earth, presumably because there was still some hope there. The pioneer of the nightmarish prospects of regimented and depersonalized worlds, Zamiatin, saw some of his gloomy

---

17. G. Popov's highly interesting article on the "administrative system" is "S tochki zrenia ekonomista," *Nauka i Zhizn'* 4 (1987), pp. 54–65.

premonitions come true in more than one country, but forty to fifty years later the same countries are on a different track. Social development made the nightmare either impossible or just provisional in the developed countries, including the USSR.

CHAPTER 10: BUREAUCRACY AND THE STALINIST STATE

A S STATED IN THE PREVIOUS CHAPTER, BUREAUCRACY, AS A problem or historical factor, did not play much of a role in Bolshevik thinking. The Bolsheviks' analysis was conducted mostly in terms of social classes, and bureaucracy was not considered a class—or was not supposed to be one. The appearance of bureaucracy as a problem (at first, as "bureaucratism" rather than bureaucracy) came with power and muddled the concepts as well as the realities. An interplay of perceptions in ideological terms with changing political realities (facts of life) is our story, as well as that of the Soviet system at large.

IN A NUTSHELL

We need to consider two key stages. The first involved the discovery of the apparatus—and its crucial force—when ex-tsarist government officials went on strike in 1918 against the new regime. In stage two, the state apparatus became a must, and the cooperation of specialists (experts), obviously from the previous regime, was a painful need and precondition for making the state machinery work. Class composition seemed to be the biggest worry—notably, because officials of the old regime, "alien" both ideologically and in terms of class, were known to epitomize bureaucratism.

For the Bolsheviks, getting "their own cadres"—with the right origin, notably, through a Bolshevik education and proletariatization (*orabochenie*)—seemed to have been a long-run solution to the problem; it proved to be a crucial task ahead. Although such a "class approach" in dealing with the bureaucratic phenomenon continued to be applied, the problem was obviously "bifocal": "proletariatization" of the apparatus (*orabochenie*) or not, inefficiency and bureau-pathology were growing, as were the numbers and costs of officials and administrations. "Bureaucratism" (and "bureaucratization") was becoming over the years a huge problem per se, but attributing bureaucratism to the legacy of the tsarist past and the country's backwardness hindered the emergence of a more potent analysis of bureaucracy as a social and political phenomenon. Proletariatization of the apparatus as the ideologically correct remedy against bureaucratism was proving perfectly useless. Just as the bureaucratic phenomenon has its own thrust and momentum, bureaucracy is more complex than only the list of its much-deplored malfunctions (bureaucratism). Many problems were not due to inefficiency and backwardness alone; they stemmed from previously misunderstood social realities, past and present. A better analysis and better-thought-out policies were needed, but this was not achieved (or seriously attempted) to the very end of the regime.

Opposing factions battled against bureaucratization, especially inside the party: the party apparatus seemed to be taking over the party and thereby deeply changing its character. This kind of discovery led those who studied Western writings or read historical works on the tsarist government to become aware of a worrisome political feature of bureaucracy, namely, its propensity to become a contender for power. The leadership, willy-nilly, did yield some ground. This was done, at first, by a slow process of offering some categories of officials rights previously reserved only for industrial workers. By the late 1920s an average official already earned much more than the average worker, and top officials earned much more than the best-paid workers. In the 1930s a "status revolution" took place that switched the orientation of the regime from workers to officials *as carriers of the state principle,* thus making them the central ideological and political mainstay of the regime. Since the state became the central tenet of Soviet socialism, the class of state servants moved to the foreground in ideology, in pace with their growing power in the state.

Full monopolization of power would be the last stage in this process, although this would happen some decades later. But ideology had already begun to follow reality in the 1920s, by trying to put a veil on the real processes at work. This strategy demanded many manipulations, "loans" from other ideologies, and an eventual dumping of the founders' creed; then, concepts such as socialism and Marxism-Leninism became, especially in the 1930s, simply coextensive with whatever the system was doing at any given time. Many of the system's chief practitioners already used other, more convenient languages and rationales—and not just in private.

Finally, class explanations were pushed aside, in substance, almost entirely. The enemy was now sought (and found) "within," serving foreign "intelligence services" from inside the party and its strongholds. Class origin stopped offering immunity: Doubting, let alone opposing; defending somebody who was accused by "the organs," as the secret services were semi-ironically called; or just formulating things differently—all were already heresy.

As class concepts died, they were replaced by the "demonization principle." Hence, the only method now was not social analysis of any kind but exorcism, a cult, and uprooting by terror: we are, of course, talking about Stalinism. Was Stalinism an emanation of bureaucracy, as was often claimed, notably by Trotsky? There is in Stalinism a considerable ambiguity here: it was undergirded by bureaucracy—of some kind at some stage—but it considered bureaucracy both indispensable (hence, the pampering of the upper layers) and unreliable.

The immensity of the problems related to the bureaucratic phenomenon is well known and has been shown through research and study worldwide. It is known that bureaucratic layers possess their own autonomous momentum (despite an image of their being impartial servants of the state), which means not just an ability to mind and fight for their own interests, but also a proven capacity to head off measures undertaken against them. This is why, despite their growing numbers, cost, and often glaring inefficiencies, they seem to defy policies and measures of control, however severe. Moreover, on an even grander scale, state bureaucracies often succeed in "taming" the absolutism and despotism of rulers by making them follow bureaucratic procedures and routines. Making top bureaucrats out of capricious autocrats would be the aspiration of a bureaucracy behind which was also lurking the potential of bureaucracies themselves to be contenders for a share, if not the fullness, of political power in the state.

Stalin studied the experience of the tsars and was aware of the tendency of bureaucracies to "regulate" absolutism. He was certainly determined not to allow this to happen to him—and was, to some extent, successful on this score. Stalinism was the big obstacle to the transformation of the upper layers of bureaucracy into a ruling class. The essence of Stalin's policy was a strategy of his own and his system's security that tended to and did take on mythological proportions. Hence, security agencies were his favorite tools of uprooting, en masse, presumed or potential enemies—notably, amidst the regime's main levers, the state and party administrations. This was the quintessential Stalinist strategy, which actually deprived the ruling party of its power and treated the state bureaucracy as a chief suspect of sabotage activities against the regime, even if they actually *were, or were becoming, the regime.*

The Stalinist method of bloody purges seemed like the ultimate weapon against the unstoppable growth, power, greed, and malfunctions of the bureaucracy. But we will be able to demonstrate the futility of "the ultimate weapon." Purges, however bloody, were entirely useless as a method for changing bureaucracy's way of being. Weber maintained that, once created, bureaucracy is very difficult to destroy—and, one can add, even to change, especially in Soviet conditions of bureaucratic monopoly over the execution of policies throughout the system. Stalin realized, maybe before others, that the bureaucracy only looked like some transparent pyramid of groups awaiting assignments and easy to control from the top. In fact, the groups tended to split into powerful, difficult-to-coordinate bureaucratic fiefdoms, each aiming at full control over its respective domain and tending, if unopposed, to tear apart the state system, rendering planning not just indispensable but actually not feasible. In sum, though, it was a monopoly over the whole Soviet system that the groups harbored, not so much by design initially but by a spontaneous thrust. When the Soviet bureaucracy, after Stalin's death, finally achieved its goals, it became apparent that it was not capable of planning. It was best at administering, rather "overadministering." The moment it succeeded in becoming *the system,* "total" bureaucratization actually turned out to have been a utopia, at least as far as the Soviet model went.

In any case, a full takeover of the system by the bureaucracy (even if they kept breeding plenty of little Stalins) was not possible, as long as Stalinism under Stalin himself existed. Stalin's image and shadow were so powerful both within and outside the USSR that most observers abroad did not imagine that the Soviet system could function without some Stalin replica. In fact, Stalin and Stalinism were replaced by a profoundly bureaucratic model, leading to a possible confirmation of the idea that Stalin himself must have been "a creature of bureaucracy." We will argue why this was not so.

STAGES AND TRENDS

The society that Lenin inherited and was burdened with after the Civil War was more primitive than the tsarist one had been. In the desperate situation, compounded by the failure of revolutions in the West, the ground was ready—whatever "ism" the central government embraced— to reproduce another version of an "Asiatic despotism." The idea of "socialization," central to any concept of the socialist ideology, thereafter took on the form of "nationalization," without reservations and nuances. Once this happened, one could observe—some even predicted—that the elites at the head of backward countries were condemned to become bureaucracies. In a devastated Russia after the Civil War, concentrating scarce material and intellectual resources at the center and, next (it was hoped), spreading the experience and competence lower down looked like the obvious strategy to follow. But it was also a prescription for the scarce intellectual forces of the country to get sucked into the governmental process and to become part of a hierarchy that had a propensity toward metastatic growth. Something quite contrary to both democratization and socialization did occur, and persisted despite the development of industry and schooling at a somewhat later stage.

Lenin must have realized this potential of his system quite early in the regime's history. He tried to escape the trap first by launching in early 1918 his idea of "state capitalism," which might, by implication, have turned around the danger of an "Asiatic" variety of despotism. The Civil War interrupted this line of thought, to be replaced by the NEP experiment—which Lenin initially saw as another version of state capitalism. Lenin's prescription now became: No third revolution.

He was, in particular, extremely worried by phenomena of bureaucratization in the new state. It was probably one of the factors that made him tell the Eleventh Party Congress that "the car does not drive at all in the direction the driver steers it"[1]—already in 1922! The Bolsheviks were still newcomers to the power game, but, unlike many of his collaborators, Lenin had the courage to admit that the state and its *apparaty* were misunderstood phenomena and, hence, capable of dragging the new regime

---

1. Lenin, *Sochineniia,* 5th ed., vol. 45 (Moscow, 1970), p. 86.

into uncharted and unwanted territory. Notably also, they threatened to carry the regime back to the features of the past, which seemed to penetrate through many visible avenues and barely visible capillaries, despite the resolve to destroy the old governmental machinery and build a new one. In fact, under Lenin and after him, the trends in the administrative machineries continued to move "elsewhere," either spontaneously or as wanted from above, by the ever more powerful new "driver."

The making of the Soviet bureaucratic self, as presided over by the party, was full of painful rifts. The experts of the previous regime (the "bourgeois specialists") were indispensable, especially in the highest and most sensitive administrations, but they could not be trusted. The rulers with good party credentials were not competent enough; they could suppress, but they were dependent on the expertise of their "bourgeois" subordinates and advisors. Both sides hated this situation. This kind of "dual power" should have subsided in due course through the creation and promotion of Soviet-made cadres, but, as we shall see, this failed to happen.

The suspicion of "antiparty" tendencies in the administrations continued unabated, despite the fact that the bourgeoisie specialists were being replaced, especially in the 1930s, by small and big bosses of a more reliable class origin. But the previous (now diminishing) internal rift was compounded or replaced by a new one: in the key administrations, where higher specialization and education were crucial, even the new bosses would still tend to be of "nonproletarian"—especially intellectual or white-collar—origin. On the face of it, this vexing problem should have been solved by a full "rehabilitation" of these nonproletarian, but still Soviet-made, officials. An ideological promotion of this attitude actually did begin, quite aggressively, in the 1920s, initially in relation to the party's own apparatus, notably, in the form of defending party bureaucrats against the attacks by intraparty opposition: they were declared by the ruling majority to be the heart of the party, and an attack against the apparatus was presented as an attack on the party, whatever the social background of the officials.

This, of course, was not a problem of just defending them from the calumnies of the critics (who had a valid point when railing against the bureaucratization of the party). It reflected a growing trend, early on in the Soviet experience, toward the making of an administrative class, inside and outside the party, ever more the real carrier of, first, the "nationalization" principle as socialism and, second, of the state as the sole guarantor of the socialist system. The redefinition of the role of the party apparatus would be followed by a similar "rehabilitation" of the state apparatus at large.

During the 1930s, governmental agencies and their bureaucracies were growing in complexity, evolving elaborate and numerous ranks and categories and an intricate hierarchical structuring. An equally intricate scaffolding of institutions was erected to master the spontaneity and boost the very low level of the performance of the apparat.

When officials from RKI, a government inspectorate, were instructed in the 1920s to inspect and study the lower apparat in the provinces, they admitted that they knew next to nothing about this apparat and what to do about improving their performance. Ia. A. Iakovlev, the new head of the RKI, admitted to being inexperienced; for example, he did not realize that no edict from the center got implemented by the lower bodies if they had not received a clear order from their direct supervisor. His pal Mikoian, the head of Narkomtorg (the commissariat at Commerce), already practiced this art very skillfully and confided in Iakovlev how this was done.[2]

But Iakovlev already knew enough to complain that the apparat seemed to be an "organized barbarity."[3] Particularly critical was the level of the lower agenices. Krinitsky, from the party's organizational department, told a conference of the Union of State Employees that these agencies—including their planning departments—had no professional preparation whatsoever. And they were the ones that fed their superiors with their ignorant reporting.[4] There are, incidentally, plenty of hair-raising stories about such reporting that could be found in the files of the central governmental agencies. Narkomfin, for example, deplored the fact that "the state of reporting from the lower local echelons . . . [was] catastrophic."[5]

Despite the reporting from below being "catastrophic," the pressure from above to report was equally bewildering. The matters that the wretched *nizovka* (local bureaucrats) were asked to report about were ridiculous and their task was impossible. Consequently, it was mostly dis-

---

2. TsGAOR, f.374, e.khr. 6, d.320, interdepartamental consultation about the lower rungs of the apparatus, pp. 91–92.

3. *Partiia v bor'be s biurokratizmon* (Moscow, 1928), p. 44.

4. TsGAOR, f.7709, 1, 2, April 1931, pp. 305–7.

5. A meeting of Narkomfin and RKI, February 2, 1931, in TsGAOR, f.374,6,316, p. 23.

regarded from below, pointing to the obvious conclusion that the top was not capable of getting its act together in coordinating the proliferating summits (*golovki*) of Moscow's offices. The development of a whole system of *uchraspredy* (personnel departments) in the state agencies aimed at training and controlling their personnel was one answer. A description by Commissar of Labor Tsikhon of his own "personnel sector" cadres and his *nomenklatura* (list of offices and officials under his commissariat's autonomous jurisdiction), found in TsGAOR (a State archive),[6] shows how intricate the organization of such a sector was. The system of *nomenklatura*—with its complexities, routines, and absurdities—is another maze. The task of defining and classifying the staffs (the so-called *shtatnoe raspisanie*) for the whole administration looks like a Sisyphean one. Frequent reorganizations and dismissals of officials (*chistki,* or purges), and countless measures to curtail, make cheaper, prohibit proliferation, and simplify, have an agitated history that has not yet been written. Over the years, different departments were established to watch over staffing—finally, in 1935, landing in a "special sector" in Narkomfin, in tandem with the STO (Council of Labor and Defense, no less)—to ensure that no administration could hire more than allowed and pay more than allocated to its *shtat,* the institution's list of personnel positions.[7]

The controls, special attention, surveys, commissions, and task forces were particularly preoccupied with the leading personnel (*otvet-rabotniki*), especially the very top (*rukovodiashchij sostav*) of, first, the top leadership in state administrations and the, next, top ranks in economic institutions. The simultaneous pestering and pampering of them—which finally resulted in both their mass destruction and, equally, a mass promoting of new ones—point to a complex and tortuous relationship and rather desperate moves. This was one important reason, though not the only one, for a flux inside the bureaucracies that was even more pronounced than in the social structure at large—a key feature of the social landscape of the 1930s.

The other key feature—which was new—was the introduction into the administration, through the party and otherwise, of many people of popular extraction. This certainly increased support for the regime among the general populace, but also caused an increased fluidity in the

6. TsGAOR, f.5515,36,6, pp. 71–73.

7. TsGAKh, f.7733,14,1043, p. 62.

ranks, as well as a lowering of the already very low educational standards, especially in the politico-administrative agencies. This made all the more painful the dependence on experts "of alien ideology," in particular in the most crucial sectors of state activity where a high level of professionalism was needed but did not exist in the party's ranks.

The methods of dispatching instructors, plenipotentiaries, and special envoys to check and recheck and, on a larger scale, the campaign style (*kampaneishchina*), were other features of policies in those years. Special task forces, under powerful troubleshooters from the Politburo who wanted to see things done "whatever the cost," were presented as the emblem of the party's administrative prowess. The same applied for "extraordinary organs" (*politotdely*) resorted to in "emergencies"—a strictly military conception, parallel to "strike units" (*udarnye gruppy*)— and asked to apply "shock methods" (*udarnost'*) as a "normal" way of acting. Such methods in those years do explain how many things were, in fact, done on the double—pointing, indirectly, to the leaders' dissatisfaction with the performance (or, rather, indolence, from their point of view) of the routine activities of most regular administrative agencies.

The government was constantly preaching that there was a need for "Bolshevik order" among personnel (*shtaty*) and their budgets, and that rationalization, simplification, and curtailment of paperwork, mechanization, and the introduction of piecework in many offices should help make the "machinery" work systematically and smoothly. The big dream of the central government comes clear in a draft of a decree by the Council of Commissars (September 1929), which required that offices achieve the following: "A firm configuration of jobs, firm composition of staffs, firm salaries for each confirmed post."[8] The predominant term is *firm* (*tverdyi*)—an aspiration obviously in reaction to the flux and the spontaneity that proved so difficult to handle. But it was an impossible dream. Routine work was inefficient and slothful, and political campaigns and shake-ups were wasteful but seemed to achieve something. Thus, the 1930s saw two Soviet models operating simultaneously, showing the inherent "split personality" of the state system, with the one part trying to shake up the other that aimed at predictable and manageable working patterns.

---

8. TsGAOR, 5515,26,31, Narkomtrud.

A more "realistic" result, with longer-term effects, was the "pampering" side of the policies. The reversal of status in favor of officials, as compared with the preferential treatment of workers earlier in the regime's history, continued more or less unopposed. Officially, it was an open, and supposedly innocent, form of "equalizing" the officials with workers in access to lodging, social benefits, and schools and, finally, in conditions of acceptance to party membership. In reality, and eventually in ideology, the trend was quite obviously not about equalizing but about producing a privileged layer and adapting ideology to the reality of the powerholding stratum of top and medium-rank officials. Making the state the centerpiece of the ideology opened the door to putting at the center of things the main state (and party) servants— the leading cadres of higher state bodies. It became official from the late 1920s on that the top-crust figures of the apparat—by now "proletariatized" and socially reliable (Soviet produced)—were to be called "the leading cadres," and hostility toward them was to be treated as antistate policy.

Moreover, it was at least semiformally declared in the mid-1930s that there was no reason anymore for the trade unions to bargain about wages: wage policies were firmly and, supposedly, safely lodged in the reliable hands of the economic management itself. Wages, an important tool of productivity, became an almost exclusive and legitimate preserve of management. Nor were the unions to fuss anymore about distortions of proletarian policies by administrators, as had often been claimed and even officially acknowledged in the 1920s. Such distortions, the new official line ordered, were now successfully overcome, and the trade union should not defend workers but deal with social benefits, cultural activity, and so on, as Stalin enjoined them to do.[9]

The less visible part of the policy went into the making, mastering, and singling out for privileges of the same "leading cadres": They were offered high salaries, sizeable premiums, thirteen months' salary, hidden perks and supplies—and enormous power. They were all very strictly controlled, but they had their own ways of amassing more power and incomes through a skillful manipulation of loopholes and structural fea-

---

9. E. Evreinov, *O svoeobraznom krizise profsoiuzov i ob ikh novykh zadachakh* (Moscow, 1936), pp. 12–13.

tures of the system. They suffered from the controls, but they also learned how to outmaneuver many of those, including the famous system of *nomenklatura*.[10] Nevertheless, the worst in arbitrary despotism made them—and, in particular, their very top layer—into those uniquely powerful slaves always on the brink of catastrophe. Their power and privileges were shadowed by a constant memento mori—until they dispelled the nightmare that filled their heads.

1937–39: KILL THEM ANY WAY YOU LIKE, STILL...

We should now propose some figures showing the growth of officialdom, first for the period 1928–39. This is only a tentative calculation of a few selected indicators, but the growth factor is quite visible. One source calculated a 15 percent (annual, apparently) growth for the 1930s, but it was not clear what categories were included. The figures come from the 1926 population census, from the one of 1959 (which contains data from the unpublished 1939 census), and from articles in *Statisticheskoe Obozrenie*.[11] The figures should be used only as indicators of trends, not as statistically warranted givens.

I have tried to single out from the broader category of "officials" data about the category of "administrative personnel," or—better—blue-collar employees (*sluzhashchie*), that also included teachers, scientists, and medical personnel, who certainly do not qualify as "bureaucrats" or "administrators." "Bosses" (*rukovodiashchie rabotniki*) include the higher or leading ranks of the bureaucratic or administrative offices. *Sluzhashchie* include all white-collar employees drawing a salary.

Thus, here are the number of those employed in "administrative offices" (*uchrezhdeniia*), the number of bosses among them, and the total number of white-collar workers in the labor force.

---

10. *Nomenklatura* relates to a system of nominations where each layer of leadership—from the Central Committee through the ministries and to heads of departments—is assigned responsibility for either direct nominations or the confirmation of candidates presented by the lower echelons. The party's control of the top echelon of officials cannot be underestimated, but many observers overlooked the complexity of the whole system and its numerous countervailing factors which, as in many other parts of the bureaucratic realm, often frustrated the controllers' intentions.

11. *Statisticheskoe Obozrenie* 5, 1928, pp. 92–94.

	ADMINISTRATIVE PERSONNEL	LEADING OFFICIALS	TOTAL WHITE-COLLAR
1928	1,451,564	600,000	3,974,836 [4.8%][a]
1939	7,505,010	1,557,983	13,821,452 [15.5%][a]

[a] *The percentages in brackets show the share of all white-collar workers* (sluzhashchie) *in the total labor force.*

In the table, the figures for "officials," as said, do not include medical, pedagogic, and scientific personnel, whom Soviet statisticians included in the *sluzhashchie* category. Neither do the figures include engineers and technicians employed in the economy who qualify for the category of "white-collar" but not of "bureaucrats" or "administrators," although many of them certainly worked in "offices." Hence, we are focusing on administrative jobs in the government machinery, meaning mostly the administrators (and their staffs) of central and local state agencies who did not directly produce goods (like factories) or dispense services (like schools, hospitals, or stores). The administrators of the latter type, though state employees in the Soviet conditions, did not belong to the state apparatus that we are trying to pinpoint. Calculations can also be made of the number of employees in the central ministries and other top agencies, as well as in regional ones. Further classifications that divide personnel into leading-administrative echelons and personnel who assisted the latter—those being subdivided into "operative" (middle-level) managers and "auxiliary clerical personnel"—are also possible, because there are figures for each of these categories. But they are rarely comparable, because of the lack of clarity in the existing data about who is included at different points in time.

It is clear from the following data that the late 1930s (1937–39) were particularly alarming for the party leadership: general employment in the economy rose 10.3 percent (mainly in commerce, education, and health), and the overall salary fund rose 41 percent. But the number of officials in administrative-managerial positions in the different government offices (*uchrezhdeniia*) rose (between March 1937 and September 1939) 26.6 percent. (The central offices of the USSR, of the republics, and lower down to districts showed a particularly alarming growth in the numbers of officials by more than 50 percent. Their salary fund grew

66.5 percent.) Even more pronounced was the increase in the number of officials in the personnel of trusts, procurement-supply bureaus, and numerous so-called cost-accounting organizations (*khozraschetnye*—servicing the economic enterprises): They grew 35.6 percent. General employment in industry showed growth of only 2.1 percent, but the number of employees in those so-called *khozraschet* organizations serving industry—in other words, those operating on a cost-accounting principle without receiving government subsidies—increased by 26.3 percent. In construction enterprises the overall number of personnel declined, but their *khozraschet* service bureaus grew 29.8 percent. The number in establishments of direct trade grew 16.1 percent, but employees of *khozraschet* 39.3 percent. The general cost of such *khozraschet* organizations grew 50 percent—all in just about two years.[12]

The breaking up during the 1930s of the big ministries into smaller ones and of the big older administrative units into new smaller districts—which continuing growth in the economy required to allow for more flexible management—resulted, again, in more growth of staffs and staffing costs, rather than in outputs and efficiency. An inflation of staffs (*razduvanie shtatov*) occurred because the new smaller agencies (*narkomaty*) simply replicated, automatically, the old, top-heavy, complicated multitier structure, which involved an enormous splintering (*drobimost'*) of supply and marketing offices (the notorious *snaby i sbyty*) and the addition of all kinds of superfluous segments of *apparaty* and all kinds of far-fetched jobs, with an ensuing growth of salaries. The "swelling" was smaller in management offices of production units than in the rest of the officialdom, but even in those offices—as well as in designer and project organizations, in the transportation sector, in urban development, and so on—overemployment and imbalances among different sectors were ripe.

In 1940 another effort was undertaken to reduce the number of officials, notably, by increasing the working hours in offices. This was decreed by the government on June 26, 1940, and was seen as a chance to curtail the staffs and make them more flexible. When the dictator departed, centralization remained and, with it, the heavy weight of bureaucracy. By then, even the serious improvements in standards of education—low standards having been an important factor in the earlier

12. E. Vasil'ev, *Planovoe Khoziaistvo* 9, (1940), pp. 27–28.

formative stages—would not arrest the ailments that kept wrecking the state agencies, among them "institutional inflexibility" (comparable to the hardening of arteries in human beings).[13] Neither would it be possible to control their proverbial *vedomstvennost'*, that is, their rather fierce departmental "patriotism." The efforts to contain, make cheaper, and curtail the officialdom through different control methods and mass purges proved to be of no avail; and the pertinent sources make pathetic reading: The authors expressed bewilderment and helplessness, from the early pronouncements of Lenin through those of Ordzonikidze, of Bukharin in 1934, and in a wealth of publications that appeared, notably, just before the war.

The enormous and unjustified growth, cost proliferation, inefficiency, nepotism, narrow-mindedness, false reporting, inflexibility, and arbitrariness defied all party and other controls. One is temped to derive the "big purges"—Stalin's recourse to the ultimate method of camps and killings—from this impotence in overcoming the bureaucratic maze and the skillful dodging of most government controls and injunctions. But physical elimination of officials did not eliminate the sociology of this layer; no purges could have done this. Material just quoted in *Planovoe Khoziaistvo* illustrates this point convincingly. The purges were a policy that had nothing to do with any serious analysis or relation to reality. The inner tendencies of higher and lower layers of *apparaty* continued, although the quality of their performance dropped sharply, as did their morale. Their ethical world and their psychological equilibrium were certainly impaired, at least in the large circles of the upper bureaucratic layers, because so many of them suffered—having been demoted, exiled, arrested, or executed. Still, their numbers kept growing, and this is why I could present my figures without bothering about the complex problem of the scale of the "turnover" inside the bureaucracy that the purges inflicted.

These traits of the bureaucracy—whatever its resemblance, in many ways, to the tsarist one—could not be ascribed anymore to "the past." They grew from the conditions then present: wholesale nationalization, the elimination of markets and of diversified sectors in the economy and society, and the administrative methods used in planning.

---

13. Marshall E. Dimock, "Bureaucracy Self-examined," in Robert K. Merton et al., eds., *Reader in Bureaucracy* (1952), p. 402.

OLDER THINKERS AND SOVIET REALITIES

A few ideas, especially from Western students of bureaucracy, can enrich the reflection on the trends we describe. Max Weber maintained that domination is inherent in any organization, especially in the big ones.[14] Smaller and simpler organizations allow democratic forms, but once they grow and get complex, a fight for power begins and direct democratic forms lose their character. Political parties are created, but those are about domination, by definition; and this trend tends to subvert democracy. A special structure for administration appears "which of necessity means the exercise of domination" and may become "monocratic" so that all the functionaries are integrated into a hierarchy culminating in one single head.[15] So we do not need Leninism to see phenomena like this.

Similar lessons can be learned from "the iron law of oligarchy," which was formulated by Robert Michels in 1915 and was documented again in the early 1930s by Max Adler,[16] who examined trends in the social-democratic parties and confirmed Michels's findings: The leadership (administration) is needed because of growth and complexity; in due course, enough wealth and power gets amassed to be worth preserving, and this weighty fact discourages policy makers from risking damaging losses. Next comes the stage when the tool gets transformed into an ideal, or aim, per se—thus actually leading to a dumping of the ideal, although lipservice may still be paid to some quite radical formulae.

Wolfgang Mommsen quotes Weber from *Wirtschaft und Gesellschaft,* in which Weber said that "a bureaucracy, once it is fully implanted, belongs to the range of social formations that are most difficult to destroy."[17] A British student of bureaucracy emphasized that bureaucracy was a work environment for millions of people. Work being formative of the very identity of individuals, the bureaucratic world is a powerful social milieu that shapes human beings as a mass. Others have contended that giant bureaucracies are on the level of government, but they are not really part of the national competition and are more a part of the domain of national

---

14. *Max Weber on Law and Society* (New York, 1954; paperback, 1967), pp. 333–37.

15. Ibid,. p. 334.

16. T. Bottomore and P. Goode, eds., *Austro-Marxism* (Oxford, 1978), pp. 229–39.

17. In *Max Weber et la politique allemande* (Paris, 1985), p. 219.

economic planning.[18] These are only a few examples from Western thinkers that point to phenomena observed in the West, anticipating, or partly in common with those observed in the Soviet case.

But in the Soviet conditions, some of the same processes went much farther: Unlike in the West, bureaucracy did become the *polity*. Hence, the bureaucratic mentality became even more powerful a factor in shaping all or most human relations. Also relevant to the Soviet experience is Weber's observation that the absolute dictator "is often completely in the power of his bureaucracy since . . . he has no means of discovering whether his policies are being enforced."[19] This does not contradict the argument about Stalin's antibureaucratic urges. Instead, it acutally anticipates much of the essence of Stalinism, leading me to my idea of "institutional paranoia" writ large: it is a sense of powerlessness, developing in the narrow leadership apex, and later in the one-man apex, that increases or persists as more power is amassed and centralized. Except that, using Weber's definitions of bureaucracy again,[20] Soviet bureaucracy was not "modern" as some were elsewhere, not "a real bureaucracy," which was normally paid in cash. In the Soviet case, the hidden privileges and supplies were actually payments *in natura*—like in ancient subsistence economies—making them into some kind of in-between formation.

It is also worth reflecting on Soviet bureaucracy's "retardation" from another angle: The bureaucrats were the guarantor and main tool in the lifting of a devastated country from misery, and they helped build a state system and its services—all run by bureaucracies. This monopoly over execution of policies was a key problem, only temporarily camouflaged by the supposed control by the party—the supposed maker, and hence "employer," of these bureaucracies. The ideological claim of workers' supervision in the "workers' state" had lost its ability to serve even as a camouflage much earlier. The monopolistic manager of all of the state's resources was executing the thrust to development; and by denying enough freedom of action to autonomous agents—factories, organizations, movements, institutions—this "manager" took direct control over the whole economy-polity-society complex.

---

18. Galbraith quoted by Jacques Elliott, *A General Theory of Bureaucracy* (London and New York, 1977), p. 329. On these points, compare p. 15 and passim of Elliott, but see also the comments on the dangers of bureaucratization, p. 344. The passage with the statement from Galbraith is quoted by Elliott on p. 329.

19. In Hans Gerth and C. Wright Mills, *From Max Weber* (New York, 1944), p. 234.

20. Ibid., pp. 204 sq.

This was bound to lead well beyond its capacity to run effectively and to control. In a system where everything is done by government agencies, not much (or nothing), except in the making of "malfunctions," comes from below. Operating on such a scale without an appropriate societal input was a mighty source of backwardness in itself. It is symptomatic that in the industrial sphere, even when machines such as excavators were available and could have alleviated the burden of primitive toil, it was reported that workers did not want to use them and managers preferred to resort to a crude labor force. That fact was noted, among other places, in a speech by a Central Committee member, Rudzutak, to the Seventeenth Party Congress.[21] He spoke of construction works, but widespread antimechanization trends could be observed in industry, culminating in a powerful thrust inside industry, from both below and above, against innovation and modernization of equipment and of administrative practices. Similar tendencies could be observed, in many ways, all over the bureaucracy.

In this context, it could be illuminating to realize the enormous weight and numbers of *praktiki,* or cadres promoted on the job to run administrations or take up engineering positions on railroads, with trusts, and in factories, but without adequate professional training. For example, they comprised 40 percent of the top and intermediate ranks of the railroads by the end of 1938, at a time when well over three-fourths of those *apparaty* were just freshly promoted to replace the thousands of purged functionaries and specialists.[22] For such cadres, except for the most gifted among them, assimilating the most superficial routines then in practice was the challenge of a lifetime.

One essential feature specific to the Soviet system is by now clear to the reader: because of the state's involvement in running the economy, the bulk of its officials of state and party administrations, the overwhelming majority of whom were party members, were engaged in the economy. We can find here the seeds of future trouble. After the elimination of the NEP, the collectivization of agriculture, and the big industrialization drive, the takeover of the economy by ministerial machineries was complete. This allowed the system to achieve, initially, important targets. But this was management without responsibility for results (except before

---

21. *Semnadsatyj s'ezd VKP(b), Stennograicheskij otchet* (Moscow, 1934), pp. 284–85.

22. *Zhelezodorozhnyi transport v gody industrializatsii USSR, 1926–1941* (Moscow, no date), pp. 309–10.

the party). And it caused the administrations to be forever glutted by functions that these kinds of agencies were not designed for.

As long as there was a Stalin at the top, he could use fear to force people to work—but not to work efficiently. His terror was arbitrary, not really a retribution for anything particular or predictable, and even the best performance was no shield against repressions. The monopoly and supposed cohesion postulated by the totalitarian model in some, at least implied, way was a fiction in these conditions: the "functions" became a basis for the crystallization of powerful departmental vested interests, and the overall system turned out extremely refractory to effective coordination. The perennial bargaining and infighting actually blocked the system's capacity to act, despite the illusion that a strong top leadership in a dictatorship—except for some areas considered top priority, mostly in the realm of security—can always have things its way.

Leroi-Beaulieu already knew how important independent courts could be for the taming of bureaucracy and, maybe, for checking some of its worst features.[23] Checking of the *apparaty* by other *apparaty* could be counterproductive. There is evidence that the key agency for such control—the RKI—was itself afflicted by bureaucratization. The idea of having such courts was a plausible one during the NEP. The reliance, though, on the party as comptroller of the apparat, with the hoped-for help from the masses, was even nearer to the hearts of a number of Bolshevik leaders. But Bolshevism was not there anymore, once the relations of power transformed the party itself into an agency badly in need of being supervised by somebody.

BORROWING FROM HANS ROSENBERG

We have already made the point that much of what was going on in the Soviet *apparaty* was universal. But producing Stalinism was another matter. When reading Hans Rosenberg's *Bureaucracy, Aristocracy, and Autocracy,*[24] one is tempted to use for the Soviet case a variation on his

23. Anatole Leroi-Beaulieu, *L'empire des tsars et les Russes,* 3 vols. (Paris, 1881–1889). This is still an astonishingly valid work. Volume 2 deals with the institutions of the state (notably, in book 4, ch. 1), with the juridical reform of the 1860s. The bureaucracy hated these reforms because they gave the courts an independence that could effectively block or thrust back bureaucratic arbitrariness and power.

24. Hans Rosenberg, *Bureaucracy, Aristocracy, and Autocracy* (Boston, 1966).

theme: "bureaucracy, partocracy, and despotism." As we are aware by now, a two-pronged process was at work in the history of the Soviet system: first, the emergence of despotism (personal power) and, second, stages in the making of something like "bureaucratic absolutism" after Stalin's death and the dismantling of the key feature of personal despotism. However interwoven, these were nevertheless distinctive and, finally, contradictory processes and models of a polity.

Before elaborating further on this duality, it is worth inserting some data on the crucial party apparatus that was also growing larger and more complicated during the 1930s. We see a seemingly incongruous development of "power lines": On one hand was the growing personal power of Stalin, who decided on everything he wanted, in all the meetings of all the bodies. On the other was the swelling (*razbukhanie*) of the party apparatus, which became unwieldy and inefficient as it was shadowing and duplicating the government machinery.[25] The apparatus of the Central Committee was endowed in 1939 with large-scale administrative departments, such as the one for "propaganda and agitation" or the Department for Cadres which, under Malenkov, had forty-five subunits.

Also in 1939, the apparatus of the Central Committee of the Ukraine employed 222 "responsible functionaries" and 90 technical workers. Unfortunately, the source of these data did not provide global figures for the party apparatus of the USSR. This was, as we know, a period when the number of ministries and so-called higher agencies in the government was growing, from 10 in 1924, to 18 in 1936, with a leap to 41 in 1940—(plus state committees with a commissariat status like Gosplan, Grain Procurements, Higher Education, Artistic Affairs—again, no numbers for staffs).[26] To match its controlling ability, the party organization below the central level also created in its apparat numerous branch departments with proliferating numbers of heads, instructors, and technical services.

The units of the sprawling administrative machinery were not enjoying delegation of powers to do the things they were created for—the opposite was true. In internal affairs everything was not just centralized

---

25. Data on the party are from V. G. Kolychev, in D. A. Volkogonov, otvet. red., *Tridtsatye gody: vzgliad iz segodniia* (Moscow, 1990), p. 24.

26. Figures on the number of ministries (*narkomaty*) are from V. P. Naumov (paper presented to the conference on Germany and Russia, held in Philadelphia, September 19–20, 1991.

but even concentrated in a tight-fisted way (*zatsentralizovano*). The Politburo meetings would deal with hundreds of items—obviously, not in any
depth—which included detailed items that did not belong to such a high
level of decision making, and sometimes not to the next lower ones.

We see, therefore, a phenomenon with a Catch-22 quality: the growing Stalinist centralization has as its counterpart, unavoidably, the
growth (overgrowth) of party and state *apparaty,* with their growing
inefficiency. But it also works the other way around: The growth of
large, inefficient bureaucracies seems to call for more centralization.

This internal contradiction of the Stalinist system was also responsible
for the "dual feature" in its modes of functioning. That is, routine and
predictability, preferred by the bureaucratic agencies, was punctuated by
the intrusion of forceful emergency or shock methods, by extraordinary
measures taken by ad hoc "special" agencies, by powerful troubleshooters delegated by Stalin, or by the Politburo after his death. This feature
will continue in the post-Stalinist regime, but in attenuated forms,
mainly in the sphere of national security.

STALIN AND BUREAUCRACY

I reiterate that Stalin was no "creature of bureaucracy," though he built
on bureaucratic structures and used them as best he could. But he may
have been their creature "by negation," in the same sense that he was, to a
large extent, dominated psychologically by the image of Trotsky and
thus was Trotsky's creature. Stalin can be seen as the Antichrist of
bureaucratic structures—and, in this sense, their product. They were
"dedicated" to him, no doubt, but this did not change the underlying
momentum of their development, which went against his system.

Stalin was, rather, the creature of his party, which he himself helped
shape as the general secretary and as master of its apparat. Although he
was not the party's founder, he overwhelmed the small group of top leaders, most of whom supported him, to become a despot dominating the
country and his associates. In this situation the problem of "taking over"
and taming the despot by bureaucracy proved impossible. The same conditions that made society fluid induced the same fluidity into the administrations and constrained their ability to solidify and defend their interests. The enormous structural shifts and a cascade of crises in the early
1930s worked in the opposite direction: They favored the establishment
of the new autocracy rather than a bureaucratic countermodel.

Another factor further deepened the oppressive-despotic features of the political system: the state that "owned and ran" the industry and the rest of the economy. The efforts in the economic field were permeated by a prevalence of state power and the spread of networks of its officials. Markets and civil society of the short-lived NEP having been pushed out, two further models of Soviet history emerged: Stalin's version of an "agrarian despotism" in the shorter run, followed by "a state-bureaucratic monopoly," after the two had coexisted unhappily for a time.

One other trait of the 1930s—the mobilizational character of much of the system's functioning, which was one component of the "dual model" we spoke about—grew from the enormous tasks and their arbitrary character. It was not and could not have been to the bureaucracy's taste, but it actually was a rather efficient antidote to the bureaucracy's predilection for routine. Shaking up the apparat—the main objective of this method— was always the first "commandment" of party bosses. The big purges of the late 1930s brought the method to a paroxysm and directed much of its fury directly against the party and state administrations.

Bureaucracy as a stratum and a powerhouse weathered this ordeal and came out victorious in the longer run, although it still managed to obtain some smaller victories under Stalin when it clipped the wings of some shock campaigns, such as Stakhanovism, which actually aimed at shaking up the bureaucrats by unleashing workers' initiative and pride. In the conditions of Soviet state ownership, bureaucracy was not replaceable. If a problem emerged and was acknowledged, the method was generally the same: Send powerful troubleshooters, the emissaries of autocracy's most reliable device, to interfere and to solve problems; but they also would end up creating an office with officials, the carriers of the routine-oriented model. This combination of contradictory pulls in the monopolistic state was at the root not only of Stalinist "supercentralization" but also of its nemesis, namely, the reproduction of the arbitrariness of the center (Stalinism was *this* by definition) by a multiplication from below of Stalin replicas at all levels of the administration ("the little Stalins"). But this underlined the paradoxical, "impossible" side in Stalinism: the capricious supercentralizer was giving away power by default; each "little Stalin" could be destroyed but was immediately replaced.

The reflection on the "impossible Stalinism" should point to a broader and peculiar set of paradoxes at work: Despotism cannot operate without shock methods (*udarnost'*); bureaucracy cannot work with them. Despotism develops hierarchy, but hierarchy cannot support despotism, which denies the importance of hierarchy. Despotism works arbitrarily and spreads its effects over the system, corrupting the *apparaty* and destroying their self-importance and their capacity to act as bodies and as powerholders. Despotism depends on, but cannot trust, the bureaucracy.

Elitization and hierarchization, whose game was power, were phenomena that were seen elsewhere. Most political organizations risk undergoing processes of this kind. Depending on the historical circumstances, most or some of the important historical tasks may still be tackled. But Stalinism became impossible because the "paradoxes" were actually an expression of powerful and contradictory forces that made the system "impossible": It stopped addressing such tasks. Instead, it found itself at odds with the better results of its own developmental drive, but also incapable of tackling the negative ones.

Over half a century, preceding and following Stalinism and maturing under Brezhnev, bureaucracy went from being a suspect and barely tolerated entity to being a partly rehabilitated one, and then to being a highly privileged but again suspect and terrorized congeries of "powerful serfs." The 1930s, which is our main focus here, was a period of social flux and of incredible turnover in society and in the bureaucracy that suffered also from its low level of professionalism and experience. In these conditions, the "third avenue"—neither working-class nor party rule— was still just a potentiality, often actually denied by some Marxists for whom a bureaucracy could never become a ruling class.

In fact, they could not yet become a solid and stable layer capable of an open and efficient defense of their rights against the party leadership. Surreptitious, less directly challenging ways were available, though. Important changes began to appear soon after Stalin's death. His despotism brought back an old trait of the erstwhile Moscovite princes as owners of all the state's lands (which were given to servants, making them into a gentry or nobility). Stalin's rule did make him into a de facto owner of all land and of the other resources, including the labor force. Once he disappeared, the collective ownership of the hierarchy's summit appeared quite clearly, but without an individual or group appropriation by key players at the top (except as manifestations of corruption, mostly as misappropriations of consumer goods). The power over the labor force also changed its character considerably, and the "agrarian despotism" period was over.

The bureaucracy now blossomed into a full-fledged ruling class. An elite was only part of it—mostly composed of the top layers of the bureaucracy—because a class is a larger and more complex social construct. The elite's power was backed by numerous lower ranks or layers inside the framework and by different social groups in the population outside it. At the same time, in the Soviet case, there was no doubt about who ran and actually owned the national economy; few other ruling classes in modern times have had this kind of monopoly. The takeover of real power in the system by the bureaucracy went hand-in-glove with its de facto emancipation from the party, including the "neutralization" and coopting by the bureaucracy of the *nomenklatura* system that was devised to control it. This happened thanks to the fact that the tool of control was also a two-way street: the controlled, as insider, can take over the tool from the inside.

The new stage that began with the elevation of Khrushchev started by reinvigorating the system and engendering a new dynamism in society and the polity, and larger internal reforms seemed imminent. But the ruling bureaucratic power grid, on its way to its own pinnacle, stalled reforms. It replaced "the cult of Stalin" by the "cult of the state," and further consequences of this change unfolded inexorably. The bureaucracy successfully eliminated the most unpalatable elements of Stalinism—notably, all those that were damaging to itself—but it also succeeded in disarming the party, by making it into its own "ruling servant." Once this was achieved, a super-monopoly ensued—a Soviet-style system of "bureaucratic absolutism" quite unprecedented in the twentieth century.[27] But this moment of supreme power also revealed that this class was not able anymore to handle any business except protecting its privileges. It had no serious leaders, and it was ideologically vacuous, demoralized, and often corrupt. The era of perestroika was a logical outcome of this situation.

---

27. The Soviet bureaucracy, although the mainstay and key feature of the system, did not attract much attention from scholars, and there are very few monographs to help produce a broader, synthesized picture. However, some recent pioneering work is William G. Rosenberg and Lewis H. Siegelbaum, ed., *Social Dimensions of Soviet Industrialization* (Bloomington and Indianapolis, 1993), in which the reader will find chapters by R. W. Davies, Don K. Rowney, Hiroki Kuromiya, Lewis H. Siegelbaum, and David Shearer on different echelons of the administration of industry.

Professor Don K. Rovney, a pioneer in the study of Soviet bureaucracy, writes about the new industrial commissariats. He also wrote *Transition to Technocracy: The Structural Origins of the Soviet Administrative State* (Ithaca, N.Y., 1989). Important pioneering insights were offered earlier by T. H. Rigby, who developed a concept of "mono-organizational society" and examined the Soviet system from this perspective. See his "Stalinism and Mono-organizational Society," in Robert C. Tucker, ed., *Stalinism: Essays in Historical Interpretation* (New York, 1977). Rigby also produced a study entitled *The Sovnarkom under Lenin*.

POSTSCRIPT

Eric Olin Wright, in his article "To Control or to Smash Bureaucracy: Weber and Lenin on Politics, the State and Bureaucracy,"[28] sums up Weber's 1917 essay on "Parliament and Government in Reconstructed Germany"and suggests that this essay is a good source to borrow ideas from when we study the causes of the Soviet bureaucracy's demise. One of the possibly crucial factors would be the party's loss of ability to produce strong and effective leaders. This would square with the broader statement—my own thesis—about the party having lost its political role and having become just a part of the bureaucracy itself.

In this case, Weber's thesis about why a bureaucracy is incapable of producing political leaders (who are supposed to be adept at formulating global policies and who mobilize the population in support of these policies) holds for the Soviet case, too. What was also missing in the Soviet case was the factor of answerability of the leadership to an electorate or an institutional system as a condition for its being "political," that is, among other tasks, capable of reining in the pernicious potentials of bureaucracy. Weber postulated the need for the leaders (who also run the bureaucracy) to be answerable to parliament, but, according to Olin—who on this point agrees with Lenin—this is not enough. The class composition (of the parliament), which Weber disregarded in this context, may prevent real, popular answerability. But this was not Weber's aim at all. Weber was interested in powerful leadership, not in the parliamentary body per se. Parliament was, for him, mainly a school from which leaders—but not real sources of sovereignty—could appear. His leaders would be "charismatic"—hence, sovereign by definition. Obviously, a "charismatic bureaucrat" would be a contradiction in terms.

The party could have played (and actually did) the role of "school of leadership" that Weber saw mainly in parliaments, and it also could—to some extent—have exercised control over bureaucracy, so long as it could preserve its suprabureaucratic (political) role, that is, have institutions that work with a modicum of democracy. We know that this feature was dwindling fast, especially during the late 1920s. It would be interesting to explore in some other context whether and when Soviet leaders were still "politicians" and when they became "bureaucrats."

28. Eric Olin Wright, "To Control or to Smash Bureaucracy: Weber and Lenin on Politics, the State and Bureaucracy," *Berkeley Journal of Sociology* 19 (1974–75), pp. 69–108.

CHAPTER 11:

STALIN IN THE MIRROR OF THE OTHER

THIS CHAPTER IS BASED, TO A LARGE EXTENT, ON ONE OF THE
insights that comparative history can offer: helping oneself to the
rich historiography of Germany and to a much better knowledge
about Hitler and his regime, in the hope of generating new ideas and
questions about the less well-known Stalin and his regime. The exercise
consists, then, in a sense, in holding the German mirror to Russia's
face—or rather to its history. In this case, we limit ourselves only to the
two dictatorships, although the same method could be applied to other
periods, too. The reader will realize that our aim here is to learn more
about Stalin, not to try to contribute to the knowledge of Hitler.

It is also quite revealing that many students of Germany use interpre-
tative constructs, specifically, concepts that can be or are already being
usefully employed in interpreting the Russian historical processes at
different periods. Ideas such as *"Gleichzeitigkeit der Ungleichzeitigen"*
(E. Bloch) or "combined development" (Trotsky), "legacy of the precapitalist past" (Wehler), "crisis of modernity" (Peukert) are "strategic"
ones in the battle of interpretations concerning the dictatorships in
question.[1]

STALIN'S CULT-AUTOCRACY

The making of Stalin's autocracy, amidst an enormous construction
effort, was permeated by destructive policies: terror, magic, and rituals,
attesting to and covering up a deep cultural and political regression and a
mighty cultural counterrevolution as destructive as the other aspects of
Stalinism. The enormous schooling effort, with its unavoidably half-
baked products, contributed to the damage, even as it lifted a multitude

---

1. For more on these topics, see David Blackbourn and Geoff Ely, *The Peculiarities of
German History* (New York, 1987), pp. 239–41 and passim. Also, see the last section of
this chapter.

of people to new positions and chances in life. All these traits were pre-conditions for the launching and results of the successful imposition of a "cult figure," who filled out the sociopsychological and political space of a country in turmoil, impressed the populace's minds, and was accepted as indispensable. Replacing Stalin seemed unimaginable.

The cult fitted the given circumstances quite naturally. There was no cult of Stalin, of any kind, before 1928; it was fabricated, as in Nazi Germany, with ever-growing doses of terror. Unlike Germany, though (except for the purge of the SA in 1934), the Nazi Party itself was not ruled internally by terror, though it was deeply authoritarian and disciplinarian. Stalin applied mass terror in the party on an unheard-of scale. And, unlike Hitler, he also terrorized his entourage: All the top leaders, from the Politburo down, were either actually executed or knew that they were candidates for the gallows at a moment's notice. This may underscore the point that the party per se was not a natural carrier of the Stalin cult—or at least Stalin did not believe it was. There was no Lenin cult in the upper ranks of the party during his lifetime; had there been, no one would have been able to engage in polemics and ideological battles with a cult figure. Yet it is a fact that most of the important leaders did not hesitate to challenge Lenin when they believed they should. Parallel to Ian Kershaw's reflection on the Hitler myth, Stalin's myth was deliberately created by Stalin himself or under his direct, supercilious supervision. He personally edited his own biography in an effort to produce a new form of legitimacy, not just in the population but, initially, even more so inside the party. That was indispensable, because the mutation into "Stalinism" consisted in abandoning the historical ideology and replacing it with another that fitted the reality and aims of a regime that was by now "moving elsewhere" very rapidly—away from Marxism and socialism, away from ideals of popular sovereignty and rule of law (the list is longer)—while still denying that the change was occurring. What better than a deified autocracy for minds that were still mostly rural or were just freshly from the countryside, shaped by tsarist traditions—a religious mentality with a deeply seated psychological need for a strong figure in times of stress—or so goes the argument quite often.

Charisma, a helpful term for leaders who were cult figures, may not be the proper term to apply to Stalin, unless we redefine it. In Weber's concept, charisma did not come with an office (like the pope's), but had to be conquered; neither did his concept have any place for terror. It was up to the leader to prove himself over and over again to his followers. There was adoration among the believers, followed either by abandonment of the charismatic leader once the spell failed or by his "routinization." Terrorizing the followers would not fit the whole concept. Stalin, at the height of his power, was hidden from his followers, and he kept people around him under the fear of death. They had constantly to prove something to him, rather than the other way round. They had all too often to prove the impossible—that they were not "enemies."

The German historical experience has examples of techniques that authoritarians used for similar needs. Hans Ulrich Wehler, a key theoretician of the thesis commonly called "the German Sonderweg" speaks about Bismarck (and others), whose policy was based on what he calls "negative inspiration": When the ability to offer positive inspiration is missing, creating images of "enemies of the empire" (liberals, Catholics, socialists, Jews) and of other nonexistent dangers, is often successfully used to shore up the power and mobilize capacities of the regime. Wehler also mentions a "structural hostility towards democracy" that characterized many nationalisms, ideologies, and some churches that engaged in spreading their "negative inspirations," notably, to serve their "structural hostility." [2] These were, unfortunately, all too often very effective policies. In view of these, as well as Russia's own precedents, it turns out that what Stalin practiced was actually a political "classic." His earlier "enemies" (foreign encirclement, capitalist hostility) were more realistic—but the later "enemies of the people" were internal, not concrete, extremely vague, and deliberately broad—anyone could fit in. This fact goes with another element of this "all-purpose strategy" (my term) that Burkhard (quoted in Wehler) described as creating "a stage of siege" as a way of ruling, which is precisely what Stalin's regime "accomplished."

The creation and use of an image of *vozhd'* (best translated by the Latin term *dux*—just *leader* would not do), based on Lenin's position and role but with considerable bending of the historical truth about the founding father, served as the stepping stone for Stalin's "cult." This was an important part of Stalin's ruling technique: he projected over time more than one image of himself. There was one, or barely one, until the end of the Civil War; another in the NEP (without Stalinism as yet); another during "the

2. Hans Ulrich Wehler, *The German Empire, 1871–1918* (Hamburg, 1985), pp. 90–94.

cult"; and what some called "high Stalinism." In any case, he was no *vozhd'* in those earlier years, and even after Lenin's death the party's activists heard from Kamenev—previously no lesser a leader than Stalin—who said, "Our party does not need a *vozhd'*." So there were some steps Stalin had to climb before being able to bestow on himself the coveted chasuble.

Behind the changing Stalin images ran different stages in the history of the system, which eventually harbored some alternative roads that could be taken. They could be deduced by studying the obstacles that he had to overcome. In each case it was some strategy others preferred. The question of whether there was, say, "a Lenin state," however short-lived, before it became Stalin's can be answered by Stalin's use of a cult as the centerpiece of the political edifice—but also by other features of his system, which I call an "agrarian despotism." If I am correct in using it in relation to Stalinism, there is no way this notion can be applied to the NEP period and its state system. It was a deeply agrarian society, but it had no despotic cult figure at the center of its political life; and however authoritarian the regime, it was nobody's "agrarian despotism." This had to be created, or recreated, first.

Nepian Russia, as it emerged from the Civil War, became again a peasant ocean dominated by communal (*obschinnye*) institutions that were made possible by the disappearance of capitalism in the revolutionary storm. The traditional traits of muzhik Russia were thereby accentuated in the early Soviet system. But, on the other hand, they now had to face a state endowed with a new vigor. One of the aims of Stalin's policies, once he was firmly at the helm of this state, was to force the peasants to shed precisely the features that their own recent revolution had underscored. But what followed was a tortured interlacing of "traditional" and "modern" features, the so-called most advanced commingling with the most backward, even barbarian ones. Furthermore, this commingling happened in the process of "the leap"—a special strategy undergirded by the gap between the social base, from which the leap started, and a state that *could* and did decide to use all its power to overcome a crisis, with the party tipping the scale toward a policy of a *ryvok*—a dash! The scale could have been tipped toward a different strategy, but once the choice was made, the Bolsheviks themselves as a party followed the liberals, the Mensheviks, and the Soviet Russians "into the dustbin of history." The "combined development" thesis, or "*Gleichzeitigkeit der Ungleichzeitigen,*" is tailor-made for this situation.

The strategies of the *ryvok* turned out to be, to a large extent, an all-out war against the peasants (they were the bulk of the nation)—thus, a "revolution," but not anticapitalist, as claimed. Anti–petty bourgeois, then? Not even this. Whatever our class analysis of the peasantry, the upshots were momentous: With coercive methods applied to the majority of the nation to keep it working, especially in *kolkhozy,* a forceful intrusion of a dynamic force into a more traditional, deeply rural (agrarian) society took place. These, then, were the circumstances in which an autocratic, personally despotic system reappeared—even if absolutism was already very considerably watered down in the last stages of the tsarist state. It manifested itself in many of the traits of the Stalinist state, all flowing from the basic premises—not just a controlled and constrained environment, but one that was still very "traditional." The depth of the cult's success in people's minds—hence, the weight of the tsarist past as one of the preconditions without which, presumably, the fabrication would have remained hanging in the air—is still a matter of conjecture.

The very making of Stalinism implied an ideological transformation, including a return to forms of nationalism from before the revolution and even to more ancient imperial themes and symbols—a perfectly fitting requirement for an agrarian despotism seeking to legitimize itself in a very shifty and explosive situation. "Socialism" would not do the trick. Magic, rituals, and, finally, "demonization" of ubiquitous subversive enemies—all equally "archaic" ingredients, although not at all rare apparitions and not exclusively Russian phenomena—were the indispensable ideological and emotional crutches. The dogmatic canonization of thought and of a leader who controlled the terms of praise that were showered on him closes the list.

The inadequacy of Leninism for the needs of the Stalinist era is illustrated by the effort the regime undertook to mobilize ideological resources entirely foreign to the initial creed. It is obvious that Stalin tried to tap political traditions, several of them simultaneously or at different times: he wanted to put to his use the aura of the great, successful, mostly "imperial" tsars; he wanted the glamor of the traditional state (with its auxiliary borrowing of church iconography for its own splendor); and, finally, he wanted to partake of the personal charisma of an anointed tsar-*batiushka,* but magnified well beyond the tsar's reach. *Rodina-Mat'* (a peculiarly Russian overemotional term for "motherland") and, later, the more politically expressive but equally emotive and mythical "Velikaia

Rus'" were taken from the tsarist-Russian heritage of obvious right-wing inspiration and were used by Stalin in an effort to gain a certain historical overinsurance for himself and his sytem. This overinsurance, or "alibi," problem is worth exploring further.

THE EVANESCENT "ALIBI"

If somebody could exact it from him, Stalin would have a lot of explaining to do as to why, having reached the top without internal terror and any "cult" around his persona, he became a bloody oppressor, found it necessary to resort to massive distortions and silencing of any criticism, and destroyed social thought, Marxism included, but still kept some feathers from it and commingled them with archaisms of all kinds. He was no founder of the party and had quite a problem with it, until he finally did produce a system, a genuine product of his own; but this was done at the expense of perverting the ideology of the founders, destroying the whole original setting of Bolshevism—in fact, betraying it. A whole system of lies had to be erected to cover up these facts. He did not and could not remain faithful in earnest to the initial evangel; his was, by the tenets of the founding ideology, a counterrevolution. Such a tortuous itinerary had to have convoluted and destructive effects—notably, what we call "an alibi problem."

It is doubtful whether building a violence-crazy superstate already existed as a hidden agenda in Stalin's mind at some early stage in his political life. He certainly had aspirations and ideas of his own at the stage of his career when he was already at the top of the party but not yet its chief. We are not yet sure how far he intended to go at that time. But there are some well-known facts that emerged as we studied nationalities and nationalism in Russia. We know from Hitler's biography that his soldiering in World War I exercised a powerful, formative influence on his personality and thinking. The most formative period for Stalin as a politician must have been the Civil War. It is here that his personal ruthlessness seemed to have shown its weight as an excellent political expedient. It is in this terrible crucible that Stalin learned the secret of victorious politics in the most daunting situations: State coercion was the secret of success; mobilization, propaganda, military might, and terror were the ingredients of power. It must have become for him synonymous with success in political leadership on a large historical arena. The debates

about the way of incorporating the different nationalities of the empire
into a common state show how those lessons of the Civil War were
assimilated by Stalin and made into the guideline for his political
choices. He was ready to make some verbal concessions—but the bottom
line had to be a highly centralized, unitary state that would not brook
any interference with its will from some spurious "sovereignties." In
these conditions the discussions about "building socialism in one country" were mostly a way of intimating that he actually assimilated the old
Russian "great power syndrome" and a readiness to lift it to unprecedented heights—in more than just his own country. It is on this plane
that he clashed quite sharply with Lenin and turned against him. But
Lenin, even when already mortally ill, was still too formidable a foe to be
challenged very openly. This is why Stalin was still taking precautions
and biding his time. It is true that the dying Lenin finally saw through
his game—but it was too late.

Let us now glean some ideas from Hitler's biographies that could be used
to cast a better light on aspects of Stalin's personality and leadership. We
know that the strands of Hitler's ideological development were coming
together at the end of his writing of *Mein Kampf* in 1924—and never
changed thereafter.[3] At the same time, the main force of his appeal and
his personal insight in recognizing the key feature of mass psychology
were also in place and rehearsed during his Munich rabble-rousing demagoguery. The lesson he learned and practiced was one: Masses do not
understand complex ideas; what moves them is hatred. This is what he
based his techniques on.

   We do not yet know that much about the stages of Stalin's political
development—except for his statism, which we discussed earlier. Whip-
ping up fear and hatred was certainly not yet of central importance in
Stalin's methods and image at the time he became general secretary; he

---

3. An important source for me, especially on Hitler's personal features, was William
Carr's *Hitler: A Study in Personality* (New York, 1973), and I drew heavily on his discussion. While working on this chapter, I had no time to read Alan Bullock's impressive
Hitler and Stalin: Parallel Lives (New York, 1992) in its entirety. Bullock provides a
panorama covering the two dictators' lives, yet without attempting to compare them systematically. In the title he correctly states that he was examining "parallel lives," and he
did so through paired chapters devoted to each man separately at approximately the
same periods. Anyone wanting to do comparative analyses will find ample information
in this book.

was to invent or reinvent these elements later. But he had to consolidate his power first, for he was far from firm in his saddle in the early 1920s. Hitler's fate, too, was still decided by others in 1932 and early 1933, mainly by those who were the players around Hindenburg. He would play with those who gave him power for some time—but would emancipate himself quickly.

A similar stage in Stalin's biography occurred much earlier. His career for a time depended on Lenin, and next it lay briefly but precariously in the hands of the Central Committee, with a deciding vote in the hands of Kamenev and Zinoviev—all at the bequest of the already deceased Lenin, who had advised the party to remove Stalin from his post. Stalin liberated himself from this cloud over his head earlier than he understood, but he still fought this past "dependence" for quite a time. And he didn't just outsmart those who helped him. He never forgave his past "dependence" on them or any debts to them.

Whatever the timing of such innermost intentions of Stalin, he did build his vision of the future around his person, and that had to be done at the expense of his movement's original ideology and leadership. He must have been driven by an enormous psychological urge for personalized power—a quest he himself was probably discovering as he went along in playing the power games as nobody else around him did. Obviously, this kind of thirst for power had to be concealed from the party's top layers—and Stalin was an accomplished master of deception. His was an image of moderation and simplicity for most of the NEP; it worked very well for him.

Internal terror, though intense, was probably less important in the making of Hitler's image; but as the integrating power of the Hitler image declined in the later stages of the war, terror was increasing. Yet miseries and terror were endured: The population, the army, and the accolytes remained faithful to the very end "because in the Führer most people found a point of identification and a point of hope."[4] In another context Carr also speaks of fear of the Russian conquest, dedication to the common ideological ground of a Greater Germany, shaking off Versailles, and so on.

At a time when Hitler was offering exactly what he promised and what the Germans adopted, to a large extent, as their own, he used and

---

4. Carr, *Hitler,* pp. 160–61.

hyperbolized Germany's preexisting nationalist, racist, and militarist traditions; worked them into a specific war- and expansion-oriented ideology—the Nazi one; and acted on it. In this process he degraded the developed country he took over and destroyed millions of people, in the service of mythical dreams. He was a real founder of his party and destroyed it, too, but only in the sense that his policies were self-defeating. Otherwise, except for the 1934 purge, he did not slaughter either his party or his collaborators. Hitler was—or became—confident and overconfident in his own and his country's possibilities and in the dedication of his collaborators.

Stalin had a tendency to test the loyalty toward him not only among the collaborators around him but also, more broadly, among the country's population. His distrust was certainly cast over the whole nation (certainly not a small burden to carry), and that is borne out by his belief in the hosts of "enemies" that his secret services were constantly instructed to keep ferreting out. This must have been actually a need, because it provided a reassurance, however fleeting. No wonder that he underestimated his country's capacity to fight (allowing us to say that they fought and won "despite him"). It all stemmed, in part, from the traits of his psyche and his mind, which could not accept reality. Most notably, he was not historically the founder of this movement, and he was taking it and the country in a direction he had to lie about: Instead of the hoped-for ever-broadening emanicpation, there was Stalinism.

"Betrayal" must have been an outrageously terrible thing for Stalin to admit; and it was none other than Trotsky, sole among the leaders of the revolution, who directly accused Stalin of being "the gravedigger of the revolution." This is why "betrayal" had to be made into everybody else's fault. This is why he needed to test the strength and moral fiber ("moral," according to his own definition) of his entourage and the people at large—notably, by the dubious test of dedication to his persona. The glorification of his greatness, genius, and, above all, his "great simplicity" in millions of speeches and pages is known to have been "commissioned," and the very terms used were screened in advance by Stalin himself.

Strong leadership could be offered by a strong government—without a deified despot, without this kind of Stalin. We can speculate that this thought occurred to Stalin, too. This is why it can be surmised that the "need" in his kind of deified leadership, though it turned out acceptable to the masses, emanated not so much from them, not even from the party, but from the top group in power—and mainly from Stalin himself. Thus, terms of adulation were one of the tests he conceived for his close collaborators. They knew it and competed in inventing ever newer superlatives in their speeches; some were very good at that. But lack of such praise (in Marshal Tukhachevsky's speeches, for example) could be and was fatal; even a sparseness of adulatory expressions was considered a "betrayal."

Thus, despite Stalin's unaccountability as the leader, there was an internal need for justification, of a compelling alibi problem, which we can discern from his supervision of the ingredients of his cult and, no less convincingly, from his drive to destroy anyone who knew or might have thought he knew him in a light that was different from what became his self-image. Thus, the cult was not just a ruling device that some dictators might have seen "instrumentally," as the only way to rule "these people." One can safely say that here was not just a calculated *arcanum imperii* to be offered to the masses so that they would behave as expected. It was generated by the psyche of a man whose vanity was insatiable (Volkogonov), coupled with a constant worry about his own security. It must have become part of the "alibi" strategy—a deeply seated psychological urge. Stalin's strategy of "producing enemies" (which, of course, Hitler also used in a phantasmagoric and murderous manner) was all turned inward, more than outward. The "sabotage" myth created the desired all-encompassing insurance policy against having to be liable for any damages. The obvious internal culprit was ever ready (vaguely attached to "foreign intelligence"), credible enough to be charged with all possible treason, and accountable for Stalin's failures. When needed, "the enemy" would just confess to anything.

But these phantasms could hit all and any institutions and personalities of the regime. The whole action was conducted in a warlike style. When in the course of war Hitler needed slave labor, he ordered people to be hauled from conquered territorties outside of Germany. Stalin's conquered territory was inside his own country, and this was where he created and used his pool of slave labor. His power inside and over his country was more absolute than Hitler's—but never so much, apparently, for him to feel that he had enough of it.

The cult capped this hallucinatory insurance policy, which served psychological as well as systemic needs. It was a unifier and a symbolic reassurance, and both dictators practiced it. But Stalin's was created by him and for him years after he was already in power; Hitler had it, at least inside the party, from the very beginning. Hitler's was also the unifying glue and mobilizer, and the "heroic" leadership that seems to be expected in tough times was "fabricated" by Goebbels and Hitler himself. Hitler, though, as we know, did it all on his own terms: a Hitler myth as he defined it himself originally. He did not hide the essence of what he was up to. His deification served a country in crisis, and although the militaristic-conquering thrust was initially kept in abeyance, it was there and clear to anyone who wanted to know. Hitler did not need an alibi; he did not perceive his aims as treasonable in any way.

Despite this, there is evidence that Hitler took care and was preoccupied with the degree of his popularity among the people. In Russia, the cult (deification) was pushed on the country from above in times of stress and fragmentation caused by the imposition of a forceful and spasmodic industrialization. There was enough fuel there to worry the leaders. Was there any relation between popularity rates and Stalin's politics of purges? We have no good data so far to answer this question, but the powerful need in "overinsuring" is, in itself, a very telling fact.

Nazism was impossible without the Hiter myth; it went with the other mythological aims that Nazism was all about. The Nazi rule could not have functioned without it, as convincingly shown by the biographer and historian Ian Kershaw.[5] The Stalin myth was indispensable to Stalin's rule. The fact that the myth could rather easily switch to "collective leadership" after Stalin's death shows that the Stalin myth was not indispensable to the system or to the party. Its importance was as a post hoc rationalization, and it stayed much longer than Stalin himself in the minds of not only the citizens but also many foreign observers. But as long as Stalin was in power, his rule was strong. He did not need, like Hitler, to produce military exploits constantly. He could be content with real or, again, mythical achievements on the internal front, the term *front* being symptomatic in this context: The internal "offensive" was conducted as a set of planned military campaigns against mythical enemies. A more "normal" authoritarianism that came after his death showed how wasteful had been the regime that had been so mightily mobilized to ensure the safety of its dictator.

---

5. I extensively used Ian Kershaw's *The Hitler Myth: Image and Reality in the Third Reich* (New York, 1987), as well as his *Hitler* (New York, 1991). In addition to being a master at intricacies of biographical scholarship, Kershaw is an excellent thinker on politico-historical systems, and his work helps us examine those comparatively.

There is no need to prove that the inner dynamic of the Nazi Party and of Hitler—war being its essence—was destructive. The same cannot be said, however, about the pre-Stalin and post-Stalin ruling party. Stalin's war against his own was an interlude, but as long as it lasted— and the same applied to Hitler almost until his very end—both personal dictatorships and myths were strong. There was plenty of support for and fascination with these leaders in both countries, and that can be measured by simple, well-documented facts: When people in Germany were dissatisfied with some of the regime's doings, they still reacted widely and wishfully by saying, "Wen das der Führer wusste" ("If only the Führer knew"). Likewise, in Russia, even sophisticated people thought, during the dead-heat of the purges, that Stalin did not know about those and would stop them if he did find out. In both cases the dictators were actually exempt from responsibility.

Stalin's biographer Robert Tucker points out in the second installment of his work that solving great state problems by killing a leader was alien to the Bolshevik Marxists, and none of them was using this method. "The only Old Bolshevik capable of 'individual terror' was Stalin."[6] Tucker said this in connection with Stalin's visit to Tomsky, the now-demoted leading Old Bolshevik, who reacted to this visit quite aggressively: He expelled Stalin from his house, cursing as he did so—and then committed suicide. Tucker went on: "The whole world would have changed in many ways for the better had Tomsky shot his visitor instead of or along with himself." Obviously, Stalin was not worried about a thing like that; he knew Bolsheviks would not do that to him. But he himself was different. And, as we said, he needed this additional psychological game to prove to himself his superiority over those "meek" ex-comrades.

A CIVILIZATION AMIDST LOW LITERACY

Data on the cultural level of Russia and of its cadres, cast light on the stage that the country was in. We offer here some additional eye-openers on this important subject. At the end of the 1920s and early 1930s, "in the majority of cases, the peasants were entering the ranks of labor being semi-literate or illiterate," according to three Soviet analysts writing in a 1988 book. They quoted a 1936 study of Stakhanovite combine drivers

---

6. Robert C. Tucker, *Stalin in Power* (London, 1991), pp. 374–75.

that showed that most of them "never read books other than manuals of their machines."[7]

The authors claim (do they still claim it six years later?) that there was a development in the countryside of a "socialist spirit" (*ideijnost'*), but in the 1930s "this new socialist *ideiinost'* overlaid a quite meager cultural soil (2–3 years of elementary schooling in the best of cases) and it acquired, unavoidably, dogmatic and vulgar features." The official Stalinist propaganda made things even worse. Still, even in those primitive forms, the kolkhozniks learned to think in terms broader than just their own district—they learned to think about the whole state.[8] We can interject that there is nothing socialist about this—but this is just an aside.

We learn from O. V. Khlevniuk that Malenkov prepared a background brief for Stalin, who needed it for the March–April plenum in 1937. It reported that among regional party secretaries only 17.7 percent had higher education, and 70.4 percent had only elementary schooling. Respective figures for city secretaries were 12.1 percent and 80.3 percent. Lacking adequate knowledge and culture, many local leaders made do through political resourcefulness and dexterity; and they surrounded themselves with gray and pliant people—as a base for their own elevation. Stalin noticed this, says the author, but actually encouraged precisely this kind of personnel policy.[9]

Such data were symptomatic for the cultural-moral background in the country—*and among the cadres.* This is important for interpreting Stalinism. But aren't we reading too much into such data? Hitler's cult grew in an educated country with plenty of excellent high-level professionals, some of them among the world's best. We know from reliable authorities that the professional academics—notably, lawyers, judges, and, equally, the scions of nobility—flocked into the institutions of the regime and offered excellent, dedicated service. It is especially interesting to note that many educated "generalists"—often excellent administrators—were particularly active in the Gestapo, the SS, and other parts

---

7. P. S. Kabytov, V. A. Kozlov, and D. G. Litvak, *Russkoe Krest'ianstvo: estapy dukhovnogo osvobozhdeniia* (Moscow, 1988), p. 210. For more data related to the educational levels of the whole population, see the introductory essay to Lewin, *The Making of the Soviet System.*

8. P. S. Kabytov, ibid., p. 209.

9. O. V. Khlevniuk, *1937-oj* (Moscow, 1992), pp. 78–79. He quoted from the party archives, Ts.P.A., f. 17, op. 2, d. 773, l. 127. Khlevniuk is a fine scholar and publicist who produces very reliable work based on solid archival research.

of the security apparatus, and many were active in planning and executing the *Endlösung* ("final solution"). The fact that such a large segment of the elite flocked into the top levels of the SS helped ennoble the service by making them acceptable as an elite service of the regime. They played a visible role in the repressive organs in the occupied territories and served not only in the SS-Führer Korps but also in the Allgemeine SS. And even if some, in private, were not really loyal to the regime, they gave the regime prestige and their talents.[10] This cannot but raise important questions concerning the relation between the level of education and political leanings and savvy.

Soviet Russia did not have at its disposal anything like Germany's intellectual resources. It had to rely, initially, on an often politically unsympathetic (and relatively small) layer of professionals and intellectuals, who were not flocking into the system and especially not into the security agencies (in which they also probably would not have been accepted). Later on, layers of their own intelligentsia would appear and their quality would improve, though quite slowly, and those went through a saga of their own. Once this intelligentsia was produced (by the regime—with some help of the older cadres, especially in the army), this intelligentsia served loyally in all the agencies; accepted the "cult," the myths, and the lies, helped spread them, and produced a huge layer of (more or less) educated Stalinists. Critical, skeptical, "internal émigrés" and outright open dissidents all appeared much later in some numbers, but the vast majority served and enjoyed privileges until the last stages of the regime—again, even as growing numbers were ever more skeptical, critical, and hostile to it.

Thus, Russia's lack of culture and cadres was insufficient for the country to have its industrial "leap forward" and socialism at the same time—so it leaped into something else. Germany went for a racist-nationalistic *Drang* for conquest; and, it turns out, high levels of development do not give any immunity against the contagious power of such ideologies. So one does not need a low-literacy country to see it adopt and spread a wave of barbarism. In Germany's case, the high level of development afforded enormous destructive possibilities for unleashing murderous myths onto the world. In Russia's case, low literacy, in a sense, imposed

---

10. All of these data are from Gunnar C. Boehwert, *The Führer State* (Stuttgart, 1981), pp. 361–73.

very large tasks but limited the possibilities of accomplishing them. This is the kind of historical bind that enhanced the role of the state but also atrociously disfigured the regime.

The subject needs more thought, because a vast improvement of educational standards did continue to play a role in considerably softening many of the regime's oppressive features and actually did prepare the ground for the regime's demise. The earlier stages of the Soviet regimes—that is, the post–World War I period—belonged to an era of dictatorships all around Russia; and studying them all comparatively can yield important insights into the genesis of such systems, at least in the given broad area. The personal aspect—that is, the role of the dictator, his cult (charisma), and so on—was a key function in all such regimes and provided some glue for the state machinery and often, probably, the bulk of the population, whom the leader helped rally behind the state. Still, Hitler's Germany and Stalin's Russia stood out quite clearly as two, in some ways, "pure" and most extreme dictatorial models and great powers.

HITLER AND STALIN — IMAGES AND MYTHS

In *The Hitler Myth,* Ian Kershaw shows that this myth—or rather "the Führer principle"—was crucial for the system, and Hitler used it in such a way that he "transformed himself into a function, the function of Führer."[11] Kershaw's aim was to contribute to the understanding of this key component of the system and to add something new to the already extensive knowledge of Hitler's personality.

All we know about Stalin, however, is the myth and mythmaking; we have little empirical knowledge about the functioning of the system or the wheels of his personal political staff—and even less about his personality. Volkogonov's biography added a lot of data previously unknown, but we still are in the dark on many points.[12] We do know fairly well, though, that, not unlike Hitler and his self-identification with the function, Stalin actually became *the system* and his personality therefore

---

11. Kershaw, *The Hitler Myth,* pp. 2–4.

12. Dmitrij Volkogonov, *Triumf i tragediia: Politicheskij portret I. V. Stalina* (Moscow, 1989). This was the first Soviet biography of Stalin that was based on a vast amount of archival material previously never seen, although his ways of using and interpreting the data are often controversial. It is in two books, with four parts, and I will quote it often, from the Russian edition. An English translation is also available.

acquired a "systemic" dimension. Kershaw's study of "the Hitler myth" was by definition an invitation to compare, not only to find common personal traits—there were more than a few—but to explore the whole politics of mythmaking in both countries, the eventual differences, and the scholarly debates on such themes.

Hitler tried to project an image of being above the fray, aloof and uninvolved in governmental dross, but somehow all-powerful and talking to the nation as though in a mise-en-scène conceived for a pagan deity. In contrast, Stalin's image was one of simplicity and, as the Soviet novelist Simonov attested in his autobiography, of a leader deeply interested with and involved in people's lives (although both Stalin and Hitler were equally detached and insensitive to human fate). Hitler was a powerful speaker-showman. Stalin managed to transform his lack of rhetorical power into an enormous asset: The brevity of his utterances seemed to convey depth, self-confidence, and wisdom—and this was an image deeply believed by many observers.[13]

It is also quite revealing that both dictators distanced themselves from the party (and officialdom) so that the blame for poor policies—even disasters—could be absorbed by others. This distance from the party was their common technique of rule. Hitler built his image at the expense of his party, as did Stalin, but also at the expense of the whole bureaucracy. In this sense, they actually did it at the expense of the pillars of their own systems. Hitler gained a lot from his first bloody purge, which was actually tiny compared to Stalin's, but it did occur before Stalin's big ones. In this case, it could have been Stalin who borrowed from Hitler rather than the other way around. On the other hand, Hitler saw Stalin's purge of the generals as utterly stupid, and he never committed anything like that; he found other ways to bury his army and his country.

For both Hitler and Stalin, dissociation from officialdom and party was a calculated move to better ground their own power in people's minds; and it was, in fact, widely accepted by the general public in both cases. In Hitler's case there were also initially enormous successes—or events seen as such—plus a sense that he moved forward without war. In fact, the racial-imperialist part in Hitler was not initially perceived fully

---

13. Konstantin Simonov, *Glazami cheloveka moego pokoleniia* (Moscow, 1990). This is an excellent source on Stalin. The writer, as an editor and a leading member of the Writers Union, participated in a number of meetings with Stalin. I relied on Simonov's impressions about Stalin as a war leader and as the "engineer" of literature.

outside the Nazi Party; but as Hitler's position rose above the party, government, and state, his innermost mythical aims of conquest and hegemony, which were lurking and waiting, could go into action.[14]

Both cases offer different versions of a "deconstruction" of the state as a rational-legal, administrative, and normally policed organization and its replacement by some kind of "privatization" of the state (Kershaw's term). In Hitler's case, his personal bodyguard became the main power behind the cult, whereas in Stalin's case, the state's security services became his personal bodyguards—and the principal base of his power. The arbitrariness of these reactions and results in both cases was a "normal" feature of an "abnormal" personalized state in which the despot himself was a crucial institution—a one-person institution, a linchpin in a dictatorial system that spun many myths but was in itself real enough.

Stalin's essential drive had nothing to do with racialism or racial superiority, with deindustrialization of "inferior" nations and the wiping out of their intelligentsia, or with war. The regime's pathologies were reserved for the internal "front," which was dominated—with well-known ups and downs—by a vicious, terroristic, large-scale war against presumed enemies, who happened to be the country's peasants, many members of its officialdom, and the best of the military, the party, and the management.

On the other hand, unlike in the case of Hitler, there was in Stalin a powerful drive to develop his country and bring it into a different age. Despite the basic incompatibility between mass slaughter of the country's elites and this building drive under Stalin, the system had yet another important act to play in the historical arena after the dictator's death. Stalin conducted his policy in a military fashion, and his terror inside his country was much broader in scale than Hitler's; therefore, eliminating some of the self-defeating murderous features of Stalinism gave the post-Stalin regime an important additional stimulus.

Stalin himself, though, ended up living in a bunker, believing only in the security apparatus, and being deranged. His state of mind was clearly dominated at this stage by a paranoid fear of his country and a view of people as unreliable and dangerous. The reason probably lies in the character of his superstate: it was—and was to stay—deeply bureaucratic, yet Stalin did not relish this reality; he felt in the bureaucrats, including those nearest to him, a force that could not like despotism. He was wrong, in the sense

---

14. Kershaw, *The Hitler Myth,* ch. 2 and 3.

that no one ever tried to kill him, but he was right in a sociological sense: they did want to do things differently and to acquire for themselves both better conditions and, finally, the fulcrum of power. Very few of Stalin's suspects were actually criminally guilty; he struck on the basis of a pathological sociology that suggested to him where the enemies *might* come from. This was one of the internal traps laid for Stalin by his Stalinism.

STALIN: PERSONALITY AND POWER

The dictators we are studying were one-man institutions of power. In such cases, personality traits and the political game the dictators play merge quite unavoidably. Nevertheless, when we study their regimes with the aim of exploring the systems they presided over and the broad political strategies they adopted, the personality issue remains backstage. When we turn to the personal portrait, details on intimate aspects come up, yet the political activity does not get relegated to the backstage. For both Hitler and Stalin, politics was the main preoccupation and obsession; therefore, the style and much of the substance of their politics could not but be deeply permeated by their psyches and characters. In regard to style, preferred stratagems, ticks and mannerisms, Hitler and Stalin, according to biographers, had many similarities.

One of them was the predilection for histrionics, as practiced by both men. Stalin biographers note that he indulged in elaborate histrionic scenes, and today we have many more detailed accounts from witnesses to illustrate this fact. An excellent source for these (and many other features of Stalin's persona) is the autobiography of K. Simonov, often confirmed or expanded by Volkogonov, as well as by other memoirists. Stalin clearly relished playing "scenes" of, say, magnanimity and thoughtfulness, accompanied by dramatic, supposedly "sudden," decisions and gestures—all prepared in advance and delivered in a deliberate, slow, and (according to Simonov) masterly way. Simonov gives an example of a meeting in Stalin's office when people of the rank of Malenkov or Molotov denounced another person actually present at the meeting, but Stalin offered himself a moment of thought and decided against the accusers. The man's life was saved, but Stalin was only pretending about not having heard the accusations before the meeting. In another story with a different outcome, Stalin deliberately minimized an incident in a display of good "paternal humor," but the culprit nevertheless disappeared the next day. Simonov testifies that "being a great actor was an intricate part of Stalin's political gift."[15]

We know that Hitler also played scenes for the audience, which, we must add, was a captive one that had no choice but to applaud. Hence, the acting talent of each dictator would not necessarily pass the test of a free public. But there was also, in both men, another facet—the darker side of the moon, when self-control would give way to terrifying outbursts of rage, which were often described and feared, especially in the case of Stalin. Even more terrible for those present, according to Simonov's account of one such incident, were cases when Stalin, in the throes of an outburst, managed to control it with great difficulty, as visible from his grimaces; the apparent restraint in fact presaged a terrible punishment for the "perpetrator." It is plausible that before Stalin acquired virtual omnipotence, he had managed to control those fits; but the effort must have been ravaging his psyche. Once he was on top and beyond control, the brakes were off—unless there was some political or personal interest to check them. Those cases might have occurred when a particular meeting was convened with an audience he wanted to impress for some reason—like representatives of the literary elite or foreign diplomats. Often the self-control was simply a part of his preferred form of revenge, which he must have been hatching patiently.

Another case worth reporting (from Simonov) concerned a young air force general who said openly, at a meeting called to investigate the causes of numerous flight accidents, that the problems happened because the pilots were forced to fly in . . . coffins. Stalin, who felt himself to be the target of the general's comment, controlled his rage, uttered some deliberately terse remark ("You should not have said this, General")—and destroyed the young man the next day. It is said also that Stalin liked to kill slowly. No doubt, he must have felt either a relish or else some kind of psychological relief in those games, as he played with the victims and waited for the moment when he wanted to strike. As far as is known, Stalin played such a game with Bukharin. Larina, Bukharin's wife, gave a vivid picture of Bukharin's slow assassination, deliberately conducted against the already broken man.[16]

---

15. Simonov, *Glazami cheloveka*, pp. 187–88.

16. See Anna Larina, *This I Cannot Forget* (New York, 1993). These are the memoirs of Bukharin's widow.

Likewise, Komsomol secretary Kosarev heard many compliments from Stalin, until one day Stalin whispered something that turned Kosarev's face livid. Stalin did something similar to Tomsky, who then angered Stalin by committing suicide "before his time." Stalin also destroyed the whole family and circle of associates of Ordzonikidze, Politburo member and head of a key industrial agency, but in the process of doing this he kept coming to Ordzonikidze's apartment, supposedly for a chat and a drink—but loud shouts (all in Georgian, incidentally) were overheard when the fiery Ordzonikidze reacted to the bloody chicanery. After one such "friendly visit," Ordzonikidze, like Tomsky, killed himself.

There was yet another Stalin stratagem of "testing" his closest collaborators—Kaganovitch, Molotov, Poskrebyshev (Stalin's personal secretary), and many others—by having their wives (or relatives) arrested for hostile activity and, probably, by making some of them sign or cosign the order of arrest. He would tell his collaborator—who did not always manage to preserve a stony face about Stalin's supposed inability to intervene—that everything was in the "impartial" hands of the NKVD. We can add this faked innocence to the histrionic mastery of the *vozhd'*. Volkogonov claimed that Stalin did not care that a figure like Ezhov (head of the secret police, 1936–38) was a brutish sadist who personally "interrogated" prisoners or was a morally rotten creature.[17] But Stalin supposedly hated weaklings—especially drinkers—and Ezhov was one of those. Stalin preferred, in his perverse way, strong-willed people (*volevye*), which meant that they could be absolutely devoted and ready to do anything for him. We can surmise that arresting or destroying a family member of his "co-ruler" from the Politburo without the latter protesting or even uttering a murmur was such a test of "character." If Molotov, Kaganovich, or Poskrebyshev had tried to defend their relatives, this would have meant they were "weak." The fact that Stalin destroyed his own wife's entire family—which was his family, too—is telling evidence of the pathological mind that is best left to the expertise of experienced psychiatrists.

A very different facet emerges when we study Stalin's working day. He had a capacity for long hours of hard work, followed by late-night libations with a few of his top lieutenants. He did not like a vast

---

17. Volkogonov, *Triumf i tragediia,* vol. 1, pt. 2, pp. 280–81.

entourage. He read quite a lot, though mostly working dossiers; Volkogonov's study of Stalin's personal files showed that he perused 100 to 200 dossiers a day.[18] Stalin's phenomenal memory and mastery of details were impressive. But his odd hours of work and sleep—the privilege of a despot—kept the whole governmental machine on alert in some way: a top official was present the whole night in any important governmental agency, and Stalin used to call in the wee hours of the morning and sternly direct the chief bureaucrat. This practice was particularly damaging during World War II when a very tired army commander tried to catch an hour of badly needed rest before an offensive.

THE WARLORD

During the war years and with Stalin's role as warlord, the features of the system and the traits of the persona blended as never before and reached their full and final shape.

Soviet armament at the end of the 1920s and the beginning of the 1930s was still on the level of the Civil War period. Russia would not have had a chance if a clash with Western armies had occurred at that time. The weakness of the industrial base was the main problem; it had no branches for aircraft, tank, car, or machine building, or for other facilities needed for producing arms. Russia was also short of metal,[19] and this was an ominous handicap. The ways of overcoming such a weakness produced heated debates, and the strategies to be adopted hinged, to a large extent, on the differing assumptions concerning the character of future wars. Marshall Tukhachevsky's views on a mobile technological war became the source of a deep-seated conflict with the narrow-minded Voroshilov, against whose views Tukhachevsky is known to have reacted in the early 1930s, in a sharply worded letter. But this was also an unmistakable gibe against Stalin that was neither forgotten nor forgiven.[20]

The destruction of the leadership of the armed forces in 1937–38, which took away about 40,000 high-ranking officers, might have grown from

---

18. Ibid., vol. 2, pt. 1, p. 340.

19. V. M. Kuritsyn, quoted in D. Volkogonov, ed., *Tridtsatye Gody,* rev. ed. (Moscow, 1990), p. 78.

20. Volkogonov, *Triumf i tragediia,* vol. 1, pt. 2, p. 76.

this or some other set of impulses and previously concealed rancors and umbrages. It was an unprecedented destruction of military cadres by their own commander-in-chief. The armed forces' backbone and brain—its strategists, industrial managers, theoreticians, and constructors—were broken at the very doorstep of World War II. It goes without saying that this carnage contributed heavily to the terrible losses of the Red Army in the first years of the war. It is true that a certain number (unknown so far) of officers and technicians were released before and during the war, but many more arrests and executions continued well into the war. Stalin's pathological vindictiveness and diffidence were probably even exacerbated as his fortunes as a war leader reached their nadir.

The problem was not, however, only in this unbelievable destruction of some of the best military men in Europe—Stalin's own. The counterpart of the gloomy suspiciousness was a "triumphalism,"[21] which was a case of self-deception (the Russian term *samoodurachivanie* sounds stronger) of maniacal proportions. Soviet military thinking under Stalin was forced to orient itself uniquely to a quick counterattack, followed by an "unavoidable" crushing of the enemy on his own territory. No professional military or anybody else could afford so much as a sigh about the power of the enemy or the recognition that the army's lack of preparation for any defensive action, even retreat, meant suicide. And suicide would have been the route for anyone who might have dared to warn Stalin about what lay ahead.

Stalin underestimated the German army's strength and did not pay attention to his (often excellent) intelligence services (he cut them down no less than he did other branches of the security system); and although he had worked very hard before the war to overcome the retardation in armaments and the relevant economic branches, these efforts, too, were marred by inconsistencies and by his preference for cronies from the Civil War and for their advice, rather than that of better qualified and abler people. His "pact diplomacy" with Nazi Germany might have been unavoidable. He was not ready for war, and the prospect of a war on two fronts (including Japan) was a nightmare, which he actually avoided (as Hitler fell into the trap). But the way Stalin played this game with Germany was lamentable, and the story is quite well known in its many aspects. Suffice it to say here that his stubborn refusal to allow the

---

21. Simonov, *Glazami cheloveka,* pp. 258–62.

military units on the frontiers, in the rear or anywhere else, to take the slightest precautions, get ready for the imminent attack, "in order not to provoke Germany" makes for very despressing reading. His self-serving confidence in his ability to outmaneuver others and to avoid ever experiencing the same was probably the reason for the state of shock and paralysis of will that struck him for about a week at the beginning of the war when he realized that all his strategies and prognostications had failed and that the Germans were already conquering enormous territories of Russia. There was at least this price to pay for the arrogant over-confidence of a man who was entirely spoiled by a political function without having to face any political contradiction.

The rumors that Stalin and Molotov discussed "a new Brest," or partial surrender to Hitler, as Beria claimed after he was arrested by pro-Khrushchev generals, may not have been true. Stalin quickly got hold of himself. But the story of the next stages of the war—until the Stalingrad victory—is one of an army that still had to learn how to fight, under a "teacher" who committed blunder after blunder of a strategic, operational, and even tactical character. He meddled heavily and in excruciating detail in ongoing war operations, persisted in many Civil War revelries (the creation of a useless Cossack cavalry was one of those), and stuck to an obtuse and characteristic gigantism that caused incredible abuse and losses in manpower.

Stalin struggled to get a handle on the situation and master a global picture of the war fronts, and—as Zhukov, Volkogonov, and others asserted—he was capable and did learn quite a lot about warfare. He even softened some of his "Stalinism" appreciably during the second, more successful part of the war. In essence, though, the man and his system continued their routine: a relentless pressure to engage in offensives without time to prepare them; identification of retreat with treason (later softened down somehow); crude, voluntaristic, and repressive methods; and the tendency to explain failure by sabotage and the incredible cruelty in treating the supposed culprits. Moreover, through special "penal battalions," barrages (*zagriadotriady*), and cleansing operations in the Red Army's rear, mounted by the security units—which otherwise participated rarely in real frontline battles—the whole arsenal and paraphernalia of a security state were mobilized against the army that was winning the war. Having been attentuated during part of the war, the Stalinist internal war machine persisted and swelled into a new draconian wave toward the end of the war, with new, elaborate chicaneries: special "filtering" concentration camps for the military personnel who were captured or just encircled by the enemy, even if they fought their way out, and suspicion toward anyone who lived in the conquered territory—and seventy million citizens lived at some time under the German occupation—provided an environment for the NKVD to operate in. The commander-in-chief suspected and fought his own no less fiercely than he did the enemy.

The study of the two dictators as warlords reveals an amazing number of features that both shared. The policy that identified retreat with treason was one of them, but it was particularly costly for Russia's soldiers and for many of its civilians. In both cases, "retreat" was taken by the two personally as an act of defiance, a personal insult for which they were ready to settle accounts with millions of people. The two did not see themselves either as leaders or servants of the state; they *were* the state. Hitler expressed this clearly to a confidant on January 27, 1944: "If the German people are not prepared to stand up for their own preservation, fine. Let them perish."[22]

Stalin did not leave any open statement to this effect, but the "discovery" of so many enemies tells the story. His policies clearly underestimated, and therefore also blocked, Russia's capacity to fight. He was—or, rather, became—essentially a *karatel'*, a Russian term difficult to translate that refers to somebody whose main business is to punish. His ignominious orders at the beginning of the war—like number 270 (issued August 16, 1941), which authorized the arrest of family members of officers who "betrayed" the country, and which deprived of aid and state benefits the families of soldiers who fell into captivity—belong to this category. Yet he presented himself to the country as a caring father. The people of the USSR thus had to endure a double calamity. They managed to fight off the invader, but they could not get rid of the enemy behind their backs and above their heads. Their adulation for their leader is another baffling testimony to the power of myths, which the dictators learned to use very successfully.

The figures on "the cost of victory" are a good occasion to reflect on a leadership whose moment of glory was also the height of its suppuration. The disproportion between the losses of both sides—in lives and prop-

---

22. A Hilgruber, *Germany in the Two World Wars* (London, 1981), p. 96.

erty—is a measure of the "extensive" character of the Russian historical effort that Stalinism pushed to the limit. The lack of consideration for human losses paralleled the attitude toward the labor force in general. I described it by pointing to the de facto distinction in the system between the attitude toward the "work force" (*rabsila*), a sociological reality, as opposed to "working class," which was used as an ideological fetish.

Stalin's way of running the war points to this personal inhumanity—that also went deep into the heart of his system. He operated with rather dehumanized ideas of numbers, of abstract blocks of "a work force" or "fighting forces" without the faintest idea about the reality of their work and action. He visited very few places where real people acted; and he never saw and never wanted to see the front and to realize what and how people functioned in real military units and headquarters. There were, I believe, only two cases of presumed visits to the frontline, but they were phony: Stalin kept at a safe distance and remained discreet, never seeing or speaking to his soldiers.

To this should be added that the industrial thrust that was so crucial for the war effort was as skewed by the methods of "planning" as the politics was distorted by its overcentralization and the very essence of despotism. The key here lies in debilitating imbalances: Armament factories were built, but in areas that were the nearest to the future front. Defense was extolled, but "strategy" was "mythologized," with only the offensive allowed to be considered—so there was no need to worry when military aircraft plants and most airfields were located too near the frontier. With defense and retreat being "forbidden" (Stalin, as we said, destroyed anyone who might have tried to contest this), there was no argument against the dismantling of powerful fortifications shortly before the war—which is what was done.

Moreover, as happened throughout the imbalanced economy, armament industries produced weapons, but not enough ammunition or spare parts for them. An endless stream of similar disparities forced administrators and chiefs to get things done by running after a tail without a head, or perhaps after a head that had lost its tail. The toll this took on the cadres cannot be quantified. We cannot miss the chance to state that there were plenty of exemplary achievements in these and other fields but that all of those required a superhuman effort, not only because of the inherent complexity of the tasks but also because of this system's inability to plan.

The other interesting feature that became particularly blatant during the war was Stalin's eagerness to almost "suck" all the key functions and positions of the state directly into his own jurisdiction. The plenitude of power he already held was not enough: He needed a direct institutional takeover on a much larger scale than Hitler was ever interested in. All the departmental boundaries between war-related agencies became so blurred that the participants in one or another "council"—all very high-ranking officials—did not know what body they were attending. Stalin alone would decide at the end of the session whether the body that was deliberating was the Supreme State Council, the Council of Commissars, General Headquarters, the Politburo, or something else again. For Stalin, these were all the same—as long as he was the boss.[23]

The megalomaniacal urge for fullness of power drove Stalin to become not only the boss of all the bodies just cited but also the supreme commander and the commissar (later, minister) of defense. It seems that his taking on anything more would have gone over the limits of the ridiculous. At the same time, Stalin's readiness to assume the title of generalissimo (not without a fake show of anger against it, followed by an "acceptance") fully justifies Bukharin's snide characterization of Stalin (in October 1929) as a "petty Oriental despot"[24]—a quite justified quip in many ways, despite the fact (maybe because of the fact) that Stalin called himself "Velikij"—The Great.

This feature of subsuming the key administration of the government under Stalin's hands-on direction—one could say, his personal property—meant that institutions could not offer any independent initiative or, in fact, do a decent job. Government leaders were paralyzed by the fear of Stalin's retribution. In principle, nothing could be done without him. Others never contradicted him, even if they knew that his assessment or decision was totally wrong. Contradicting or correcting him could mean death or a prison camp. Simple demotion would have been an act of charity. A leadership engaged in amassing so much power could not but abuse it, almost by definition. This also was a predictable impediment to grasping reality. This fact offers an additional illustration of the idea proposed elsewhere in this book that bureaucracy's takeover of power after Stalin's death brought, curiously enough, a quite meaning-

---

23. Volkogonov, *Triumf i tragediia,* vol. 2, pt. 1, p. 271.

24. Ibid., pt. 2, p. 41.

ful emancipation of the state apparatus and an interesting improvement in the life of the population.

The story of the preparedness—or lack of it—for the war, the lamentable policies of forbidding any action to counter the imminent German attack, a persistent mania to stage offensives without any good strategic reasons or enough time for preparations, the terroristic and dishonest punishing of officers for Stalin's own failures, and the mass persecution of "deserters" or war prisoners or just people who got out of an encirclement constitute both a deeply depressing tale and an indictment of Stalin's regime. The tale of how people lived through all of this is equally grim.

The people, the army, and the generals were all "guilty" by definition; hence, the key in treating the soldiers—as with the labor force—was *silovaia,* punitive, brutal, and ugly. Stalin believed in the glitter of his cult and in his infallibility and (through a seeming political miracle) made the masses and many of the elites believe in it, too. Even the terrible price of his failures did not shatter this image—critics of Stalin knew that they would have no chance with the public, much less with his security agents. The regime's security was therefore foolproof, and the enormous security apparatus and precautions were actually, to a large extent, superfluous. When we eventually get data on the number of people in the security services, it may turn out again that even in this domain, Hitler's regime was much more "economical" in terms of the number of secret service agents per thousand inhabitants. Stalin, who not only personified but privatized the system's institutions, was losing control over his actions and his mind as he was succumbing to the folly of trying to control everything.

THE OVERLORD OF THE ARTS (LITERATURE)

Our source here is mainly the autobiography of K. Simonov, a fine and honest person and an avowed and naive Stalinist. Simonov illustrated in his self-searching memoirs the depth of dedication to Stalin and an almost total disregard of the most monstrous aspect of Stalin's leadership by a whole generation of Soviet intellectuals—even if many of them, including Simonov himself, knew from some personal experience that their position was extremely fragile and that they could be crushed at a moment's notice. The liberation from Stalin's spell that began only after his death was a painstaking path that Simonov described in his memoirs.

They remain an important document about this sinister spell and about many honest people's difficulty in shedding it.

The breathtaking building sites (*strojki*), the victories in war, and the credible and desirable vision of a great man ("warts and all") were important factors in the acceptance by people such as Simonov. Also, many an unassuming but bright lad ascended to positions of national glory, and this was a powerful contributor to their succumbing to Stalin's cult. These people did not yet know or understand the Stalinism we are talking about, the other side of the moon. When Stalin was already an acknowledged leader, Simonov's cohorts were fifteen; and when Stalin died, they were thirty-eight years old. The images and the ethos that were propagated by the regime had nothing to do with the massive slave labor or other iniquities; instead, the young followers saw and experienced an impressive ethos of building the country and serving the upward movement of an awakening giant, in a spirit of romanticism and moral integrity. It was therefore painfully dispiriting to them to discover that this ethos had its much darker counterpart.

The frequent meetings with Stalin on problems of literature, in which Simonov participated together with other leaders of the Writer's Union (he recorded the content of those meetings by making personal notes immediately after each one), give an excellent picture of this aspect of Stalin's activity. Stalin showed an amazing knowledge of all aspects of literary affairs, including a detailed mastery of the content of novels. This was a degree of expertise that Simonov called "bewildering."[25] The meetings with the representatives of the Writer's Union, Simonov surmised, helped Stalin—who did not go out very much, if at all—to gauge the moods of the intelligentsia. He also meddled in minutiae of literary life and discussed to whom should go prizes, premiums, blame, and censures. He personally nominated leaders and editors (and the deputies) of literary journals, commissioned novels and plays on specific subjects, demanded that authors make changes, and unhesitatingly told writers when he thought their work was no good. Simonov himself had to write a novel on a specified theme. Stalin needed a prestigious author to help him promote his policy "against kneeling before the West" after the war, an attitude that Stalin considered dangerous. Simonov obliged and got a "Stalin prize" for it, but he later viewed this as a moral low in his life.

---

25. Simonov, *Glazami cheloveka,* p. 142.

Since Simonov gave us a sense of what Stalin liked or criticized and expected from literature, we can very effectively discern Stalin's political methods: He personally controlled minds (or tried to) and instilled ideas by dictating how history should be written, as well as literature, films, and music. According to Volkogonov's biography of Stalin,[26] a personal assignment of this type—a novel, a play, and, we could add, Stalin's own biography or the noisily trumpeted *Short Course of the History of the Communist Party of the USSR*—was one of Stalin's methods in shaping the spiritual development of the nation in the direction he wanted, especially in terms of a constant readiness to battle the "enemies of the people." But literature certainly played a special role.

This type of supposedly sophisticated personal leadership (which was also so destructive of cultural life) had no parallel, to my mind, in Hitler's actions. His regime also dominated culture, but without any detailed or, perhaps, personal interference from Hitler. Ideology and censorship were probably enough for him, and he relied on associates to deal with such matters. Their task was self-evident for the members of the Nazi creed.

THE OLD TYRANT

World War II devastated Russia, but it legitimized—or relegitimized—Stalin's rule. At the same time, the backward-looking traits (especially the inability to move the country out of its rut) and deep obscurantism of his regime were thickening. This can best be illustrated by the 1946–48 "cultural" policies that came to be known as *zhdanovism*. Stalin's imposition on a multinational country of a chauvinist anthem extolling "Velikaia Rus'" was the last chapter of his and his system's degeneration. The fact that it went with a virulent display of anti-Semitism makes the character of his rule quite transparent.

Hitler was destroyed by the war, but the economic system of Germany was preserved, although not intact. Germany could come out (with Western help) after the war and rebuild a supermodern economy (as could Japan); hence, fifty years later Germany seemed almost to have won the war. Self-sustained growth and an ability for renovation were the secret. In contrast, the Soviet system managed to create a backward superpower—a very Russian historical syndrome.

---

26. Volkogonov, *Triumf i tragediia*, vol. 2, pt. 2, pp. 33–34.

After the victory in the war, Stalin reacted viscerally against any sign of "toadying to the West" among his citizens. He certainly perceived it as a blow to his prestige and a real defeat in victory, insofar as millions of his soldiers saw the conquered living so much better than the victors. Stalin needed his intellectuals (many of whom he suspected of getting contaminated), and he mobilized people like Simonov and Erenburg to battle this scourge.

The victory in the war "froze" Stalin and his system; he was not ready to change anything.[27] Becoming a victorious world leader had a "mummifying" effect on him—exactly as reaching a superpower position and other big achievements had a numbing effect on his successors.

In January 1948, Stalin personally ordered the making of new camps for "Trotskyites." He also required "prisons for special tasks" and other high-security institutions, becoming at this stage a *karatel'* par excellence. Volkogonov, who studied Stalin's personal files, says that his attention was concentrated mainly on security agencies. As usual, he dealt with these matters in great detail, and he pampered and extolled, decorated, and promoted security personnel (especially the NKVD and NKGB).[28]

Stalin did not write diaries, but there might have been a file that Beria eventually snatched from his office when Stalin lay in a coma.[29] Doctors were not called to help him, thanks to a Beria maneuver: Stalin had refused to see doctors and had listened to Beria's advice about some home-made remedies for his illness. Beria probably sensed that Stalin plotted against the old guard, including Beria himself. It is also quite obvious that with the "security" obsession of the aging and ever more deranged, irrational, and anti-Semitic Stalin Beria's control over details of Stalin's life must have been growing. He even managed to convince Stalin that his two most faithful servants—Poskrebyshev, his personal political secretary, and Vlasik, the head of his bodyguard—had to be fired. These two were certainly well enough informed to make Stalin suspicious of Beria's manipulations. Stalin's emphasis on the security agencies gave Beria his place of choice among Stalin's top lieutenants—but the murky ground could become a bog for anyone.

27. Ibid., pp. 20–23.

28. Ibid., p. 132.

29. Ibid., p. 45 and passim. The story of Beria's doings during the last hours of Stalin's life is not yet documented convincingly.

Simonov described Stalin's last appearance at the Central Committee meeting on October 16, 1952, where he shocked the audience by savagely attacking Molotov and Mikoian, hinting that they would not be reliable and staunch successors to him. Beria might have deduced that he was in danger, too. When the same Central Committee adopted another Stalin idea—a new and much larger Presidium of the party—it was immediately apparent that the members of the old Politburo were a minority in the new ruling body, and this was a possible sign of Stalin's intention to eliminate the old guard altogether in his next move. During the same session (he spoke one and a half hours in a session that lasted two and a half hours) he played his last histrionic number by offering his resignation, which was duly rejected by unanimous vote.[30]

In the last of his nightmarish affairs, Stalin arrested a group of the Kremlin's mostly Jewish doctors, accused them of plotting to assassinate leaders, and had them tortured to extract confessions. This was a telling testimony, if one more was still needed, to the old dictator's pathology and the flotsam of a decomposing regime—the last gasp of a deranged and hate-filled executioner. Self-isolation was part of the final period in old Stalin's life; hence, he might have fallen prey to Beria, who was responsible for his well-being and security.

WHAT DID COMPARISON AFFORD?

The economic development of Germany after the mid-nineteenth century brought about a limited parliament and pressure for strengthening the Rechtstadt, but the political framework remained an authoritarian monarchy. The latter, even if getting ever more ensnarled in capitalism, was nevertheless an older German product. Different parts in society hesitated between the authoritarian and the democratic streaks that the historical process contained, settling with Hitler at a time of crisis, then switching to democracy (with the help of the occupying Allies) after Hitler's regime was smashed.

Modern scholars of Germany have used terms such as "combined development" to characterize this phenomenon (where newer and older layers and traditions combine in unpredictable ways). They were unaware, probably, that this was also a concept on which Trotsky

---

30. Simonov, ibid., pp. 211–16.

depended heavily in interpreting tsarist development, notably, in the introduction to his history of the revolution, written in 1930 and first published in 1932.[31] Trotsky referred to Marx's term "uneven development," which he reformulated into "combined development," and proceeded to explore the effects of this "law" in Russian history, showing the merging of the most modern with the most archaic traits in systems that attempt speedy modernization. Interestingly enough, he did not apply this scheme to Stalin's Russia, for which it was almost tailor-made, probably because Stalinism was not yet sufficiently crystallized in 1930.

In any case, if Blackburn and others tend to see this phenomenon as universal and not unique to Germany—which is true—I would nevertheless keep but qualify the term *unique*. The broad "mechanism" is common, but the forces participating in the making of the crises and their outcomes are not the same in all cases. Older national traditions, precapitalist in their origin—however reworked by the impetuous development of capitalism—continued to affect the next chapters of both German and Russian history. German capitalist development before World War I strengthened the authoritarian state; in Russia, such development weakened it. In Stalin's Russia, capitalism was thwarted, thereby opening even broader the gate for the impact of the more primitive past on the emerging Stalin regime. In Brezhnev's Russia (and even earlier), "civil society" also made its appearance (under the impact of urbanization), in the condition of a "mellowing authoritarianism" accompanied by a weak pressure for a form of limited democracy but more visible pressure for a system resembling the authoritarian German Rechtstadt.

Be that as it may, this bundle of ideas is relevant to what we handle in this chapter and book because, as it turns out, terms used by different schools to grasp the historical development of Germany, especially its Nazi phenomenon, are also applicable and can be used in analyzing Soviet Russia and particularly Stalinism. Uneven, discrepant movements of different layers and dimensions of a society, and the ensuing tensions and crises they created, were equally crucial in both systems—although the general formula must be provided by the empirical materials taken from the historical environment under study. The problem of crisis, so obvious a precondition for the rise of Nazism to power, also plays a role in the key chapters of the Soviet experience. Again, the cir-

---

31. Leon Trotsky, *The History of the Russian Revolution* (New York, 1980), pp. 3–15.

cumstances are changing, but at each stage it was the intrusion of a powerful impetus into a given, already at least partly imbalanced (hence, crisis-prone) situation—like capitalist development in tsarist Russia, the industrialization drive at the end of the NEP, and the massive urbanization in the post-Stalinist USSR—that created powerful crises. Both the German and the Russian dictatorial systems belong to the class of phenomena engendered by deeply imbalanced historical circumstances and representing fairly primitive forms of statehood and political leadership endowed with the most modern tools of technological development. The fact that one regime was served by a capitalist economy and that capitalism was evicted in the other is an additional topic that complicates our reflections about perspectives in Russia and elsewhere.

Returning to the central topic of this chapter, we realized that, according to the most recent biographies, Hitler was not suspicious of his entourage and did not fear for his safety: he was actually loyal to his old comrades in arms, and they reciprocated with unswerving loyalty. Nor did he fret about the fidelity of the masses, although he was very concerned about his popularity. As long as he was successful—and even beyond—the devotion to the Führer held fast. These statements about Hitler underscore the fact that Stalin had a very different attitude toward his entourage, and they force us to ask why that was so.

It turned out that his position inside the regime was different from Hitler's. Hitler felt safe, whereas Stalin did not—and not just because of fear of assassins. There was a peculiar element of insecurity in the psychology of Stalin's despotism—notably, because of what we called an "alibi" problem—that Hitler did not suffer from. This had nothing to do with Stalin's actual safety—no one ever attempted to kill him—although any critical statement, especially any texts critical of him, were perceived by him as a call for a terrorist act. This brought us to the problem that Stalin had with his ideology but that Hitler did not need to be bothered about. Stalin operated with a complicated ideological hybrid that suffused the cultural and political life of the country with a thick fog of hypocrisy, and he was successful beyond belief: Had anyone attacked Stalin for his crimes, even with facts and figures in hand, this would have provoked a violent reaction from the public and an even worse one from the secret police. And there were still plenty of supporters and defenders left years after his death to muddy the waters of the perestroika, despite the many disclosures of hideous facts, beginning with the famous "secret speech" of Nikita Khrushchev in February 1956.

The answer to this success lies not so much with one or another ideology, but with the production and efficacy of the cult, which can work with different ideological garments. The comparison required us to look into this problem. Both dictators built up a personal cult, and each identified his own "Führer principle" with the state—each *was* the state—but as we studied them as leaders, we discovered again a host of differences. We noticed, for example, the difference in the use of terror by the two protagonists. Hitler used it predominantly outside his country and not at all in his party, though he took care not to give the party members more power than he thought necessary. In contrast, Stalin's enemies were inside, and they were mostly invented. Stalin faced a task of building up the country's economy and defense from a quite low point; Hitler did not need to handle such a task. We also notice that while the "essence" of Hitler's national socialism was actually war, conquest, and racial superiority, Stalin's warfare, before he had to face Hitler's attack, went inward—against his people and his party.

We also encountered in both cases the "personalization" of state power—that is, a psychological phenomenon that makes the dictator identify himself with the state, but in the sense of an actual mental appropriation. In Stalin, who could not content himself with the essential levers of power while otherwise remaining above the fray, we observed the additional propensity of laying his hands directly on institutions and their functions and titles—and thereby emptying them of their institutional rationality. His path consisted either in a personal accumulation of chairmanships (as during the war) or in piling impossible tasks upon the government agencies and forcing them to cope (and to lie) under the terrorist whip of a ubiquitous secret police.

Hitler's ways had the same effect on the machinery of the state as a whole, but not because Hitler wanted a direct, hands-on possession. He left the governmental agencies more or less intact, with their ministers at the head, but he messed them up by improvising extragovernmental institutions, making the ministries almost redundant, and concentrating war making in his own hands. Unhappy as the Nazi ministers might have been with Hitler, they personally did not have to live with the threat of the Gestapo hanging over their heads (unless they engaged in real plotting against Hitler). In sum, Stalin was a tyrant who was actually running (administering) the machine of the state, whereas Hitler ruled over it but did not run it in the same way.

All of these points lead us to explore a kind of "political psychology" of despotism—*psychopathology* is a better term—an obvious theme to handle in cases when power is "privatized" to such an extent that one person's psyche permeates the political realm. Here we notice that Hitler and Stalin both fed their psyches with a motivator: What Jews and anti-Semitism were to Hitler, Trotsky and Trotskyism were, plausibly, to Stalin—some kind of mythical and monstrous darkness that they both needed and supplied themselves with, to whip up or justify their own demonism. In the case of Stalin, who personally also supervised literature, history, and so on, "privatization" of power and his ways of exercising it gave us an additional insight into this ruler's mind.

The two minds in question, despite a number of interesting similarities—including the "privatization" phenomenon—differed considerably. Some of the similar features stem from the inherent imperatives of despotic rule—from the psychology of the position, rather than from their psychological makeup. Additional but related comparative dimensions open up in this context, namely, the mythologies and myth making involved in both dictatorships. Hitler's and Stalin's power and myths turned equally around their own cults—that much is clear. But the ideological content was different: In the one case, it was German racial superiority and war, with war as the measure and filter of all things; in Stalin's case, it was about a magnified vision of the Russian state—the statism principle writ large but shaped by him personally.

There was actually no idea of a successor in either case and quite naturally so: One does not bequeath a cult of one's own person. The privatization of the system in both cases was such that history seemed to be beginning and ending with the two. Each cult therefore had an ingredient of "eternity" in the eyes of its carrier, who did not have a place for his own mortality in his system. In both cases, though, the public "bought" the idea—and this is perplexing. It must therefore be said that in each case the public, or segments of it, played a role not only in "buying" the cult but also in building it up. Hitler's ideology and cult were built from the preexisting ideological matrix of the German right and conservatism. "The Hitler myth," explains Ian Kershaw, did acquire the power of transcending the miseries of everyday life, and it caught the minds of a prominent sector of the bourgeouis intelligentsia and middle class, which contributed to its legitimation.[32] The propaganda minister who produced the cult succumbed to it himself, as Goebbels's diary shows.[33] The years 1935–36 witnessed a considerable erosion of the "cult"; but Hitler forbade anyone to bring him reports about corruption and other trouble,[34] and things began to "improve" also in his own psyche: From March 1936 (when the Rheinland was recovered) it could be observed that Hitler himself became a victim of "the Hitler myth"—or a "victim" of "Nazi propaganda." The day he began to believe in the Hitler myth marked the beginning of the end of the Third Reich.[35]

We have no doubt that Stalin also believed in his own cult, although we cannot say that this identification began with his own propaganda. Stalin's cult was erected on an authoritarian scaffolding that was initially inspired by popular emancipatory ideologies. Stalinism meant the takeover of this predecessor and a refocusing of it around the centrality of the state and then on an amalgamation of older traditions and ideologies of imperial statism, including the sacrosanct principle of "the one and indivisible"—the tsarist postulate for imperial Russia—in Stalin's own interpretation.

If both dictatorships still responded to the manifestations of "combined development," Germany after the war probably escaped the spell of this "law." Russia, on the other hand, even well after the war—despite the victory and the shedding of much of Stalinism—is still in the grip of the ancient "curse." Our comparative inquiry helps us to ask why and to offer a few answers.

---

32. Kershaw, *The Hitler Myth,* p. 70.

33. Ibid., p. 71.

34. Ibid., p. 76.

35. Ibid., p. 82.

THE SPRINGS OF DEMISE

CHAPTER 12:
NATIONALISM IN OUR TIMES

The Case of Russia

THE WAVE OF NEW NATIONALIST MOVEMENTS AND NEW states that began with the splintering of the USSR is a part of a rather modern phenomenon, dating from about the mid-nineteenth century. A particularly intense wave occurred in the aftermath of World War I and another in the so-called decolonization after World War II. The current wave—including the fragmentation of Yugo-slavia—is a quite intense one and exhibits some similarities with the post–World War I situation. Old empires were dismantled to be transformed into a string of independent states, and the recent dismantling of what is called "the last old empire" returned the political map of Eastern and Central Europe to its post-1918 shape. At the same time, new independent state formations appeared in the Caucasus and in Central Asia, further expanding international strife and nationalistic passion into areas that seemed settled and relatively calm.

The impression of time crawling backward is disquieting, as nationalist movements in Central and Eastern Europe, seconded now by the post-Soviet accretions, began their new independent journey. All too often they are turning for inspiration to images and heroes from the past—and thus to old enmities and conflicts. President Woodrow Wilson's idea of national self-determination and Lenin's program of a federation of Soviet states are put again, by history, before a jury: Did they succeed or fail? Tito's work, the most successful exercise in "de-Balkanizing the Balkans," is in ruins—but it is not a thrilling sight. Did these waves enhance freedoms, open new vistas and chances, or expand international cooperation and peace? Did they bring much luck to the numerous decolonized African nation-states? Do they help the reform process in the countries of the former USSR? These are quite pertinent questions, but whatever the answers (my own are all in the negative), the fact remains that nationalism is a powerful reality and is here to stay. It is a complicated and tenacious problem: Ethnic and national varieties are facts of social life, responding to deep human, social, and psychological needs.

Nations are in many ways "imagined communities," and they cannot justify themselves without "getting their history wrong."[1] But many other social phenomena are "imagined," too—that is, ideologically constructed from sometimes arbitrary assumptions and unverified facts, not to mention obvious falsehoods—and they can, nevertheless, become powerful forces. Myths of all kinds—and *myth* is the right term for an "imagined" reality—are mighty movers, and many ideological monsters of our times were built on "errors" but were "real" phenomena nonetheless. In fact, the more mythical the character of their claims, the more shattering may be their impact. Nations, their cultures, and their self-consciousness are thus a relatively recent but complicated multidimensional phenomenon with a dynamic of its own that is neither easily understood nor readily mastered—especially when a nation's leaders think they can best master only by unleashing.

Our problem, though, is not "nations" or people's need to identify with or belong to what is eventually a sovereign and independent state. Our problem is "nationalism"—an outgrowth of the things just listed. Nationalism is all too often endowed with destructive and aggressive urges and invariably linked to exclusion, oppression, racism, and fascism—rather than to the enhancement of freedoms, which is the official objective. Obviously, various ethnic groups or nationalities have fought oppression and achieved autonomy or independence, and have eradicated blatant and subtle discrimination. Such acts of liberation have allowed a certain state of dignity that oppression denies its victims. In many cases, though, this uplifting has been followed by one group assuming superior-

---

1. Ernest Renan's 1881 lecture at the Sorbonne, "Qu'est que c'est une nation?" is quoted in E. J. Hobsbawm, *Nations and Nationalism since 1780: Programme, Myth, Reality* (New York, 1990), p. 2. See also Benedict Anderson's *Imagined Communities: Reflections on the Origins and Spread of Nationalism* (London, 1983), a widely read book.

ity and running roughshod over others. Thus, nationalism leads to abuses of newly won freedom and itself becomes an oppressive force. The production of virulent nationalisms, irredentism, and, broadly, failed and backward-looking nation-states obviously poses many threats.

ARE UNIVERSALISM AND PARTICULARISM POLES APART?

To interpret the nationalist flare-up, let us first consider the reflection on this theme by the British philosopher Isaiah Berlin. In an interview entitled "Two Concepts of Nationalism,"[2] Berlin extolled human variety, specificity, and diversity as the real essence of the human condition. In contrast, according to him, the failed ideas of the Enlightenment that preached universalism, progressivism, and generalized values and reason are deformations of this essence—ones, in fact, that led to the Soviet totalitarianism that collapsed. In this perspective, Marxism, which shared the misperceptions of the Enlightenment, is also declared dead (hopefully for good this time, especially since the USSR is no more).

Berlin does not relish the outpouring of chauvinism, strife, and hatred that virulent nationalism has caused and keeps causing. He overlooks the fact, however, that many gloomy results of nationalism have had nothing to do with the collapsed Soviet totalitarianism, which Berlin seems to have seen as the cause of all evil. Also, it is difficult to see how ideas of enlightenment could have engendered such phenomena. But the result, he admits, is bleak, and no solution exists as long as there are no common values to make these nationalisms yield to shared cooperative attitudes. What, though, are those common values that are missing? Are they not precisely the substance of "universalism," which Berlin finds bankrupt and prone to create slavery? I leave him with his contradictions: nationalism is life itself, as against the presumably false abstractions of the Enlightenment; yet nationalism is a pest that cannot be contained without some of the abstractions—and, I would say, the internationalism that is not just an abstraction but a principle crucial to human existence.

It is difficult to understand the implied logic that nationalist demons would not have existed or would have been less pernicious if Marx had

---

2. *New York Review of Books,* November 21, 1991, pp. 19–23.

not launched his class struggle or inspired (as he supposedly did) the Stalinist empire. Whether stated or implied—quite independently of what
one thinks of Marx 121 years after his death—an analysis that focuses on
a preference for "specificity" over "universalism" is missing the whole
drama: specificity turned loose lies at the heart of this nationalism,
destroying values that are, precisely, universal and equally essential to
the human condition. I find it appropriate to add here a conclusion by
E. J. Hobsbawm from a recent study: The contemporary flare-up of
nationalisms is a phenomenon to be taken seriously, but it reflects the crisis "of the old Wilsonian-Leninist ideology and programme," because
the relevance of "nation" and "nation-state" to the political and economic structure of the globe "is sharply diminished";[3] hence, this phenomenon is an additional international problem.

My life in seven different countries has turned out to be an experience in
"comparative nationalism" and a personal verification of the thesis that
nationalism sometimes solves important problems, especially when a
national movement fights against discrimination and oppression. But
almost invariably, once such a movement acquires the coveted status of
independent nation-state, yesterday's victims victimize others, and the
apparently liberating character of nationalism shows its true nature.
Nationalism, of course, is not one thing but a panoply of phenomena and
movements; and, to my mind, many of those, however much they build
on ethnic, cultural, or linguistic features inherent in human societies
(and are therefore indestructible), are not about them or for them: The
essence of the nationalist frame of mind and thrust is that it cherishes one
type and, hence, no variety at all. This is why taking nationalism, which
is essentially about excluding, for a legitimate expression of an intricate
human principle of diversity and the urge for belonging is misleading.
Nationalism is, to the contrary, the perversion of a principle that cannot
be guaranteed without regard to the principle's universal quality.

   "Exclusionism" in its different forms—at a time of a particularly complicated interconnection and interdependence in world affairs, where
solutions lie mainly in accommodations and cooperation—is a counterideology. It is pushing the clock back by offering solace and security
where they cannot be found anymore—in an escape into particularism.

---

3. Hobsbawm, *Nations and Nationalism,* pp. 163–64, 177, 181.

Exclusionism consists of transferring values (often mythical) of tribal or clan solidarities and cohesion, or family values of love based on blood links, onto big ethnic-political aggregates. This is an ideological exercise that often does succeed, to a point and for a time. And this is precisely why it—and the causes that lead to it—have to be taken seriously, to avoid a host of pernicious effects that block human cooperation.

The argument against making particularism into a virtue has to be supplemented by a warning against erring in the opposite direction. The Soviet system erred blatantly in its disregard for the importance of "the local," the specific, the ethnic, and the different, but it was not a reaction against the abuse of universalism by those different particularists. The reason for this Soviet attitude stemmed from a blend of a bureaucratic preference for uniformity—which is a different category altogether—with an ambiguous game of hide-and-seek with a particular type of nationalism.

The predilection for the grand scale so characteristic of the Soviet regime engendered a propensity to produce and impose uniform solutions from the center onto the whole country. This was the regime's best way of simplifying action and of ensuring the execution of policies and control from above—with control sometimes more avidly sought than the production of action itself. This became blatant when the regime spun into a fatal decline. The same tendency had existed there before, but it had been less obvious while the still-dynamic system could boast of many successes. But as the world around and the social reality inside were getting ever more differentiated and complex—hence, unresponsive to inadequate, standardized simplifications—the huge Soviet power-hub began to stall. The restriction of centralized uniformity to only one or a few spheres of social life and governmental action would have been unavoidable and could have been tolerable. But the society-wide imposition of uniform policies from a greedy control center inevitably caused an accumulation of problems.

The case of the Soviet nationalities is a particularly telling example of the inadequacy of an overcentralized state for handling a national maze. Nationalities in the USSR were characterized by a growing differentiation of local conditions. Officials trumpeted a growing homogeneity and declining strife as the prevailing trends and main achievements of their system. This stance was a predictable position to be taken by notorious oversimplifiers, but it was also an obvious humbug. Irrepressible local differences and the center's dream (or pretense) of uniformity were constantly at odds.

In Stalin's times the prevailing tendency consisted in suppressing. Khrushchev's and Brezhnev's policies became much more flexible and sometimes even elicited more flexible responses from Moscow. In fact, officials increasingly were delaying, turning a blind eye, maneuvering politically, and combining pressure with negotiations—but without affecting in substance the irresistible and spontaneously evolving sociopolitical relations in the republics and elsewhere. Standardized, "made-in-Moscow" policies were losing their grip. The corrupting impact of the peculair nemesis of Soviet statehood—namely, the powerful centralism that was breeding "multicentrism" (*mnogotsentrie*)—finally paralyzed the very center itself. The trend applied also to the national republics, which were all too eager and were appropriately constituted to gain for themselves as much as the center would concede, willingly or unwillingly. These trends that were produced in the republics complicated indigenous constellations of power, moods, and ideologies. On the one hand, the growth of their national intelligentsia produced national leaders and enough candidates for most jobs, making the previous professional superiority of the ethnic Russians a thing of the past. On the other hand, especially in the Caucasian and Central Asian republics, traditional family and clan networks were still powerful enough to penetrate the state and party *apparaty* and "coopt" them for all practical purposes. These were the so-called local mafias—alliances of state-party leaders with local clans and black-marketeers, who tended to hold real power in such republics.

This picture has to be retouched further by the realization that after Stalin's death there were areas and periods in the realm of national policies that enjoyed calm and looked promising, especially in the cities. At such times one could observe in Russia and in the republics a widespread expression of satisfaction with the interethnic relations. A good study of what people remember today about the national relations in the past might reveal a widespread feeling that things were rather smooth and friendly and that a sense and acceptance of a Soviet supra-ethnic commonality was in fact present and at times growing. If research can prove this assumption, which I conceived on the basis of quite numerous conversations in Moscow with well-informed people of different ethnic origins, we would have to add this, too, to the file on Soviet nationalities.

"WE SHOULD GET TOUGH WITH LENIN"

The Soviet nationality complex is one of the burdens of Russian history, even if it was willingly assumed by the regime. It was inherited from the tsarist empire and was expanded under Stalin, after World War II, into a complicated "bloc," well beyond the historical frontiers of Russia. This burden contributed to the heavy weight the regime had to carry, but it was far from being the main shaper of that burden. In a national mosaic such as the Soviet one, it was more difficult than elsewhere to produce a feeling of patriotism, the indispensable unifying glue in political entities; and in the USSR this feeling had to be state (not nation) oriented. The education and propaganda sought therefore to instill in the multiethnic population an allegiance to an obvious, common rallying symbol: the state called USSR was the natural banner for this purpose. This was a quite plausible objective that was also practiced in Western Europe and elsewhere.

However, the USSR also had harbored Soviet-style protostatehoods, themselves potential (it not always actual) carriers and breeders of national aspirations, ready to turn into nationalisms; and this situation was deplored equally by Stalinists and Russian nationalists. They bewailed this as a legacy of Lenin, who supposedly had imposed it on a reluctant Stalin and had almost toppled him for having become, according to Lenin, worse than a traditional "Russian bully." As previously unknown materials keep emerging from the Russian archives, it becomes clear that Stalin not only criticized "the old liberal" but actually despised him and saw a need "to be tough with Il'ich."[4] This quarrel between Stalin and Lenin had many underpinnings, but it broke into the open early in the history of the regime in connection with the way of constructing the USSR and fitting the nationalities into it. Behind the battles about constituting such an unusual agglomerate into a common political unit lurked the broader problems of the very essence of this state, its ideology and message.

---

4. This is an exchange of notes between Stalin and Kamenev during a Politburo meeting, September 28, 1922, where Kamenev stated: "[Lenin] goes to war in defense of independence" (of Georgia, in this case); and Stalin answered: "I think we need to be tough with Il'ich." For an invaluable collection of materials on the history of the national problems, see M. K. Gorshkov, V. V. Zhuravlev, and A. P. Nenarokov, eds., *Nesostoiavshijsia Iubilej: Pochemu SSSR ne otprazdnoval svoego 70-letiia?* (Moscow, 1992), p. 114.

Bolshevism split at this juncture into different strategies and ideologies. Conservative nationalists from the non-Bolshevik camps would not share Lenin's intention to get rid of Russia's image as a prison of nations; they would deplore "the catastrophe" and disgrace of having cut "Mother Russia" into pieces and of having created states for the minority nationalities, each of them a potential source of separatism and disintegration. Nationalists and Stalinists agreed on this point, quite early on, and here was the source, however remote, of the alliance between squads of party members and rabid nationalists, who often parade their unity and slogans in the streets of Moscow these days.

Thus, interestingly, two (if not three) historical intuitions were at work when the USSR was created in 1923–24. One was represented by Stalin and his allies, and was encapsuled in his "autonomization" plan, which postulated a simple incorporation of the various nationalities as autonomous units of the Russian republic. There was no doubt about the meaning of it: a federation would hamper the freedom of action of a centralized and unitary state, on which Stalin had set his eyes, probably under the impact of the Civil War, if not earlier. With his political instincts, Stalin anticipated the potentials of nationalism that federated republics would harbor; he preferred conditions that would encourage a "melting pot." This American term was not in the political vocabulary in Russia, but there was another: The preferred perspective envisioned the "merging" (*sliiane*) of nationalities, sometime in the future, into one nationally nondistinct collectivity. Pressing more or less hard into this direction might have had, as some hoped (Stalin was no doubt one of them), the same effect as "the melting pot."

The ailing Lenin woke up rather suddenly to the dangers of such incorporating of various nationalities into Russia. In fact, he already had had some misgivings about being too hard on the nationalists, and on Mensheviks, too, in Georgia somewhat earlier. But now he realized that the policies already in place were going in the wrong direction, even before the USSR was created. It would look like the continuation of the old Russian system, and he argued—in a highly emotional pitch (especially in his memorandum on nationalities)—that this was not the face a revolutionary country should show, especially to the awakening East. Stalin and his ilk emerged in Lenin's mind as a bunch of "Great Russian bullies" about to take over the party for good. During the debate on nationalities at the Twelfth Party Congress, the influential Old Bolshevik N. Skrypnik (a Ukrainian leader who later would become a member of the Central Committee of the Soviet Communist Party) followed the same line, accusing the party at large of being infected with Great Russian (*velikoderzhavnyj*) nationalism. He was exposing the usual method of such circles—Stalin's among them—of hiding their own "nationalist deviation" by emphasizing the dangers of the "local nationalist deviation." Skrypnik was not the only person to give vent to such misgivings about the nationalist leanings in the party.[5] Two other strong voices were those of Christian Rakovsky, a Central Committee member who joined the opposition led by Trotsky, and Mirza Sultan Galiev, a Tatar communist leader.[6]

The line Stalin was adopting in those early years later blossomed into a system of absolute power that endeavored—without real success, in the longer run—to empty of its content the structure called USSR. This was the structure that "the old liberal" Lenin wanted to be "a federation of equals." "Old liberal" was an irritated gibe against Lenin's policies that Stalin launched in a private note, not in Lenin's face. Stalin mocked this tendency of "playing around with independence."[7] this view toward nationalities led him into an ever-deepening identification with the classical themes of the Russian extreme right, which came to fruition after victory in World War II. At that time it erupted in the form of a virulent anti-Semitism, which was the worthy accompaniment to an equally virulent Russian nationalism that was epitomized, through chanting about the glory of *"Velikaia Rus',"* in the new national anthem—a symbol par excellence of Russian chauvinism. This also meant that Stalin opted for the biggest nationality as his power base and was ready to suppress by force the probable reaction of the other nationalities against the unabashed self-professed superiority of "the big brother."

There were ups and downs in juggling with the national policies after Stalin's death, but *"Velikaia Rus'"* stayed. Finally, a very strong "Russite" trend kept emerging and made a powerful nest for itself at the very top of the party. Forceful Russification would have been the obvious strategy of such a trend to prevent the minorities' cravings for independence.

---

5. See *Dvenatsatyj S'ezdVKP(b)*, 17–25 aprelia 1923 g., Stenograficheskij otchet (Moscow, 1869), pp. 569–73.

6. For excerpts of the debates on nationalities during the Twelfth Party Congress, see Gorshkov et al., *Nesostoiavshijsia Iubilej*, pp. 201–14.

7. Ibid., p. 108.

This might have been the right way to rally Russian nationalism behind the regime—on condition of actually aggressively fomenting it—but this was certainly not the right way to incorporate the minorities and dampen nationalism in the republics. The vision of "Soviet patriotism" had little chance to develop under such an explosive banner.

Another way would have involved abandoning the unitary and centralized state as Stalin wanted that, plus reforming and strengthening the federation. The Lenin legacy of national republics—imposed on the unwilling Stalin when he was not yet powerful enough to have everything to his liking—implied a serious potential for a considerable delegation of powers, decentralization, and vitality of the federal principle. But the Stalin-legated centralism of a unitary state would not let it happen. The actual result was a hybrid: Moscow-controlled power, as Stalin wanted, but with the preservation of forms of national statehood for the main nationalities, as Lenin insisted on (in part, almost from his grave). These contradictory forces battled it out and produced a national policy full of zigzags and inconsistencies, as documented by Ronald Suny, an American specialist on the nationalities of the USSR.[8] However curtailed, the republics were appropriate politico-administrative units for achieving a federal structure. They were a base for the preservation of the nationalities and held a potential, as Stalin's political flair signaled to him, for expanding their Soviet-style nation-states into independent countries. It is such a mischief that Stalin or other fans of Great Russia wanted to prevent by "merging" the nationalities in a unified state, with paltry autonomies thrown in for consolation. A real federation having been discarded, the potential for a break-up of the union had to be taken seriously.

THE MANY SOULS OF THE PARTY

A "hybridization" of ideologies by and inside the party corresponded to the juggling of contradictory policies in relation to nationalities. The party was never really monolithic. Enough variety and factionalism existed in the ranks and among the leaders in the early stages, but the party managed, nevertheless, to preserve a considerable degree of unity. "Monolithism" was a later addition, a Stalinist one, when it was imposed

---

8. From Ronald Suny's series of lectures at Stanford University, which appeared as *The Revenge of the Past: Nationalism, Revolution and the Collapse of the Soviet Union*, Foreword by Norman M. Naimark (Stanford, Calif., 1993).

and made into the highest principle of party life. But instead of strengthening ideological "purity"—which monolithism was supposed to serve, thanks to administrative pressure by "a secretarial ladder"—ideological monolithism broke down. Additional ideological "products" were introduced by sanction from Stalin and his entourage, who felt free to use different ideological symbols (languages) simultaneously, according to their predilections and political expediency, without bothering about contradictions among them. Debate was not possible, so contradictions and plain nonsense—whether accepted by the public, as was often true, or ignored by them, as also happened—could float around in the official world. Opponents existed, of course, but they would not last or would not "go public."

The Imperial Great Power image and nationalism were cultivated by Stalin's regime from the mid-1930s on, and it certainly was quite an independent and ideological entity, coexisting supposedly with what the "Short Course," the official history of the party, wanted the citizenry to learn. The official textbook's connections with Marxism were a caricature, whereas the parallel extolling of powerful and cruel tsars, however spurious in itself, was an unmistakable orientation, backed by intense propaganda. But the "Short Course," with its perverse falsifications of history, was contributing its part by offering an ideological foundation for the whole era of hysteria against "the enemies of the people." To my mind, this concoction of "enemies" was again an ideological brew in its own right, the real heart of Stalinism and specific to it. But yet another broader, somewhat less discernible line of thought and ideological orientation was connected to the growing centrality of the state, as best represented by the term *statism*. Stalin promoted his own version of statism, and "the cruel tsars" now became an ideological ingredient of such an orientation. The country's growing bureaucracy—as one would expect—made it into its own credo, then preserved and developed it after Stalin's death. Statism was yet another ideology in its own right that could live with and use equally well some supposedly socialist slogans (nationalization) and traditional Russian authoritarian themes (though not necessarily the images of autocrats).

After Stalin's death, several ideological currents existed and acted insidiously and surreptitiously—until they dared to come out into the open. Hectic social change in the Soviet Union after Stalin produced a re-emergence of a kaleidoscope of ideological and political "undercurrents" in society and had its repercussions in the ruling party itself: more than ever before, it became in those years, amidst the rank and file and inside the apparatus, an agglomeration of ideologies, trends, and streams—not at all the "Marxist-Leninist" monolith that kept being proclaimed by East and West. Some Marxist-Leninist devotees—whatever this might have meant at that time—were present among members and especially inside the ideological apparatus, but it is not clear whether they were the preponderant factor even there. Rather, as said earlier, a variety of ideological streams and cliques coexisted in a tenuous state of balance—sometimes turning into conflict—partly hidden from observers' eyes and at times actually becoming quite visible.

A version that some mistook for Marxism-Leninism was actually a remodeled Stalinist statism and was becoming a sizeable force not only in the upper echelons but also in the lower ones. Its proponents used Lenin's name, but what they meant was their devotion to the deeply authoritarian patriotism and expansionism. This brought them easily into an alliance with a more traditional, strictly Russian chauvinism of the Great Power brand, which did not care for Lenin or anyone similar. They respected Stalin, though not for his presumed "socialism." This meeting of hearts was not accidental, because broad layers of *apparaty* (and even broader layers in society, especially among intellectuals) actually believed in "statism." This was the real thing for them, because this was what they practiced, cherished, and tried to preserve.

The ideology and practice of statism could be presented in military-patriotic, technocratic, or neo-Stalinist versions, or in a mixture thereof. To its supporters this might have seemed like the rediscovery of a safe ideological position, with which they probably hoped to bolster the system. But such "rediscoveries" of old but fairly bankrupt planks were part of a general decadence of the regime that not only spread demoralization and corruption but also created a moral vacuum and a growing delegitimization of much of what was officially preached or professed. The ongoing economic decline was a catalyst for such trends. In the 1960s and especially during the 1970s, it became obvious to some observers abroad and to analysts inside that the regime was heading toward a full-fledged and generalized crisis.

Those who drew such conclusions were, nevertheless, rather few. But the ideological confusion was obvious, especially among the intelligentsia, even if they did not yet discern its full meaning. The growing sense of the inadequacy of the official ideological formulations and the stagnation of the institutions pushed many people to look for ways out, first, in different ideological allegiances and identities and in programs for the revitalization of the system. This was happening not only in different intellectual circles and other social layers but also among the political leaders and their administrations.

The regime, as we know, used a number of modern ideological and practical themes, or progressive slogans, going from themes of the Enlightenment to Marxism and Socialism to the big trends and themes of the contemporary civilization, with the techno-scientific revolution as its driving force. Although such themes served the regime in different ways and at different times, they failed to prevent its decline. The quite effective suppression of open opposition and debate, which might have challenged the regime on its own grounds, had a deeply corrupting and perverting effect on the best and most forward-looking ideas. No serious scholarly and cultural reflection about the complexities of our times or about political imperatives—unless exercised privately by individuals or semiprivately by scholars in some institutes—was made available at times when such tools for self-examination were urgently needed. It goes without saying that no socialist or Marxist thinking existed, especially when growing numbers of intellectuals were reacting to such thinking as an official sham and were looking to different traditions, either pre-revolutionary or Western, to guide them. Broadly speaking, the system was "successful" in blocking intellectual life and thought, leaving the country with a menacing deficit of thoughtful leadership, which has been sorely missing in the new era.

It is worth interjecting that during the 1960s, in the framework of the open and internal debates on economic and other reforms (fully supported by Prime Minister Kossygin), the intellectual and professional level of the participants and the level of their commitment and hope were impressive and promising. But this movement of what came to be called "the men of the sixties" (still among the best of those active in the 1980s, but by then tired and old) was throttled after the supression of the "Prague Spring" in 1968. Thenceforth, there was a paucity of forces and thinkers capable of offering ideas for reforms and convincing ideologies of emancipation to a population that was rather well educated and urbanized but politically and ideologically impoverished.

This situation accounts for the fact that the search for ways out of the crisis and the critique of the regime were in many cases shallow and quite often merely backward. For some circles, this was a rush for Western models and inspiration—but with little knowledge and experience for a critical assimilation of Western realities. It meshed with an equally impetuous rejection of the realities of the USSR and of anything that was done in it during the whole post-1917 period. In other circles (sometimes in the same ones, after people had sobered up from their initial infatuations), there was not only a violent reaction against the "Westernizers" and their presumed servility before the West but also a search for ideological roots and inspiration—not to mention solace—in the past, which meant, mostly, religion and nationalism.

This kind of ideological pluralism, both in "undercurrents" and in increasingly open currents, actually contained a whole panoply of nationalisms, many of them exhibiting little taste for democracy or openly hostile to it. This is one of the main reasons for their hostility toward the West. This means that those were frankly authoritarian currents, which included semifascist or fully fascist and obsessively anti-Semitic ones, plus many atavistic attitudes of "prerevolutionary" vintage. This view was rooted in stories such as "The Protocols of the Elders of Zion" or in the related idea that the main antagonism of modern times is one between Slavdom and Judaism, with the latter seeking to control the world from its base in the United States, which Jews supposedly control already. Such views began to develop and appear, more or less on the surface, at least by the later 1960s, continued outside and inside the higher and lower spheres of the decaying Soviet system, and are now open for everyone to see in today's Russia and all around it—sometimes even in journals and reviews bearing the same names as twenty-five years ago.[9]

---

9. A good example of such opinions and of their persistence is a paper by a Russian researcher presented to an October 1992 symposium on "The Russian Independent Institute of Social and National Problems." He expanded on the evil role of foreigners in depressing the Russian nation and concluded that "the process of the development of Russian national self-consciousness, in condition of Russia's re-entry into the international division of labor" will be complicated, especially since it will take place in the framework of the historical quarrel between two superior ethnic entities: Judaism, which has already reached its full blossom, and Russian culture, which is still developing but is already a dominant genotype. The Judaic ethnos—so runs the argument—replaces nowadays the German one and actually does dominate the United States. See *Obnovlenie Rossii: Trudnyj poisk reshenij* (Moscow, 1992), p. 31. The speaker, F. E. Sheregi, is a member of this institute, but the editors distanced themselves from his opinions in the English summary of the proceedings (p. 186).

It was in the late 1960s that an ideology of Russian chauvinism, anti-Semitism, and expansionism began to be preached quite openly, especially by a group that some analysts called the "Russity." They were writing in a number of official party publications in the 1960s and 1970s—notably, *Molodaia Gvardiia, Nash Sovremennik, Moskva*—with writers and editors such as Shalmaev, Lobanov, Vikulov, and a host of others who not only preached their fare but aggressively attacked the best representatives of contrary views.[10] They sometimes incurred a mild censorship from, say, the ideological department, but, basically, nothing happened to them; they could continue their propaganda in the same or in other, equally important outlets. On the other hand, supposedly important party officials who tried to attack them from "older" positions of internationalism lost their political power.

The case of Alexander Iakovlev, then the acting head of the Propaganda Department (and later a close advisor to Gorbachev), is a good example. He attacked the Russity sharply in the press, but he was soon sent to the Russian Embassy in Canada. He was later recalled to an influential position when Andropov began his brief spell of party leadership and was viciously smeared by the same Russity in a gossip campaign. The same clique was responsible for the defeat of Alexander Tvardovsky's editorial career in the periodical *Novyj Mir*, which played a remarkable role as a bellwether, provided a critical and innovative approach—often labeled "liberal"—to the country's problems, and had a deeply democratic potential and appeal.

The conclusion is obvious: The differences between an Andropov and those who tolerated and encouraged rabid party nationalists at the party's top positions, in the Central Committee and the Politburo, were very serious indeed. We do not yet have a clear picture of who was what in the leadership, but many clearly were looking for a replacement of the standard ideological credo. The mentor of the nationalists was probably Suslov, the secretary who oversaw the whole ideological sphere. He paraded at the same time as the official "theoretician" of Marxism-Leninism, but it is obvious that he and Iakovlev, and eventually also

---

10. Material on these trends and periodicals can be found in Edward Allworth, ed., *Ethnic Russia in the USSR: The Dilemma of Dominance* (New York, 1980); and Alexander Yanov, *The Russian Challenge and the Year 2000* (New York, 1987). For a chronological history of trends in Russian nationalism, see Stephen K. Carter, *Russian Nationalism, Yesterday, Today, Tomorrow* (New York, 1990).

Andropov, were not the same Marxist-Leninists. It stands to reason that in different conditions they would not have belonged to the same party.

On the whole, the majority, at least in the party's upper stratum, were conservative authoritarians, and there was no thick wall between them (even if some Marxist-Leninist terminology still appeared in their speeches) and other conservative creeds or different versions of nationalism, often with an orthodox religious coloring. It can be argued that, by the late 1960s, those people, even highly placed ones who could be called "Marxist-Leninists," did not have the upper hand or had lost it.

There were in the party also various reform-oriented leaders, even "party democrats"—although certainly just a minority at the top. The initial Gorbachev wing happened to be such a minority in the party's upper reaches, that surprised the conservatives, who found themselves duped. But this just underscores the fact that the USSR was not ruled by some left-wing party or ideology—that much should be spelled out, even if many, for some mysterious reasons, believe otherwise. Very influential in the party was a conservative wing that opposed any reforms and leaned even more toward a Russian nationalism of a rather gloomy variety, thus replicating the ideological development of Stalin at the ebb of his life. The party's ability to offer something else was clearly declining, as was the whole system. Whether the party understood this or not, nationalism looked like a policy of last resort for at least a strategically important part of the apparatus.

In view of the politico-ideological trends just described, it becomes clear that the nationalist and conservative forces inside Russia under Yeltsin's presidency are not of very recent vintage. Their roots go far back into Russian history, but the direct influences were the years of "stagnation" during the previous three decades and the ideological amalgam that came to dominate the party at that time. This was part of the propitious ground for breeding decadent streams and moods, heavily borrowed from the least-appetizing prerevolutionary traditions, and transmitting them to a "post-Communist" Russia beset by crisis and vulnerability. This is why, when ex–party members (many of them old *apparatchiki* in all the parties) today fill key governmental jobs, go to churches, produce privatizations (sometimes for the benefit of their own private businesses in tandem with black-market or outright ganster types), and preach "democracy and anti-communism," along with several varieties of nationalism (including some that smack of fascism), their actions do not represent mere conformism, bad faith, or trendiness. This behavior is a reflection of what these people were or were becoming while still inside the party and still extolling the Marxist-Leninist or "socialist" qualities of the regime. Many of the same people now repudiate those features or even loathe them—apparently, with a good conscience—and turn to backup positions they had been cultivating for quite some time.

Some Russian, as well as anti-Russian, nationalists see the central weakness of Russia and the source of its woes in its "weak national self-consciousness." The Russians are a "sick nation," or, as E. Allworth put it, "Russians remain an ethnically underdeveloped people"[11]—so runs this diagnosis. But this point is argued, characteristically, from contradictory positions. The nation is sick because Russians saw themselves as an "imperial" nation and took that for granted. For some non-Russian nationalists this was an ugly feature that was, by definition, common to this nation of oppressors. Those who see the Russians' "imperialist" orientation as the root cause of a weak national identity sometimes quote ethnographic surveys of the 1970s and 1980s, which reported that, when asked about their national identification, most Russians said "Soviet" (*Sovetskie'*). Most nationals in the republics cite their own ethnicity as their identity. According to surveys, a Georgian or Uzbek would rather identify with his or her nation and republic. Such responses of Russians (presumably living in the other republics) are supposed to hinder or dilute a Russian national identity, while also being, purportedly, an expression of an imperialist self-image.[12]

Another Russian-nationalist version perceived Russians as being too tolerant, too much influenced by the hordes of "foreigners" living amidst and around them. This trend convinced the Russians to cleanse themselves, reaffirm their own identity, and stop—as some say—"all this pernicious national intermingling." Views of Russia as an "infirm nation" suffering from the absence of a self-confident national identity would also lead some of the nation's proponents to argue that such "infirmity" explains the revolution and the victory of Leninism. The proof of the

---

11. Allworth, *Ethnic Russia,* p. 34.

12. G. Lapidus, V. Zaslevsky, and P. Goldman, eds., *From Union to Commonwealth: Nationalism and Socialism in Soviet Republics* (Cambridge, 1992), contains a contribution by the Russian ethnographer L. Drobizhevz, "Perestroika and the Ethnic Consciousness of Russians," with data from ethnographic surveys on national attitudes of Russians and other nationalities (pp. 98–111).

whole thesis is easily found in the visible, even dominant presence of non-Slavs and non-Christians in the Bolshevik government.

Open or camouflaged xenophobes do not care for the fact that the so-called Bolsheviks—as any Communist government is, according to them—"corrected" this situation a long time ago: The post-Stalinist central bodies were not only *Judenfrei* but were also deeply Russified, with mostly a strong admixture of Ukrainians and White Russians, themselves Russified and at most "closet ethnics." More ironic and probably more shocking for ignorant defenders of their nation's "purity" would be the fact that the Russian nobility and gentry (the nation's most conservative political leaders), including the tsarist court, were ethnically mixed, carrying German, Muslim, Polish, Finnish, and Moldavian names. Jewish names were more frequent on the left and among the liberals. The extremist-pogromist "Black Hundreds" and other groups of this kind were led, again, by Russified ethnics, including some of Jewish origin.[13] As we already quoted, "getting their history wrong" is in fact typical of enraged nationalist propagandists.

Laments about Russians being meek and smothered by others come from Russian nationalists who feel themselves neglected or assailed by pressures and insults showered on them by the ever more aggressive national minorities—or the majorities in their own republics. Interpretations of this kind are supported also by some anti-Russian nationalists who may feel that a Russian xenophobic nationalism would tend to dump the empire and further weaken Russia by antagonizing also the minorities inside Russia itself. To some, the collapse of the USSR and a further fragmentation of Russia proper may appear to be the best guarantee for their own independence.

Some voices from abroad join the debate on nationalities and nationalism and actually support the different nationalist currents—disregarding their xenophobic and other unsavory features—because they see in that brand of patriotism the best ideological buttress against communism or any other left. Such voices join those on the inside who do not like the presumed lack of nationalist ardor among many Russians. It smacks of a danger of "cosmopolitism"—a code word among extremists, whether of the "Zhdanovite" or of the "Black Hundred" minting, for Jews—as well as for liberal and left-leaning intellectuals.

---

13. See Dmitri E. Pospelovsky, "Ethnocentrism, Ethnic Tensions, and Marxism-Leninism," in Allworth, *Ethnic Russia,* pp. 124–25.

Appeals of this kind—including calls for "national purity" and "strong national identity," and for a "return to sources," "to the national soil" and "heroic past," or to the lost Grand Russian glory—against plots from the outside and from inside, including the menace of "international Zionism"—are typical ingredients of a radical, even conservative right (or for that matter, any right anywhere). They are never too far away from racism and fascism, and their advice is never really "innocent." Even without the empire, Russia continues to be an interethnic country. The ideologies in question are a sure prescription for a further decomposition of Russia, because its minorities will be matching manifestations of such a Russian nativism with their own.

ARE THEY ETHNOCENTRIC, IMPERIALIST, INTERETHNIC, INTERNATIONALIST?

The problems of Russians did, in fact, stem in many ways from the imperial appetites of the system and its propaganda. Traditionally, Russia's international position loomed larger than its economic wherewithal—and this, sooner or later, involved enormous cost and considerable fragility for the tsarists and, finally, for Soviet Russia. Ideologically, Soviet Russia was not what it officially claimed to be: therefore, it suffered not only from an economic deficit but also from a moral-ideological one, both of which were harmful for the country. Peddling mythologized and hybrid values to feed the self-consciousness and psyches of a multiethnic country had a great cost attached to it, for the citizens and the regime. The appeal of the regime was therefore "schizoid": It praised and built its identity and world thrust on the USSR, but for this approach to be or look sincere, Russian nationalism had to be kept at bay, lest the regime wreck the Soviet Union by fomenting a nationalist backlash from the republics. Or the regime veered to an opposite policy of basing the entire system on the interests of the most powerful nationality.

When discussing the first swing of the pendulum, some writers argued that depriving Russia of the same institutions that the others had—especially a national party—hindered better interrepublican relations.[14] Granting Russia the status of a nation-state, similar to the status of the other republics, would allow the emergence of a more genuine federal-

---

14. S. Bialer, "Comment: The Impact of Common RSFSR/USSR Institutions" in All-worth, *Ethnic Russia,* p. 199.

ism. It could have put an end to an omnipresent Russian superiority that parades hypocritically as a carrier of internationalism. Others maintain that it is always the strongest nationality that poses the greatest menace to a federation—and this has to be kept at bay.[15] In Yugoslavia, for example (as Bohdan Denich described), the precautions taken by Tito consisted of putting breaks on the Serbs, the biggest nationality in that country. The same, Denich implies, should have been done in Russia.

In the meantime, this debate became purely historical, but nationalists keep slogging it out. The old USSR does not exist anymore because of Lenin's "antinational perfidy," as some Russian nationalists say. Offering statelike structures to the ethnic minorities produced poisoned fruits. Despite all the obstacles put in their way, those republics offered their nationalities almost all they needed to keep alive the dream of independence and to actually get it. At the same time, Lenin's heirs denied the Russian nation what those minorities got. Assessing such arguments, as far as they go, against Lenin depends on how we rate other available policies that the critics have in mind. Was Lenin wrong in wanting those national protostates? Was a unitary state better and feasible? Was it right to give Russia something less?

In fact, the lament about the Russian nation being deprived of attributes that others had did not seem to bother too many people. Even if they did not have their own national party, Russians dominated the All-Union Party, and it is questionable whether average Russians felt unhappy and nationally deprived because they did not have a Communist Party of the RSFSR with its own Central Committee. All the institutions in Russia were Russian, there was a government of the Russian republic (RSFSR), and every Russian knew that Russia was the leading nation in the USSR and that the leadership of the CPSU was predominantly Russian.

This leadership, on the other hand, whether it chose to control the Russian nationality by containing and restricting its powers or preferred to "bribe it" by adopting some of its worst nationalist prejudices, was not interested in letting appear a mighty Russian Central Committee of a Russian Party that could undermine the parallel leadership of the CPSU, also mostly in Russian hands. These leaders preferred to reserve this dangerous power for themselves; after all, they were a dictatorship that minded its dic-

---

15. Cf. Bohdan Denich, "Dilemma of the Dominant Ethnic Group," in Allworth, *Ethnic Russia,* pp. 315–24.

tatorial business. But would a Russian Central Committee grant Russians more freedom than others had in their republics? So the pressure for such a party might have come from a layer of *apparatchiki* who would gain many good positions if a Russian Republican Party bureaucracy was created, under the very ceiling of the All-Union Party hierarchy.

It is true that economic difficulties did create in some circles a resentment against the fact that some republics fared much better than Russia, and a growing faction in the party leadership might have used this as an argument for a change of orientation they were envisaging: to bow to a certain realism and reorient the ideology, in the wake of Stalin, toward the strongest nation, superior to others in terms of space, numbers, historical traditions, and military and scientific weight. This would mean that leaders of this persuasion would begin to cultivate their own image as pure Great Russians. Ethnic Russians already dominated the leading agencies; and some of them, as we already know, flirted with a "heavy" Russian nationalism, often of the crudest type, and believed this to be the safest way of keeping the mighty Russian base on the side of the party— or of the leadership of the right kind. The mythical *"Velikaia Rus'"* that Stalin personally put into the anthem—real dynamite as far as other nationalities were concerned—remained in the anthem after Stalin's death, except for the excision of his name as the one that "raised us all."

This was now to be seconded by virulently chauvinist trends inside the party, in party journals and newspapers. Preaching the need to "strengthen the military-patriotic education of youth" or extolling the *Rodina-Mat'*—which is untranslatable, though "Mother Russia" gives an idea—could seem, to a fervent Russian nationalist, an unambiguous call to be patriotic. But this was not really a call anymore that would put the USSR above anything else. The Uzbeks, who would be asked to be "militarily patriotic" for the USSR, knew well that for many Russians and party bosses it meant "Velikaia Rus'." Thus, the Uzbek intellectuals or officials, faced with the need to serve the world thrust of *Rus'*—the ancient ancestor common to the Russians, Ukrainians, and White Russians—might have, in this situation, preferred their own myths of a powerful conquering nation (which Uzbeks had been part of many centuries earlier) and to ask: "Who do those corrupt Russians think they are? We were and can be conquerors ourselves."[16] Achieving national

---

16. This is based on my conversations with Uzbek officials in Moscow.

independence was thus for many officials a stepping stone to proving their national virility by claiming an ability to conquer and oppress somebody else. There were other reactions to the signs of Russian nationalism in the Moscow upper echelons, and they were unambiguous in their readiness to dump the USSR and to rule the others as normal provinces—an old dream of conquerors.

However, events after the perestroika took an entirely different turn. The republics quit the USSR and declared their independence, whereas many Russian nationalists and large layers of the population have preferred in recent years to get rid of the imperial burden by letting the republics go and turning their attention to internal problems of Russia proper. In fact, one can say that Russia, not Armenia and Azerbaijan, actually undermined the USSR. Whatever else such action was, it cannot be qualified as imperialist; it was, perhaps, a stroke of realism. At the same time, an expansionist wing parades in the streets, denounces "treason," and demands the reconstitution of the USSR. It is this theme that produces much of the "curious" alliance of orthodox Communist Party members (of a Stalinist or neo-Stalinist mold) with nonparty or normally antiparty chauvinists. It is not "Marxism-Leninism" that is their common ground; it is the dedication to an old-fashioned imperial statism. In fact, as already suggested, this orientation was part of the ideological amalgam that flourished inside the party, with a growing preference for cladding the expansionist self in rather ancient garments.

But was the Russian national conscience imperialist in its essence, as some writers claim? Other writers contest this. One opposite and popular conception has it that the Russians themselves suffered from the imperialism of the USSR, which put a heavy burden on the Russians. A subtheme, already alluded to, is the complaint that the USSR denied the republic of Russia (RSFSR) the same attributes of self-government that were granted to all the other republics. What is meant here is the fact that Russia proper was not allowed to have its own national party with a central committee at its head, party congresses, and control of the republic by such bodies. These two assertions require some comments.

Some Russians were indeed perceiving themselves as part of an "imperial nation." They denied others the right to go their way, or they saw others as inferior, in need of a big brother. The so-called mission that the "big brother" is called on to play—as known from other imperial experiences—also had its proponents, including a genuine expansionist trend among some Russian party members. But the existence of such attitudes and circles may not reflect fully what the multiethnic reality of their country meant for many, if not most, Russians. Millions of them, in my opinion, took the multiethnic reality for granted as a normal and acceptable way of being, even as a reason for priding themselves in actually sharing this feature. This aspect was not related to ideas of a "Russian mission" or to imperialist cravings, and it certainly was no case of "sickness." Although "exclusivist" or nativist nationalists hated this widespread attitude of Russians and saw in it some kind of infirmity, it is not too difficult to return the compliment to them. It is my contention that the so-called "sick" attitude among many Russians (and others) was valuable and, rather, a sign of good health. The considerable force of such attitudes can be gathered from Gorbachev's 1991 referendum, when the country was asked whether it would approve a reformed USSR that offered full guarantees of national and other rights to all republics: 127 million people voted in the referendum; 112 million—76 percent—said yes.[17]

It is therefore unwarranted to talk about imperialism as a national feature. Parts of the Russian public might have gotten corrupted by the imperial expansion and practices of their country, and they are the ones who chant for the reconstitution of a Russian-dominated USSR. But the multiethnic reality of their country and the international cohabitation in the framework of the USSR produced more than one kind of consciousness. The fact that so many quickly accepted making Russia "independent" and letting the others go their own ways, does not point to very deep imperialist appetites, even if the adoption of an independent Russia without the USSR is often accompanied by a "good riddance" argument—a nationalistic, but not imperialist, reaction. But this is not the only argument among the public for letting the others out. Granting them their independence is seen in some circles as the best way to restore a common international entity. This motivation may not necessarily be the one of a minority; there are still many people who wish to reconstitute a federation, for reasons far removed from imperialism and nationalism. The arguments of a Yakovlev against the "Russity," which I talked about earlier, were based on an antichauvinist and anti-imperialist position. There was a pro-USSR school inside and outside the party that was not Russian nationalist, but I have not seen any research on this trend.

---

17. A. Nenarokov, sost., *Nesostoiavshijsia Ivbilej,* ibid., p. 436.

All in all, the existence of the USSR bred currents bent on domination, assimilation, and Russian superiority, as against quite different currents that accepted intermingling and political coexistence as political and human values. The latter currents neither suffered nor should be "diagnosed" by quack-healers as deficient in their national dignity. Such an attitude was actually an antidote to imperialist appetites and nationalist fervor, which were detrimental to the interests of an internationalist agglomeration. It should be added that relations among the nations of the USSR, although shifting and sporadically marred by tensions, enjoyed periods of calm, cooperation, and a perception that the cohabitation is livable and positive. Instead, it is itself the proddings for the Russians to shape a "healthy" nation by cleansing ethnically that are pernicious. National interaction, cohabitation, cultural curiosity and exchange are the essence of human life. The idea of some ethnic-national neatness is a pathology.

WHOSE CONSCIOUSNESS IS IT, ANYWAY?

The assessments and opinions I discussed earlier about Russians' perceptions of themselves and the state of their national consciousness are rarely buttressed by firm data and good research. These are impressions and conclusions I formed from reading various publicists' or politicians' papers or ideologically motivated preconceptions that represent the views of the authors involved—but do not say much about the real subject in question: the multitude called "the Russians." Themes such as the "national spirit" or "national character" belong to the domain of arbitrary and, at best, impressionistic views that intellectuals and propagandists produce or invent according to their moods; to the features they observe in themselves, among circles of friends; or to thoughts they imbibe from an influential writer. "The Russian Idea," a theme best known from the writings of the religious philosopher Berdiaev,[18] is suffused with the philosophy of Dostoevsky. And no writing of this kind ever tries to prove to what extent the Russian peasants—without whom thinking about "the Russian nation," or even "the Russian idea" would make no sense—actually shared the features that intellectuals postulated or whether the two groups saw things in the same way. Of course, the publicists sometimes have been satisfied that "consciousness" can be pro-

---

18. Nikolai Berdiaev, *Russkaia Ideia* (Paris, 1971).

duced by leadership and intellectual groups and that the masses will follow. It does, in fact, happen often in this manner—the public is sometimes swayed and is never asked again what they think. Still, the prevalence of ideas among the population can nowadays be tested by surveys
and research, including public opinion polls and results of elections and
referenda, and claims to representing people's minds can be verified.

But there is a specific difficulty in ascertaining popular opinions amid
the crisis and uncertainty that Russia and the surrounding area are suffering from these days. Any findings may express no more than passing
moods—not necessarily structured and permanent ideological and
political entities, which actually do not yet exist. The ephemeral appearance and splitting of political parties are evidence of this flux. The same
applies to different forms of nationalism and the difficulty of gauging
their popularity. This seems a propitious ground for demagogues and
false prophets, as well as for irrational mass reactions.

We observe, for example, that economic misery and unsettled political
conditions induce Russians to react negatively, if not violently, against
people with Caucasian features, who dominate the Russian open, semi-
legal, and illegal (but always very expensive) markets, especially in the
capitals. Russian scholars call such predictable nationalism *bytovoi,*
related to an aspect of "everyday life." In a situation when millions of
Russians feel unsafe because they find themselves unwanted foreigners
in the same republics from which those merchants come to trade in
Moscow, the seemingly ephemeral type of nationalist reaction can easily
grow into something more powerful; agitators who would like to thrive
on such moods are available. The danger of a virulent nationalism in the
population at large cannot be dismissed. As the situation deteriorated—
since the election of Yeltsin—Zhirinovsky gained almost a quarter of the
(poorly attended) parliamentary election in December 1993. In conditions of a continuing crisis and a growing mass of people in despair, such
an outcome was to be expected. But shouldn't we also remember the 76
percent that voted for a federation of free republics two years earlier?

Therefore, we must exercise caution when drawing conclusions on
the matters under discussion. All kinds of rebounds and turnabouts are
possible; opinions and moods in this country are fluid and uncertain. No
hypothesis can be excluded—including, of course, the menace of a violent nationalist and proauthoritarian backlash. Still, one should not
dwell on these dire outlooks too much: the turn-for-the-worse scenario

has not happened yet. In an anti-Russian country like Lithuania, whose nationalist leaders so recently won the coveted independence from the USSR, the rout of the same leaders and the victory in the latest elections of the country's new president, Brazauskas, was spectacular and entirely unexpected. He was the head of the Communist Party, which he managed to reform, opposing both too speedy "marketization" and the previous strongly anti-Russian line. Something similar happened recently in Latvia, too (but that nation is less friendly toward its Russian population). There are counterparts to Brazauskas in Russia, too—of several types and hues. Moreover, when one listens to or reads what the different nationalists preach to the Russian people, one first must realize that they are not united and they do not preach the same thing. It is plausible that people in a state of despair may want to clutch onto simplistic cures, often based on and appealing to irrational reflexes that are stronger in unsettled than in more stable circumstances.

The promise of gathering people in a reassuring citadel surrounded by mythical enemies constitutes irrationality. The cure proposed in such cases seems painless, because the proposed operation is to be performed on somebody else's body. But there is a trap in all such ideologies: They are very poor "equipment" for handling the problems of a continent in crisis; they have no answer to the real problems of Russia. Their "remedies" were already tried out in Russia and elsewhere, and those led to catastrophes. Russia's national problems cannot be solved by anything that preaches exclusivity and superiority. Russia itself is a mini-USSR, and there is no escape from this fact except through cooperative approaches—or a bloodbath.

As we already know, some nationalists do not like the fact that large layers of the Russian population perceive their national existence as part of a multiethnic framework. If such opinions actually are really widespread, this would mean that many Russian citizens do understand that national identity and many other moral and ideological problems that plague Russia do not have any "national" solution at all—certainly not a nationalist one. In their dealings with the nationalities inside Russia and in the former USSR, they are doomed to practice a healthy dose of internationalism; otherwise, the decomposition will become irreparable. All the players in this area share a common danger—the danger of becoming versions of banana republics (even if bananas do not grow there).

I have more to say about the crisis in chapters 13 and 15. Dangers exist, but we have no reason to exclude the prospect of recovery. A faltering

Russia may continue to splinter, not just along ethnic divides but also along the lines of normal, ethnically Russian administrative regions that experience a powerful centrifugal pull, which the enfeebled Moscow government has trouble with. The recovering Russia will face a twin metamorphosis: by shedding its empire and its imperial aspirations, it can become, for the first time, a nation-state of sorts; but it also can help reorganize the whole area of the former USSR on a nonimperial basis. In this process, the concept of a "nation-state" may take on a different form, one of an "inter-nation-state." Russia's internal mosaiclike structure—replicating the previous broader, international complex—demands a special political entity. Dumping powerful, ideologically loaded, and deceptively obvious shibboleths such as "nation-state" and adapting to a more complex reality are neither easy nor common steps, especially when imaginative elites are a rare commodity and the phony internationalism of the previous system has pushed people to a reactive nationalism.

WITH ALL DUE RESPECT, IT WAS NOT THE NATIONALITIES...

The downfall of the Soviet system and the dissolution of the USSR contained interactive processes that need to be isolated and examined separately. This is true because some authors today see the pullout of the nationalities—certainly a factor in the decomposition—as the main cause of the Soviet regime's downfall. It is the nationalities, some claimed—and some had even predicted—that buried the system. It can be plausibly argued that the exit of the nationalities dealt the coup de grace to Gorbachev's government, but it was not they who caused the downfall: It was the decline and de facto downfall of the regime that gave them the chance to leave. It was not the Russian problem, in itself, or "the poisoned fruits" of Lenin's republics. There is no doubt that "Lenin's legacy" and its persistence in the structure of the USSR kept the nationalities alive and even developed them and their nationalisms, but the ailments of the bureaucratized Soviet-style systems were similar everywhere—whether they had or did not have similar national problems. The complaints of national republics were often similar in substance—although more deeply offended, because of the additional national charge—to the complaint of many purely Russian administrative regions.

The USSR, like the Russian empire, was created by Russia and from Moscow. It was difficult to miss the importance of the multiethnic relations, because already in the early 1920s the way of incorporating the nationalities into the state system was a test for the very character of a state to emerge, and it revealed important political cleavages inside the party and the political alternatives available to the country. But the same choices and political preferences were expressing themselves in debates about peasants, planning, industrialization, the party's internal regimen, and devolution of power to just any—not only ethnic—regions. The choices about nationalities and the way of running them added sharpness to the dilemmas and to the character of the regime in future years; but the battle of the centralizers for a powerful center in a unitary state, as opposed to other versions of authoritarian rule, was a battle about all the basics.

The system did not become deeply bureaucratized because of the need to control nationalities; it controlled nationalities, as well as the economy, culture, and the rest, because it was bureaucratic—and for this there were many reasons. When, in the course of its development, it began to stagnate and lost the capacity to reform, it kept, in turn, losing control over all those spheres—including the nationalities. In the final analysis, the regime stumbled and fell because of its bureaucratic essence. If anything, the way the economy was handled would have priority in analyses of the causes of the downfall. The top-heavy center—one of the key characteristics of the Soviet superstate—reached a situation where it could not solve the issue of nationalities or anything else. It could not handle the economy, for instance, because it lost the capacity to formulate policies and to impose them on its own institutions. It was the center that could no longer retain the state-partocracy that many of the smaller republics continued to have in power. The republics still kept coming to talk and sign, even when all that was left of the center was a lonely Gorbachev. They left when the USSR was not coping with anything else—especially with Russia itself. This does not mean that if Russia had remained strong, it could have continued the empire. Russia could have remained strong or recovered only if it had reformed itself deeply; thus, the empire would have ended anyway.

The interrepublican relations were bound to be reformulated, like most of the other components of the system. There is sufficient evidence that without this downfall of the center (and even during the process of its downfall) most of the republics had a majority who supported the continuation of a union, appropriately redefined. Hence, as far as the bulk of the population was concerned, the acceptance of a redefined federation was quite possible. However, such a change would have required the presence of a widespread political will and enough political potency in Moscow, but that was already on the wane. A parallel development could be seen in 1917 when, initially, most ethnic areas and the bulk of their populations were content with autonomy and expanded their aspirations as the regime faltered. Then, as now, it was the renegotiation of the rules of the game that was inescapable—but not the rush to independence. The role of the different local elites, using Moscow's weakness and rushing toward power in their own separate states, was crucial, as is often true in nationalist movements. Therefore, nationalism in most republics—including the Russian one itself—was not as powerful or massive as some claimed. The Moscow vacuum created the change and with it, the appetites.

In sum, the national structure of the USSR was just an explosion waiting to happen, but it did not happen just because it was waiting. The subsequent dissolution occurred with an ease that was deceptive. The republics are not coping with their predicament, and they are still looking to Russia and keep coming to negotiate and renegotiate cooperative arrangements—even though Russia itself is in trouble and is not yet able to offer very much.[19]

---

19. Jan S. Adams, from Ohio State University, concludes: "The role of the Commonwealth defined broadly as a means of multilateral cooperation—an integrative process—is very much alive. The integrative imperatives that coexist with aspirations for national sovereignty among the former Soviet republics are the prime force drawing the Commonwealth countries together" ("Will the Post-Soviet Commonwealth Survive?" occasional paper, Mershon Center, April 1993).

BIBLIOGRAPHY

*What follows is a list of the books and articles I read while working on this chapter,
which is based on a paper for a conference on nationalism in Central and Eastern Europe
that took place in the French city of Le Mans, in December 1992*

ALLWORTH, EDWARD, ED. *Ethnic Russia
in the USSR: The Dilemma of Dominance.* New York, 1980.

ANNANEPESOV, M. A. "Prisoedinenie
Turkmenistana k Rossii: Pravda
Istorii." *Voprosy Istorii,* no. 11 (1989), pp.
70–86.

ETIENNE BALIBAR AND IMMANUEL
WALLERSTEIN. *Race, Nation, Class—
Les Identités Ambigues.* Paris, 1990.

BERLIN, ISAIAH. "Two Concepts of
Nationalism: An Interview." *New York
Review of Books,* November 21, 1991,
pp. 19–23.

BILINSKY, YAROSLAV. "Mykola Skrypnik and Petro Shelest: An Essay on the
Persistence and Limits of Ukrainian
National Communism." In Jeremy
Azrael, ed., *Soviet Nationality, Policies,
and Practices.* New York, Praeger, 1978.
pp. 105–43.

BOTTOMORE, TOM, AND PATRICK
GOODE, TRANS. AND EDS. *Austro-
Marxism.* Oxford, 1978.

BRIGHT, CHARLES, AND SUSAN
HARDING, EDS. *Statemaking and Social
Movements: Essays in History and Theory.*
Ann Arbor, Mich., 1984.

BROMLEJ, IU. V., GLAV.RED. *Sovre-
mennye ethnicheskie protsessy v SSSR,* 20e
izd Moscow, 1977.

CARTER, STEPHEN K. *Russian Nationalism: Yesterday, Today, Tomorrow.* New
York, 1990.

CONNOR, WALKER. "Ethnonational-
ism." In Myron Weiner and Samuel
Huntington, eds., *Understanding Political Development.* Boston, 1987.

DEBRAY, REGIS. "Marxism and the
National Question" (interview with
Debray). *New Left Review* 105, Septem-
ber–October 1977, pp. 25–41.

DIMANSHTEIN, S. "Ten Years of
Nationality Policy in the Party and the
Soviet Government." Trans. Y. Bilin-
sky from *Novyj Vostok* 19 (1927), pp.
I–XXII.

HAUPT, GEORGE, MICHAEL LOWY,
AND CLUDIE WEILL, EDS. *Les marx-
istes et La question nationale, 1848–1914.*
Paris, 1972.

HOBSBAWM, E. J. "Some Reflections on
the Break-up of Britain." *New Left
Review* 105, September–October 1977,
pp. 2–23.

———. *Nations and Nationalism since
1780: Programme, Myth, Reality.* Cambridge, 1991.

KOZLOV, V. I. *Natsional'nosti SSSR,
Etnodemograficheskij obzor.* Moscow
1982.

LAPIDUS, GAIL W., AND VICTOR
ZASLAVSKY, EDS. *From Union to
Commonwealth: Nationalism and Separatism in the Soviet Republics.* Cambridge, 1992.

LIKHACHEV, D. S. *The National Nature
of Russian History.* Columbia University, Averell Harriman Lecture, New
York, November 13, 1990.

NENAROKOV, A. P., SOST. *Nesostoiavshijsia iubilej. Pochemu SSSR ne
otprazdnoval svoego 70-letiia?* Moscow,
1992.

NETTL, J. P. "The National Question."
Appendix 2 in *Rosa Luxemburg,* pp.
843–62.

OLZACK, SUSAN, AND JOANNE
NAGEL, EDS. *Competitive Ethnic Relations.* New York, 1986.

"Pamyat'." *Nationalities Papers* 19, no. 2
(special issue) (Fall 1991).

PIPES, RICHARD. *The Formation of the
Soviet Union.* Cambridge, Mass., 1964.

RAANAN, URI, ED. *The Soviet Empire: The Challenge of National and Democratic Movements.* Lexington, Mass., 1990.

RAANAN, URI, ET AL., EDS. *State and Nation in Multi-Ethnic Societies: The Breakup of Multinational States.* New York, 1991.

RAEFF, MARC. "The Style of Russia's Imperial Policy and Prince G. A. Potemkin," in G. N. Grob, ed., *Statesmen and Statescraft of the Modern West.* pp. 1–51. Barre, Mass., 1967.

SCHMEMANN, SERGE. "Ukraine Facing the High Cost of Democracy—Birth Pangs of a Nation." *New York Times International,* November 6, 1992, p. A1.

SUNY, RONALD GRIGOR. *The Making of the Georgian Nation.* Bloomington, Ill., 1988.

———. "Rethinking Soviet Studies: Bringing the Non-Russians Back." Paper presented to the Kennan Institute, Washington, D.C., July 24, 1992.

SUNY. "Nationalism and Social Class in the Russian Revolution: The Case of Baku and Tiflis." In Ronald Suny, ed., *Transcaucasia.*

Nationalism and Social Change: Essays in the History of Armenia, Azerbedzhan, and Georgia. pp. 239–58. Slavic Publication. Ann Arbor, Mich., 1993.

SUNY, *The Revenge of the Past: Nationalism, Revolution and the Collapse of the Soviet Union.* Foreword by Norman M. Naimark. Stanford, Calif., Stanford University Press, 1993.

THADEN, EDWARD C., ED. *Russification in the Baltic Provinces and Finland, 1855–1911.* Princeton, N.J., 1981.

YANOV, ALEXANDER. *The Russian Challenge and the Year 2000.* Trans. Iden J. Rosenthal. New York, 1987.

W E CAN FOLLOW SEVERAL LINES OF INQUIRY IN EXPLORING
the springs of the regime's downfall. In this chapter, however,
the emphasis will be put on how the mainstays of the regime's
dynamics and power turned sour in the process, each one separately and,
finally, all of them en bloc. This statement is made in order to avoid an
impression that decline and decomposition are all that the Soviet phenomenon had to offer. The full apprehension of this historical period
demands several journeys from the present back into the past and from
the beginning of the regime (if not earlier) into the present, in order for
valid conclusions to be reached. But it is the "autopsy" approach that pre-
vails in this chapter.

I will observe, in particular, the importance of interconnections and of
the reciprocal reinforcement that occurs between the two parts of the
equation known as the "political economy." Economics and politics in
this system were an amalgam, with some features specific to the Soviet
case. An important factor that makes all these phenomena best analyzed
as a "political economy" is not just state ownership but also "party leadership." The political will is one of the initial factors of growth. But the
model chosen, as I have already shown, turned out also to be one of overall bureaucratization. We have to examine how these and other features
in the system's functioning led to the loss of dynamism and, especially, of
its ability to respond to change and to the growing complexities of Soviet
and international reality. It is this complex that we are trying to track
down, by exploring different threads of which it was composed—and
the price tag attached to each one of them.

THE HISTORICAL UNDERPINNINGS OF FAILURE

A historico-sociological parenthesis is indispensable to an exploration of
some "historical underpinnings" of the overall process or, in other
words, the legacy of history relevant to our key problems. The trends

that eventually damaged the regime began to develop, first, inside the planning-managing grid and, next, or parallel to it, in the broader social landscape. We are familiar with the peasantry-versus-state dichotomy during the New Economic Policy (NEP). The bulge that cities created in the rural landscape was there already, but urban areas were still far from predominant. What was predominant was a two-layer social "duet" composed of the peasantry, as described earlier—some 80 percent of the population—and the state bureaucracy, which was leading the state organs, supported by workers and other city dwellers, most of them employed by the state. We therefore can still, at this stage, include them in the category of "state and state-dependent sectors."

That was the situation during the NEP. During the accelerated industrialization of the 1930s, this social landscape was transformed, for the most part, into a three-layer "triad." This triad advanced in many ways, according to widely accepted standards, yet it carried a very low cultural potential in all its layers and, hence, was amenable to being easily used for or induced to support deep political and cultural regressive waves. The prime social component of this fateful triad of the 1930s was still the peasantry, which was considerably shattered by collectivization but was far from having been transformed or "re-educated." Despite the introduction of tractors and combines, the peasants continued to work largely with their hands. Through the effects of industrialization, a growing mass of new workers—the second component of the social triad—was now replacing or supplementing the traditional physical labor of peasants with an equally physical industrial labor—a fast-growing but poorly educated and low-skilled mass of *chernorabochie,* which has remained the hallmark of the Soviet working class.

The third layer consisted of the sprawling officialdom, with a problem parallel to the one that afflicted the workers: Officials were either of low literacy in the lower administrative rungs or of poor professional qualifications, even in the higher rungs of the political and industrial administrations. The vast category of *praktiki*—that is, people who grew on the job, from the ranks and from the party, but without professional training— were, in a sense, the counterpart in the techno-structure of the unskilled *chernorabochie* of the shop floor. After Stalin this constellation kept evolving in the course of hectic urbanization waves, but the making of an overgrown bureaucracy and the perpetuation of large layers of low-skilled workers and employees did not stop. The old triad of Stalin's age was partly superseded by a more modern social and professional profile, but it partly reproduced itself in the form of the *mekhanizm tormozheniia*—the bundle of vested interests that thrived on the stagnation (*zastoi*).

The problem of skipping stages and moving directly to "socialism" from a precapitalist society (which is the backdrop to the type of precipitated social changes just described) was often debated among Russian social democrats, including the Bolsheviks. But "skipping" does not allow a country to leave all of its legacy behind. In fact, even when supposedly skipping stages, the system was at the same time perpetuating an extensive, peculiarly Russian, "quantitative" orientation, as I argued in chapter 4. Those were certainly features "imposed" by genuine historical limitations, but the choice of strategies added their weight, too. Alternatively, one could argue that those historical features favored certain strategies over others.

The theme continues to be a fitting subject for reflection. But the Russian case also raises a somewhat different aspect of the historical legacy—namely, the cost of destroying capitalism prematurely, so to speak, or preventing its reappearance after it was set back. Lenin began to grapple with this problem almost as soon as he found himself in power. It is worth recalling the shock he caused in early 1918, when he suddenly began to claim—and preach—that a version of state capitalism needed to be applied in Soviet Russia and that this approach should be declared programmatically as the main strategy for a lengthy transitional period. (Later, during the transition to the NEP, his search went for a different compromise that could be dubbed a "co-op capitalist" one, though this term is an interpretation of mine and was never used by Lenin.)

It is still a matter for debate—as it was inside the party during the 1920s—whether the continuation of the NEP could have prevented the new turn, with its excesses and enormous cost. The fact remains that the NEP was actually discarded, creating shock waves that engendered or deepened the rifts and constant "maladjustments" among the economic, administrative, and political spheres in the system. The results were, in the longer run, staggering. First on the list was the wholesale bureaucratization, which also generated a host of consequences. In its overblown appearance, it was strictly related to broadening "nationalization," first, and then to the elimination of markets—or "overplanning," which was the other side of the coin of "entmarketing" the economy—that is, eliminating the market and replacing it with administrative methods. Bukharin clamored in 1928 against this overplanning and against the elimination of small-scale production and producers operating in the markets. Such a policy, he warned, would cause "a colossal growth of officialdom"[1]—and he did not need to take this idea from Max Weber. The phenomenon was blossoming all around and would reach unheard-of proportions, which Bukharin described in 1934 in his *Izvestiia* article with a barely concealed sense of horror.[2] Something new and unusual was occurring: The emerging bureaucratic system became the arena and the substitute for "economics." Because state agencies replaced a market mechanism, *they* became a *sui generis* economic mechanism—notably, through their "planning system."

Some general features should be interposed briefly at this juncture.

1. This was a system geared to the large-scale state interest, to huge projects—at least after the system emerged as a well-crystallized entity. It thought in global terms—state, classes, the world—but it had no thought and little to offer in terms of individuals and groups, the small-scale environments in which people live. It had a fairly adequate airplane communication system, but no roads to connect villages and townships. It had cosmic programs (and phraseology), but not enough day-care homes to accommodate the children of working mothers. Hence, a woman emancipated enough to have a professional life, whether in branches requiring hard physical labor or sophisticated scientific activity, had to continue after her workday to toil in unpaid household chores, which, amidst the prevailing standards of living, amounted to a household serfdom.

2. Our reflections about the character of the small-scale production in Russian agriculture, with its weak marketability, are important in this context, too, in yet another way: Against the social background of a muzhik country, the idea of direct state takeover of the whole branch of agriculture or the whole economy—in fact, the running of the whole economy "directly" from the center, without markets—looked rather natural and appeared clearly superior. Ideological and pragmatic considerations were also a factor. Large-scale forms were superior, presumably by definition; they spelled progress. Small-scale ones therefore needed to enlarge their scale—an idea that is not always false, in itself,

---

1. Bukharin, "Notes of an Economist," *Pravda,* September 30, 1928.

2. Bukharin, "Krizis kapitalisticheskoj sistemy i problema kul'tury," *Izvestiia,* March 30, 1939.

but had devastating effects when it was clumsily generalized into some "law" or "principle" and was executed by direct state takeover.

3. The list of "mytho-positions" such as those in the previous points is long, but the conclusion is one: to the central power structure, human life, initiatives, values, personality, and community all belonged to the "small-scale" human dimension. But was there not a party that was reaching out tentacularly into so many small nooks of social (sometimes even personal) life—at least in intention? Why could the center not concentrate on the grand design and leave the human, local dimension to the care of the local party? On paper, this was what the local party had to do. However, it could not, because the human dimension is as "political" as the grandiose scale is, and maybe even more so. Meanwhile, the party was evolving into a Soviet-style state organ, responding to the logic of a centralized bureaucracy, rather than to the social dimensions of the real Russia.

4. The predilection for the grand scale bred a rather natural propensity to produce uniform solutions, from the center onto the whole country, as the supposedly best way of simplifying action, execution, and control from above. Control was sometimes more avidly sought than the production of action itself, especially when factors of decline began to squash the sources of dynamism. But the international scene and society inside the country were getting ever more differentiated and complex, hence ever less responsive to inadequate standardized simplifications. The "grandiose" dimensions were becoming inadequate for a modernizing or modern society—contrary to the expectations of people who reflected a localized and fragmented rural reality of the past.

5. At the same time, the development that geared the system toward the supposedly grandiose also led to the preponderance of the administrative over the political dimension in the party and the system. It actually amounted to the disappearance of politics in the party parallel to the disappearance of planning in the plan. Not only the citizenry but also the party members were barred from meaningful participation in politics. The call of the erstwhile "democratic centralist" opposition, in 1919–1920, to allow autonomy to local party organizations, if only in the sphere of executing important decisions, was disregarded. The locals were becoming politically impotent; they could not react meaningfully to the problems around them by engaging in debates, programs, and political contests. They were more important for a time

than the local state administrations; yet in a broader order of things, they were just appendices to the central state administration—not members of a political party. I return to this theme later.

6. The same point can be restated from another angle, one also relevant to the administrative function: the penchant of a bureaucratic administration toward centralization has as its counterpart the unwillingness and, soon also, the inability to respond to complexity by offering individual, social, and even bureaucratic agents enough autonomy to allow them to handle their tasks. The bureaucracy thereby condemned itself to deciding and running everything through and by bureaucratic agencies, especially by their summits—ultimately, an impossible task. Had this been so in only one or a few spheres, however important, it could have been somehow tolerable. But the production of uniform policies for all the crucial spheres of life could not but end up in accumulating problems without solving anything, because nothing was "uniform" in reality.

The case of the nationalities is a good example of the enormous inadequacy of such responses. Nationalities in the USSR, by definition, were characterized by growing differentiation and variations of the local circumstances. At some times, after Stalin's death, the center did conceive of policies that took cognizance of local conditions, but more often it yielded to and tolerated the trends that developed locally as a fait accompli, rather than accepting them as a base for policies. On the whole, though, the lines of action were standard, "made-in-Moscow" ones. The production of uniform policies was the rule; flexible responses were usually offered stealthily. (This was discussed in greater detail in the previous chapter.)

The "nationalization" that occurred with the onset of the Civil War was one of the costs to be paid for eliminating capitalism. It so happened that this principle, often considered socialist by definition, suited the ruling networks very well as they constituted themselves partly during, but mostly after, the Civil War: those were bureaucratic-administrative layers, not a large class, or not yet. In the longer run, this principle became the sine qua non for those layers, because their power over the economy (and the system) was based on it and gave them, as a bonus, a socialist claim and pedigree to bask in. Otherwise, the "bosses" were also free to use other ideologies—and they did just that.

Wholesale nationalization produced the state ownership that, over time, took on in practice the form of the ministerial (*vedomstvennyi*) quasi-owners. We will argue that these supposed servants of the plan tended to and finally succeeded in splitting the economy into administrative "fiefdoms" and fragmented the center and its ability to impose its policies. These trends could barely be papered over or even camouflaged by the protracted and, in time, notorious coordination (*soglasovyvanie*) that became the hallmark of the Soviet administrative process—or by the mirage of planning. The term *mirage* is in order—the USSR spun many mirages in areas where hard-nosed realism should have prevailed.

The unified system of state ownership helped to produce over time the bloated centralism that, in turn, bred the multicentrism, in politics as well as in the economy, which was alluded to earlier. The growing congestion of the center and of the whole bureaucratic machinery was the predictable price to pay. Once "centralization" overstepped some kind of limit, the centralized machinery became "overcentralized" and a process of fragmentation set in, along ministerial divides, and eventually clogged and blocked the center into immobility. State agencies, most of which enjoyed the status of ministries, acquired—or, rather, usurped—ever more independence. What could be simpler, ideally, than to supervise from the center the actions of *golovki* (top management) of even a hundred ministries and assure a well-coordinated whole?

In reality, those ministries, owners of vertically organized branches, could *talk* about coordination in the center and *read* a commonly discussed plan, but they ran their fiefdoms single-mindedly, refusing to cohere even at the Moscow hub of power. They became a system of fragmented units that did not communicate with each other except through the "coordinating" activities, intrigues, and infighting at the top. Their cooperation in common "planning" became more formal than real, whereas real deals among them were conducted informally, if not illegally, in the framework of some kind of a mutilated bureaucratic stock exchange. They dealt in favors, goods, and influence and in an endless process of "coordination" that produced more immobility at the top than meaningful action. Elements of competition existed among them, but they competed for a bigger share in investment capital to be extracted from the center, not for a better performance of their branch or of the center.

As the Soviet scholar V. P. Shkredov claimed in an unjustly forgotten book,[3] "nationalization" cannot function before its time. Ownership can easily become fictitious, and the management that is built on it can be wasteful and ineffective if there is no compatibility of sorts between the key requirements of an economic system—the technological where-withal, the quality of labor and management, pay-and-incentive schemes—and the capabilities of the overall administrative system (based on this kind of ownership claim). Economic agencies, deprived of the right autonomies that market conditions offer, cannot reach the maturity (and complexity) that would justify and enable a degree of planning by some central authority.

Obviously, what Shkredov meant, or what we can deduce from his argument, is that wholesale nationalization and the concomitant direct management by state appointees did not respond to the state of develop-ment of the "production forces." It could be decreed juridically, but it was "premature" economically and unmanageable socially (because of a lack of cadres, among other things). And it could, as it did, engender "production relations" that turned into powerful breaks on the economy and into a momentuous disfiguring of the political sphere. Shkredov, whose book was published in 1967, did admit that there might not have been much of choice in the initial stages, but he hinted that the practice lasted too long.

Following this frutiful line of thought, we can state that some of the effects of the "premature nationalization" were mended after the Civil War. Grain requisitions that were practiced during the Civil War were called "War Communism" after the policy itself was dumped, and the antimarket ideology took at least a less prominent position with the advent of the NEP. But it was eliminated, in substance, during the five-year plans—another case of a strategy adopted "prematurely," if one assumes that some presumed maturity can ever occur that would war-rant a fully marketless economy. But both of those premature efforts had momentous effects, because they inculcated in the state a propensity to get "inflated" and offered the right conditions for this to continue unabated.

---

3. See Shkredov, *Ekonomika i Pravo* (Moscow, 1967). I quote this book in my *Political Undercurrents in Soviet Economic Debates* (Princeton, N.J., 1974).

Here, the socialist credentials of these ideas may be quite misleading. The historical milieu allows us to trace them, instead, to the older Russian political and economic reality of the prince as owner of the whole land, as I maintained in the chapter on "Soviet socialism." On top of this, yet another illusion was added that, again, did seem to present a semblance of socialist credentials: the center claimed that the direct administrative takeover of the production of use-values and their distribution "according to the needs" in mostly "natural" (that is, physical) units was a superior principle of economic and social life. The "mediated," indirect exchanges of goods through markets and price systems, so ran the ideological argument, must create social polarization, a class society, and a capitalist system. Although such an idea is defensible, it remains a fact that the Soviet "unmediated," "planned" system did create on its own, albeit in a different form, not just a polarized society but a malfunctioning, imbalanced, and sterile economic system. And the "direct" appropriation and distribution of products that was supposed to be superior was actually the principle that operated on any manor of the Middle Ages, as well as the *pomest'e* of a nineteenth-century Russian serf-owner.

The elimination of capitalism and of markets that were supposed to be superseded by "postcapitalist" planning methods produced, one could say, a string of spectacular achievements, which turned into a cascade of ironies. Over time, it came to look as if the evicted markets were exacting their revenge in many ways, not only in the form of black markets but in *sui generis* multilayered markets that operated, on a large scale, from below, among the state enterprises. This trend appeared early in the functioning of the enterprises in their effort to get the needed equipment for the factories through barter between enterprises and thereby overcome the deficiences of the official supply system. Before the war, severe laws had already been issued against this kind of activity. The government could have, instead, introduced a market-style organization for purchasing equipment, which many reform-minded economists constantly clamored for, and thus could have saved the managers, to say the least, from constantly courting disaster by resorting to *blat* (favor trading); hoarding of reserves, especially materiel and labor; and a host of other informal or illegal remedies against malfunctions of the system. These practices smoothed the process to some extent, but they inevitably entangled the system in more damaging malfunctions on a gigantic scale because of the constant clash with the principles and practices of central planning.[4]

In view of the fact that the badly needed link for a normally functioning cooperation among specialized economic agencies was missing—namely, a "normal" market—the operating units were prompted to exercise the (denied) autonomy, by pseudomarket devices, in ways that accumulated waste and evolved into an overall model that resembled the Parisian Place de l'Etoile: all the main economic and political pipelines ran to and from Moscow. The story of the Soviet economy can be a variation on the theme of what actually did arrive at the center from the periphery and of what actually did reach its destination in the periphery, when moving from the center or at its behest. What got lost en route is quite a story.

Let it be said, as a parenthesis, that markets are older than capitalism; they are an economic mechanism that did produce and does produce capitalism, but any contemporary economy shows an enormous growth of nonmarket factors. Likewise, an ever-growing "socialization" of economic assets is observable and, hence, the phenomenon of constant infringement of the "social" on the supposedly strictly "private." From this point of view, it would have been much more profitable for a country that proclaimed socialist aims to have had a "market economy" and to have tried to plan it (which needed to have been done and could have been planned), rather than erecting an administered bureaucratic juggernaut that was not a viable economy and, in fact, could not be effectively planned. It could only be administered, sometimes with impressive results, but also damaging imbalances and the waste. The reason thereof lies in the lack of sufficient elbowroom for economic agents and the inability to mind costs. When one does not know what things cost (and may not even be interested in knowing), there can be no economic planning.

It is interesting to note that a radical such as Trotsky understood these problems perfectly well. The supposedly reckless industrializer, in a series of letters to the Politburo in 1923, hammered the point that without scrupulously minding costs in the management of state industry, the industrialization process would result in a massive waste of national

---

4. These phenomena were studied by a number of Western economists, including Joseph Berliner, Gregory Grossman, Paul Gregory, Holland Hunter, Jaum Jasny, and Alec Nove.

wealth. And this view was in addition to his well-known postulate, formulated in 1925, that the planners should use prices of the world markets in setting indicators for internal planning. Ideas expressed in his speech to the fourth Congress of the Komintern in late 1922 and a brochure published in 1923 make clear that, for him, planning could not be "hatched in offices, based on abstract communist preaching."[5]

In his Komintern speech, Trotsky corrected the prevailing view that the NEP was mainly a concession (through markets) to the peasantry: it was equally important as a policy for industry that would have to operate on markets for a long time. "The market will remain a regulator of the national economy for a long time to come," Trotsky said. The state industry could not be developed without this; orders from above were not good enough. The work of every enterprise had to be controlled from below, by the markets; and focus on the markets had to be decisive during the lengthy transition period. "If every enterprise is to become an integral part of a unified socialist organism functioning according to plan, a great preparatory work of the market mechanism is needed that will take a lengthy period of time."[6] One did not have to be a "moderate" to understand things like that—although, of course, no one knows what kind of economy would have emerged from such a "transitional" orientation toward markets.

What did emerge over the years when a market mechanism was discarded and "planning" reigned supreme allows us to say two things: first, that there can be no viable economy when the interests of the producing units and those of the managing structure (superstructure) are clashing; second, whenever they get reconciled, that happens at the expense of the consumer (which means, after all, the national economy at large). So the planning system, another piece of the mechanism, was yet another casualty of the initial hopes and would be added, finally, at some moment of history, to the list of "mirages": It was to become a system of controls expressing the interests and abilities of a particular type of bureaucracy,

---

5. Trotsky, *Novaia ekonomicheskaia politika sovetskoj vlasti i perspektivy mirovoi revolitutsii'* (brochure) (Moscow, 1923), pp. 21–23. It is known that Lenin read and praised this publication and asked the Politburo to publish 200,000 copies of it. For Trotsky's letters to the Politburo, see volume 2 of the extremely useful collection of Trotsky documents, in four volumes, compiled by Iu. Feldshtinsky, *Kommunistichaskaia oppozitsia USSR, 1923–1927* (Vermont, 1988).

6. Trotsky, ibid.

and this controlling was inimical to granting substantive forms of autonomy for the base. Without autonomy, there were no initiatives from below, except when people feigned to work for the plan but defended themselves from it by whatever means necessary. The characteristic modus operandi of the economic management was the call to do things "whatever the cost," and much of the economic activity during Stalin's time, and to some extent later, was conducted as a string of emergencies. When things became more routinized in most of the economy, some priority sectors (war and cosmos) continued to operate on the "emergency" line, which severely hampered the rest of the economy.

As the role of price (cost) became marginalized, quantity became the natural method for fixing targets and controlling the outcomes. With an inbuilt propensity, in an expanding economy, for those targets to proliferate and for the focus on quantity in the planning to become obsessive, quality became the victim of such planning. These developments not only engendered an illusion of control (which was dear to the bureaucratic mentality) but also transformed planning into an empty claim. And they eventually resulted in "the disappearance of planning in the plan,"[7] as described in chapter 5.

The overcentralization and the ensuing fission of the center, which rendered it incapable of mastering its own state apparatus, created another incongruence: the loss of an identifiable boss (*khozian*) in the overmanaged and overcontrolled systems. This points to the last "mirage"—but a weighty one—that we need to consider: "fictitious ownership." The nationalized, overcontrolled, and overplanned system (the "overdoing" in Soviet experience is part of the interlocking causes and effects to which we can now safely add the term *overcentralization*) caused the *khoziain* (boss) to preside over an unbelievable *bezkhoziastven-nost* (mismanagement). So much bossing occurred that a real and effective boss disappeared, although everyone had more than one superior, which was a calamity in itself. Nobody was ever responsible for wasteful, reckless, or criminal decisions. Such statements are not just theoretical deductions; these were real laments to be heard all over the huge territory: "Who is responsible?"—followed by a desperate, "You will never find anyone responsible among them!"

---

7. See *Slavic Review* 32, no. 2 (June 1973), pp. 271–87, a comment on Holland Hunter's illuminating article about "The Overambitious Soviet First Five-Year Plan."

Why did this situation happen? In all probability, responsibilities overlapped too much, too fluid a demarcation of prerogatives existed, and too many participants were involved in the *soglasovyvanie* process, which smothered both energetic action and clearly defined responsibilities impossible to achieve. The theme needs further study, but one conclusion is self-evident: If no one is responsible, then there is really no boss either. These are all parts of the same syndrome and of the political economy under scrutiny here. The powerful boss was losing control over the functioning of the economy, without anybody else gaining control—except for the old-fashioned historical force of spontaneity.

THE EFFECTS

As stated already, the bureaucratic penchant toward centralization engendered an unwillingness, and soon also an inability, of people to respond to complexity by doing anything other than stifling the powerful societal input (including that of the administrations themselves), without which a modern system (or any system) cannot function. What was actually being created was the concentrated power and an over-centralization that could not but lead to more of the same at the top and to a whole system of disequilibria below, that is, in the economy and society. These mortal viruses were inbuilt into the economic system from the outset of the famed *strojki* (building sites) during the first five-year plans.

Constantly emerging bottlenecks and imbalances signaled the presence of those dangerous viruses even in those years. The accumulating problems in factories, cities, the countryside, neighborhoods—including sprawling corruption, growing disparities, neglect, and social injustice—all kept growing, despite the "presence" of the party (as well as other controllers, informers, and analysts), presumably "everywhere." Finally, one could speak about an aberrational economy where more waste than useful production was coming from the factories. A deadly slowdown and the inability to reform, especially since the scuttling of the partial reforms of the 1960s, allowed an obvious conclusion early on: the demise of such a system was only a matter of time.

The position of the party and its obvious inability to make any difference in the growing and deepening manifestations of crisis and decline had much to do with the stifling of the party membership, parallel to the process that kept consolidating the party apparatus into an insulated social and political power hub, being supposedly on top of both the party and the state. But the process we observe was also surreptitiously working for a reversal of roles: instead of a one-sided domination of the state by the party apparatus—there was such a period, too—the party administration was absorbed by the state bureaucracy. It would remain a key administration, on top of other administrations, but the wheel would turn by at least 90, if not 180, degrees: the political sovereign would end up serving as the spokesman of the supposedly subordinate sphere— instead of serving as spokesman for its membership and for broader social interests. The famous (and often overstated) power of the *nomen-klatura,* designed to control the composition and loyalty of state officials, became counterproductive, too, by reinforcing the reversal of the roles. It assured all top bureaucrats the neutralization of the politico-ideological factor that made the party apparatus a censor that did not have much to censor anymore. This enabled the big apparat to subdue, for all intents and purposes, the small apparat, however important its administrative role still was.

The key feature of the system—the ownership of the whole economy under centralized management—was in itself the root cause of the "gigantism" that served as a starting point for my argument. Concentration of the ownership (without any important market sectors, except the kolkhoz markets and—unavoidably—the much bigger black one) produced the "economization" of the political system—and, significantly, of the party itself. This in turn caused the spreading of the "economistic" methods (counting quantities, prescribing qualities, setting targets, and heavily controlling or censoring the outcomes) onto other spheres of the system, especially science, education, culture, and ideology. This "politicization"—in the sense of state ownership, control, and direct managing of those spheres—caused "depoliticization" of all the spheres, in the sense of forbidding the citizenry's political participation or any other political action.

We already know that the same trend worked inside the ruling party. Not only the rank and file but even layers quite high up in the administrations were denied a serious role in the political process, even though the latter played a weighty role in the execution of policies. And this fact reinforces a point I have made in other chapters: Too much political power can kill the political process—and the carrier of this power itself. At this juncture it is almost a redundancy to remind ourselves that the political agency, whatever its importance, loses its potency too. Important but impotent? Yes. When the upper crust of a bureaucratic world becomes its spokespersons, that crust becomes entirely dependent on them. In a nutshell, an agency once so dynamic in Soviet society lost the capacity even to cut through the red tape; it became part and parcel of the red tape. Such was actually the situation toward the end of the regime.

It was not always so, or not exactly so. There were stages in the development of such phenomena, and those have to be studied and discussed; but they are not easy to outline as yet because a more detailed study that would show such stages has not been conducted. But when it happens, we are already in full *zastoj* (stagnation). For all practical purposes, the state machinery had nobody above it anymore; it answered only to itself—which was as good as to nobody. At that moment, it was already adrift—huge, heavy, powerful, and immutable, but, in fact, dead. The cause of death can be briefly described as *demesure,* or an overdose of its own essence, that is, allowing its inner self to be stretched to the limit of its "logic." Growth became overgrowth and, finally, downfall.

This paradoxical knot of problems allows us to say that although an "autopsy report" is a good focus for reflecting on the factors of the system's historical exit, it may still be premature to reach convincing conclusions about the system's "death." An "autopsy," after all, is a metaphor. A system is not an individual, and a change of systems does not eliminate historical continuities that tend to reappear in the most unexpected and circuitous ways. This is why we need to see the product of the ongoing reformist efforts first; only then will we know what actually did or did not finally recede into the past.

WHY DID IT LAST?

The substance of this specific "political economy" was what sustained the system. And the system lasted, and at some times thrived, not solely because of terror, as some have simplistically concluded. Terror actually subsided and changed forms appreciably after Khrushchev came to power, although the overall system of controls continued to be a key feature. Indoctrination, monopoly of propaganda, and—mainly under Stalin—terror and fear are part of this story. For many, especially among the elites, declarations of faith and admiration for Stalin and the system could easily be just a defensive behavior. If research becomes possible, the weight of this factor will emerge more clearly. But this is not the sole ingredient that shaped the outcome. Many attest to the fact that during and after Khrushchev's reign, widespread fear did subside and even disappeared in the population and in most elite groups.

The system lasted, first, because of and thanks to a very feverish and dynamic leg of its history, which laid the base for a powerful state. Achievements on the battlefield and in the international arms race followed, and they added to the factors that we can call "laurels" on which the system began to rest. These achievements were certainly products of a considerable dynamism that the Soviet system did command for some time, but they contributed to the conservative bent in the regime characteristic of winners of great battles. They tend to lull rulers away from vigilance, dim their awareness of decline, and block the readiness and ability to engage in reforms. All seems well to them, and they do not notice that the sources of dynamism are withering away and that the previously efficacious controls are beginning to act counterproductively. It seems reasonable to wait for the 1970s to begin the count of the full *zastoj*—even if blocking mechanism, which we outlined, had begun operating much earlier.

POSTSCRIPT:
PARTY AND POLITICAL LEADERSHIP

Interesting food for thought on the difference between bureaucrats and political leaders is contained in an article by Eric Olin Wright entitled "To Control or Smash Bureaucracy: Weber and Lenin on State, Politics and Bureaucracy,"[8] in which Wright referred to Max Weber's 1917 essay on "Parliament and Government in Reconstructed Germany." (Wright summed up Weber's article but did not give a clear source of it.) It seems that one could borrow ideas from this article to explain some of the causes of the Soviet bureaucracy's failure. My own "depoliticization" thesis led to the conclusion that once the party lost its political character, the party leadership lost the character of a political leadership and became itself just a part of the bureaucracy.

Weber explained that political leaders must have the capacity to formulate global policies and mobilize the population in support of their

8. *Berkeley Journal of Sociology* 19 (1974–75), pp. 69–100.

policies. Bureaucrats, part of a hierarchical structure, are not trained or recruited for this kind of action. A bureaucrat is not submitted to the same type of answerability that political leaders are or should be bound to, as a condition of their being "political" and, hence, capable of reining in the pernicious potentials of bureaucracy. Weber contends that such leaders (who have jurisdiction over administration) should be answerable to parliaments. On this point, Olin disagreed with Weber and pointed to the class character of the parliaments, which Weber did not bother about, though it could be a screen preventing popular answerability.

This is contentious terrain. In the authoritarian environment we are studying, the making of political leaders and the control of the bureaucracy were possible inside and through the party as long as the party could still preserve its suprabureaucratic (political) role—that is, the working of its institutions—with a modicum of democracy and a good knowledge and contact with the population. We know that such aptitudes were dwindling fast. It is interesting to explore when party leaders were still political leaders and when they became bureaucrats. In the Soviet condition, a process was at work that assured the leadership of an enormous concentration of power—thanks especially to the overall "nationalization" of national productive and reflective assets. This "depoliticized" the system to such an extent that it made the party actually lose power. (These ideas were explored in an article published in Italy but not included in this volume.)[9]

---

9. Moshe Lewin, "The Party in Power—Realities and Surrealities," in Marcella Flores and Francesea Gori, eds., *Il Mito dell'URSS: La Cultura Occidentale e l'Union Sovietica* (Milan, 1990), pp. 259–68.

WHENCE THE CRISIS?

TODAY, RUSSIA IS NO SUPERPOWER ANYMORE. IT HAS NO functioning economy, no functioning state, no system, and it is not in the news that often anymore. Russia is a nebulosity at this time in its history, engulfed in a deep crisis that makes reality look like a surrealistic nightmare, which could be the basis for many dire predictions. But the crisis is real, and it is indeed fraught with some worrisome prospects. It is not easy to analyze the character of this crisis; there are no obvious tools for doing so, and the available ones are not all equally good. The concentration on a few leaders—even if they (or one of them) seem to be the only key players—is not enough. Obviously, it is easier to relate to personalities by hating or liking them, whereas "crises" and "processes" are impersonal and demand reflection, not emotions.

The prevailing feature of the current situation is its "fluidity." By saying it is magmatic, we dramatize without exaggerating. This is why it is so difficult to distinguish between bubbles on the surface and hard realities. Reevaluating history, including some of the themes I dealt with in previous chapters, is indispensable. A crisis, after all, is part of a historical flow, and what caused the previous system to fall continues to affect the ongoing ordeal. It is also worth repeating that the system was not what it claimed to be. But the ideological fabrications were dangerous to the previous system, because too much camouflage denied its members the knowledge of what it really was. The system probably did belong to something "modernizing," but curiously unmodern. Its leaders belonged to the class of bureaucratic industrializers; but, unlike the Japanese leaders, for instance, the Soviet ones also insisted on running and owning the economy. The crisis was therefore one of a bureaucratic system of a category to be defined. It does not help that, except for a few pioneering efforts, we do not have enough scholarly studies of the Soviet bureaucratic phenomenon.

Yet the well-sheltered system of privileges—which worked independently of performance, lacked any direct political challenge of importance, and quickly squelched any opposition that arose—was a facade that made the sinking ship look like some glorious *Sputnik*. (The *Sputnik* was no accident, but it does not change this verdict and does not remove the system's deep streak of archaism, inherited from Stalin's times.) The Soviet ruling class was not the first such group to have mistaken sclerosis for a simple hangover. The sources of dynamism were getting ever more tightly clogged by a constituency that blocked reforms and the indispensable adaptations to the real world. Self-renovating and self-sustaining "mechanisms" became loose—and, finally, lost.

So a good handle on the system's past and its main features can help us better place the ongoing crisis in some framework that would make its unfolding more understandable. I found it useful in this book to single out and depart from the grand wave of social mutations related to the urbanization of much of the USSR that brought much of the country nearer to—and even, to some extent, integrated it in—the Western reality. At the same time, the country's affinity with the rural-muzhik past was being severed. For a state system that was founded on a social base still powerfully rooted in a millenary tradition, difficulties kept accumulating at the intersection of these connecting-disconnecting lines, with the West and with the past; meanwhile, the social reality of the last forty years was impetuously changing. A transition on this scale—and so recent—from one sociohistorical era to a very different one can explain many social, cultural, and ideological vagaries, especially the inadequacy of an ideological bridge called "Marxism-Leninism," which was so precariously suspended over a human landscape in flux. The search for new or old identities in different, often quite old creeds and the leaders' ideological maneuvers and hesitations between a certain type of Soviet internationalism ("the Soviet nation") and several versions of nationalism—including the pro-*Rus'* chauvinism—in search of a unifying social and imperial idea were all manifestations of a loss of vigor and of structures in trouble. Many factors that played a role in the making and unfolding of this system now had a hand in its undoing. Some even contributed to the making of a new order.

A "blissful" ignorance of social and political realities of the country was a chief cause and sign of the regime's decline. That ignorance, together with other features to be discussed, has perpetuated the crisis since the regime's downfall. When the reformers came to power, they were groping, moving blindly. How much knowledge did Gorbachev have of the real situation, including of the institutions supposedly under his command? How much knowledge and theoretical grasp of the system did the intellectual-professional classes have of the realities, in conditions of limited possibilities for research and debate? A good understanding of the previous system was missing, and this alone was a powerful impediment to reforms. But the difficulty was magnified by the next hurdle—lack of good knowledge of the systems that were supposed to be used as models for replacing the old—and this problem does not need belaboring now.

Western knowledge of Russia was, naturally, much better than in Russia itself, but the extent of that knowledge has also been tested by recent events. There was, in fact, no Western prescience about what was coming in Russia, because most Westerners had no conception of a historical process, of the interconnection between different historical dynamics and their impact on the previous system and on the brewing crisis. As often happens, the result was a mistaking of descriptions of troubles for analysis. A lot of energy went into producing a counterideology, or "unmasking," although a continuous unmasking eventually stopped producing real knowledge.

The prevailing tendency among experts on Russia was to concentrate on state action and on the leadership, which seemed—especially to the proponents of the totalitarian conception—to be the sole acting force. Or, the state is no more than a participant in processes composed of actions and reactions from a welter of other participants—from society, the economy, and the culture—who complemented, neutralized, sometimes perverted, or simply annulled actions and intentions of the government. Although "state" and "bureaucracy" are often taken for a single, hyphenated entity, state bureaucracy is also a complex social reality, with spontaneous internal trends interacting with other social pulls and pushes. In sum, the overall picture is commanded by processes that, in general, are poorly controlled, or spontaneous.

And yet the Soviet historical process—which should have been the overriding theme and approach—was mostly moving "elsewhere." This applied to the times of Lenin, of Stalin, and of their heirs, and still holds true today. Such statements have nothing to do with denying the power of states and leaders, but those have to be seen on a broader canvas where states may become less potent, even impotent. Looking at Russia and all the other republics, no one can afford to deny this kind of statement. At a certain stage, the system's power hub—even if it still looked immutably imposing—did not control events anymore. It was not a problem of personalities or poor policies. Impersonal factors that seemed to be "planned" never stopped working at their own pace—they could not be suppressed—and they kept producing sociological, economic, and ideological trends among both the general populace and the elites. The appearance of dissidents signaled such changing attitudes, and more involved studies have shown those trends to have been widespread.

It was a measure of history's malice that a regime so heavily addicted to "planning"—that is, administratively controlling—became blind and helpless when facing phenomena that could be handled only by political—or, rather, politico-democratic—means. By denying political involvement to society, the system denied itself the capacity to enter the modern era. In these conditions, the reliance on the efficacy of security agencies and their intelligence services, characteristic of conservatives and "security" states anywhere, proved "brilliantly" its bankruptcy. As "stagnation" set in, difficulties kept accumulating and were swept under the carpet, and the regime's decadence spread a deep crisis of values all over society—a political and moral vacuum that exposed the regime and that struck the whole "official" world in the first place.

The scarcity or absence of theoretical and political thought that would handle the complexity of today's world blocked the search for programs of change—a search that was either discouraged or forbidden anyway. With the "factor of ignorance" reigning supreme, the system was sliding into a generalized crisis it wanted to ignore.

Subterraneanly, privately, in academic closed seminars, in spontaneous conversations, and even in governing circles, a search for ideologies to revive the system (or to combat it) and for ways to escape the economic marasmus (actually, from an impending catastrophe) was going on, from the late 1950s well into the 1960s—in other words, well before the coming of the perestroika. During the 1960s, the essentially economic debate that burst into the open in hundreds of publications still exhibited a considerable vigor, but the effervescence was throttled after the "Prague Spring." A few years later the same fate befell the Kosygin reforms, which had allowed such debates to flourish. From then on, the "stagnation" (*zastoj*) that set in also depressed scholarship and idealism, and demoralized forces that would have otherwise been able to offer ideas of emancipation to a population that, although educated and urban, was left politically, socially, and ideologically impoverished.

All this points to a conclusion that the situation in Russia is not a product of recent years alone; its roots go far into history. But the ideological amalgam and vacuum I alluded to earlier were particularly luxuriant during "the years of decay" (*zastojnye gody*), which produced decadent moods, adopted some of the least appetizing prerevolutionary ideologies, and legated it all, finally, to today's crisis-ridden "post-Communist" Russia.

A STATE IN SEARCH OF A POLITY — AGAIN

It may be useful at this juncture to add an idea that can contribute to the diagnosis of the previous ailments—and to a reflection on the possible cures: "A crisis of a state without a political system" is a notion that was implied in the description of the previous regime's difficulties. This is a part of the "total success" story of the bureaucratized and, for all practical purposes, "de-ideologized" system—not that there were no connivances and social groups involved actively or by default in supporting the regime. But it was nevertheless the case of a state that was, or became, almost self-contained as a power structure and treated societal factors mainly as the receiving end of its efforts at manipulation and control. Signals from outside back into the system were received and often caused some decisions in response; but the regime's state administrations were not surrounded by relatively autonomous or independent societal organizations and movements that were free to compete, contest, and actively participate in the political system. Such could have been, as they are elsewhere, the media, professional associations, cultural movements, political parties, churches, or trade unions. Those are components of a viable political system, in which state institutions and emanations of civil society not only do the primary job of socializing the citizenry into a given system but also participate in a system's politics. Seen from this angle, the Soviet state managed to become a state without a political system, because even if organizations of this type existed, they still were supervised as, basically, auxiliary state agencies that received instructions on what to do. This situation began to harm the regime and denied it renovative power. Hence, the cure would demand creation of a state that is also a political system, in the sense of incorporating (and developing) a civil society, especially the elites and leadership networks that are indispensable for the running of a modern system—even if not necessarily, or not exactly, a Western-type democracy. The exclusion of the larger public from the political process ended in the exclusion of the ruling networks from history. The so-called success I have been discussing consisted in the system preventing alternative institutions from emerging in its midst, making the rather sudden collapse—not caused but exposed by Gorbachev's opening of the dams— into such a complicated crisis.

Another aggravating circumstance resided in the character of urban society as it surged ahead amidst restrictive deficiencies inherent to the Soviet conditions. The intensity and novelty of millions of peasants' transition into urban environments were magnified by numerous impediments that the restrictive Soviet system put in the way of efforts to establish communal links—and autonomous institutions that are indispensable for the making of a viable urban organization. Strong incorporative powers that help people find their place, gain a sense of belonging, adapt to a new culture and its values, and develop organic ties would provide an intolerable competition to a struggling and aging party-state agglomerate. The weakness or absence of such solidifying and uniting factors in Soviet cities made Soviet urbanization into a fragmenting and uprooting experience that contributed to a massive sense of helplessness and vulnerability and that blocked the appearance of a more vigorous urban culture.

All of these problems were and still are very real, as psychological and sociological studies of Soviet urban societies have shown (or will show). But the required knowledge has to be acquired on the go—and this does happen—as evident from various publications that translate many of the best products of Russian and other republican research appearing in the press and in scholarly periodicals.[1] The required knowledge has to be

---

1. The catalogues of the publisher M. E. Sharpe (Armonk, N. Y.) contain a list of reference works and journals that specialize in translating Russian (and other) articles in law, philosophy, economics, and other fields.

acquired rapidly, "on the go," as it were, because the problems are pressing. But once we realize the depth of the difficulties, we can imagine how
such a string of tremors contributed to the global character of this har-
rowing "global crisis."

WHY IS THIS A GLOBAL CRISIS?

We are well aware by now that nothing happened in the USSR "suddenly"—neither the decomposition of the regime nor the wave of
reforms nor the dismemberment of the USSR. What was sudden was
the appearance of most of the diseases on the surface and simultaneously.

The crisis took some decades to develop, and it stands to reason that it
was already in an acute state when we saw Brezhnev, already dead for all
practical purposes, traveling to represent the USSR in Germany. The
fact that he was replaced, consecutively, by two mortally ill general secretaries adds another touch to the morbidity of the situation. In view of
those facts, the complexity of the current crisis is an effect of the inherited
long-term decay, which is exacerbated, I contend, by the efforts to get rid
of the old structure and to replace it with something else.

The global character of the crisis was also a legacy of the thorough
bureaucratization of almost all aspects of the previous system. If this
bureaucracy was all-pervasive, so also would be the crisis of its system.
What deepens the bewilderment—and illustrates one of my contentions—is that Soviet bureaucracy constitutes one of the most glaring
gaps in our knowledge of the Soviet regime. When the center began to
falter, all of the potentially cetrifugal pulls—especially the republics,
which had previously been kept at bay—erupted against the "centralism" of Moscow. The disaggregation testified to the fact that the regime
kept accumulating problems without solving them—which always
makes things explosive when the walls come tumbling down.

One upshot of an all-encompassing system going belly up is that the
replacement has to be, so to speak, reinvented in all substantial aspects
and walks of life—preferably, almost simultaneously—from the economy to schools and political institutions, from citizens to leaders. The
blueprints, cadres, and authoritative leaders that are indispensable for
such a vast endeavor only begin to appear. Worse, a legitimate state capable of effective action is barely in its infancy. An exaggerated centralism
is not really the problem anymore; it is replaced by the lack of a strong

center, with literally thousands of central edicts being shelved by ever more disdainful regional leaders.

Such a crisis is not, of course, routine, and precedents from other global crises can be instructive. Various "times of trouble" (*smutnoe vremiia*), or periods when Russia found itself in a "systematic void," can be evoked: The peasant wars in the eighteenth century, less shattering, but menacing nonetheless; the 1905 revolution, which brought the monarchy, for a moment, to a standstill; and the horrendous years 1917 to 1921, when the monarchy collapsed and the bloody Civil War ensued are further examples that have nothing to concede to the *smutnoe vremiia* of the early seventeenth century. We are facing a new "time of trouble" quite different in many ways from the preceding ones, a time without a civil war or a revolution, but of an unparalleled complexity nevertheless.

In all previous instances there was also, sooner or later, a recomposition of the pieces into a new functioning entity, and it is important to know how and through whom this occurred. The current crisis in Russia does continue, however, as long as a credible political agency or alliance of forces is not yet visible and does not take over convincingly. As one might guess, this has not yet occurred: politically coherent forces that should have provided the country with programs to sustain the change and recreate a system are missing. The ones that do exist are still groping, splintered, and poorly led. Still, there are people in governments and local assemblies who are trying to provide leadership. Curiously, however, most of these leading figures, central and local, who are already involved in reform efforts come from the previous system. Later I return to this point and reflect on some of its implications.

GORBACHEV AND THE INTELLIGENTSIA

It befitted the character of this sytem that Gorbachev's initiative came almost as a coup from above, which was made possible by the pyramid-like (*verkhushechnyi*) character of the party-state. Basic decisions—including the selection of Gorbachev for the top office—could be made by a narrow circle of leaders. The results of the coup must have surprised even its top architect, who felt compelled to "open up" the system ever more (more than he might have initially intended) and produce the exhilarating moment of freedom. But it also created a moment of truth that confused the proponents and startled all the conservative forces—

the entire constituency making up the "breaking mechanism" (*mekha-nizm tormozheniia*) on which the regime rested. There was no reason to believe that the latter would not fight back; likewise, there was no guarantee that the reformers would be united and would know what to do and how to do it. In fact, both the former and the latter did happen.

The coup from above, by Gorbachev, was followed by a chaotic anti-system urge from below. When the controlling mechanisms began to weaken, all the woes of the country that kept accumulating under the heavy cover of the regime's monopoly—all the wounds, neglect, and despair, and all that was in need of urgent mending—came up to the surface, with devastating effects and a multidimensional complexity. This was unavoidable, and actually indispensable, in the given situation: The country had to learn the full scope and depth of its problems, which it had not realized before.

The results of opening up the sluices of glasnost' were twofold. First, the chaotic situation did not seem to respond to any orderly, step-by-step policy of reform. Preserving the state and just "coopting" civil society as a way of reinvigorating the system—as Gorbachev might have initially hoped for—proved impossible. The old state system was economically and politically insolvent, and it began to fall apart even before the appearance of new institutions ready to step in and run the economy, reform the educational system, preserve the culture, reconstitute the state, handle the various nationalities, reform the judiciary, and respond to a value crisis. Listing all this makes us realize that such an avalanche was, by definition, beyond any leader's capabilities. In fact, it was also beyond the capabilities of the existing elites, especially the Soviet intelligentsia, at least in the short run.

Second, the declaration of glasnost' allowed the intelligentsia to assume an enormous influence in shaping perceptions of reality. But the propensity of many among them to spread gossip and to react hysterically helped inflate the country's miseries to apocalyptic proportions, accompanied by the most dire predictions. Their efforts were so effective that we did not even notice that the scene, however agonizing, was at the same time astonishingly calm throughout at least the Slavic parts of the former USSR. Now there is trouble aplenty, but there are no rivers of blood, no mass disorders, no civil wars, and only one right-wing coup, which petered out in sixty-two hours. We are even tempted, thanks to the insistence of doomsayers, to ask why something does not happen, as opposed to what we are now seeing. For a crisis of this magnitude, it is the relative calm and the lack of massive disorder that are remarkable—although the continuation of the decline and growing despair may well lead to much more dramatic events.

Some other legacy of a difficult history must be at work when influential circles of the Moscow and Petersburg intelligentsia indulge—with almost a masochistic glee—in gloomily predicting either the coming of the "wild Russian jacquerie" (the much-discussed *Russkii bunt*), or the return of a Communist dictatorship (although if a dictatorship does appear, it will be far from anything Communist). The contribution of some of the media and many of the intelligentsia to a panicky view of things is undeniable. They have played a role in an extremely dangerous loss of credibility of even the new institutions of state power introduced by the reforms, especially through their almost automatic support for any movement toward separatism (some, of a pernicious kind), which many offered during Gorbachev's presidency. In fact, they almost talked themselves and the country into having those calamities that they so assiduously predicted.

The unmasking of past atrocities, iniquities, and corruptions had a liberating effect initially. The settling of accounts with an ugly past through condemnation and repentance might have delivered minds and souls from a national nightmare. Unfortunately, in many quarters the denunciation soon became a strategy and a way of thought that testified to an addiction to "negationism." An unending list of atrocities and injustices committed under Stalinism was not followed by analysis. For some, in both East and West, an atrocity is never atrocious enough: If evidence shows there were several million camp inmates, these people insist that there must have actually been double or triple that number. To them, half a million or a million executions sound like a mere apology for murder, so they conclude that there must have been millions more. Those who use this very disturbing tactic cannot live with the truth—which was atrocious enough without being inflated.

The worst aspect of this phenomenon was the political use of the Stalinist atrocities. The furious onslaught against the state by the independent press and "radicals" from the intelligentia of the capitals, initially quite justified and refreshing, went further than was good for the country. The switching of much of the anti-Stalinist fury onto Gorbachev pointed to their sterility. Many seemed to have expected to be given, by a Gorbachev or by anybody else, an instantaneous flourishing Western democracy and abundance, which nobody could have actually delivered without switching from denunciations to positive, patient political activity. The intelligentsia's ineffectiveness and disorientation were part of the crisis, instead of a remedy for it. Negationism continued to prevail even in the programs for change and for alternatives that did begin to emerge.

On one hand, there was an uncritical acceptance of Western models, based on limited knowledge about them and on an almost mechanical acceptance of positions that were the opposite of what the previous regime had done (or what it claimed to have done). This went with a wholesale rejection of all the achievements of the post-October 1917 period. In some circles, another "strategy" appeared that consisted in "swerving away" from the recent past and turning for inspiration to the prerevolutionary times by adopting not only older-style nationalisms and orthodox religion but also various atavistic creeds—most of them more or less fiercely antidemocratic and rather frankly authoritarian, including a fascist variety thrown in for good measure. These ideologies also were and are deeply anti-Western and are fiercely opposed to the internal Westernizers, thus restoring an old quarrel that has dominated Russia's political thought since Peter the Great, if not earlier. We know that such currents were developing in Soviet Russia since at least the 1960s.

Despite this critical assessment, we should not forget many impressive acts of courage and works of intellect and integrity by these or other parts of the same intelligentsia, whether dissidents or intrasystem critics, or by the core of people who are desperately fighting today to get their country out of its misery. But since mediocrity and demagoguery always sound louder than serious thought and actions, we would like to caution amateurs who would hastily rewrite history that they will be forced to rewrite it again, and probably quite soon.

Returning to the leading personalities, we can observe how the "personal" and "impersonal" are intertwined in the flow of historical events. It is the latter that makes the environment in which the leaders act, but their actions—or even inactions—do count. Gorbachev could launch his initiatives because he had the commanding position at the top of the party-state pyramid. His power was partly real, since he had enough of it to launch reforms; but it was partly fictitious, largely because of the inertia, disinterest, and ineptitute of the *apparaty* and others who could—and did, to a degree—block any reforms. Launching a new course was a necessity in order to avoid a collapse, but once the sluices were open and never lowered again (to Gorbachev's enduring credit), a collapse occurred anyway. This was true because the sources of his power were also the carriers of the system's disease.

With glasnost' proclaimed and maintained, and parliaments— another Gorbachev novelty—springing up on the level of the USSR and in the republics, the overcentralized system, with its impotent center and its apparat, had to go. Therefore, Gorbachev was, from the very beginning, sitting on a glacier that had to melt.

Gorbachev's mastery of zigzagging was one reason for his survival in the whirlwind. Initially, he reacted boldly to the country's historical agenda, launched an enormous enterprise, and never retreated from the essentials of the ongoing changes. That was the "Gorbachev phenomenon," step one. The crisis would not have turned so devastating if history had moved according to a well-synchronized timetable: One train leaves, the other comes in, exactly when needed. But history was not working in this manner. A leader appeared unexpectedly from an apparatus that specialized in producing apparatchiks and then rose like a meteor on the world arena. But instead of mustering mass support for a program of reforms, he found himself almost in a lonely solo performance and at moments even seemed a pathetic figure.

Gorbachev's departure from the scene by the fiat of institutions created (or abolished) by the perestroika signaled the "end of the phenomenon"— though a pretty remarkable one. A more reliable judgment, however, must await the later stages of the ongoing transformation.

Boris Yeltsin, a product of some of Gorbachev's blunders, is an interesting phenomenon in his own right, and his own stamina cannot be disregarded. Yet his ability as leader is still unclear, which is why doubts about how long he will last continue to grow. As with Gorbachev, the perceptions of the man keep changing: despised, distrusted, adulated, and at some point even crowned "King Boris the Mighty" by columnists—but this icon of King Boris is already forgotten. The latest referendum, in May 1993, supposedly restored his aura over and against the Parliament that challenged his strategy of reforms and was dispersed by canon fire in September 1992. But the new Parliament, installed in December 1993, dealt a heavy blow to the party of Yeltsin's main supporters, elected an anti-Yeltsin majority, and forced on him a change of course, away from precipitate and radical "marketization" policies. The same elections startled even inveterate Russian pessimists by producing an unexpectedly strong showing for the rightist extremist Zhirinovsky (23 percent of the vote). Many have blamed Yeltsin-backed policies for this outcome. Stopping the drift and reversing the trend of decomposition would itself be a great achievement, but there are very deep doubts in Russia as to whether Yeltsin is really the man of the hour, whether this can be done under his leadership. He is widely considered to be lacking the necessary qualities to lead the country in crisis and, even worse, many perceive him as "finished" already.

What comes next remains to be seen. The shifting situation at the moment of this writing cannot be our main preoccupation here, but the mercurial nature of the leaders' political fortunes is, for the time being, a structural feature that seems to wear leaders and other cadres down— and *this* is of interest to us. Yeltsin's leadership and the changing perceptions of him are best examined within the framework of an inquiry into the constraints inherent in this unprecedented historical situation— which one might call magmatic for its unpredictable shiftiness and fluidity. The task of leaders who try to run the country amidst a deepening crisis is formidable. As I write these lines, the story is still unfolding.

IS ONE "RIGHT" REPLACING ANOTHER?

We noticed that the Soviet system underwent a set of metamorphoses, leading it—ideologically and politically—away from its initial, clearly left-wing positions and role to an equally clearcut conservative (some would say right-wing) orientation. It became evident to anyone willing to see that the officially proclaimed ideology was not viable anymore. The real "working" ideologies in the ruling state that actually clashed with each other consisted of several versions of Marxism-Leninism that were getting watered down in the process—while the nationalist streams kept getting stronger. Another minority, much weaker than the Marxist-Leninist ones, was a reformist, democratic, more or less socialist wing, which was not very visible for a long time in the post-Stalin regimes. It is easy to show that in the early stages of a still-dominating ideological purity and commitment, the greatest pressure was exerted against old right-wing and other currents of the previously ruling classes, and also against different competing "leftists." The later stages saw the official policies turning to a systematic destruction of any kind of left, with a selective de facto tolerance of different nonleftist currents, although the more outspoken of those were also suppressed. It is therefore no surprise that the Soviet system became a cemetery for Marxism and socialism as schools of thought, since they would obviously become dangerous by unmasking the regime from inside—as was already happening in the 1920s.

Against this background, the Westernizing ideologies—procapitalist, prodemocracy, and pro–human rights (initially, the last two were more pronounced than the first)—were genuinely advanced and liberating compared to the oppressive system. Today's political effervescence among the elites and in the general public, and the appearance and disappearance of political currents and parties are important themes: What are the different right-wing and conservative formations? What is meant by "liberal," "democratic," or "left-wing" self-images?

Die-hard proto-Stalinists who became allied with fairly rabid nationalists thickened the gloomy picture of a rising right. And Zhirinovsky's success a few years later seemed to surpass all the predecessors from this disquieting constituency. At the same time—as we already argued in connection with the ideological trends among the intelligentsia—the previous regime's official sham ideology (its claims to socialism, Marxism, an orientation toward labor) was taken at face value by many proponents of the new trends, many of them active in Yeltsin's entourage. Having more often than not been among the adherents—even stalwarts, of the previous regime—they should have known better what the regime really was and what creeds they had professed, openly or tacitly, in the past. But the ideological swerve against socialism, now presented as the source of all evil, was playing a specific, often deliberately intended role: It helped them to move toward positions acceptable to the centrist and conservative circles in the West or to conservative circles within Russia. By fighting the supposedly socialist regime of their past, as some dangerous factor or menace to the reforms, they made it difficult to found the type of left that had never been acceptable to the previous regime; and one that would have been a dangerous competitor for the struggle for power in today's Russia.

However, such positions abound in paradoxes. By rejecting socialism

and by equating it with the Soviet regime—and, moreover, by expressing this criticism in old-fashioned anticommunist terms—many intellectuals automatically came to endorse Western practices already long
discredited in the West and disdainfully discredited some of their country's own achievements and valuable experiences, which they may now
badly need. The result illustrates well what I have called "the ignorance
factor" and have described as a further manifestation of the crisis:
Numerous initially influential (or still influential) circles made an imaginary "socialism" they had neither managed nor known into the basis for
a movement toward a capitalism they misunderstood—a very flimsy
intellectual foundation indeed for building a new and better system.

What many of them were adopting was, at best, an already outdated
neo-liberalism that leaned more to its right-wing versions. Thus, for a
time at least, they probably created a strong right (or a different version
of it, as a Western political barometer would probably register it), even as
they were getting yet another right (of a different authoritarian-statist
vintage)—but both profoundly anitsocialist. Now there is also a very
patchy and peculiar "center" that stands between two "rights," rather
than between a right and a left, because there is not much of a structured
left remaining in the Soviet Union—the previous system energetically
took care of that. In the meantime, the battle of two rights (and a center)
for control of Russia is a paradoxical, but not really puzzling, result of a
regime that was already decomposing for some time and had left this
kind of legacy. But this will not last either; a deeper differentiation and a
reconstitution of, probably, several lefts is to be expected, especially since
some of the current promarket reforms, as they were initially practiced,
kept causing more and new political alignments.

Developments among the members of the previous ruling party continue to be of interest. We hear mostly of the perverse alliance between
Communists and extreme nationalists—which is actually not a big surprise. But all over the country, efforts are being undertaken to found or
consolidate political organizations, including different left-wing orientations, but almost invariably in political groupings that, so far, evince a
high degree of ephemerality and splintering. It is also equally interesting
to follow the different study groups, think tanks, and political associations that reflect on and prepare reform projects, inside and outside of
academic structures, with different political colorations to them.

It is difficult, maybe even impossible, at this time to discern the contours of future political alliances and of forces capable of reconstituting a political system that would be different from some pessimistic, if not sinister, alternatives often discussed. Obviously, Russia's survival depends on the restoration of a viable state. This was the problem on the agenda in 1917; it was then solved by the Bolsheviks. In 1930 it was done by the Stalinists. Who will do it next?

CRISES, ANTIDOTES, AND POTENTIALS

The crisis we observe in Russia today is already a protracted one. We can assume that there will also be a "postcrisis" Russia, but it is not yet clear how and when. A few preliminary questions would help us reflect on the "anatomy" of the crisis. If "anatomy" is a useful enough metaphor, there must be some "internal patterns" in a crisis—however baffling this may sound when talking about what looks like an unstable mess. But we must ask: Is it always the same mess? Are there any stages in the ongoing crisis?

The depiction of woes and fragmentations, however real, may be erroneous if one gets caught in the unending stories that are available and mistakes the symptoms of crisis for its explanation. Despite the lamentable picture on the surface, the crisis produces not just woes but also, as we know, parliaments, elected local governments, a multitude of social, professional, and cultural organizations, an independent if financially strapped press, numerous businesses and economic institutions, and parties of all hues. Much of this happens through a spontaneous process, independent of governmental policies.

These developments give us ground to speak about two distinct bundles of factors that shape the ongoing events; those are overlapping for the moment, but they can and must be distinguished. The first includes manifestations of the decomposition of the old, the results of the fracturing and centrifugal pulls made possible by the weakening of the previously powerful regime, as described in earlier chapters. The other concerns governmental and spontaneous activities aimed at creating a new system, of which I just mentioned a few.

The concentration on the personality of leaders, as noted, comes to us easily but is quite misleading: The problems concern nations, elites, and strong social movements. Rebuilding a system, an economy, or a national mosaic and curing endless ills are not and cannot be just tasks to be handled by a leader or two; such efforts are a test of the stature, nerve, and stamina of the country's elites, whoever they are. They are the ones who are passing the exam; the test of a leader is of a different sort altogether.

A second bundle of factors is engendered by the efforts to reform, especially by measures to introduce a market economy—such measures being crisis makers in their own right. The overlap of the two crisis makers—decomposition and recomposition—is responsible for the lamentable state of affairs that demoted Russia from its superpower position and made it into a "beggar country." But the two stages have a different character, and they should not be misread: the one denotes agony of the old; the other, birth pangs of a new system. The crisis is obvious, deep, and complicated, but the making of a new system is occurring though without obvious contours, which makes the process tough on the participants and a difficult hurdle for observers.

The prevailing tendency in the first years of Yeltsin's presidency was to look for shortcuts or miracle cures in the form of "one-liner" programs, such as "privatization," or "marketization" delivered as a "shock-therapy." Indulgence in a primitive and belated "anticommunism" also belonged to the makeshift weapons in the sphere of ideology and politics. The accompanying widespread popular despair and apathy are also a factor, though these belonged to the first bundle of factors that contributed to blocking the mainsprings of recovery.

Is the given moment, which looks like a void in terms of renewal strategies, the eye of the hurricane or the bottom of the slope? Or are those still manifestations of a preexistent and deepening crisis? The latter is an acceptable diagnosis: the perestroika prompted the *unraveling* that brought to the surface all the ailments, and there were more of those than the country bargained for. If so, this was an important historical job—unintended, of course, yet a precondition for handling the problems. The old system was diseased and had to go, and the problems had to come up and be faced before the process of addressing them seriously could start. This would mean that the eye of the hurricane (though not all kinds of trouble) might be behind already. The five to six years that brought it about were not too long a period for a continent to realize what its ailments really were and are. Finding the remedies and applying them may require more than five to six years. There are ubiquitous signs that people are sobering up from all kinds of excited and "radical" moods. The real dilemmas can now be faced: A strong leadership is needed, but how can a dictatorship be avoided? Freedom and sovereignty should be established for nations, but how can devastating nationalisms, as well as catastrophic and useless conflicts, be avoided? How can markets be introduced without ruining the populations, as well as weakening central and local authorities?

Obviously, today's flux contains more than one potential outcome. The historically shaped area probably carries in itself more than one road and outcome, including some of a very disquieting variety—as is often the case in many societies. The task of finding and choosing the strategies and models that could tip the scale in favor of one or another of the competing potentials is for those people and networks of leaders. We therefore have to observe the groups competing for power and for strategies without losing sight of the spontaneous action of millions of people on the immense territory. A multitude of individuals, groups, and institutions in the centers and, mostly, locally are doing things that address more than mere survival: They also are deliberately trying to find solutions for problems in their purview.

The seeds and shoots for these solutions—and of the future—must already be right there in the present. But they cannot be made to grow without mass involvement of citizens and the appearance of broader action-oriented political associations.

The perestroika unveiled the weakness of political will and the inability *as yet* to produce impressive political movements, programs, and leadership of substance. The political weakness of the intelligentsia of the capitals and an inheritance of a diseased system are part of the problem. The force of the younger generations is not visible yet and remains largely untapped, and the chasm between generations is frequently discussed and much deplored. Nevertheless, the composition of the Parliament elected in December 1993 as well as political initiatives around the country permit us to see that some older and many new, actual *and* potential driving forces are already in place or in the making, and many new faces can be expected in the arena quite soon.

CHAPTER 15:

CONCLUDING THE UNCONCLUDED

LET US RESUME THE LINE OF THOUGHT THAT WAS PRESENTED in the introductory essay to this volume and was broken down into different aspects for further examination in the chapters. This was a broad explanatory scheme, with different subthemes that helped to account for the ups and downs of Soviet history. The observation of changes in the socioeconomic sphere showed a momentous reversal of the "big developmental vectors" that occurred over the whole span of Soviet history, which had two main stages. The first stage depended on a social structure that was dominated by, basically, two main "players": the poor, slow-moving, conservative, even backward-looking rural society—the bulk of the nation at that time; the other was the rather modern, future-oriented state and its appendages, including the urban centers, which were capable of—and hell-bent on—implementing dynamic programs of economic development.

Stage two was reached some fifty years later when the character of the players and their relative internal dynamics changed profoundly. It was now a predominantly urban society (and a growing one)—a complex structure not comparable to the preceding one. This society faced a powerful bureaucratic state that was conservative and stagnating, yet was trying to rule over an entirely different population. Between these two disparate stages and social realities lies the development of a state that was going through two political regimes: The one dominated by "Stalinism" was replaced by another one I call "bureaucratic absolutism." The two were different but were related by an important common set of features and trends that turned out to have been crucial and, finally, fatal. That is, between the two different stages unfolded a bureaucracy and its internal dynamic and logic of an overall owner-manager, the main carrier of a party-state machinery, and, in the final stages, a full-fledged ruling class.

This system's strengths and woes correlated with the changing social landscape. The system was still dynamic as long as the bureaucratic structure was running a basically rural society—as is still the case in China. The steam began to run out of it as the rural component kept declining—or, as the urban one kept growing. This correlation allows one to state the obvious: Soviet-style bureaucratic absolutism could not run a modern urban society. It was, as I contend, too archaic for this task.

Such were the historical circumstances that contained several outcomes. One of them was the clash between a more primitive social bedrock and an aggressive modernizing state that produced massive change and social promotion (and demotion) for millions of people. These circumstances are at the heart of the big battles over ideology and politico-economic strategies—which, incidentally and contrary to less discerning views, produced several Leninisms before the onset of Stalinism proper. The clashes I am talking about took on acute forms in the 1930s, and they contain the "secret" not only of Stalinism but also of its own final failure. Those were enabling, though not necessarily predetermining, conditions for the Stalinist takeoff and its main emanation, namely, the Stalinist state.

This outcome demands, of course, a more involved study that would consider not only the input of current events but also conjunctures of personalities and of crises, which permeated the whole process.

Examination of the making of several crises, including the latest and fatal one, reveals a specific manifestation of what I call "the reversal of vectors": The system's sources of strength were turning sour. Springs of dynamism and renovation in this system began to weaken. During the last two decades, signs of decay spread over most institutions of the regime. In this time of stagnation, called *zastoj,* social transformation proceeded at a hectic pace and was marked especially by wave after wave of urbanization. In the institutional setting of the state, the key features were overcentralization and the top leaders' efforts to preserve the old-fashioned, traditional ways throughout the vastly differentiating new society. The system had its roots in and drew much of its inspiration from the old bedrock that still prevailed during every leader's first steps on the ladder of power, but this bedrock was disappearing at a disconcertingly fast pace. In the preceding chapters I described trends inside the state and the party and examined the idea of a bundle of factors that produced an ever-deepening "internal trap," which undermined the regime. The trap led to the incapacitating power glut at the top, finally causing the peculiar downfall of a system that was not really toppled but, rather, collapsed.

These features, and not "the ruling working class"—obviously a nonsensical ideological concept—are the departing points in the analysis. Soviet history, which began by claims to a "workers' state," actually reproduced its working class in a renewed form of a "proletariat"—in the sense of a dominated labor force deprived of political rights and of class representation. The trade unions were state controlled. Although a proletariat was recreated, there was no recreation of a capitalist class or of capitalism. Instead, there was this bureaucratic state and maze, its upper layers becoming a full-fledged ruling class that controlled the state, the economy, and the redistribution of the national product. But all this proceeded with a parasitic bent: The social layers that undergirded this bureaucratic state coagulated into vested interests bent on perpetuating irresponsible power, irresponsible economic management (without cost) at the top, and an unproductive, poorly paid, but unexacting labor force, both at the lower ranks of the bureaucracy and in the lower strata of the productive system.

Consequently, the making of a parasitic bureaucracy, inimical to creative talent, was paralleled by the production of a massive low-key labor force in the economy that acquired its own vested interest in the ensured minimal standards of living this regime afforded them. But they also epitomized and became part of a *mekhanizm tormozheniia,* a good Russian term denoting the social mechanism that puts brakes on change and that produced, over the years, the interests vested in ongoing decay. This is how the foundation was laid for "the problem": This outwardly successful colossus was not actually capable of self-sustained growth and renovation in either the economic sphere or the political one. Its thrusts forward were politically managed and pushed at an economic cost that had its limits, whereas in Germany, for example, the system was endowed with such renovative power, which Hitler's wars did not destroy. So, quite obviously, very different historical mechanisms were at work in the two countries.

In a book written years ago, I pointed to *nekaia zalimitirovannaia sistema*—the late V. S. Nemchinov's term—meaning "a straitjacketed, highly fettered system." I also projected that term onto the polity, and especially the party, to conclude that as the economy was succumbing to its internal "imbalances," the party was losing the art of conducting politics.[1] *La demesure* was another term I found very fitting as I tried to grasp the particular features of the system, in which everything was exaggerated: overcentralized, overinvesting, overplanned, overpropagandized, and politically underdeveloped, to say the least—in fact, it was fully depoliticized. The system was losing out on all those points where it was "overdoing," but they happened to be its hallmark. No wonder the regime's main tools of power were in trouble. Power was slipping away.

THE SYSTEM'S MINEFIELDS

We can now briefly encapsulate again the historical "internal trap" that undermined this system. The Soviet economy worked for "the plan" (for the state, for politics)—not, in substance, for the consumer, who had very little say or control (notably, because the political party was a notorious "depoliticizer"). The plan, as administered by governmental agencies, "knew" mostly quantitative targets; it did not know quality. Thus, the supposedly supermodern planning operation ended up in continuing a Russian historical tradition of the "extensive," low-productivity mold.

The growth and role of bureaucracy in the system, which thrived on the aforementioned features, stemmed from the side effects of the state's sudden imposition of large-scale industrialization on a prebourgeois peasant society. A spontaneous, almost "natural" massive overproduction of bureaucracies followed, as predicted by critics. As the political agency that once could control them was itself sucked into the bureaucratic maze, bureaucracy enjoyed full freedom from political responsibility and was exempt from responsibility for the results of its economic activity. These were two crucial "freedoms" that made the economic system into a really *political* economy and therefore a pseudo-economy. We clearly see at this stage why this was so. Lack of interest in cost was part of this "freedom." Things do cost, of course, but—here was the crunch—to the administrative makers and shakers who gave the orders, costs were of no concern. Their positions and privileges were ensured,

---

1. Moshe Lewin, *Political Undercurrents in Soviet Economic Debates* (Princeton, N.J., 1974), reissued as *Stalinism and the Seeds of Soviet Reform* (New York, 1991), p. 145; V. Nemchinov, *Kommunist*, no. 5, 1964, p. 76. The article by Nemchinov, a leading proponent of reforms, contains a devastating critique of the Soviet economic model.

whatever the problems in the economy or the troubles and miseries for consumers—and however gloomy the future. The forecasting of the future was firmly controlled, monopolized, and censored. So the future seemed to have been ensured, too.

One of the forms of insurance consisted in an almost total success in preventing the emergence, inside or outside the system, of any viable and sufficiently vital backup mechanisms that could offer alternative ways of doing things. This made the system difficult to replace and even made it hard for people to imagine alternatives. But, ironically, this "success" was self-defeating. An unstoppable process was at work that made the powerful boss, in the absence of viable forces ready to oust him, insensitive to cost or to consumer demands and unable to conduct reformist policies, which caused an atrophying of the regime's vital functions and ability to act, to ensure a modicum of technological innovation, provide goods for the population and inculcate in it common values.

With these problems went the immobilization of the center, the "feudalization" of the system by powerful bureaucratic agencies. The sociopolitical consequence of it all was that the whole system became parasitic. History, quite obviously, could not be planned by such methods, although those held sway. This is what I meant by saying, at the start of this conclusion, that key features of the regime's ups and downs correlated with the unfolding of a bureaucracy operating as owner-manager of the economy and polity. Under this kind of aegis, the economy was not run according to an economic rationale and the polity did not respond to the political imperatives of the country. Logic, or interests and views of the bureaucratic owner-manager, was the imperative—and this "logic" was strained to absurd limits.

The time of reckoning had to come sooner or later, and it did come in an unusual scenario that, mercifully, did not involve a civil war. As there was nobody to challenge the system seriously, it was not toppled but withered away, because it reached the limits of its viability. Therefore I conclude that it died from natural causes. The same factors, though, that caused this downfall made the emergence of a new system so devilishly difficult. Another unusual feature in this situation—one of a growing list—is that the actors who are trying to do the job of reforming are often the ones who ran the previous show.

WHY WAS THE SYSTEM "ARCHAIC"?

I keep underlining the *archaic* features of the regime, although the term is not precise. *Precapitalist* is also usable, but only if the most advanced market economies with democratic political systems serve as the measuring rod. Too many capitalist economies have oppressive, primitive political systems. *Archaic* is easy to understand when we consider the empirical data on the results of the Civil War. That war caused, I contend, an "archaization" of the country, which took a giant step back during World War I and the Civil War. And the peasantry reacted with an "archaization" of its own: It took shelter by retreating into an older, self-sufficient shell dominated by its traditional system of land communes. The argument about archaism is also implied in my assessment of the Stalinist system as one form of an "agrarian despotism." Only the term *agrarian* may need an explanation; *despotism* is obvious.

I see Stalinism as one more—the last—version of a rural nexus writ large, a political system clashing with the country's rural backbone. In the process, the system got reincarnated as an "agrarian despotism," in which the mythologized ruler "above" is followed below by a more or less regimented peasantry—a rightless mass of citizens flanked by a veritable slave-labor sector. A cultural counterrevolution and return to primitive ideologies of the past complete the picture. The term *archaic* applies, of course, to the ruler's despotism, with arbitrariness as a key element. Capricious rulers have included pharaohs, Russian tsars and sultans, Renaissance princes, and desert sheikhs; but with Stalin an additional and aggravating dimension existed: Stalin had at his disposal technical means no pharaoh or sultan ever possessed.

Initially, though, industrialism actually buttressed the state's authoritarian features, because industrialism, in its own way, was also deeply authoritarian, as in any other system. In the meantime, the "cult" of Stalin added another, mythological prop from an equally old arsenal of political rule; and, once entrenched, Stalinism became marked by a perverse animosity and destructive fury against the most advanced products of its own developmental policies. Science and the intellectuals, culture and political thought, strong and independent-minded personalities, the world of the arts—all were heavily blocked and damaged by primitive indoctrination and coercion.

The bureaucracy, after Stalin, was emancipated from a terroristic rule of Stalinism before anybody else, with the whole country benefiting from it, too. Yet archaic traits persisted in the "liberated" and expanding bureaucratic octopus. A low-productivity economy and a massive denial of political and other autonomies reproduced again, though in less destructive forms, the contradiction that had plagued Stalinism: an inability to live with the products of its modernization, especially industrialization. But Stalin's successors also felt menaced by the mighty wave of urbanization and tried to maintain controlling shackles and ideological manipulations that naturally had an archaic ring to them. These leaders were blocking their country from entering a different stage that was knocking at the door.

In light of what we now know of the system—at least in the interpretation that is presented here—should we speak about Russia being engaged in "a transition from socialism to capitalism"? It was tempting to use such a title for this concluding chapter, but the idea is misleading: the implied approach misses the whole point in the actual development and the essence of the real "transition." My argument is that Russian capitalism was still poorly implanted and that it collapsed in the revolutionary storm, leaving Russia, in substance, in a fully precapitalist mode. This is why the switch, say, from the NEP to the Stalinist state led from one precapitalist system to another, and, finally, after Stalin, to a third that would be the last. The technology and science, as well as many other aspects of the industrial civilization, were similar to those in the West; but the system, in this last leg, was still precapitalist, not only because it had no democratic institutions (not all capitalist market economies have them) but because its polity had archaic features that were part of a family of premodern, even ancient despotic and absolutist practices. Ubiquitous controls, the denial of freedoms, a police state (without the breaks offered by even a conservative Rechtsstaat, which Prussia and Germany were known for), the muzzling of culture, and ideological narrow-mindedness all point to a peculiar industrial, yet archaic, configuration. We can therefore discuss to what class of political systems this case belongs. But whatever the answer, the affinities with old authoritarian and absolutist precapitalist regimes is too obvious to be disregarded.

THE SYSTEM'S "MATRESHKA"
— A CRISIS IN A CRISIS

The crisis the USSR was ushered into was not only a result of the accumulating imbalances by a regime that could not change any more but also a continuation, in a sharper form, of what was brewing over a good quarter of a century. What at the beginning of Gorbachev's leadership might have seemed a reparable crisis within some structures exploded into a "global crisis." The features that define this crisis as global can be visualized as follows: Because the economy was fully etatized, the collapse of the state system damaged, rather than liberated, the economy. The state system collapsed without leaving an heir. The downfall of the state-run economy left the country without a strong state—and without an economy. Yet even now, as the crisis goes on, the country continues to vegetate on the previous system's structures—or, rather, on its remains—because the essential features of a state monopoly could not yet be reformed. This is one of the instances of continuing the crisis of the past. Although these remnants are for the moment vital, they are in fact still diseased—perhaps even more than in the past—and will remain so as long as they are not incorporated into a new functional system.

Unfortunately, much of the new market economy is not very healthy either: it still is, to a large extent, of the speculative-parasitic variety.

This accounts also for the growing fissures that make the specter of more fragmentations (of Russia itself) very menacing. Society is ensnarled in a deep value crisis—that is, moral marasma, apathy, despair, young people's lack of interest, and the spread of pernicious, backward-looking moods are all evident.

It is amidst this kind of moral and general crisis that Russia is trying to "reinvent" itself as a system: a state, an economy, ideologies, political parties, and moral values have to be reformed, restored, or created. So far, Russia does not appear to be succeeding in these tasks. But it is also more than probable that we, the observers, are too much in a hurry to see things happen there. Recreating a sociopolitical self on such a scale is devilishly complex, so it is not a job for the fainthearted and the neurotic.

The new system cannot be merely imported or "invented." It can only be "reinvented" from the given material, which consists of many past experiences, institutions, and traditions that some people hate and others like too much.

Even if the previous regime failed to prepare alternative political cadres to serve as its own successors—if not as its gravediggers—many of those who now head the renovating efforts did come from the party and its apparat. Obviously, these had many useful features and people (as well as some less useful ones), but we can surmise and should expect that certain features of the product of a rather lengthy history will survive. We therefore have to qualify the idea, expressed earlier in this chapter, that "everything" must be reinvented. The previous regime has gone—or almost gone—but only as an entity, as a model; the new model will incorporate much of the past because the past, or enough of it, has not gone away. The presence of the *apparatchiki* on all levels of government reminds us of the role of the "bourgeois specialists" in the earlier stages of the Soviet regime: They played a crucial role (not yet sufficiently explored by research) in transferring governmental experience from the past to the new state. Yet there is an obvious difference—the "bourgeois specialists" were hired experts, whereas the *apparatchiki* of the defunct Soviet system are actually in power.

Are they contaminated remnants of the past who will taint the process or useful nuggets that were available in the old system and can be useful to the new one? In any case, the preservation of these cadres was made possible by the peaceful dissolution of the previous regime: A civil war would have made such a result impossible. The *apparatchiki* do, in fact, fulfill an important transitional job, although this is fraught with some worrisome carryovers. The new cadres and faces that are being seen already in the provinces and in the urban centers—many of them thirty or so years old—will decide, either consciously or inadvertently, what will be used or will prove irremovable from the various pasts available. Will it be something from the older political culture, Russian and Soviet, or from the national culture in general? From the Soviet industrial system or from the better kernels of the previous bureaucracy—or perhaps from the "second economy"? In the current situation, the presence of some of these "pasts"—in judicious doses, one hopes—actually provides indispensable building blocks. This is why attention should be paid to important elements of historical continuity that do not break so easily or should not be wantonly broken. The Bolsheviks paid a price for wanting to "break the whole machine" before constituting a new one, and they quickly found that this was a blunder—hence their switch to collaboration with bourgeoisie specialists. It is interesting that the "impetuous" reformers of today did not learn the lesson until the December 1993 elections had routed them. Even the breakup of the USSR should be examined from the viewpoint of powerful continuities: the republics did not always insist on total independence, but when they finally got the chance and did sever the unity, historically created links and interests did not disappear, either as sources of danger or as stimuli for restoring some form of federative ties.

I do not wish to overstate the power of the past. A past is not eternally the same: "New pasts" and new histories are in the making, and already plenty of novel features have developed in Russia and in the former USSR area, and they will continue to do so.

Democratization, for instance, though it is not firm enough so far, is a novelty. The economic system will not be the same; the old one has died, and cannot be resurrected. New and younger generations are joining the political process to replace the "democratizing *apparatchiki*" of today. What the younger leaders carry in their rucksacks is not yet known to us, or to them. In any case, the magnitude of the problems that Russia and the former Soviet republics are facing can be handled only by mass activity and leadership groups. Hopes and cravings for "a leader" are expressions of immaturity; it is crucial that new political leaders come in through elected bodies and parliaments, thus elections can be decisive in shaping this process. Conversely, weakening these still-fledgling institutions can do enormous damage to prospects of an orderly recovery.

One very powerful and pernicious tradition must continually be kept in mind: "statism," a master ideology and practice addressed in a previous chapter. What makes it particularly sneaky is the way in which it can be clad in different ideological garbs and can pass easily from one regime to another. Statism has very solid historical roots, and it is precisely the weakness of the current statehood that produces a large breach through which the deeply authoritarian statism—a state of mind as well as a set of political practices—can be smuggled back in and can throttle the emancipatory aspects of the current reforms. There is enough political and ideological nostalgia, including among people parading as reformers, to conjure up a monster, intentionally or otherwise. A strong state can emerge by producing a "political system" instead of a structure of dominance that once again denies politics to its citizens. A slippage into the latter is possible because, historically, capitalism emerged everywhere from certain more or less favorable preconditions. The weaker such pre-conditions are, the larger the role of the state. Tsarist Russia—and even more so, the Soviet system—grew out of this kind of deficiency.

In the meantime, the pressure to slow down the pace of the reforms, which has been ascribed uniquely to "conservatives," may be more meaningful than just a conservative nostalgia for the old regime. As one batch of reforms begins to look problematic and demands some rethink-ing, the battle will continue not only between a "radical" market orienta-tion and a social one that wants to cushion the blows, but also between a tendency for wholesale borrowings from the West—or from one of its embellished images—and a more selective combination of borrowings from the national heritage and from others throughout the world. A third alternative refuses any Western input, does not like aliens, and looks to the "national past" as the main source of inspiration.

A persistently dogmatic mindset among Russia's intellectuals and leaders is also a huge hindrance for the formulation of realistic reform programs. Although the old system fell apart, the dogmatic minds remain intact. These people refute the ideological claims and pretentions of the previous system, yet they have tended to replace them with new ones. An "ideologized" search for solutions is posing a great danger for the reform process. The predilection for "unmasking" is easily mistaken for studying. The defenders of the old and the proponents of the new have, supposedly, a firm grip of one thing: the old system. They suppose that this is the one thing they know well. Therefore, some still cling to it, or rather to one of its ideologies. In contrast, others produce their pro-grams of change by mechanically turning to a polar opposite: everything was state owned before, so all should be privatized now; everything was planned before, so all should be market now. Such mindsets are not con-ducive to serious programs and strategies of change.

Programs of change can easily become merely another ideology rather than a judicious approach to a complexity that calls for open minds.[2] A program will not work if it does not offer an integrated set of responses to the challenges of the real world. It has to address all sectors of the economy (private, state, foreign, mixed), including the indispensable

---

2. The production of an "ideology," instead of a program for economic change, is ana-lyzed by Jacques Sapir in his excellent study of the current situation in the former USSR, *Feu le système Sovietique? Permanences politiques, mirages économiques, enjeux stratégiques* (Paris, 1992).

financial and monetary aspects. The legal backing for the economy's needs and, more broadly, reforms of the law and the judiciary must be part of the package. The political institutions and the problems of regions and nations must be considered, too. Of course, all of these things do not have to be done simultaneously; some timetable will be needed. But rejecting the very idea of planning amounts, in these conditions, to creating a new chaos when trying to escape the current disorder.

If appropriate, practices and experiences of the previous regime should be used, provisionally or permanently. In the meantime, spontaneity reigns supreme, with some going in the right direction and some in the wrong one. The weakness of the elites and of the state system may push Russia into a capitalist model, which would again be followed by social convulsions, but ones worse than the crisis that Russians are now enduring. Although the many dire predictions of impending catastrophes have not come true, the unprecedented crisis—in which the country does not really have a system but is surviving on remnants of the past and a miraculous elementary family-and-neighbor mutual-help economy—does not allow for too rosy horoscopes. There is no reason, on the other hand, to become obsessively pessimistic. I have mentioned before various promising activities and signs of resourcefulness and an ability to survive, and there are many more positive examples that cannot be described fully here.

ADVICE TO THE ADVISORS

One particular danger is worth singling out. The whole area is open now to foreigners and seeks their help, input, and advice. Such outside help is extremely important, but it can become meddling. The international situation, always a crucial factor, is even more important for today's enfeebled Russia and other areas of the former USSR. If the West has too many of its own difficulties—if, for example, Western Europe gives in to its nationalisms or the United States fails to execute its own necessary reforms—the scenario for Russia would be even more complex. On the other hand, in an atmosphere of increased international fragmentation, a new configuration of blocs and alliances is to be expected, to counteract the effects of a conflict-prone situation. Russia may find a niche for itself in one such alliance and, through it, a place in the international community. Even a still-struggling Russia can find new support for itself but inept meddling may not only push it in an unwanted direction but also stimulate extremist forces internally. This is why external political intercessors must not press their own choices too hard onto a volatile country and push it in the wrong direction. Unfortunately, the logic of an old-fashioned power game calls for meddling as the very wisdom of statehood, by definition.

One particularly ill-advised activity is the peddling of poorly defined Western solutions and concepts, which may actually be very controversial in the West itself. Taking sides in internal political battles between representatives of bona fide interests and alternatives without understanding the character of the main players and the whole situation is also quite imprudent. The widely promoted notion of "democracy" means for a Westerner the way institutions of his or her own country work; democratic institutions might be quite different in other areas. Russians, given their traditions, could easily support a "democrat" who, in fact, might turn out to be authoritarian, even repressive—a phenomenon that has been seen in many places.

Another idea that may easily be misleading concerns forms of transition to a market economy. If "nonmarket," utterly bureaucratized economies calling themselves "socialist" no longer have much of a future (China is a separate problem of interest), the unqualified promotion of "free market" economies is misleading because such economies must be appropriately and firmly controlled, rather than merely set free. The nonmarket factors in any developed economy are powerful and growing in importance, but it is imperative to ensure that those factors remain responsive to social will, that is, to democracy—which is far from being the case. Important as the marketization measures may be in themselves, one discerns behind the underlying rationalizations East and West a lack of awareness of the complexity of modern economies, in which market and powerful nonmarket components interact and the state has an enormous role to play in regulating, and often actually planning, economic life.

Experts must be sure that they are giving the right advice. Where do people acquire the expertise that authorizes them to counsel a whole system on how to become another one, especially amidst an unprecedented transition? The counseling about the introduction of "capitalism" or a "market economy" often amounts to a proposal for "shock therapy." The counselors seem to forget that capitalism took between 500 and 150 years to emerge, and that this process involved countless shocks. The prospect of a miracle being performed in 500 days, give or take, can leave an observer breathless, but it can do even worse damage to a whole country.

The other "trifle" that is sometimes forgotten is that there certainly are different capitalisms—Brazil, Great Britain, Japan, the United States, and Mexico are all capitalist. The term *capitalist* is linked to stories of success, crisis, stagnation, and failure. Which outcomes will occur in Russia and other parts of the ex-Soviet area? Systems and economies can and should be presented by means of strict respect for hard facts; unfortunately, expositions of economic systems are riddled with ideology. One has to be sure that any advice offered on subjects of this nature avoids ideological distortions and embellishments. In addition, there are signs that the market economies worldwide are in the throes of profound changes. Russia, which always was a stage behind, may enter capitalism through a wrong door—the one that is already disappearing—and then have to play catch-up once again. Moreover, a broader and more intricate caveat is in order when offering foreign experience for use in a different historical milieu: Transplants of such experience may be even trickier than transplants performed on human bodies. Rejections may endanger whole societies, not just individuals.

RESTORING A STATE COMES FIRST?

The different, sometimes menacing alternatives are anxiously discussed in Russia, though they have not yet been clearly evaluated: Is a Japanese-style state capitalism appropriate? A Brazilian solution—glittering downtowns with enormous shantytowns—isn't it, unfortunately, one of the potentials? How can Russia avoid this and achieve something more humane and democratic? These are awesome problems, and the main political forces now in power have not yet gotten a handle on the alternatives.

Today's diminished and enfeebled Russia will continue to sink if it does not restore a functioning system. How can serious economic reforms be conducted without solving the problem of power—its pattern and sufficient legitimacy? It is very easy, for example, for Americans to tell Yeltsin he must control inflation before he can get the promised $29 billion, but what if he has no power to do this?

Obviously, a state without an economy cannot function. Reciting the story of Russia's potential—its size, riches, and so on—will not bring about needed changes. If Russia is to face the complicated world successfully, a different sort of polity should emerge where the societal input is powerful and society's political role is potent. With a recovering economy and a re-emerging polity, Russia will become an important power again, and soon. The political and economic changes can be instituted almost simultaneously, but a credible political force must come first.

The state, however rudimentary, has often pulled the system's other components out of the crisis at hand. And that must be true now, too—although, in a fragmented society, the state may resurrect a recurrent historical paradigm of a strong state and a weak society. So even if the present is miserable, such a future is not a consolation.

Much depends on who reconstitutes an action-capable state at a critical time like that. In "the times of trouble" (seventeenth century) it was a social movement, under Minin and Pojarsky, that sparked the process. Who can and will do this now? This is a crucial question. Although everybody talks about the state of the economy—and rightly so—politics, not the economy, is the first priority. These issues are central to the ongoing conflicts in today's Russia; and they are fraught with potential menace, notably a repetition of one of the past strangleholds.

Russia is, in fact, underdeveloped again and lagging, and it was accumulating signs of a new underdevelopment for quite a time. This is the paradox of its history: Some of the most successful catch-up efforts have ended up, again and again, "in the red." My essays underlined the recurrent phenomenon of "accentuated retardation" at the end of the NEP, in the Stalinist period, and, finally, in the Brezhnev "stagnation." And this phenomenon is still apparent today.

History does not go away; it stays with us in many ways—and it had better be mastered. The wholesale rejection of the postrevolutionary past that many Russians engage in is a largely impotent verbal act. Making sweeping rejections without good knowledge is a prescription for destroying what works and replacing it with what does not. This happened after October 1917, for instance—and on a grand scale. Nevertheless, it is better to realize that the Russians do have a past that was not all dark, and that today they do have a better-educated population, with pools of talent that are not yet fully deployed. But change is coming. Russia is relearning how to become and be a nation, a state, and a system. In such a situation menacing slippages can always occur, and the prospect of remaining weakened for some time is serious. But not everyone is demoralized, ready to sell out and run.

One can risk a very general prediction: For better or for worse, the system that will emerge in Russia will be different and distinctive—yet it will be a national dish, *à la russe,* and not necessarily ominous. Some think that the process will last many years, which certainly seems likely, given the magnitude of the task. What many people do not realize, however, is that in today's slump, a set of small improvements can have a powerful magnifying effect and go a long way in lifting the spirit of the population. Contours of the new system that are now barely visible can emerge as a functioning system in a few years—there is no need to talk about decades.

Since the political configuration of the country is still in the making, though, and the current stage is far from sealed, the burdens of Russian history are not yet safely behind. But the laboratory of history is certainly working. The country's political complexion may still change several more times.

The factor of "spontaneity" is crucial. Observers have reported widespread pessimism, inertia, and despondency, but such conditions are far from being the whole story: so much happens in local governments, in and around schools, in business initiatives, in study groups, in action committees, in neighborhood associations, and in a multitude of professional unions. There are tens of thousands of these entities, and they constitute an important process that will shape the future no less than the political enactments of the government will. They may actually, sooner or later, contribute to the emergence of a stronger leadership and help to restore regional and national voluntary and cooperative organization—and thereby prevent a damaging fracturing of the country and preserve the enormous potential of this continent. There are millions of people for whom elections, parliaments, constitutional rules, and the quest for the rule of law are attractive. This attitude may get strengthened in the next couple of years—and may remain potent. Similarly, the habits of social activity, from the communal and local to the national levels, are vibrant. We do not see enough reports about the numerous professional, cultural, and political associations, in the capitals and in most provinces, that are energetically handling their problems and those of the country. There are also a growing number of entrepreneurs, an interesting press, and mass movements concerned with ecology, education, and the problems women face. They are not powerful enough, and the economic situation is bleeding them all; but they are potentially strong enough to mobilize millions of people. The new and novel urban milieu allows us to entertain the hope that the positive reform "process" may this time be powerful enough to avoid the historical precedents, especially the relapses into underdevelopment, which I described as one of the "burdens" of Russian history. The current crisis, hopefully, may be the last version of just this kind of relapse.

The interpretations of the relevant past (of Russia, of the cold war, of the whole twentieth century) are inevitably part of any reflection on our times. The making of a world economy and an interdependent world—an epoch-making, though not a recent phenomenon at all, in fact, was seen, thanks to the changes in Eastern and Central Europe, as a step into a new world order in the making, one that would replace the cold-war blocs. But this hope was recently marred by a disquieting comeback of so much that is antiquated and backward-looking, and not only in the former Soviet area. The ideological veils and political shortsightedness inside and outside Russia collude in blurring the fact that the world is one, that the fortunes and misfortunes of states and systems interact and change seats. Atavistic nationalisms parading their ominous fare in Europe and elsewhere exacerbate, rather than alleviate, the hurdles of a complex and all too often jittery world. The old imperial games of big and small powers are no answer either—and are by now useless. It is true that the "new world order" that was optimistically predicted in Gorbachev's heyday now looks more like a *sauve-qui-peut,* breeding helplessness and pessimism. But it is also true that the acceptance of a new agenda is imperative, and powerful forces are pushing for it, in order to match the fact of international interdependence by institutions and policies that would insure a modicum of coherence to that agenda.

WHO TOPPLED WHOM, LOST, OR WON?

The system, as I have claimed, died "from natural causes." Such statements offend those who prefer some heroic myths about their role in toppling the regime. But it is better to confront the truth: No one toppled it; it fell from its own excessive weight. Even the August 1991 coup by the nostalgic old-regime supporters petered out without much counterpressure. Yeltsin's appeal to the population to go on strike went unheeded and was superfluous. The regime succumbed to its internal sclerosis, which made it incapable of handling the overall complexity.

This is what did the trick—not any particular enemy. A toppling of the regime by force or a military conquest would probably have had quite a different outcome, but neither of those events actually happened.

Some continue to claim the credit for "toppling communism," maintaining that it was the cold war and the arms race that led to victory. Were this true, it should have happened much earlier: The superiority of the West over the Soviet bloc in economic, technological, and scientific resources, in manpower and standards of living, and in domination of propaganda warfare were overwhelming. But the depth of the West's ideological commitment was problematic, as is illustrated by the big "love affair" with China once it split from the Soviet bloc. China and its regime were for many years adopted by the West lock, stock, and barrel: Its communism, prison camps, and human rights record were disregarded, and it was praised as much more rational and forward-looking than the USSR. There is no doubt that the Chinese regime benefited from this anti-USSR alliance with the West or that its position in the world (as well as internally) was strengthened—and it continues to be quite strong. So much for the toppling of communism.

The cold war acquired its own momentum, which became more important than any particular ideology within it—this was true for *both* sides of the contest. This is why the appearance of Gorbachev and his surprising policies in favor of stopping the arms race made him at that time into the most popular leader in the world and certainly a winner, not a loser. His actions exposed the futility of the cold war and implied that both contestants were actually losers, whereas the winners turned out to be the two vanquished World War II aggressors—they avoided excessive militarization and were able to pour their resources into their economies. The "winners" of World War II, on the other hand, were transformed into superpumps for a monumental squandering of their wealth. It was obvious that Gorbachev's moves to end the cold war caught the "cold warriors" unawares and produced a considerable consternation among their ranks—if indeed it was a victory, they did not immediately acknowledge it. Certainly, it was unwanted. The arms race was, of course, more onerous to the Soviet side, not only because it had a weaker economy but also because its overall economic system had a built-in propensity for wastefulness. The old system certainly lost. What is problematic is the idea of a winner.

The unraveling of the Soviet system began with Gorbachev's launching in earnest his reforms of internal democratization. It can be argued plausibly that the cold war delayed Soviet reforms and even prolonged the stranglehold of conservative *apparatchiki* and their allies. Reforms were needed, and there was an interesting effort to introduce changes in the economic model in 1965, under the aegis of Prime Minister Kosygin; but the conservatives scuttled this effort, prolonging their grip on power. They thrived on the cold war. A less conflictual international environment would have diminished the importance of the military-industrial complex and would have demobilized "the mobilizers"—that is, the image of the enemy and the force of the appeal for a patriotic rally against him. Perhaps the Eisenhower-Khrushchev détente, a casualty of the downing of the US reconnaissance plane over Soviet territory in 1961, might have had a chance of stopping the race when the whole ICBM arsenal on both sides did not exceed fourteen or sixteen rockets. In such a case, in an international environment of increased economic and cultural exchanges with the West, the structural inadequacies of the Soviet economic system would have been exposed much earlier and the cover-up that "patriotism" offered to the regime's conservatives would have lost its appeal. The 1965 reforms could have continued and deepened, and the transformation of the Soviet system—or its demise—could have proceeded apace and in a less convulsive way than was to be the case in the early 1990s.

This reasoning does not claim anything more than plausibility—but it is sufficient for arguing against the seeking of false laurels in the cold war. These deflect the attention from grasping the Soviet phenomenon as a system that managed, especially since the early 1970s, to self-destruct in a relentless, obsessive way, and, further, from understanding that the foes of the Soviets—the United States, primarily—also kept damaging themselves without realizing this for some time.

These are points not to be missed by students of systems and of the factors that produce crises. The weight of international factors is powerful, and Gorbachev's moves only underscored the enormous changes that had been in the making for quite some time; they were not sudden. Moreover, they concerned the whole world, not just the USSR: they certainly created considerable confusion and loss of direction also among the former adversaries of the USSR.

It was the vast historical changes—not any particular country, or this or another leader—that shaped the new international reality. Against such a backdrop, it is only a slight consolation for the self-proclaimed winners that the crisis has, so far, been more devastating to the other side. The surprising result of the increased complexity of the world is that no matter who the losing side may be, everyone must pay. The current sorry state of Russia and the rest of the former USSR is actually harming everyone, making any self-satisfied pronouncements quite misplaced.

However controversial this may sound, the game on which many became hooked—the cold war and its addictive effects—lasted too long. Could the cold war not have been stopped earlier? Did the obviously superior side not feel too happy with this game? Did that side not know that it was superior, and by just how much? How could the weaker side have been made into the supposed main player? These questions are intriguing, and there certainly are specialists who could find the answers for us. But the historical agenda is broader and urgent. The so-called new world order (or mess) is the agenda, and the effects of the recent past (that is, of the last half century, or perhaps even of the whole century) are still being felt. As the ex-Soviets endeavor these days to shift to capitalism amid great distress and dire forecasts, the cold war is confirmed by historians and political theorists as a remarkable half century of potential apocalypses that the protagonists managed to contain.

POSTSCRIPT:
WHY THE CHINESE MAY STILL SUCCEED

The Chinese experience over the last decade, with its growing market economy and a seemingly remarkable economic growth rate, is a fascinating event that makes us wonder why Russia could not act in the same way. It may well be that it is too early to draw conclusions from this "Chinese way," but a few remarks come to mind. The Soviet experience with the NEP seems a plausible point of comparison with the Chinese policy, which looks like the NEP writ large; the circumstances surrounding the introduction of the two policies have some important elements in common. The Chinese policy's background was certainly a series of crises (the Great Leap Forward, the Cultural Revolution), and there were many inadequacies in the state sectors.

However, China still has what Gorbachev's Russia did not have anymore—a huge peasantry that not only supplies the country with food but is probably a reassuring mass that allows the authoritarian system to face emerging new social strata and private sectors without being unduly alarmed. There is another important difference: Soviet Russia did not succeed in attracting foreign capital, though in the 1920s it did try to achieve this with "foreign concessions." China, on the other hand, enjoys a massive influx of Asian investment capital—and increasing amounts from the West—to the extent that some Taiwanese, South Koreans, and others have transferred their factories to China (where labor costs are lower), though they may be running them from their home headquarters.

Furthermore, today's international environment is different from that of the 1920s, when Russia was, for the West, an ideological and political novelty and a menace. And Russians themselves never stopped seeing the peaceful 1920s as a breathing space between large-scale wars, especially ones waged against them. It is different these days for China, seen from both inside and outside its borders. In addition, the Chinese system has been in place barely forty-odd years—it is some thirty years younger than the Soviet system. In the latter case, there was more time for many self-defeating features of the system to reach their plenitude; the Russians drove their statism, including nationalization, to its limits.

On the other hand, a superpower position, the international competition, and the transformation of the population into a predominantly urban one do not yet apply to China, or not to the same degree that they do in the former USSR. More important, China stopped the statization process by renouncing, first, the more utopian Great Leap and, later, other extremist policies in the countryside; and China is now allowing a large-scale market economy with growing private sectors to develop. The latter point is crucial. Paradoxically, then, by remaining more backward than Russia but renouncing extremist policies in time to push toward a wholesale statization, China preserved its capacity to act and to execute important policy changes. This was also the case with the still-backward and devastated new Soviet state, which could lead and change strategies and did this several times over, although in quite contradictory directions. It remains to be seen whether successful marketization will bring about a democratization of the Chinese system, its "re-Staliniza-tion," or even a considerable transformation and reinvigoration of the authoritarian state in the wake of economic success. These are all plausible possibilities for the not-too-distant future.

In brief, Russia had enough time to go too far. The Chinese seem to have arrested the urge of their bureaucracy to metastasize beyond repair. Thus, they retain, in a still predominantly rural country, the capacity to rule and tolerate—or initiate—important reforms.

The Scope of the Stalinist Gulag

FORCED LABOR

Using criminal labor for building important economic objects was suggested by N. Ianson, the commissar for state inspection of the Russian republic (NK RKI). In a letter to Stalin, Ianson suggested that criminal labor be used to open new areas of the country for economic exploitation, for work on construction sites, lumber cutting, and road construction. This idea was put into practice during the 1930s.[1] The first "regulation" on labor camps appeared on April 7, 1930. The first forcible use of mass labor for colonizing faraway wilderness did not involve inmates but, rather, the uprooted ("dekulakized") peasants, who were not sent to camps but were exiled to forced settlements—although under the authority of the Gulag administration. They became so-called *spetsposelentsy,* and later I have more to say about this type of repression. According to criteria that applied at that time, a figure of 4.6 percent was employed by government offices to estimate the ratio of "hostile classes" (*klassovo-vrazhdebnye elementy*) in the population of 160 million, "dekulakization" and other types of "cleansing" probably achieved this "norm." Victims of "cleansing" in the early 1930s, in addition to the kulaks, consisted of smaller waves of arrested Nepmen, ex-members of other parties, internal party opponents, ex–tsarist officers, ex-Whites from the Civil War—all of whom took the road either to camps or to places of exile (*ssylki*), as did the kulaks. Thereafter, the contingents of those condemned to forced labor grew at the expense of broad categories vaguely qualified as "enemies of the people," or "saboteurs." These people came from all walks of life and were sentenced summarily—without even a Soviet-style due process—to labor camps for various,

1. V. P. Danilov and S. A. Krasil'nikov, eds., *Spetspereselentsy Zapadnoj Sibiri, 1930–vesna 1931* (Novosibirsk, 1992), pp. 13–14. In early 1930, this principle was applied in the labor colonies of the NKVD with sentences up to three years, and in the ITL camps under

mostly fictitious crimes.[2] A still-unknown number of them were equally summarily sentenced to death.

This kind of terroristic treatment of layers upon layers of the population was not the result of a "good idea" suggested by a commissar. It grew out of policies and practices that were characteristic of the forced tempos of the "planning era," and thus were mobilizational and coercive by definition. The policies of collectivization and dekulakization, the first large-scale acts of coercive social transformation, served as a training ground for making people do under duress what they had done before without any state coercion—namely, work. The Gulag system, based on such policies, flourished, especially after 1933, and has since become, for some, the hated symbol of an oppressive regime and, for others, a hotly defended practice—at least initially. Estimates of the numbers of people incarcerated or executed in the Gulag became ammunition in an ideological battle that raged before and even more intensely during the cold war, even when the forced-labor phenomenon took on, after Stalin's death, quite a different dimension. Recent publications from the Russian archives, based on previously secret and quite credible reports of the security agencies themselves, allow us to obtain a more realistic picture of the number of inmates of the "Gulag Archipelago." However, convincing data are not yet available for the number of executions, especially during the bloody purges of the late 1930s—often referred to merely as the Bloody Purges, to distinguish them from any other action using the term *purge*.

Numbers per se were not what counted in assessing Stalin's system, though. The enormous exaggerations that became, for some, almost a credo and a means for testing other people's dedication to democracy were an independent phenomenon that may be worth exploring on some other occasion. But this phenomenon did not contribute to the study of the grave and intricate problems related to Stalinism and to the Soviet system at large, an endeavor that required painstaking weighing of evidence.

OGPU when the sentence was over three years. NKVD also initially ran the special kulak settlements, but it was turned over to the OGPU in the spring of 1930. At that time, the NKVD camps contained 600,000 prisoners and the OGPU ones, 160,000. In 1934 the OGPU was "dissolved," but in fact it took over the NKVD, which now contained the Gulag administration—with all the types of imprisonment and deportation settlements being concentrated under this roof.

2. Kuritsyn, in Dmitrij Volkogonov, ed., *Tridtsatye Gody* (Moscow, 1990), p. 89.

CAMP INMATES AND THE FIRST DEPORTATION:
THE 1937 CENSUS

The first reliable figures on the camp population appeared in a study of the 1937 population census, its materials, and its ill fate. As is well known, the government declared this census to have been "an act of saboteurs" (*vreditel'skij*), voided it, and then conducted a murderous purge of an unknown number of statisticians who had not found population numbers the government expected. Materials of this census remained unpublished until these data were discovered and made public in 1990. They also included, for the first time, the secret but official data from the Defense Ministry and NKVD's Gulag, both of which were obligated to deliver to the Census Bureau of Gosplan's Statistical Service (TsUNKhU)—and, obviously, to Stalin and Molotov—many statistical data on people under their jurisdiction. The discovery was made and reported in a series of important articles entitled, characteristically, "A Half-Century of Silence," by the scholars B. V. Zhiromskaia, Iu. V. Poliakov, and I. N. Kiselev.[3] A year later, most (or much) of the census material was also published by the Academy of Sciences in a statistical handbook.

The Gulag statistics for 1937—as shown in the handbook—reported 821,000 inmates in camps, 375,000 in colonies, and 545,000 in ordinary prisons. There also were 916,800 "deported settlers" (*trudposelentsy*), half of whom (probably) were in Gulag-supervised settlements (*kommandantskie poselki*) and were included in the contingents that the NKVD (Commissariat of the Interior) registered in 1937 for census needs. The others were registered personally by census takers, because their civil rights had already been restored to them.[4] But we know from elsewhere that later came a hardening (*uzhestochenie*) of official attitudes toward them, and by 1939 all such settlers were counted by the Gulag system. So

3. Iu. A. Poliakov, V. B. Zhiromskaia, and I. N. Kiselev, "Polveka molchania: (Vsesoiuznaia perepis' naseleniia 1937go goda)," *Sotsiologicheskie Issledovaniia,* no. 6 (1990), p. 3; 21, no. 7 (1990), pp. 50–70; and no. 8 (1990), pp. 30–52. I learned belatedly about Robert E. Johnson's Introduction to "A Half-Century of Silence: The 1937 Census" (*Russian Studies in History* [Summer 1992]).

4. *Vsesoiuznaia perepis' naseleniia 1937: kratkie itogi* (Moscow, 1991), pp. 17–18. An interesting introduction is provided by Zhiromskaia and Kiselev. Previously secret memoranda and an explanatory apparatus are appended. Data supplied by Defense and NKVD to the Census Bureau are on pp. 160–81.

we can, for our purposes, add this figure in full to the Gulag contingents for 1937, as did V. N. Zemskov,[5] who found more detailed material than the three authors of the article on the 1937 census. Their data were from the Statistical Service located in TsGanKh, whereas Zemskov got his data directly from the files of NKVD-MGB in TsGAOR that contained the *spetskontingent* NKVD, that is, the contingents of those who either worked for or were inmates of the Gulag and had to be recounted directly by the Gulag administration, then a subdivision of the NKVD.

According to a government instruction concerning census taking of populations under Gulag jurisdiction (*po osobomu spisku Gulaga*), the Gulag had to include in its data the personnel (*shtat*) of the NKVD; the guards; militarized fire brigades; some police cadets serving in camps, prisons, colonies, and building sites; and all the prisoners, whether already sentenced or under investigation. The "deported settlers" (*trud-poselentsy*)—mostly kulaks at that time—who resided in areas under Gulag jurisdiction (*v zonakh, trudposelkakh Gulaga NKVD*) were also counted by the Gulag. All kinds of deportees (*Ssylnye, trudposelentsy*) who were under NKVD jurisdiction, but not in those *zony* (areas under Gulag jurisdiction), as well as those of them who had their civil rights restored, were registered by census takers like all other citizens.[6] I will say more about these "deportees" later.

It turns out that the NKVD-Gulag administrative staffs were called, for census purposes, *spetskontingent A*. Camp and prison guards were *spet-skontingent B* (with the Russian sound of *B*), and the inmates were in the *V* category (with a Russian letter that looks like *B*). We thus learn for the first time how many people the Gulag system really employed or incarcerated in each of these categories. But, first, it is worth making clear in passing that all the categories in the Gulag's domain were included, though not openly, in the overall published population statistics, without specifying how many people were actually imprisoned. The 1991 handbook of the 1937 census explains how this was done. Guards and civilian employees (called *spetskontingent B*) in camps, prisons, and *spetsposelki* entered the general census figures under the professional or social positions which they reported having belonged to. Prisoners under investigation (*podsledstven-*

---

5. V. N. Zemskov, "Gulag—istoriko-sotsiologicheskij aspekt," *Sotsiologicheskie Issle-dovaniia,* no. 6 (1991), pp. 11–21, continued in no. 7 (1991), pp. 3–15.

6. Ibid., no. 6, p. 17.

nye) also declared as their profession the one they had exercised before their imprisonment. Prisoners sentenced to prison terms in "normal" prisons did not answer the profession or social group question; they responded simply "Inmate" (*zakliuchennyj*). Youth in colonies for minors answered "Vospitannik." Prisoners in camps and colonies (*spetskontingent V,* using the sound for the third letter in the Russian alphabet) gave the names of construction sites or organizations they worked for as inmates—but not the social group they belonged to. They appeared in the published statistics in the general category of "others" (*prochie*). In such a way, the totals on professionals and social groups in the census included the victims of political repression or of criminal justice. By similar devices, the army was also included in the total population figures.[7]

The precise numbers for the "secret" categories are now available from the same and other sources.[8] At the beginning of 1937, the army had in its ranks 1,682,569 people—including probably people in the navy. On February 7, 1939, Defense reported a figure of 2,100,233 people,[9] including ones in the navy. In 1937 there were in the Gulag a total of 2,389,570 inmates for the whole V category in all the types of detention places,[10] plus the B category—guards and hired punitive personnel, police cadets, and militarized fire brigades serving in all the penitentiaries.

In 1937 the A category had 270,730 people.[11] All in all, NKVD reported in 1937 a total of 2,660,330, including those in the V, A, and B categories. For the 1939 census the NKVD reported a total population of 3,742,434 people, including, again, the "A" and "B" personnel.[12] The "handbook" containing the 1937 census explained that this *Kontingent A* included central and local administrations of the NKVD, the NKVD's

---

7. *Vsesoiuznaia perepis'*, pp. 231–32, note 19.

8. Ibid., p. 164.

9. Poliakov et al., no. 8., p. 43.

10. *Vsesoiuznaia perepis'*, p. 173. Some Gulag statistics single out three types of camps. The tougher camps were the ITL (*isprevitel'no-trudovoj lager*), ITK (*ispravitel'no-trudovaia koloniia*) housed prisoners with lighter sentences, and the smallest contingent was in colonies for juvenile delinquents. Sometimes all three were lumped together, and the deported "special settlers" were also included. We can now distinguish between these categories and present data for all of them.

11. Ibid., p. 174.

12. Poliakov et al., p. 42.

own military units, and the frontier guards (it would be helpful to find out what the exact number of frontier guards was). As of 1939 there were 365,839 officials and officers[13] among the "A" agency administrative personnel. Hence, an additional 100,000 or more people were recruited into the NKVD apparatus to support the purges—assuming that the number of frontier guards remained unchanged.

The three authors who provided these figures estimated that on the day the census was taken (January 6, 1937) there were 1.8 million inmates in the Gulag. In 1939 their number grew to 2.6 million. V. S. Zemskov, a researcher and historian at the Academy of Sciences, adds more clarity to the numbers of these authors, who had problems with assessing whether NKVD figures included the *spetsposelentsy* category and what the exact number of guards included in the total was. Thanks to his NKVD materials, Zemskov arrived at the following data on inmates and deportees for January 1, 1937, and January 1, 1939, respectively:

TABLE A.1

	1937	%	1939	%
IN CAMPS	820,881	30.9	1,317,195	44.6
IN COLONIES	375,488	14.2	355,243	12.0
IN PRISONS[a]	545,000	20.5	350,538	11.8
Trudposeleniia	916,787	34.4	938,552	31.6
TOTAL	2,658,156	100.0	2,961,528	100.0

[a] *Prison figures are for April 1, 1937, and January 1, 1939 (Zemskov, pp. 74–75).*

These are numbers of inmates and deportees (who were, nevertheless, a category apart from camp inmates). The deportees lived and worked in settlements, not camps, and resided in their own lodgings, which were not surrounded by walls and guards. Excluding those "deported," Zemskov found somewhat more camp inmates than the three authors had found in 1937—but several hundred thousand fewer for 1939. Obviously, categories A and B are excluded from table A.1. Zemskov found data for 1940 that reported 107,000 armed guards (including 12,000

---

13. Ibid., p. 45.

selected from among the inmates themselves) and 1,668,200 prisoners
(March 1); 107,000 guards constituted 6.4 percent of the whole camp
population. According to him, the same 6.4 percent can be assumed valid
for 1937 and 1939. That would give, respectively, 111,447 and 129,470
guards in all the prisons and camps.

THE GULAG, 1934–54

So much for the figures revealed by the two "excavated" censuses. What
about the years before and after these censuses were taken? The best and
most credible material so far was offered by Zemskov in a series of valuable articles, from which I have borrowed liberally.

First, though, we need a detour to another serious author who has
reflected on the data about victims of terror. Such data have been the subject of heated—often venomous—exchanges in ex-Soviet writings. One
point of contention remains the number of those engulfed by the 1937–38
purges. O. Khlevniuk, a historian and journalist known for his balanced
approach, quotes Roy Medvedev (who thought that 5 million to 7 million
people were repressed for political reasons in 1937–38 alone) and then a
legal scholar and historian, A. Dugin, who challenged Medvedev's numbers. According to Dugin, the number of the repressed was "at least ten
times smaller."[14] Khlevniuk recalculated Dugin's numbers of political
prisoners in camps and claimed that not just "counterrevolutionary
crimes" but also so-called "socially harmful" and "socially dangerous"
(sotsial'no vrednye and sotsial'no-opasnye) categories, as used in the Soviet
criminal code, must be added to the tally of "political prisoners"—which
Dugin did not consider. Such an addition would mean that for January 1,
1937, there were 104,826 plus 103,513 (for a total of 208,339) political prisoners; and for the beginning of 1939, there were 454,432 plus 285,831 (a
total of 740,263)—still a far cry from Medvedev's millions.

Khlevniuk, however, also wants to add considerable numbers of those
who were en route to camps. He contends that some "enemies of the people" were not fully registered (nedouchitivalis') because they were on the
roads when the reports (spravki) were compiled. Many testimonies led to
the conclusion that the number of deaths from hunger, cold, and illnesses
during transport was particularly high. (I must note that while the latter

---

14. O. V. Khlevniuk, 1937-oj (Moscow, 1937), p. 154.

is correct, the number of people en route to camps would have shown up —minus deaths—in the figures of the next year. Whether such deaths would have been included in the total of reported deaths is not yet possible to know.)

Figures for mortality also need closer scrutiny. Documents show, said Khlevniuk, that the mortality rate in camps for 1937–38 was 5.5 percent to 5.7 percent of the total inmate population per year. Khlevniuk also brought up the problem of executions during the same Great Purges. Data supplied to Khrushchev in April 1954 assessed them at about 700,000 for 1921 to 1953. Other figures from the secret police given to the Central Committee's plenum in 1954 spoke of 600,000 executions, specifically, during 1937–38. It is also known that many family members of those sentenced as "enemies of the people" were punished by deportation. So the scope of repression during the two years cannot be expressed in hundreds of thousands, but in millions.[15]

Again, though, we must recognize that such conclusions depend on the type of repressive measures Khlevniuk has in mind when he talks about "millions." If he was referring to all those incarcerated as well as all those deported to coercive settlements from 1937 to 1939, then he is right. As noted earlier, there reportedly were almost three million people in 1939 in camps and settlements, but that figure includes criminals and a sizeable population that was exiled between 1931 and 1933. On the other hand, it is unclear whether the 600,000 executions—if this number can be taken as final—should all be included in the camp population, because it is unclear whether they were first shipped to camps and executed later, or whether those were executions soon after the death sentence, without a stay in the camps.

So much for Khlevniuk's corrections and legitimate misgivings about the still-unsolved questions regarding the purges; as yet, there are no data that would provide the answers. But even corrections (upward), which good data would eventually allow, would not substantively change the emerging estimate of the scope of repression during the 1930s, which is our main focus here. Such an estimate is obtainable now, thanks to the census figures, some still-unverified KGB publications, and the work of Zemskov, to which I now turn again.

Zemskov's article, entitled "Gulag: A Historico-Sociological Aspect,"

15. Ibid., p. 156 and passim.

is the first text that could, justifiably, carry such a title. Zemskov begins by debunking all overinflated numbers.[16] According to Medvedev (whom Khlevniuk had quoted earlier) the number of Gulag inmates in 1937–38 should have grown by millions. In fact, nothing of the sort occurred. From January 1937 to January 1, 1938, the number grew from 1,196,369 to 1,881,570 and fell, by January 1, 1939, to 1,672,438. However, 1937–38 saw a flare-up by several hundred thousand, not by millions. The number actually compiled by the security services of all political prisoners for the years 1921 through 1953 reached 3.8 million, most of whom were punished by administrative fiat. This was the memorandum (*spravka*), also mentioned by Khlevniuk, that Rudenko (the prosecutor-in-chief), Kruglov, and Gorshenin (the heads of the security services) prepared for the Politburo (for Khrushchev) in April 1954.

The agencies that inflicted the most such sentences were, mainly, an array of "special," extrajudicial administrative bodies of the NKVD, called *Kollegii, troiki* (the so-called *Osobye Soveshchania*). These rendered 2.9 million sentences out of a total of 3,777,380 sentences, including 642, 980 death penalties (shooting), 2,669,220 sentences to time in camps and prisons for twenty-five years or less, and 765,180 sentences to forms of exile (*ssylka i vysylka*); 877,000 sentences were rendered by courts and military tribunals, including the Special Collegium (*Spets-kollegiia*) and the Military Collegium (*Voen. Kollegiia*). (The jurisdiction and differences among these bodies belong, partly at least, to jurists of the breed who imagined Kafka's *Trial*.)

Just before the *spravka* was delivered to Khrushchev on February 1, 1954, there were still in the camps 467,946 inmates accused of counter-revolutionary crimes, and an additional 62,462 such offenders were *v ssylke*—that is, sentenced to additional punishment after having served their camp sentences.[17]

These are already very big numbers, but claims of there having been 5 million to 7 million in 1937–38 alone make no sense to Zemskov. He thinks that the figure given by Kriuchkov (the last KGB chief under Gorbachev) of one million arrests for 1937–38 is corroborated by the existing Gulag statistics. He then goes on, using official, previously secret

---

16. Zemskov, "Gulag," no. 6, 1991.

17. Ibid., p. 12. On this page Zemskov also gives a wealth of details about sentencing by different bodies.

documents, to refute Shatunovskaia, who claimed—on the basis of some
KGB document that supposedly had disappeared—that from January 1,
1935, to July 22, 1941, 19,840,000 were arrested as "enemies of the people" and 7,000,000 of them were shot, with the rest perishing in camps.
Zemskov claims to have irrefutable information that between January 1,
1934, and December 31, 1947, 936,766 prisoners died in the Gulag camps
of all causes—and this number included fatalities among common criminals.[18] Shatunovskaia's data, then, which were quoted in the West, were
for him nonsensical. In another of his articles,[19] Zemskov took to task
Antonov-Ovseenko, who certainly did not find any of his figures in the
archives. He spoke about 16 million inmates supposedly imprisoned in
camps in the autumn of 1945, when there were in fact 1.6 million in the
camps at that time. Zemskov used NKVD-Gulag materials from
TsGAOR to which he had privileged access.[20] His totals agreed with the
numbers from the 1937 census found in TsGANKh, as well as with figures Ezhov sent to Stalin and Molotov at that time.

Zemskov also contested the often-quoted figure provided by Robert
Conquest (in his 1968 book *The Great Terror*), who believed that the
number of inmates in camps and prisons reached 9 million in 1939, compared to 5 million in 1933–35 and 30,000 in 1928.[21] In fact, camps,
colonies, and prisons in 1940 contained 1,850,258 prisoners. The Soviet
author Chalikova claimed that there were between 8 million and 12 mil-

---

18. Ibid., p. 13. Zemskov offers plenty of tables to back up his contentions. We know that
O. Khlevniuk had some doubts about Zemskov's data, but he certainly would not have
endorsed anything remotely resembling Shatunovskaia's figure.

19. *Istoriia SSSR,* no. 6 (1991).

20. He was not allowed to give file numbers, but these files may be accessible by now. See
Zemskov, "Gulag," no 6. (1991); a critique of Conquest and Chalikova is on p. 10. The
figures are on pp. 11–18. After this appendix was already drafted, G. Rittersporn kindly
allowed me to preview a paper by J. Arch Getty, Gabor T. Rittersporn, and V. N. Zemskov, "Victims of the Soviet Penal System in the Pre-War Years: A First Approach on
the Basis of Archival Evidence" (*American Historical Review* 98, no. 4 [1993], pp.
1017–49), which contains a wealth of statistical material never previously available in the
West, and some of which I am also using. Still, my own appendix and presentation does
not necessarily overlap with their material.

21. These are figures quoted from Zemskov. When perusing Robert Conquest's *The
Great Terror: Stalin's Purge of the Thirties* (rev. ed. [New York, 1973], p. 452), one can find
that Conquest was inclined to accept that there were 8 million camp inmates in 1938. In
his appendix A, where he examines terror casualties, he tends to vote for an even bigger
number: around 12 million for the end of 1938—presumably not including common
criminals (p. 708).

lion for 1937 through 1950. In fact, again, the biggest number for any year between 1934 and 1953 in the Gulag was 2,561,351 inmates on January 1, 1950. In his secret speech, Khrushchev also deliberately exaggerated when he declared that at the time of Stalin's death there were 10 million in camps. Copies of the briefs (*dokladnye zapiski*) of the Ministry of Internal Affairs that were given to Khrushchev can be seen in TsGAOR: they informed him that on January 1, 1953, the Gulag's camps and colonies kept 2,468,524 prisoners.

TABLE A.2: PRISONERS IN THE GULAG
(AS OF JAN. 1 OF EACH YEAR)

YEAR	IN ITK[a]	INCLUDING CR[a]	IN ITL[a]	TOTAL
1934	510,307	135,190 (26.5%)	——	510,307
1935	725,483	118,256 (16.3%)	240,259	965,742
1936	839,406	105,849 (12.6%)	457,088	1,296,494
1937	820,881	104,826 (12.8%)	375,488	1,196,369
1938	996,367	185,324 (18.6%)	885,203	1,881,570
1939	1,317,195	454,432 (34.5%)	355,243	1,672,438
1940	1,344,408	444,999 (33.1%)	315,584	1,659,992
1941	1,500,924	420,293 (28.7%)	429,205	1,929,729
1948	1,108,057	416,156 (38%)	1,091,478	2,199,535
1949	1,216,361	420,696 (34.9%)	1,140,324	2,356,685
1950	1,416,300	578,912[b] (22.7%)	1,145,051	2,561,351
1951	1,533,767	475,976 (31%)	994,379	2,528,146
1952	1,711,202	480,766 (28.1%)	793,312	2,504,514
1953	1,727,970	465,256 (26.9%)	740,554	2,468,524
1954[c] (APRIL)		448,344		1,360,303

Source: TsGAOR, NKVD Fund, (code number not given), quoted in V. Zemskov, *Istoriia SSSR,* no. 5, (1991), p. 152.

[a] ITL (*ispravitel'no-trudovoj lager'*) was the camp proper. ITK. (*Isprav.trud.koloniia*) was a camp for lesser offenders, who were tranferred to the Gulag jurisdiction in 1934. CR meant those sentenced for "counterrevolutionary crimes," and these data are their numbers and percentages of ITLs totals. These figures do not include administrations and guards.

[b] Figure for camps and colonies

[c] Zemskov's figures for 1954 are incomplete, so only partial data are cited for that year.

The same article has a detailed year-by-year table for 1934 through 1953 (and I added 1954 data from another place in the same source) that deals with ITLs, ITKs, and the totals (see table A.2). There are also absolute figures and percentages of those sentenced for "counterrevolutionary" crimes, but in the ITLs alone. Separate data are given for inmates in regular prisons, for 1939–1948; they, too, belonged to the Gulag administration and have to be added to the totals of inmates. I am examining only a selection from these data, mainly to allow the reader to get a sense of the size of the Gulag's repressive empire and, in particular, the number of political prisoners (as the secret police defined them) being held. (Khlevniuk and Zemskov did warn that corrections of the police figures are needed—and did, in fact, propose them.)

In trying to get an inkling about the size of the imprisoned populations, I also borrow from Zemskov's tables of inmates incarcerated in prisons between 1939 and 1948 for January and December of selected years only, and group them in table A.3.

TABLE A.3: INMATES OF PRISONS

YEAR	JANUARY	DECEMBER
1939	350,538	186,278
1941	487,739	247,404
1946	261,500	290,984
1948	275,850	230,614

Source: TsGAOR, NKVD Fund (code number not given), quoted in V. Zemskov, *Istoriia SSSR,* no. 5 (1991), p. 154.

The majority of these prisoners usually ended up in camps, so they can be added to the overall prison-and-camps population for each respective year.

The real scope of repression through deprivation of freedom must, however, include those who were deported and sent to remote places for a term or for life. Although not equivalent to prison or camp, this was a severe enough punishment; and, as noted earlier, such exiles were included in the Gulag census, in part in 1937, in full in 1939. The Ministry of the Interior continued to maintain jurisdiction over them, but they were not located in the Gulag "zones," and their legal status was changing over the years. Still, they were victims of a severe, terroristic punishment and have to be included in the figures that interest us.

Here I will focus on their overall number for July 15, 1949, when it reached 2,552,037 people, and for January 1, 1953, when the total was 2,753,356 in all places of deportation. These numbers include the whole population—men, women, and children—on whom this punishment was inflicted. Zemskov's articles on these categories were a real break-through because he offered enough data to reconstruct a revealing profile of these populations.[22]

With the addition of the deported, the number of people who were denied their freedom between 1949 and 1953 by all the system's forms of repression totaled 5,183,772 inmates in 1949 (I used here the number of prison inmates in 1948; the one for 1949 was not available) and 5,221,880 in 1953—including here the Gulag and the exiled alone, without the regular prisons, whose number was not available for this year. An arbitrary 240,000 may be assumed, for the sake of rounding up, however approximately, a tally of 5,461,880 people—inmates and family members—including many criminal offenders (roughly, below 2 million for 1948 and over 2 million for 1953). Among the exiles there were also offenders who would be punishable in any other country. This would still leave us in each case with several million who were wantonly accused of imaginary crimes or whose actions would not have justified so much as a civil suit elsewhere.

GULAG — AN "ALL-PURPOSE" INFRASTRUCTURE

Zemskov's papers provide also previously unknown data for prisoner turnovers in the Gulag—that is, the number of those being released and coming in, and categories of crimes they were punished for, as well as the regional dispersal of the camps. We also get, for the first time, some NKVD data on mortality in camps over the years. From 1934 to 1947, 963,766 prisoners died more than half—53.6 percent of this total—died during the war years (1941–43).[23] The numbers for political convicts have to be revised upward, as O. Khlevniuk suggested, by assuming the exis-

22. V. N. Zemskov, "Spetsposelentsy (po dokumentam NKVD-MVD)," *Sotsiologich-eskie Issledovania,* no. 11 (1990), p. 12.

23. Zemskov, "Gulag," in ibid., no. 6, pp. 13, 21 (for the number of deaths in camps), and ibid., no. 7, pp. 3, 7.

tence of some additional, though smaller, numbers among prisoners in the "colonies" and prisons and still more among other categories considered "criminal."

The same author provides yet another set of data on the infrastructure of the camps. On March 1, 1940, the Gulag had 53 principal camps, with numerous smaller branches, and 425 camps of the lighter ITK variety, as well as 50 colonies for juveniles. The Gulag also reported 90 kinderhouses, with 4,594 children whose mothers were prisoners. The picture did not change much by December 1, 1944, when there were 53 ITLs (camps), but 667 branches and 475 ITKs (colonies). The novel features this time were probably represented by 17 camps with harsher conditions (s usilennym rezhimon) and by 5 more for punitive hard labor that were introduced in 1944 (the tsarist term katorzhanie was applied to these inmates)—all included in the general ITL category.

In July 1946 the USSR also had 514 prisons, including 504 general ones, 2 internal ones (operated by MVD, the Ministry of Internal Affairs), and 5 prison hospitals. One can hear rumors in Moscow (though spread by people with some knowledge) that a certain number of "special-special" prisoners were not reported anywhere, by order from above. But the sources think that this concerns a few thousand inmates; hence—if at all true—this would not change the overall picture significantly. Another piece of information that needs further clarification concerns special tribunals that operated inside the camp system and sentenced people to death there. Are these deaths included in the 963,766 casualties reported for 1934–47? Perhaps, but there is no way, so far, of knowing.

The Gulag system also contained the so-called spetskontingent NKVD—not to be confounded with the prewar use of this term. During the war it came to mean a network of special "filtration camps" (their name changed several times). It was run by a department in the NKVD (later called otdel proverochno-filtratsionnykh lagerej). People in many different categories transited through those camps: (1) soldiers and officers who broke out of encirclement, (2) those who served as policemen under German occupation and other categories suspected of collaboration, (3) men of draft age who stayed in the occupied territories, and (4) Soviet intelligence and reconnaissance officers (!) who were parachuted or otherwise sent behind enemy lines but were now submitted to the degrading "filtering."

From their inception at the end of 1941 until October 1944, 421,199 were taken into those camps, and 335,487 were "filtered out." Most of those "verified" in this way returned to the army, some went into the army's punitive battalions or into industry, some served as camp guards, and some were arrested by military counterintelligence (Smersh). Beginning in 1946 the filtering action was transferred into the Gulag. During 1946, 228,000 repatriated Soviet citizens were "checked out" in this way. Their number dropped to 4,727 by September 1, 1947.[24] The "inventiveness" shown by the punitive administration in coming up with ever more differentiated institutions ready to inflict growing degrees of harsh treatment was supposed to match the flourishing phantasms of the political leadership about ever meaner "enemies." Their supply was not allowed to dry up.

FORCIBLE SETTLEMENTS: THE KULAKS

According to I. E. Zelenin, there were approximately 900,000 kulak families in 1927, with a total of about 4.5 million people. The number of such families shrank to between 600,00 and 700,000 after "extraordinary measures" were applied to them during the 1928 and 1929 grain procurement campaigns. In 1930 and 1931, 381,000 families were deported, and another 200,000 to 250,000 families "dekulakized themselves" (*samoraskulkachilis'*), which, in most cases, meant that they fled from their villages.[25] In 1932, according to V. P. Danilov, 100,000 more families were sent away from their villages. The *samoraskulkachivanie* occurred largely among the 400,000 to 450,000 families that were grouped (by a special commission) in the so-called Category III and were initially allowed to stay in their localities (after a partial confiscation of their belongings). But most of them fled, creating a substantial component of "the flight from the countryside" that Stalin complained about. In sum, some 1.1 million to 1.2 million mostly prosperous family farms were destroyed during collectivization, and their members (5.5 million to 6 million people) were exiled or fled in an effort to shelter themselves from persecution. "Real kulaks" among them, according to Zelenin, were no more than half this number.[26]

---

24. Ibid., no. 7, pp. 4–6.

25. I. E. Zelenin, "Osushchestvlenie politiki 'likvidatsii 'kulachestva kak klasa'," *Istoriia SSSR,* no. 6 (1990), pp. 43–44.

26. Ibid., pp. 43–44.

Zemskov confirmed Zelenin's numbers for those deported in 1930 and 1931, and then brought in a mass of new data. An official policy of colonizing the North[27] through forced population transfer (*pereseleniia*) created, on the receiving end, the phenomenon of "special settlements" (*spetsposeleniia*). The Russian government decreed on August 18, 1930, that the NKVD would be responsible for running them. NKVD's policy toward the deportees was dictated by their function as a future labor force. Hence, a liberal attitude toward those unable to work prevailed, and NKVD officials protested against deporting people who were too young or too old to work—and in general against wreckless exiling of people without providing them the supplies stipulated by law, thus causing illnesses and many deaths. Documents show that NKVD was protesting not only illegalities committed against but also neglect of these people.

"Nevertheless, this colonization was executed with unusual cruelty," said Zemskov. By July 1938 there were 180 district and 800 village NKVD "command posts" (*komandatury*) that handled 1,741 labor settlements (*trudposelki*). The Gulag was running this sytem centrally and locally through its network of special departments (*otdely mest zakliuchenia i trudposelkov UNKVD*). In character with the vagaries of the Great Purges, many of the Gulag administrators who oversaw the kulak colonization (*kulatskaia ssylka*) were themselves purged for having, supposedly, favored the enrichment of the kulak settlements. "Enrichment" aside, this *ssylka* did, in fact, settle down by 1935; and, relatively speaking, the *ssylka* created for themselves more normal living conditions (*obzhilas'*).

As a result, many improvements occurred, including a surplus of births over deaths. At the same time, the government kept issuing legislative acts that restored civil rights to growing numbers of the exiles.[28] The first step in this process was made by a 1933 decree that restored the rights (to vote, to study wherever they wanted) to children of the exiles. On May 27, 1934, the government restored civil rights to many adults, but not the right to leave the settlements. From 1936 on, all the exiles were registered on voting lists; and from 1939 on, a partial return of passports began. Some people started to leave the places of exile.

In the early and mid-1930s the exiled population continued to grow, as

27. V. N. Zemskov, "Kulatskaia ssylka' v tridtsatye gody," *Sotsiologicheskie Issledovaniia*, no. 10 (1991), pp. 4–7. Ample relevant documents, including ones on epidemics and living conditions, are in Danilov and Krasil'nikov, *Spetspereselentsy*.

28. Zemskov, "Kulatskaia," pp. 7, 11.

did cases of authorized departures. From 1934 to 1938, 31,515 people were released as having been deported wrongly; 33,565 more left to join foster parents. Thousands of young people were allowed to leave to pursue their studies, to marry a free citizen, and so on. As yet, though, the very existence of a sizeable "kulak exile" was not seriously dented.

The first legal enactments that opened one of the main channels for the subsequent liquidation of this *ssylka* was an enactment by the government, on October 22, 1938, ordering the issuing of passports to the children of all the exiled adults. Any sixteen-year-olds who were not involved in criminal activities stopped being registered on the ledgers of the Gulag. They now could receive passports and leave. Considerable numbers were now leaving, among them invalids, whom the NKVD authorized to go by a ruling of June 3, 1939. Nevertheless, the number of exiles was still growing in the first quarter of 1941—from 930,221 to 960,133 inhabitants. During those months, 77,703 newcomers were brought in, from different categories, as against 47,791 people who left. In the beginning of the war, requests to leave ceased, and many people even asked to return to the settlements so they could continue being exempted from the draft.[29]

Among the 936,547 labor-settlers registered in places of exile on January 1, 1942, 93.1 percent were ex-kulaks, 64,696 were other types of deportees, such as peasants who failed to deliver procurement quotas and others who were deported from cities, mainly in 1933, in connection with the passportization drive. They would be sentenced to three to five years of imprisonment, and the verdict would be commuted to deportation to forced settlements. Still others were deported, mainly between 1935 and 1937, when western frontier zones were cleansed of "unreliable" elements. On April 11, 1942, came the decision of the Supreme Defense Council to draft ex-kulaks into the army.[30] This opened up an entirely new chapter in the life of such exile communities, a topic that needs further research.

The number of families exiled before 1934 was 381,026, with a total population of 1,803,392 people. Their colonies were first called *spetspereseleniia* and later *trudposeleniia,* and from 1944 on were rebaptized as *spetsposeleniia.* It is unclear what purpose this bizarre play with terms served.

---

29. Ibid., pp. 12–13, 17–20.

30. V. N. Zemskov, "Spetsposelentsy," *Sotsiologicheskie Issledovaniia,* no. 11 (1990), note 24.

Whatever the names, we know that these settlements were populated (on January 1 of each year) by 1,317,022 persons in 1932, by 1,142,084 in 1933, and by 1,072,546 in 1934. This was in the framework of this first forced colonization policy. On July 1, 1938, a population of 997,329 people was recorded as residing in 1,741 labor settlements (*trudposelki*). In addition, hundreds of thousands attempted to run away from the settlements, especially from 1938 to 1940, and the majority succeeded; but this is a separate matter. Most of the ex-kulaks exiled between 1929 and 1935 were later "removed from the deportation lists"; between 1941 and 1948, 810,614 ex-kulaks were liberated.[31] Toward the end of the war, the "kulak exile" as a penal system was actually resorbed—even if many did stay on in places they had initially been exiled to.

In light of such data, Solzhenitsyn's claims that fifteen million *muzhiki* were pushed out to the tundras during the 1930s,[32] which some authors spread around as reliable information, was an exaggeration that would have liquidated much of the Soviet army even before the German attack. The real numbers—probably one tenth as large—were sufficient to indict the government in sabotaging the country's well-being and security.

OTHER "SPECIAL SETTLERS"

Without the Soviet phenomenon of "deportations," for which kulaks served as a large-scale precedent, a realistic picture of the character and scope of repression during the 1930s and 1940s cannot be obtained. But first we have to learn another batch of terms from the lexicon of the Stalinist mass terror. There were different categories of deportation. *Spetsposelentsy* were those deported for a term as stipulated by the sentence they received (*na sroka*). *Ssylnoposelentsy,* on the other hand, were exiled to some specific area without the right ever to return home (*na vechno*). *Ssyl'nye* were those who were sent into a place of exile (*ssylka*) to serve additional time, after having served the initial prison or camp sentence.

There was another variation on the theme—the *vyslannye* (*administrativno vyslannye*), the mildest of the deportation categories. These people would be deported from their habitat and sentenced to live anywhere but

---

31. A. Solzhenitsyn, *Arkhipelag Gulag,* vol. 1 (Moscow, 1989), p. 34.

32. Zemskov, "Spetsposelentsky," p. 4.

"minus three" or "minus seven," that is, anywhere but in one, three, or even seven specified places (usually important cities). V. N. Zemskov, in a paper entitled "*Spetsposelentsky*" (based on NKVD-MVD files), offers ample data on these penalties. After the kulaks, a wave of Poles appeared in 1940 and 1941 whom the Polish government used in the 1920s to colonize areas in its newly recovered East. There were also refugees and tens of thousands of other Poles—for a total of 380,000—from the areas the USSR incorporated in 1939 and 1940, including a wave of Lithuanians. In midwar, most of those were released, and two Polish armies were created, though not without suffering serious casualties, as was well known for years and is now confirmed by documents found in the archives. More than 20,000 Polish officers, plus some officials and landowners, were summarily executed before the Russo-German war and were buried in mass graves in Katyn and several other spots. Later in the war, whole ethnic groups were deported to *spetsposeleniia* again. In late August 1941 this fate befell 949,829 Soviet Germans, who were joined, from 1945 to 1948, by 120,192 more.[33]

In 1943 and 1944 hundreds of thousands of other ethnic groups who had been accused of treason were exiled to the East, from the Crimea, Kalmikia, and Northern Caucasus. Stalin personally supervised these deportations and praised the security force officers who executed these operations. About 650,000 people were deported from Northern Caucasus, in three military-style operations that necessitated an army of 100,000 soldiers from the security forces and 19,000 NKVD and Smersh (military counterintelligence) operatives.[34] There also was deportation of Tatars, of Lithuanians and other Balts, and of people from the formerly Polish territories, after they were retaken from the Germans. Pitched battles were raging there between the Soviet Army and Lithuanian and Ukrainian partisans.

The end of the 1940s saw a hardening of the regimen and penalties in the places of exile, especially for people who tried to escape. In 1949, smaller numbers of "unreliable elements" from the Black Sea littoral—Greeks, Turks, and "Dashnaks" (nationalists) from Georgia, Azerbaijan, Armenia, and Northern Caucasus took the road of the "special settlements." On January 1, 1949, the registers showed 2,300,223 deported settlers, including 1,835,078 of those "forever," and 465,145 for a term.

33. Dmitrij Volkogonov, *Triumf i tragediia: Politicheskii portret I. V. Stalina,* vol. 2 (Moscow, 1989), pt. 1, pp. 257–58.

34. "40-50-ye gody: posledstviia deportatsii narodov," *Otechestvennaia Istoriia,* no. 1 (1992), pp. 122–43, esp. data on p. 142.

A more recent batch of documents from the archives of the MVD, retrieved and published by the historian N. F. Bugaj,[35] allows me to sum up numerically the whole trail of repression through deportation between 1941 and 1948. All in all, 3,266,340 people were exiled and forcibly resettled during this time span, 215,242 newcomers were listed (some of them were, probably, the newborn), and 1,226,162 left. Among those who left, 883,102 were released from the forcible settlements and 309,100 died. The documents give a grim picture of the living (and dying) conditions of the settlers, especially during their initial state of shock.

While insisting on the fullest possible assessment of the scope of repression,[36] I cannot leave without mentioning the considerable shrinking of these punitive actions in later years. The extensive exiling would disappear altogether, camp populations would dwindle, and the political category would change in both scope and character. This inversion of the process can be traced from the following data.[37] Between July 1, 1954, and July 1, 1957, 2,554,639 people were released from the "forced settlements." The last releases occurred beginning in 1960, when people were being granted the right to return home. The whole phenomenon of "special settlements" actually disappeared, although not the penalty itself; individual deportation, which lingered on, comprised by January 1, 1959, 9,363 people. Those were supposedly tramps (*brodiagi*) and some counterrevolutionaries (87 such cases). Also, the *ssylka* as an additional penalty after the camp sentence—far from anything enlightened in sum, but now a comparatively marginal punitive practice—continued.

A similar "inversion" can be traced during the Khrushchev period regarding the Gulag population. Zemskov's second article on the Gulag[38] gives an overall number of 2,528,146 inmates for January 1, 1951, including 994,379 in colonies. Of this total, 579,918 prisoners (including 103,942 in colonies) were sentenced for "counterrevolutionary acts," giv-

---

35. Zemskov, "Spetsposelenetsky," pp. 8–9, 11, 13. He also gives ample statistical data. See also note 26 for data on different waves of deportation from the Caucasus.

36. V. N. Zemskov, "Massovoe osvobozhdenie spetsposelentsev i ssylnykh (1954–1960)," *Sotsiologicheskie Issledovaniia,* no. 1 (1991), p. 20.

37. Zemskov, "Gulag," ibid., no. 7, pp. 12, 14, and passim.

38. *Sotsiologicheskie Issledovania,* n o. 7, 1991, p. 12. For the subsequent information see p. 14 and passim.

ing a table that presents a breakdown by charge and sentence. Detailed figures follow, showing the stages of political prisoners' massive liberation from camps, as ordered by Khrushchev, and the shrinking of the whole "counterrevolutionary" category after the Twentieth Party Congress (1956–59). On January 1, 1955, there were still 308,089 of those; but by April 1, 1955, only 11,027 remained, and their representation in the overall camp population dropped from 33 percent to 1.2 percent.

It should be remembered that the post–World War II "counterrevolutionary" category included many collaborators with the Nazis, insurgents, and traitors—mostly real culprits—but they too benefited from Khrushchev's amnesties, whether they were in camps or in the places of deportation where most of them were usually dispatched.

CONCLUSION

How many people were executed? This question was posed earlier in this postscript. All the official figures—computed initially by the secret police's leaders at the request of Khrushchev's government and presented in full secrecy—spoke about some 700,000 to 800,000 who were executed for presumed political offenses. This was said to have covered the period from 1921 (some quote 1927) until the end of 1953. These data were part of the broader information given by the same source on all those who were sentenced for "counterrevolutionary" offenses during the same years, mostly by "administrative" (that is, "expedient" procedures) conducted by "special" bodies and, much less frequently, by the regular court system. Some observers assume that most of those who were executed—possibly about 600,000 people—perished during the Great Purges, or somewhat later in the camps. That is also supposed to be the number cited by security agencies in a memo to the Central Committee.

If there is no proof for a higher number, why would such figures be insufficient? Artifically blowing them up hinders efforts to get the most realistic picture possible of the events we are trying to grasp. Other motivations might have guided the less naive among those who preferred flying statistical kites to the responsible business of looking for evidence and proof. Those disturbing and pathological phenomena of dictatorship have to be seen for what they were in order to face them and draw some lessons from them.

The "apocalyptic" number-crunching also has the curious effect of making the crimes in question suddenly look small. The toll that the rulers inflicted on the population was enormous, not only in sheer numbers but also in terms of cultural, psychological, and political damages. Both the sense of horror and the historical task of studying this horror and placing it in some flow of things is not diminished just because the relevant numbers are smaller than those dreamed up by people with fertile imaginations.